Encountering Islam on the First Crusade

The First Crusade (1095–1099) has often been characterised as a head-to-head confrontation between the forces of Christianity and Islam. For many, it is the campaign that created a lasting rupture between these two faiths. Nevertheless, is such a characterisation borne out by the sources? Engagingly written and supported by a wealth of evidence, *Encountering Islam on the First Crusade* offers a major re-interpretation of the crusaders' attitudes towards the Arabic and Turkic peoples they encountered on their journey to Jerusalem. Nicholas Morton considers how they interpreted the new peoples, civilisations, and landscapes they encountered, sights for which their former lives in Western Christendom had provided little preparation. Morton offers a varied picture of cross-cultural relations, depicting the Near East as an arena in which multiple protagonists were pitted against each other. Some were fighting for supremacy, others for their religion, many simply for survival.

NICHOLAS MORTON is a lecturer in History at Nottingham Trent University. He is the author of many works on the crusades and the military orders including *The Medieval Military Orders* and *The Teutonic Knights in the Holy Land, 1190–1291*.

Encountering Islam on the First Crusade

Nicholas Morton

Nottingham Trent University

CAMBRIDGE
UNIVERSITY PRESS

CAMBRIDGE
UNIVERSITY PRESS

University Printing House, Cambridge CB2 8BS, United Kingdom

Cambridge University Press is part of the University of Cambridge.

It furthers the University's mission by disseminating knowledge in the pursuit of
education, learning and research at the highest international levels of excellence.

www.cambridge.org
Information on this title: www.cambridge.org/9781107156890

First published 2016

Printed in the United States of America by Sheridan Books, Inc.

A catalogue record for this publication is available from the British Library

Library of Congress Cataloguing in Publication data
Morton, Nicholas Edward, author.
Encountering Islam on the First Crusade / Nicholas Morton, Nottingham
Trent University.
New York : Cambridge University Press, 2016.
Includes bibliographical references and index.
LCCN 2016018908   ISBN 9781107156890
LCSH: Crusades – First, 1096–1099.   Islam – Relations – Christianity –
History – To 1500.   Christianity and other religions.
LCC D161.2.M68   2016   DDC 956/.014 – dc23
LC record available at https://lccn.loc.gov/2016018908

ISBN 978-1-107-15689-0 Hardback

There are, I know, those who prefer not to go beyond the impression, however accidental, which an old work makes on a mind that brings to it a purely modern sensibility and modern conceptions; just as there are travellers who carry their resolute Englishry with them all over the continent, mix only with other English tourists, enjoy all they see for its 'quaintness', and have no wish to realise what those ways of life, those churches, those vineyards, mean to the natives. They have their reward. I have no quarrel with people who approach the past in that spirit. I hope they will pick none with me. But I was writing for the other sort.

C.S. Lewis[1]

[1] C. S. Lewis, *The discarded image: An introduction to medieval and Renaissance literature* (Cambridge: Cambridge University Press, 1964), p. x.

Contents

Figure and Tables

Figure

Tables

Acknowledgements

I started to chew over this topic about five years ago when pieces of evidence started come to my attention which simply didn't fit the current interpretations of Christian attitudes towards Islam at the time of the First Crusade. Since that time I have had many conversations on this topic and shared ideas with a wide range of colleagues working on this area, whose thoughts and criticisms have been absolutely foundational to the creation of this book. To all of you may I offer my heartfelt thanks.

I would particularly like to recognise the assistance I have received from Jonathan Phillips and Elizabeth Lapina, whose suggestions and criticisms have been extremely valuable. I'm also deeply indebted to my long-suffering reviewers, whose feedback has been so very helpful.

To the CBRL I owe a particular debt of gratitude for their ongoing support for this project. Back in 2013 they were kind enough to pay for me to visit Jerusalem where I was able to share some of my earlier ideas at their Kenyon Institute. I found many of the questions I was asked at that time to be extremely helpful and illuminating.

One of my key challenges in building this project was to devise and prepare my methodologies and theoretical lines of approach. I spent the better part of the summer of 2012 mulling over these issues and I am particularly grateful to Judith Rowbotham, Andrew Jotischky, and Robert Irwin for their input at this time. My further thanks goes to Paul Crawford, Ian Wilson, Simon Parsons, Bernard Hamilton, Benjamin Kedar, Adrian Boas, Thomas McCarthy, Bill Niven, and Mark Dickens for their kindness and support with the project's later development.

To my family, this book comes with my deepest love and thanks.

Note on Translations

In this work I have translated many passages from their original languages into modern English. Nevertheless, where a good quality translation already exists, I have tended – not always – to use the existing translation rather than creating a new one. There seems little reason to replicate work.

Introduction

During the First Crusade (1095–1099), a motley assortment of pilgrim armies left their homelands and loved ones to attempt a journey of over 2000 miles to distant Jerusalem.[1] Most died along the way. The few who survived found themselves encountering places, cultures, and peoples that were often simultaneously foreign and familiar. On the one hand, they had been hearing about Jerusalem and the Holy Land from the cradle. This was the land of Christ's birth, life, passion, resurrection, and ascension. On the other, it was wholly strange, populated by communities whose culture and outlook on life was so very different to their own. They saw crocodiles, great snakes, and lions. They ate sugar cane and dates. They learned the feel of silk. These were landscapes under non-Christian rule and the pilgrims soon found themselves: conducting diplomacy with the Fatimids of Egypt, negotiating with the Arab dynasties of Syria, and fighting wars against the Saljuq Turks. For the majority of pilgrims the sense of dislocation brought about by these events was considerable. How they coped with the transition into this new, unfamiliar, and often hostile milieu is the subject of this book. It shall explore how they drew upon the received wisdom of their former lives, their lived experiences, and the guidance they sought from eastern Christians on the road, to understand the Turkish and Arabic peoples of the Near East.

Within the odyssey that was the First Crusade, the pilgrims encountered many different societies, but the people who filled them simultaneously with the greatest dread and the deepest admiration was the Turks. The encounters that took place between these two very different peoples warrants the closest attention not least because they had so much, and yet so little, in common. Firstly, there were the crusaders. Theirs was

---

[1] The straight-line distance from Paris to Jerusalem is 2068 miles. L. Ní Chléirigh has recently reaffirmed that the First Crusade *was* understood by participants to be a 'pilgrimage' expedition, answering several critics on this point. See Léan Ní Chléirigh, '*Nova Peregrinatio*: The First Crusade as a pilgrimage in contemporary Latin narratives', *Writing the early Crusades: Text, transmission and memory*, ed. M. Bull and D. Kempf (Woodbridge: Boydell, 2014), pp. 63–74.

1

formerly the static existence of agricultural communities whose elites fought small-scale noble vendettas, enjoyed jocular entertainments, and steadily accumulated spiritual and material capital from one generation to the next. Still, they were also a people in transition because suddenly, for the first time in centuries, they were taking the road in almost migratory numbers; an agricultural people on the move. Then, from the opposite direction came the Turks, only a few decades removed from the Central Asian steppe. Their horizons were radically different. The waves of nomadic Turkic tribesmen emanating from the great Asiatic grass sea broke on many shores and China, Persia, and India lay on their mental skylines. Theirs was a world of movement, of vast distances, of self-sufficiency and the battle for survival against the forces of nature. Dismissed by almost all their agricultural neighbours as barbarians, the Turks were also a people in transition. Like the crusaders they were newcomers to the Near East and, having conquered many lands, their leaders were slowly evolving from tribal chiefs into settled rulers; the tribal and the shamanistic were merging with the Islamic and the Persian. In some respects it is hard to imagine two more different peoples belligerently making 'first contact' during the First Crusade and yet they also had so much in common.

They were both conquerors, intent on taking and holding land. They both found themselves governing many native peoples who reacted to their rule in similar ways: some fled or died upon their swords, others attempted to manipulate them to their own ends, some even came to them for sanctuary; all had to come to terms with their new masters. The Turks and Franks also recognised much that they admired in one another. Whether landowning knights or tribal warriors, these were societies which valued their arms and mounts and both saw these similarities in each other. The more optimistic even speculated that they might somehow be related. Both were martial peoples who celebrated war and interpreted its outcome as spiritual judgement.

The convergence of these complex and disparate peoples, both of whom were midway through rapid social evolutions, is a fascinating affair. It defies reduction or easy categorization. Their interactions are as composite and varied as the thousands of individuals involved. The matter is complicated still further by the fact that the Turks and Franks encountered one another in the great arena of history: the Near East. These confrontations took place within a battered and partially subdued landscape of Byzantine, Syrian, Fatimid, and Armenian societies, which were themselves perched upon the ruins of classical empires, Old Testament kingdoms, and fallen Islamic dynasties. During the crusade, all these societies – past and present – made their influence felt, whilst no living society was left unaltered by its passing.

This study will explore the crusaders' relations, whether belligerent or more pacific, with the Muslim (or in some cases partially Islamified) peoples of the Near East. It will demonstrate how the pilgrims reacted and responded to the different ethnic groups they encountered and examine how they made sense of these interactions through the lens of their own prior experience and world view. Crucially, it will demonstrate how they came to rely upon eastern Christians for guidance and information upon the world of the Near East. At a macro level, there will also be discussion upon the longer-term effects of the First Crusade upon western Christendom's broad engagement with the Islamic world.

The complexity and richness of the interactions that occurred between Christendom and Islam during the early crusading period (eleventh–twelfth centuries) is one of the great attractions of this study area. The vibrancy, brutality, and diversity of the relationships and perspectives which emerged at this time – whether on the frontiers, or within academic or mercantile circles – have led many scholars to ponder how the various Christian protagonists perceived their Muslim neighbours.

The current academic pugilists weighing into this particular ring hail from many different schools of thought with each bringing their own methodologies, insights, and assumptions to bear. All approaches have produced their distinct results and many studies have sought to describe the conceptual lenses through which medieval Christians viewed their Muslim neighbours. These differing scholarly approaches to inter-faith relations at the time of the early crusades will now be reviewed.

To begin, there are the historians of the Crusades and the medieval Mediterranean, specialising in the crusading movement and Christendom's southern frontier. This is a large group whose publications are typically empirical and inter-disciplinary in approach. Outputs from this school of thought are generally characterised by a close examination of the textual primary sources arising from multiple cultures spliced with a readiness to incorporate findings from archaeological and art history studies. When they touch upon the question of Christendom's relationship with Islam, in an eleventh/twelfth-century crusading context, most will stress the diversity of frontier interactions – friendly and hostile – between Christians and Muslims throughout this period, drawing attention to the many commercial, diplomatic, and social links that evolved alongside the frequent military encounters.[2] The First Crusade is

---

[2] For an excellent and recent example of a work which stresses the diversity of the connections established across the faith boundary, see Epstein's recent study (although unlike many other authors in this field he does show some willingness to engage with post-colonial theory). See S. Epstein, *Purity lost: Transgressing boundaries in the eastern Mediterranean, 1000–1400* (Baltimore: Johns Hopkins University Press, 2006). Many crusading histories take this (or a similar) view; see, for example, C. Tyerman, *God's war:*

generally given as a high point of inter-civilisational hostility followed by a period of accommodation as the campaign's survivors were forced to come to terms with the business of ruling large Muslim populations in the Neat East.[3] When defining the crusaders' perspectives, typical points of reference include the Muslim nobleman Usama ibn Munqidh and his friendship with the Templars, the Spanish pilgrim Ibn Jubayr's remarks about the many Muslim communities living peacefully under Frankish rule, the treaties made between Franks and Muslims during the First Crusade, the First Crusade's Jerusalem massacre (1099), and William of Tyre's praise for the Turkish ruler Nur ad-Din. The compilation of such points normally generates a mixed picture in which religious hostility and inter-cultural interaction lie side by side. Historians raised in this school also tend to reject the idea that the First Crusade and the subsequent period of Christian settlement in the Near East (following the First Crusade) can be characterised as an all-out inter-civilisational battle for supremacy. Köhler in particular has stressed that it was pragmatism and *realpolitik*, rather than confessional divisions, which determined the political decisions made by Muslim and Christian leaders.[4]

Such historians have, however, typically been cautious in engaging with hypothetical models, particularly post-colonial theory. One feature of the voluminous research produced by these academics is that whilst many studies have offered insights into the first crusaders' attitudes towards Islam, it is only in the last few years that any full-length studies have appeared on this subject.[5]

Another group of scholars to contribute to this discussion consists of those who research Christendom's general relationship with the Islamic world during the medieval period, embracing all regions, contexts, and frontiers. Naturally, they are painting on a broader canvas, and the Crusades (still less the First Crusade) represent only one component in their

A new history of the Crusades (London: Allen Lane, 2006), pp. 126, 192; T. Asbridge, *The Crusades: The authoritative history of the war for the Holy Land* (New York: Ecco, 2010), pp. 122, 176–183; T. Asbridge, 'Knowing the enemy: Latin relations with Islam at the time of the First Crusade', *Knighthoods of Christ: Essays on the history of the Crusades and the Knights Templar, presented to Malcolm Barber* (Aldershot: Ashgate, 2007), p. 25.

[3] See, for example, J. Phillips, *Holy warriors: A modern history of the Crusades* (London: Vintage Books, 2009), p. 38.

[4] M. Köhler, *Alliances and treaties between Frankish and Muslim rulers in the Middle East: Cross-cultural diplomacy in the period of the Crusades*, trans. P. M. Holt, revised by K. Hirschler (Leiden: Brill, 2013), passim.

[5] M. Völkl, *Muslime – Märtyrer – Militia Christi: Identität, Feindbild und Fremderfahrung während der ersten Kreuzzüge* (Stuttgart: Kohlhammer, 2011). Another excellent full-length monogragh which considers the representation of Muslims both in the crusading chronicles and *chanson*s is A. Leclercq, *Portraits croisés: L'image des Francs et des Musulmans dans les textes sur la Première Croisade*, Nouvelle Bibliothèque du Moyen Âge XCVI (Paris: Honoré Champion, 2014).

wider field. The great founders of this research area were Norman Daniel
and Richard Southern, whose famous studies have become sounding-
boards for later historians. Scholars in this area, following their illustri-
ous forebears, have made a particular study of Christendom's leading
intellectuals and their engagement with non-Christians. Bede, Peter the
Venerable, Joachim of Fiore, Francis of Assisi, James of Vitry, William
of Tripoli, Dante, Ramon Lull, and Riccoldo of Montecroce are typical subjects of discussion.[6] Moreover, whilst crusade historians tend to
concentrate on the cut-and-thrust of frontier life, academics in this field
have engaged deeply with medieval intellectual attitudes towards Islam
the religion and the stereotypes surrounding the identity and person of
Mohammed. A key figure in this area today is John Tolan, who has
focused his attention on such subjects, particularly attitudes towards
Mohammed (although he does also deal with frontier relations).[7] For the
most part, the conclusions reached by historians in this field tend to be
darker than those reached by scholars of the Crusades, stressing the sustained hostility felt by medieval contemporaries towards non-Christian
religions (particularly Islam). Tolan ends his major work, *Saracens,* pondering the notion that medieval Christianity's claim to be the universal
truth inevitably provoked its adherents to denigrate non-Christians.[8]

Given the common interests between these schools of thought and
crusades historiography, it is remarkable how little interaction there has
been between them; they rarely reference each other's works or engage
with each other's major debates. Perhaps this lack of communication
is explained in part by a readiness among scholars in these fields to
engage more enthusiastically with theoretical models. Edward Said's
arguments, particularly those propounded in his *Orientalism* (1978) have
found a more receptive – although not uncritical – audience among such
scholars.[9]

---

[6] The classic works which laid the foundations for this field of study are R. Southern,
Western views of Islam in the Middle Ages (Cambridge, MA: Harvard University Press,
1962); N. Daniel, *Islam and the West: The making of an image* (Edinburgh: Edinburgh
University Press, 2009).

[7] J. Tolan, *Saracens: Islam in the medieval European imagination* (New York: Columbia
University Press, 2002).

[8] Tolan, *Saracens*, p. 283.

[9] See, for example, Tolan's remarks: J. Tolan, 'Afterword', *Contextualizing the Muslim other
in medieval Christian discourse*, ed. J. Frakes (New York: Palgrave Macmillan, 2011),
p. 171; Tolan, *Saracens*, pp. xvii–xix, 280–281; J. Frakes, *Vernacular and Latin discourses
of the Muslim other in medieval Germany*, The new Middle Ages (New York: Palgrave
Macmillan, 2011); S. Akbari, *Idols in the East: European representations of Islam and
the Orient, 1100–1450* (Ithaca, NY: Cornell University Press, 2009), pp. 5–14. For an
excellent and very thought-provoking survey of the key writers in this field, see K. Skottki,
'Medieval western perceptions of Islam and the scholars: What went wrong?', *Cultural*

A linked group of scholars are those who research the depictions of 'Saracens' contained in the *chansons* and epic verse of the Middle Ages. These *chansons* concern many aspects of medieval life, telling tales of heroic quests, courtly knights, and evil beasts. Among these tales, depictions of warfare against 'Saracens' appear regularly. The *Chanson de Roland* and the *Chanson d'Antioche* are the two works to receive the greatest attention with regard to the First Crusade and many studies discuss their interpretation.[10] Key explanatory tools, commonly employed in research on these sources, are notions of alterity, in particular the use made by medieval Christian writers of hostile representations of the 'Saracen other' to demarcate their own identity and that of their co-religionists. In recent years there has been a lively debate on the precise nature and structure of such models of medieval alterity, which in their most basic form posit an opposition between contemporary representations of 'white', 'light', 'handsome' Christians fighting 'black', 'dark', 'ugly' Saracens, the purpose attributed by scholars to such representations being the reinforcement of Christian group identity.

A particularly sophisticated example of such debates can be seen in Akbari's *Idols in the East* in which, in a wide-ranging discussion (covering the period 1100–1450), she breaks down the medieval discourses on Islam into their component parts, arguing that such representations were a hybrid formed from multiple strands of thought. These include the conviction that geography and climate determine the behaviour and physiology of different peoples (including 'Saracens'); the fundamental medieval belief that Islam was an erroneous and carnal faith; respect at a intellectual level for some aspects of Islamic philosophy (drawing primarily on Roger Bacon and Dante); and, in a crusading context, the importance attached to the sanctity of Jerusalem and, by extension, the belief that any non-Christian presence was inherently a pollutant. This is her lens. She sums up this perspective describing persuasively how medieval Christians were 'at once attracted and repelled, fascinated and

---

transfers in dispute: *Representations in Asia, Europe and the Arab world since the Middle Ages*, ed. J. Feuchter (Frankfurt: Campus Verlag, 2011), pp. 107–134. See also Blanks's survey: D. Blanks, 'Western views of Islam in the pre-modern period: A brief history of past approaches', *Western views of Islam in medieval and early modern Europe*, ed. D. Blanks and M. Frassetto (Basingstoke: Macmillan, 1999), pp. 11–53. Other studies that have influenced the theoretical approaches employed to the study of European attitudes towards Islam include: C. Bouchard, *"Every valley shall be exalted": The discourse of opposites in twelfth-century thought* (Ithaca, NY: Cornell University Press, 2003); D. Nirenberg, *Communities of violence: Persecution of minorities in the Middle Ages* (Princeton, NJ: Princeton University Press, 1996).

[10] For a starting point on *chansons* concerning the crusades, see Danial, *Heroes and Saracens*; Akbari, *Idols in the east*. See also Leclercq, *Portraits croisés*.

disturbed' by Islam and the Orient.[11] Within this, she draws deeply
upon notions of alterity, showing how such models developed over time,
but making the fundamental point that 'through defining Islam, then,
medieval Christians were able to define themselves.'[12]

Another much-debated theme within this research field concerns the
identification and definition of the two dominant strands within Medieval
European discourses on Islam (and their inter-relationships). Norman
Daniel labelled these as 'official' and 'unofficial' approaches. The 'official' view was that of the Church and its major writers, engaging with
Islam on a spiritual level and seeking to situate Muslims within their theological world view. The 'unofficial' perspective was that depicted in the
chansons and romances so beloved by knightly elites, telling tales of heroic
battles, beautiful maidens, and treacherous 'Saracen' kings. These two
narratives, which existed side by side in medieval society, adopt rather
different stances in their approaches to the Muslim world and are distinct from one another in many respects, especially in their intended
audiences, narrative objectives, and basic knowledge. Certainly, Norman Daniel stressed the differences dividing them.[13] Nevertheless, in
recent years, his view has been moderated somewhat by Akbari in the
earlier-mentioned *Idols in the east*. She makes the point that these twin
narratives may have had individual qualities and yet there were clear inter-
relationships between them. In a similar vein, this study will demonstrate
that clerical views informed the *chansons* while chivalric notions manifested themselves in more scholarly texts.[14] Moreover, this work will
draw upon this debate primarily in its aim to confirm that crusading
texts represent – to varying degrees – syntheses of these two strands.

The final group to be considered here could perhaps be described as
'world' historians, or at least those concerned with the development of
civilisations over the *longue durée*. These are scholars courageous enough
to propound overarching theories spanning many centuries and conti-
nents, and who approach the Crusades as one component phase in a far
broader trajectory. Edward Said is an example of one such writer, and
whilst he actually says very little about either the Crusades or the medieval
period as a whole, his major work, *Orientalism*, lays out a broad schema
for understanding western attitudes towards the 'Orient' (and Islam in
particular), stretching from the classical period through to the modern
age. His basic point is that western European approaches to the 'Orient'

---

[11] Akbari, *Idols in the east*, p. 279.
[12] Akbari, *Idols in the east*, p. 281 (see also p. 216) and *passim*.
[13] N. Daniel, *Heroes and Saracens: An interpretation of the chansons de geste* (Edinburgh: Edinburgh University Press, 1984), pp. 1–2.
[14] Akbari, *Idols in the east*, pp. 201–203 and *passim*.

have been moulded by a long-standing paternalistic discourse which is inherently hegemonic and which asserts an arrogant sense of imperialist supremacy over the 'non-European' other.[15] Given that he touches upon the Middle Ages, it is necessary for medievalists to consider the relevance of his arguments.

Having said this, engaging meaningfully with Said's views on the medieval era is problematic. The gist of his thesis is rather blurred at times.[16] In some places Said argues that Europe's medieval (and ultimately modern) encounter with Islam was dictated in part by a deep sense of fear emanating ultimately from the rapid Islamic advances into Europe during the Early Middle Ages.[17] On other occasions, however, he talks about a long-standing Western supremacist and hegemonic stance towards the 'Orient' propagated during the medieval period but dating back to the classical era. The union of these two impulses, both the fear of the invaded and the arrogance of the supremacist, one must conclude, cumulatively laid the foundations for a modern European perspective. This summary is problematic; at best it is a line-of-best-fit. Said's arguments are mercurial. Said continually describes long-standing western attitudes in *imperialist* terms (manifesting a confident will to dominate and codify the Islamic 'Orient') and he builds many modern perspectives on medieval foundations. Even so, he simultaneously provides strong grounds for viewing medieval Europe as the *subaltern* in this civilisational relationship in that he acknowledges that for much of the medieval period Christendom was weaker, in retreat, and driven by fear of its Islamic neighbour.[18] Consequently, Said's views surrounding the medieval period are hedged with ambiguity in that he presents Europe both as the imperialist and the subaltern. This creates a tension in his argument, which is not fully unpacked.

On these grounds, it is rather difficult to know how to approach and employ Said's *Orientalism*. It has been too influential to ignore and yet the hostility with which he offers his views contorts so much of his thesis. Still, this present work is not intended as a full-length critique of his argument.[19] It would be more positive to extract from his argument that which is relevant to this present study. Some component parts of Said's ideas, which either relate to, or encompass, the medieval period warrant

[15] E. Said, *Orientalism* (London: Routledge and Kegan Paul, 1978).

[16] R. Irwin, *For the lust of knowing: The orientalists and their enemies* (London: Penguin, 2006), p. 284.

[17] Although this really only comes fully into focus in an afterword written in 1995: E. Said, *Orientalism* (London: Penguin, 1995), p. 344. In this he follows: Southern, *Western views of Islam*, pp. 3–5.

[18] See Tolan, 'Afterword', p. 175; Akbari, *Idols in the east*, pp. 7, 9.

[19] For a detailed critique, see Irwin, *For the lust of knowing*.

closer attention. The notion that Christendom's approaches to Islam were driven by a spirit of fear is worthy of closer inspection. Likewise, one premise that undergirds *Orientalism* is the fundamental conviction that Islam was *important* to western Europe. After all, Said characterised the 'Orient' (exemplified by Islam) as Europe's 'great complementary opposite'.[20] The question of whether Islam occupied anything like so exalted a position within medieval European thought-worlds will be considered in full.

Another key writer to offer a model of comparable breadth is Samuel Huntington. A major line of argument in his famous *Clash of Civilizations and the Remaking of World Order* is that there has been a historic faultline between western Europe (and latterly America) and the Islamic world: 'each has been the other's Other'.[21] The essence of his thesis is captured in the following sentence:

So long as Islam remains Islam (which it will) and the West remains the West (which is more dubious), this fundamental conflict between two great civilisations and ways of life will continue to define their relations in the future even as it has defined them for the past fourteen centuries.[22]

In short, it is/has been a sustained and existential battle for supremacy.

For him, the primary building blocks of the modern world are the relationships between civilisational units: western Christianity and the Islamic world representing two such units. Naturally, Huntington was writing predominantly about contemporary affairs, but the relevance of his theory to this work lies in his attempts to present his 'Clash of Civilizations' between Christianity and Islam as a permanent civilisational truth spanning back to the seventh century. Like Said, in his main work, he passed very rapidly through the crusading era but his thesis still poses important questions, perhaps most importantly: did the First Crusade create/propitiate/dilate a Clash of Civilisations between Christianity and

---

[20] Said, *Orientalism*, p. 58. This is a notion that has been contested by Irwin who wrote: 'Islam did not feature largely in medieval European thought. It played, at best, a minor role in forming the self-image of Christendom'. Irwin, *For the lust of knowing*, p. 53.

[21] Huntington's main publication on this topic has been S. Huntington, *The clash of civilizations and the remaking of world order* (London: Simon & Schuster, 1996) (quotation p. 209). This quotation seems to override Huntington's earlier observation made on page 21 that global civilisations pre-1500 were only intermittently in contact with one another. This work is an expansion on his earlier article in *Foreign Affairs:* S. Huntington, 'The clash of civilizations', *Foreign Affairs* 72.3 (1993), 22–49. Bernard Lewis had already been making arguments in a similar vein, even to the point of using the term 'Clash of Civilizations', in his article: B. Lewis, 'The roots of Muslim rage', *The Atlantic Monthly* 266.3 (1990), 47–60 (cited by Huntington in *Clash of civilizations*, p. 213).

[22] Huntington, *Clash of civilizations*, p. 212.

Islam? Or is this kind of terminology unhelpful when bringing the events of this period into focus?[23]

Said's *Orientalism* and Huntington's *Clash of Civilizations* are among the few major 'world history' theories to really provoke a response from medievalists concerned with Christian/Islamic relations (even some historians of the Crusades have taken notice). Indeed, medievalists have been debating this kind of theory long before Huntington's *Clash of Civilizations* hit the press. The question of whether the First Crusade and the establishment of the Latin East provoked a long-standing and vicious conflict between two diametrically opposed religious/civilisational forces, each bent on the other's destruction, has been batted about for centuries. Notably, in 1991 (only two years before Huntington's first article on this theme), Michael Köhler instigated a frontal assault on this same notion.[24]

One of the dangers with characterising entire schools of thought *en bloc* in this way is that naturally such broad generalisations fail to recognise the individuality of specific authors. To those writers who feel corralled and misrepresented by this brusque sweep through the historiography, may I offer my apologies. Nevertheless, such an approach is necessary. The question of the crusaders' attitudes towards – and treatment of – Muslims is one of the most sensitive and most contemporaneously contentious of topics. The number of historians to pronounce their verdict is legion and it would be impossible to do justice to each. It was tempting, when writing this book, to confine research solely to works produced by historians of the Crusades. After all, they are the most tightly engaged with the First Crusade sources and their immediate contexts. Still, such an approach

---

[23] Interestingly it is much harder to find medieval historians who support the notion of the Crusades as a 'Clash of Civilizations' than it is to find those who refute it. Menache described the early crusades in this way, but only in passing. S. Menache, 'Emotions in the service of politics: Another crusading perspective on the experience of crusading (1095–1187)', *Jerusalem the golden: The origins and impact of the First Crusade*, ed. S. Edgington and L. García-Guijarro, *Outremer: Studies in the Crusades and the Latin East III* (Turnhout: Brepols, 2014), p. 235. I suspect that the refutations offered by crusades historians are not offered predominantly in response to scholarly texts which support the idea but, rather, to answer ideas currently in circulation within the modern media. Certainly when Paul Crawford rejects the notion that the Crusades instigated such a 'clash', he is primarily responding to conclusions reached by the modern media and politicians: P. F. Crawford, 'The First Crusade: Unprovoked offense or overdue defense', *Seven myths of the Crusades*, ed. A. J. Andrea and A. Holt (Indianapolis, IN: Hackett Publishing Company, 2015), pp. 1–28. I am grateful to Professor Andrea and for being given a glimpse of the pre-publication proofs of this work. For discussion on popular cinematic representations of the Crusades, see N. Haydock and E. Risden (eds), *Hollywood in the Holy Land: Essays on film depictions of the Crusades and Christian-Muslim clashes* (Jefferson, NC: McFarland & Company, 2009).

[24] Köhler, *Alliances and treaties.*

would fail to take into account the sheer density of interest in this area; or the contributions made by other academic circles.

So what does a *new* book on this subject have to offer? This topic may be well trampled, but there is still much that can be said.[25] There are foundational questions here that reward closer inspection. To take one example, historians are generally comfortable describing the crusaders fighting their battles against the *Muslim* Turks. Nevertheless, this presupposes that Turks can unproblematically be characterised as 'Muslims'. Recent research has demonstrated that the Turks were only partially Islamified by the end of the eleventh century and they still retained much of their shamanistic spirituality and steppe culture; thus, even the basic binary that the crusade was fought between Christians and Muslims requires reconsideration. Thus, key questions to be considered here include:

- How far had the Islamic religion penetrated among the Turks by the time of the crusade? (i.e. were the crusaders actually fighting 'Muslims'?)
- Did the crusaders view the various peoples they encountered in battle simply as undifferentiated 'Muslims'/'Saracens' or were their perceptions and approaches founded more on their foes' ethnic identity, i.e. Turkish, Arabic, Kurdish, and so on?
- Did the crusaders draw solely upon their own traditions when attempting to identify and interpret the Turkish and other Muslim peoples they encountered? Or did they seek guidance from eastern Christians/Muslims?
- Had any news of the Turks penetrated western Europe in advance of the crusade? (And by extension, how much were the crusaders told about the Turks during the recruitment phase of the campaign?)
- Were western Christendom's secular and ecclesiastical elites any more interested in 'Saracens' after the crusade than before?

By exploring these questions, new dimensions to the crusaders' attitudes towards the peoples they encountered during the crusade will be

---

[25] Examples of articles that provide an overview on this topic include: B. Hamilton, 'Knowing the enemy: Western understanding of Islam at the time of the Crusades', *Journal of the Royal Asiatic Society* 7.3 (1997), 373–387; M. Jubb, 'The crusaders' perceptions of their opponents', *Palgrave advances in the Crusades*, ed. H. Nicholson (Basingstoke: Palgrave Macmillan, 2005), pp. 225–244; J. France, 'The First Crusade and Islam', *The Muslim World* 67 (1977), 147–157; R. Hill, 'The Christian view of Muslims at the time of the First Crusade', *The eastern Mediterranean lands in the period of the Crusades*, ed. P. Holt (Warminster: Aris and Phillips, 1977), pp. 1–8; N. Housley, 'The Crusades and Islam', *Medieval Encounters* 13 (2007), 189–208. There are also the monographs mentioned earlier.

identified, drawing out unexplored aspects of their thought-worlds, their sources of inspiration, and their lived experience.

Another conviction that is often communicated – whether explicitly or implicitly – in studies on this subject is the belief that 'Saracens' were vital to western Europe's identity (and therefore to that of the crusaders) by providing the essential 'other' against which Christendom defined its own identity. The roots of this theoretical approach – going back to Friedrich Hegel – lie in the notion that individuals or societies construct their own identity by defining it *against* that of enemies or strangers (i.e. 'I know who *I* am, because *I* am not *you*'). In a similar vein, as Said commented when speaking broadly about the European identity: 'the Orient has helped to define Europe (or the West) as its contrasting image, idea, personality, experience'.[26]

Methodologies of this type have been employed in many contexts and have been applied to a wide range of civilisations. The idea that the 'self' acquires meaning through its comparison against the 'other' has clearly spoken deeply to many people.[27] Clearly it has explanatory power when discussing human nature (as many studies – including those discussed earlier – have shown), but this kind of approach can be taken too far. At times, historians have placed the self/other model at the very heart of Christendom's identity: that is, Christendom's core identity was defined by its sustained opposition to Islam.[28] Identity is complex and the product of many influences. Antagonistic neighbours, and the hostile stereotypes that are formed to characterise them, may play their part in shaping a society's character but to position their influence as the fundamental fountainhead of identity is too reductionist. Most contemporaries living away from the frontier in medieval Europe could have passed their entire lives without ever meeting a Muslim, still less living in fear of imminent attack. For them at least, Islam could not have been much more than a

[26] Said, *Orientalism*, pp. 1–2 (see also p. 58).

[27] For wide-ranging discussion on this theme, see A. Classen, 'The self, the other, and everything in between: Xenological phenomenology of the Middle Ages', *Meeting the foreign in the Middle Ages*, ed. A. Classen (New York: Routledge, 2002), p. xi.

[28] For example, Blanks and Frassetto remarked 'to be sure, there were other elements that went into the construction of the Western identity: Europe was also the product of internal colonisation and cultural assimilation. Yet the encounter with the Muslim "other" was elemental to the shaping of the Western world view'. They later observe that 'the Muslim became, in a sense, a photographic negative of the self-perception of an ideal Christian self-image'. D. Blanks and M. Frassetto, 'Introduction', *Western views of Islam in medieval and early modern Europe: Perception of other* (Basingstoke: Macmillan, 1999), pp. 2–3. Some historians have, like me, expressed concern at this kind of approach. See, for example, N. Berend, 'The concept of Christendom: A rhetoric of integration or disintegration?', *Hybride Kulturen im mittelalterlichen Europa: Vorträge und Workshops einer internationalen Frühlingsschule*, ed. M. Borgolte and B. Schneidmüller, Europa im Mittelalter XVI (Berlin: Akademie Verlag, 2010), p. 60.

distant name for some faraway people; certainly it is stretching credulity to believe that 'Saracens' would have served as their major point of reference when framing their identity. A broader model of identity is needed.

One area of expansion, discussed in this work, is to explore the role of alterity on a spiritual level. To date, when academics have applied notions of self/other to their work, they have done so almost entirely on an earthly plain. Human identity is formed when defined *against* other communities, religious groups, genders, classes, or social cadres, or in some cases the landscape. Nevertheless, human beings are not solely earthbound; they are also deeply spiritual. For the citizens of almost any civilisation in any era the main yardstick against which individuals have measured their own/their society's character has not been the hostility of unfriendly neighbours but the moral ideals of their God/scriptures. Medieval Europe is a classic example of such a society and the determination to live out the example of Jesus Christ (operating as a positive 'other') was perhaps the single most commonly held objective for contemporaries. For some, this was a goal of fundamental importance; for others, it was a labour that consumed their entire life.[29] The underlying driver of identity and morality here is not 'I know that I am good because you, my hated Muslim enemy, are evil', but rather 'I know I am fallible because You, Jesus, are perfect and I aspire to be like You'. One of this work's most important contentions will be that the crusaders' spent far more time seeking to imitate Christ's perfection – and failing, even in their own eyes – than they did preening themselves over the vices – supposed or otherwise – of their Muslim foes.[30] Their depictions of Muslims by contrast will be shown to be little more than a collateral by-product of the primary engine of identity: the relationship between medieval Christians and God.

This work will begin (Chapter 1) with a brief overview of relations between western Christendom and the Muslim world from the seventh century through to the eve of the crusade. The intention here is to provide a benchmark against which the events of the crusade and the attitudes of its participants can be compared. Later sections will then discuss how the Church and proponents of knightly culture encouraged the peoples of western Christendom to view and approach both Muslims and other non-Christians during this central medieval period. The following chapter

---

[29] The concept of God as the 'other' is one that historians have only just begun to explore, but this approach is still not unprecedented. See Classen, 'The self, the other', xli–xlii. See also the edited collection: *The otherness of God*, ed. O. Summerell (Charlottesville: University Press of Virginia, 1998).

[30] William Purkis has already conducted some ground-breaking work on the important of imitating Christ within crusader spirituality, see W. Purkis, *Crusading spirituality in the Holy Land and Iberia, c.1095–c.1187* (Woodbridge: Boydell, 2008), *passim*.

will then open discussion on the crusade itself, exploring its objectives and how Muslims were presented during the recruitment phase (Chapter 2). This discussion will then lead into an analysis of the crusaders' attitudes towards – and interactions with – the various Muslim peoples they encountered on campaign (Chapter 3). The next phase of this investigation considers the period directly following the crusade, asking how monastic writers and theologians attempted to make sense of the information brought home by the returning crusaders about their enemies (Chapter 4). This will be succeeded by discussion on the First Crusade's impact on Christendom's long-term relationship with Islam (Chapter 5).

One of the dangers with studies on a theme of this kind is that there is a temptation for authors to draw a hard line around their chosen subject material (in this case, attitudes towards Muslims/Islam) and then to treat this strand as a discreet entity that can be studied in isolation from the wider matrix of crusading thought. This is problematic because by segregating a theme in this way, the various links which both contextualise this topic and locate its significance within a wider mesh of ideas are either impoverished or lost. This work by contrast analyses the crusaders' approaches to 'Saracens', Turks, Arabs, and so on as component parts in their broader thought-worlds, establishing how this aspect of their experience related to their wider ideas concerning their objectives and sense of purpose, eschatology, personal spirituality, theology, miracles, visions, and geographical awareness. This stance has been adopted because it is often the interactivities between these linked ideas that draw out their deeper meaning. There are, however, a few topics which are not analysed in detail here – even if they formed part of the underlying investigation – largely because they have been discussed so exhaustively elsewhere. The various parities between the crusaders' attitudes towards Muslims and Jews, for example, represent one important theme which is not fully examined in this investigation. The crusaders did, on occasion, make such linkages and Baldric of Bourgueil sums this up clearly when he wrote of Jews, heretics, and Saracens that 'everyone calls [them] enemies of God'.[31] Nevertheless, there are many works which discuss this subject and it is towards the more uncharted regions of the crusader experience that we shall steer our investigation.[32]

---

[31] BB, 19.

[32] The classic work on this subject is R. I. Moore's *The formation of a persecuting society: authority and deviance in Western Europe, 950–1250*, 2nd ed. (Oxford: Blackwell, 2006). See also J. Tolan, 'Introduction', *Sons of Ishmael: Muslims through European eyes in the Middle Ages* (Gainesville: University Press of Florida, 2008), pp. xi–xiii; J. Riley-Smith, *The First Crusade and the idea of crusading* (London: Continuum, 2009), p. 54; J. Riley-Smith, 'The First Crusade and the persecution of the Jews', Studies in Church

Terminology: 'Saracens', Turks, and Muslims

For the most part, this work will abide in its terminology with the long-standing conventions of modern historiography. Terms such as 'Crusade', 'western Christendom', and even 'Europe' will be employed throughout following customary scholarly practice, even if this usage is not without its objections. It is well known, for example, that the varied assortment of armed pilgrim groups which set out for the east following the Council of Clermont definitely did not refer to themselves cumulatively as the 'First Crusade' or identify participants as 'crusaders'. These terms are the inventions of later generations and yet they are ubiquitous in scholarly works. Their value lies primarily in their concision, in that they permit authors to communicate a widely understood concept without the tedium of unnecessary circumlocutions. Thus, they will be used throughout.

A particular problem for this present work lies in defining the various Muslim groups encountered by the crusaders during their journey to Jerusalem. Even the terms 'Muslim' or 'Islam' create issues because, in an assessment of European perspectives, they are anachronisms. The name 'Islam' entered the French vocabulary in the seventeenth century and the English lexicon in the nineteenth. 'Muslims' are first referred to in both languages only in the seventeenth century.[33] Earlier terms found commonly in western European sources include 'Saracens', 'Hagerenes', and 'Ishmaelites'. These are all words which have biblical roots. The term 'Saracen' long predated the rise of Islam and was disseminated across Christendom in large part through the efforts of St Jerome.[34] It began as an ethnonym for the nomads of Northern Arabia, but later acquired specific biblical connotations. Gradually during the patristic era a consensus emerged among Christian writers that the term 'Saracens' related back to the story told in Genesis 16–17 about Abraham and Sarah. These biblical chapters describe how Abraham and his wife Sarah could

---

history, ed. W. Sheils, 21 (1984), 51–72; D. Iogna-Prat, *Order and exclusion: Cluny and Christendom face heresy, Judaism, and Islam (1000–1150)* (Ithaca, NY: Cornell University Press, 1998), pp. 275–322; B. Kedar, 'De Iudeis et Sarracenis: on the categorization of Muslims in medieval canon law', *The Franks in the Levant* (Aldershot: Ashgate, 1993), pp. 207–213. For a recent summary of the historiography on the anti-Jewish massacres of 1096, see J. Bronstein, '1096 and the Jews: A historiographic approach', *Jerusalem the golden: The origins and impact of the First Crusade,* ed. S. Edgington and L. García-Guijarro, Outremer: Studies in the Crusades and the Latin East III (Turnhout: Brepols, 2014), pp. 117–131.

[33] J. Tolan, G. Veinstein and H. Laurens, *Europe and the Islamic world: A history* (Princeton, NJ: Princeton University Press, 2013), p. 3.

[34] K. Scarfe Beckett, *Anglo-Saxon perceptions of the Islamic world*, Cambridge studies in Anglo-Saxon England (Cambridge: Cambridge University Press, 2003), p. 22.

have no children, so Sarah suggested to her husband that he should father a child by his Egyptian slave girl Hagar. Hagar duly conceived, but then began to treat her mistress with contempt, provoking Sarah to drive her away. Following the visitation of an angel, Hagar returned to Abraham and bore him a son named Ishmael. Thirteen years later, God then blessed Sarah who bore a son named Isaac. The earlier-mentioned names 'Hagarene' and 'Ishmaelite' – so often applied to medieval Muslims – reference the belief that these peoples were the descendants of Hagar and her son Ishmael.[35] The term 'Saracens' was also deemed to relate to this story because medieval authors interpreted it as representative of a false claim made by the 'Saracens' that they were actually descended from Sarah and not from Hagar. There is no evidence to suggest that Arabs ever actually applied the name 'Saracens' to themselves, but this explanation for the term was widely referenced in western Europe.[36] Isidore of Seville, for example, offered two explanations for the term 'Saracens'. The first was that it derived from the 'Saracens' claim to be descended from Sarah. His other explanation, which he seems to have rated rather less highly, was that the name alluded to the Saracens' Syrian origin and was a garbled form of the word *Syriginae*.[37]

For present purposes, although these names have the virtue of being contemporaneously relevant, they are still generally unsuitable for the modern historian of the First Crusade. The first crusaders hardly ever used the terms 'Hagarene' or 'Ishmaelite', so these words bring us no closer to their thought worlds. The name 'Saracen' is equally objectionable because it is loaded with the expectations, beliefs, and interpretations of the medieval and early-modern periods.[38] Such polemical freight is undesirable for a historian, who wishes solely for a term that essentially denotes a medieval Muslim.[39] Consequently, the terms 'Muslim' and 'Islam' will also be used throughout this work, with references to

[35] See, for example, Bede's commentary on Genesis: Bede, *Opera pars II: Opera exegetica 1: Libri quatuor in principium Genesis*, CCSL CXVIIIa (Turnhout: Brepols, 1967), p. 201.

[36] Scarfe Beckett, *Anglo-Saxon perceptions*, pp. 93–95, 200–212.

[37] Isidore of Seville, *The etymologies*, trans. S. Barney et al. (Cambridge: Cambridge University Press, 2010), p. 195. A slightly different origin for the name 'Saracens' can be found in the eastern Christian tradition. John of Damascus felt that this name referenced the idea that Sarah had sent Hagar away destitute from her home, see St John of Damascus, 'On heresy', *St John of Damascus: Writings*, trans. F. Chase jr, The fathers of the Church XXXVII (Washington, DC: The Catholic University of America Press, 1958), p. 153.

[38] Scarfe Beckett has shown that this term had pejorative connotations from as early as the eighth century in Anglo-Saxon territory. Scarfe Beckett, *Anglo-Saxon perceptions*, p. 1.

[39] For excellent discussion on the problems involved in using this term, see Frakes, *The Muslim other*, pp. 39–40.

'Saracens' offered in inverted commas; to indicate that whilst this work will utilise contemporary terminology it does not advocate its polemical import. It should be reiterated, however, that in today's lexicon the term 'Muslim' draws a fairly distinct ring around the adherents of a specific religion: Islam (although this is itself problematic given the various groups and sects that are encompassed by this term). To medieval writers the boundaries between the 'Saracen' religion and generic paganism were far more muddied and obscure than the use of the more modern term 'Islam' might imply. Typically, writers saw no objection to describing all non-Christians as 'pagans', 'heathen', or 'gentiles', and all three of these terms appear frequently with reference to Muslims in chronicles written throughout the medieval period, including those for the crusade.

Digging deeper, this work will also consider the crusaders' attitudes towards various sub-groups found within the Islamic world, specifically different ethnicities. The discussion will focus in particular upon three groups. The first of these is the collection of predominantly nomadic tribes, which under the leadership of the Saljuq family, invaded the Near Eastern region in the early-mid eleventh century. It is customary – both for modern and medieval writers – to refer to such peoples as 'Turks'. Still, this monolithic term obscures the very real diversity of the many pastoral peoples who participated in the Turkish-led tidal wave which broke over the Near East. These invaders were not solely Turkic, nor were they entirely under Saljuq command. Even twelfth-century medieval European contemporaries could make distinctions between 'Turks' and 'Turcomans'. Having said this, the chroniclers for the First Crusade – like the writers from many other Christian and Muslim traditions in the Near East – were unanimous in their use of a primary all-encompassing term for all these peoples: 'the Turks' (*Turci*). As we shall see, they could also use other names such as 'Parthians' or 'Persians', but these were generally simply alternative 'catch-all' terms which made no attempt to identify sub-groups. Given that this work is committed to exploring the crusaders' attitudes towards the various peoples they encountered, it will follow their terminology.

Two other peoples encountered by the crusaders to be considered here are firstly the Egyptian Fatimids and their subjects and secondly the long-standing Muslim communities of Syria and the Levant. To take the first of these, Fatimid Egypt was a reasonably cohesive political entity in the eleventh century and so, in a political sense, it is reasonable to refer to Egyptian peoples, particularly Egyptian armies and their leaders, as the 'Fatimids'. Even so, again a note of caution must be added in that the Fatimid caliphate (and its armies) incorporated many different religious and ethnic groups. Armenians, Turks, and Sudanese warriors marched in their ranks and there were Christians, and Jews who called Egypt home, albeit under Muslim rule. Thus, when this work refers to 'Egyptians' or 'Fatimids', these distinctions remain.

The final group is the most problematic. It comprises those Muslims of Syria and the Jazira who had been subjugated by the Turks during the eleventh century and who, by the time of the First Crusade, had either fallen under Turkish control or who maintained an uneasy quasi-independence. They were generally identified by the crusaders with the names 'Saracen' or 'Arab'. As stated earlier, the former of these terms is the most problematic for use in this present work, not least because it was sometimes applied to the Turks.[40] The term 'Arabs' is more appealing as a descriptor for this group (essentially, non-Turkish, Arabic-speaking Muslims in Syria), although it too must be nuanced and contextualised before it can be used effectively.[41] One of this term's strengths, for our present purposes, is that it is relatively unburdened with the same kind of emotive baggage that surrounds the term 'Saracen'. Another lies in the fact that the term 'Arabs' was employed extensively by the crusaders themselves to describe Muslim peoples living in this same area.[42] It is also reasonably historically accurate. Before the advent of the Saljuqs, the Syria/Jazira region had been dominated by a series of Arab tribes and ruling families: the Banu Kilab, the Banu Uqayl, the Banu Mazyad, the Banu Munqidh. Some of these Arab dynasties remained reasonably cohesive even after the Saljuq invasions, some offering determined resistance to their Turkish overlords that rumbled on long in to the twelfth century. The crusaders dealt frequently with these tribes and families and consequently it is not unreasonable to refer to them collectively as 'Arabs'. Certainly the famous Muslim historian Ibn Khaldun uses this terminology in this context when he discusses the Turkish conquest of the Near East, writing:

Then the days of Arab rule were over. The early generations who had cemented Arab might and founded the realm of the Arabs were gone. Power was seized by others, by non-Arabs like the Turks in the east.[43]

These points notwithstanding, the limitation must still be added that the ethnic and religious map of Muslim communities in this region was hardly monochrome. There were Sunnis and Shias as well as many

---

[40] Völkl, *Muslime – Märtyrer – Militia Christi*, p. 219.

[41] Tyerman makes a similar differentiation: Tyerman, *God's war*, p. 125.

[42] Having said this, it has been noted that in the early-medieval Anglo-Saxon sources, the 'Arabs' and 'Saracens' were treated very differently from one another creating, as Scarfe Beckett points out, 'the almost total distinction between them'. Scarfe Beckett, *Anglo-Saxon perceptions*, p. 182 and *passim*.

[43] Ibn Khaldun, *The Muqaddimah: An introduction to history*, trans. F. Rosenthal (Princeton, NJ: Princeton University Press, 2005), p. 25.

Islamic minorities, most famously the Nizaris (more commonly known as the Assassins), in this same area whose distinctiveness is obscured by a single blanket term. Many centuries had elapsed since the early Arab conquests and in the interim a variety of peoples from different ethnic backgrounds had adopted Islam as their faith, who would not necessarily have described themselves as 'Arabs'. Even so, with these concerns in mind, and because this study wishes to engage with attitudes of crusaders, who were generally unaware of these more detailed ethnic/doctrinal distinctions, the term 'Arab' will be retained to define this group, following their terminology.

Methodologies

Methodologically this work will traverse much thorny ground. Perhaps the two most controversial issues discussed are those of trans-cultural borrowing and reality/representation. The first of these is essentially the process of identifying whether a particular idea, technology, symbol, or practice was borrowed or copied by an individual from a neighbouring society, rather than bring the product of their own imagination or traditions. This issue occurs frequently in this study because it is often necessary to establish which ideas the crusaders borrowed from the Byzantines/Armenians/Syrians and which were the product of their own experiences and background.

The second issue (reality/representation) is the question of whether a description offered by an individual about a different person or society should (a) be interpreted as a fabrication intended for polemical/apologetic purposes or (b) be accepted simply as a statement of observed fact, or (c) be presented as an admixture of the two. For example, when a crusader describes a Turk, attributing all kinds of behaviours and qualities to him, can any part of his description be taken seriously as reflecting reality? or must it simply be assumed to be a hostile representation? This work's approach to these themes will now be discussed.

Trans-Cultural Borrowing[44]

Much of the thinking on this particular methodology has recently been helpfully unravelled by Kedar and Aslanov and the theoretical approach employed here follows their recommended framework. Fundamentally,

---

[44] This section draws directly upon the following article: B. Kedar, and C. Aslanov, 'Problems in the study of trans-cultural borrowing in the Frankish Levant', *Hybride Kulturen im mittelalterlichen Europa: Vorträge und Workshops einer internationalen Frühlingsschule*, ed. M. Borgolte and B. Schneidmüller, Europa im Mittelalter XVI (Berlin: Akademie Verlag, 2010), pp. 277–285.

they offer four scenarios in which it is possible to conclude that an act of transcultural borrowing has taken place. The first three are as follows.[45]

1. If we are explicitly informed that an act of trans-cultural borrowing has taken place case.

    (i.e. Anna Comnena specifically informs us that Alexius Comnenus warned the crusaders about Turkish military tactics. Thus it is reasonable to assume that the crusaders 'borrowed' this knowledge.)

    ... and we are convinced that the author is not trying to lie

    (for the sake of argument, Anna could have made this statement, not because she knew it to be true, but to attempt to underline the crusaders' ignorance and their dependence on her father's guidance).

2. If a distinctively named 'cultural trait', which appears in one society, suddenly appears in another under the same name.

    (e.g. several crusading chronicles use the term 'Azymites' to describe Armenians serving the Turks. This is a Byzantine pejorative term, not used widely in the West, which implies that the crusaders' borrowed it).

3. If the introduction of a new 'cultural trait' follows a recognised pattern of geographical diffusion.

    (e.g. several authors connected to families with strong links to Byzantium – i.e. the Normans and the counts of Flanders – sometimes used distinctively Byzantine terms when describing the Turks, such as 'Persians'. These authors had not visited Byzantium in person, nor is any specific link attested between their works and Byzantine originals, even so, they are located in regions or social circles where many Byzantine traits are known to have been diffused. On these grounds it seems likely that they inherited these terms from these sources).

These approaches are reasonably straightforward and provide strong grounds for proving transmission. The fourth of Kedar and Aslanov's 'rules' concerns instances where a historian believes that an act of trans-cultural borrowing has taken place but none of the earlier rules apply (i.e. the act of borrowing is not stated explicitly; there is no distinctive 'borrowed term'; and it does not form part of a known pattern of diffusion). For example, Chapter 3 will discuss how Fulcher of Chartres used the term '*Turci Orientales*' in his history. This could mean nothing more than 'Turks from the east', but it could also reference the Byzantine practice of dividing the Turkic peoples into western and eastern halves: Eastern Turks (i.e. Saljuqs among others), Western Turks (i.e. Hungarians). The term, however, is not distinctive enough to be sure that this act of

---

[45] The examples are my own.

borrowing has taken place. Fulcher does not state that he has borrowed it, nor does it appear in any other chronicle (thus none of the earlier rules apply). In such cases, Kedar and Aslanov offer various grounds which can strengthen the argument that an act of borrowing has taken place: if the trait 'borrowed' by society A closely 'resembles' originals in society B; if the trait 'resembles' the originals on which it was based in more than one respect; if it can be proven that the borrowed trait post-dated the creation of the original; if the 'borrower' had access to the culture from which it was borrowed. Ultimately in these circumstances it is necessary for historians to make their case and arguments (such as the earlier discussion on Fulcher of Chartres) can often only be advanced tentatively.

Reality and Representation

The question of whether 'Western' Christian descriptions of the Muslim 'east' can have any factual basis is contentious territory. It is an issue that Said returns to time and again in his work *Orientalism*. Although his argument on this point is multifaceted, he summarised his view with the greatest clarity when he wrote: 'we need not look for correspondence between the language used to depict the Orient and the Orient itself, not so much because the language is inaccurate but because it is not even trying to be accurate'. For him, 'western' portrayals of Muslims are merely artificially constructed caricatures, seeking to amuse, frighten, or instruct their European audiences, and acquiring currency through centuries-long repetition. Any moments when they might reflect actuality are simply coincidental.[46]

Likewise, historians interested in the transmission of textual tropes from author to author over the centuries often treat descriptions (e.g. of Muslims by western Christians) as manifestations of long-standing polemical or theological discourses, which can be traced back for centuries. In studies of this kind, the significance of such tropes lies in their long-standing thematic development – handed down from generation to generation – while the possibility that they might in any way reflect the author's actual lived experience is not central or, in some cases, not even considered. In many instances this is an entirely appropriate approach. As we shall see later, the widespread conviction among western European authors that the Turks employed poisoned weapons seems to have been founded on descriptions of Parthians offered in Virgil's *Aeneid*; certainly this identification has little basis in reality. This example bears

---

[46] Said, *Orientalism*, p. 71. See also: Frakes, *The Muslim other*, pp. 13–17, 36.

out the idea that, in this case at least, it is the discourse that shapes the perceived reality rather than vice versa.

Still, the crusaders had actually travelled to the east and to believe that *all* their descriptions of Muslims contain no empirical reality would necessitate turning a blind eye to a substantial portion of the evidence. In the following discussion, it will be shown just how accurate and precise crusading authors could be on many points. The crusaders learnt a fair amount about the nature and composition of Turkish weapons and showed some precision in distinguishing between broad ethnic groups. They also made some attempt to understand Turkish and Arab dynasties and their recent history; thus in many cases their observations need to be taken seriously as genuine attempts to report events faithfully. Even some of the more hostile-sounding charges levelled against the Turks cannot be simply batted away as unfounded polemic.

Let us take, for example, the accusation made by Baldric of Bourgueil that when the Turks invaded the Byzantine Empire during the late eleventh century they turned some churches in Asia Minor into stables for their animals/horses.[47] *Prima facie* this report can be easily dismissed. Baldric was writing a long time after a crusade in which he had not participated. Moreover, this complaint forms part of his version of Urban's Clermont address – a sermon often labelled as a self-evident piece of propaganda. Still worse, the claim that 'Saracen' peoples turned churches into stables appears in earlier apocalyptic sources; a link that may indicate that Baldric was drawing upon long-standing eschatological traditions concerning the Muslim 'other'.[48] A different, but equally damning, piece of evidence is that this same accusation also appears in the *bella parisiacae urbis* concerning Viking depredations; possibly Baldric manufactured this detail to equate the two.[49] There are admittedly other crusading authors who also report this Turkish practice, but these are mostly authors who were connected with Baldric and his work in some way – so they are automatically rendered suspect.[50]

These are formidable objections. Still there are stronger grounds for accepting his statement. Writers from several different cultures, or writing works wholly unconnected to Baldric, describe the Turks acting in this

---

[47] BB, pp. 6, 7.

[48] J. Rubenstein, *Armies of Heaven: The First Crusade and the quest for the Apocalypse* (New York: Basic Books, 2011), p. 123; Scarfe Beckett, *Anglo-Saxon perceptions*, p. 157.

[49] Abbo of Saint-Germain-des-Prés, *Viking attacks on Paris: The bella parisiacae urbis*, ed. and trans. N. Dass (Paris: Peeters, 2007), 62. For discussion: E. Lapina, *Warfare and the miraculous in the chronicles of the First Crusade* (University Park: University of Pennsylvania Press, 2015), 95.

[50] GN, p. 101; OV, vol. 5, p. 16.

way. The Georgian *History of David, King of Kings*, depicting events during the reign of Malik-Shah, reports the Turks using churches as stables, as does the continuator of Frutolf of Michelsberg's chronicle.[51] Another Syriac chronicle, admittedly discussing later events, offers a similar report in a description of the events that followed Zangi's capture of Edessa.[52] It might also be added that large buildings might be deemed suitable for stabling horses by those who were unconcerned about their spiritual significance. In light of the cross-cultural agreement on this point it seems reasonable to take seriously the notion that Baldric's report was founded on a factual report. This example serves as both a caution against dismissing the crusaders' statements too swiftly as 'representations' and it underlines the corroborative value of texts from different cultural traditions. Throughout this work, the observations, allegations, and statements made by the crusaders will continually be compared against those made by Armenian, Arab, Coptic, Georgian, Byzantine, and Syriac authors, on the principle that if two or more authors from different cultural backgrounds corroborate one another on a point of specific detail then the possibility has to be entertained that their claims are factual.

The task of distilling reality and representation becomes even more complex when it is considered that a single story or piece of evidence may contain blurred shades of both. Let us take, for example, the many stories told in crusader chronicles about the Turkish commander Karbugha and his preparations for confronting the Franks at Antioch in 1098. Several chroniclers claim that, shortly before his march against the Franks, Karbugha's mother visited him in Aleppo, warning him strenuously against this course of action. She is said to have conducted astrological observations which showed that his cause was doomed. As with the earlier piece of evidence, there are strong grounds for rejecting this story – either partially or completely – as fiction.[53] It might be asked, for example, how a crusading chronicler could possibly have known that a conversation had taken place between the Turkish general and his mother in a distant

---

[51] 'The history of David, king of kings', *Rewriting Caucasian history: the medieval Armenian adaptation of the Georgian chronicles*, trans. R. Thomson (Oxford: Oxford University Press, 1996), p. 311; S. Vryonis, 'Nomadization and Islamization in Asia Minor', *Dumbarton Oaks papers* 29 (1975), 50–51; *FE*, p. 132.

[52] *Anonymi auctoris chronicon ad A.C.1234 pertinens II*, trans. A. Abouna, Corpus Scriptorum Christianorum Orientalium: *Scriptores Syri CLIV* (Leuven: Secretariat du Corpus SCO, 1974), p. 100.

[53] Rubenstein, describes it as 'almost surely wholly fictional': Rubenstein, *Armies of Heaven*, p. 209. Murray takes a similar view: A. Murray, 'The siege and capture of Jerusalem in western narrative sources of the First Crusade', *Jerusalem the golden: The origins and impact of the First Crusade*, ed. S. Edgington and L. García-Guijarro, Outremer: studies in the Crusades and the Latin East III (Turnhout: Brepols, 2014), p. 201.

city, let alone how he could have acquired the precise wording of their dialogue. In addition, as Hodgson has insightfully noted, Karbugha's mother is portrayed carrying out several roles commonly associated with exemplary descriptions of western Christian women, especially those of an advisor or protector.[54] Likewise, as we shall see, the story forms a component part in a much wider polemical narrative found within these crusading chronicles which describes a dawning awareness among the Turks that God was fighting for the crusaders; hardly a point that inspires confidence in the tale's basic accuracy.

These factors need to be treated with the utmost seriousness when weighing the value of this narrative, yet there are also some points that speak in its favour. For example, there is nothing especially unlikely about a Turkish commander seeking astrological guidance before battle. Describing the final phases of Shihab al-Dawla Qutalmish's rebellion against Sultan Alp Arslan, Ibn al-Athir explained how before the clinching battle in 1063 Qutalmish sought astrological guidance. Like Karbugha his observations told him that defeat was at hand; a prediction he apparently took seriously enough to abandon any hope of a victory.[55] Moreover, in the early stages of the Turkish conquest of Persia, the leaders Tughril, Chagri, and Yabghu are said to have consulted an astrologer who foretold their future conquest of Khurasan.[56] More importantly, Ridwan of Aleppo is known to have employed a court astrologer, raising the possibility – however remote – that this was the very person consulted by Karbugha.[57] Whilst these points do not specifically corroborate the crusaders' claim that Karbugha sought pre-battle astrological guidance, they at least demonstrate that such an act was entirely in accordance with standing practices. Consequently, when judging the likelihood that this tale possesses any factual basis, at least in outline, the only conclusion that can be drawn is that it is 'possible'.

To take a final example, the *Gesta Francorum*, along with several other chroniclers, describes the Fatimid army marching into battle at Ascalon (12 August 1099) under a banner surmounted by a golden apple (*pomum*

---

[54] N. Hodgson, 'The role of Kerbogha's mother in the *Gesta Francorum* and selected chronicles of the First Crusade', *Gendering the Crusades*, ed. S. Edgington and S. Lambert (New York: Columbia University Press, 2002), pp. 168–172. On her subsequent representation in *chansons*, see Leclercq, *Portraits croisés*, p. 107.

[55] AST, p. 151.

[56] A. Peacock, *Early Seljūq history: A new interpretation*, RSIT (Abingdon: Routledge, 2010), p. 125. For descriptions of the pre-Islamic Turks' shamanistic practices see: Ibn Faqih al-Hamadhani, 'On the Turks and their lands', *The turkic peoples in medieval Arabic writings*, trans. Y. Frenkel, RSIT (Abingdon: Routledge, 2015), p. 49. See also: P. Golden, 'Religion among the Qıpčaqs of Medieval Eurasia', *Central Asiatic Journal*, 42.2 (1998), 207–209.

[57] AST, p. 294; Kamal al-Din, 'Extraits de la Chronique d'Alep', *RHC: Historiens Orientaux*, vol. 3 (Paris, 1884), p. 590.

aureum).[58] This seemingly innocuous report of a golden apple may well be a piece of bland reportage, simply reflecting observed experience; alternatively, it might represent an attempt to communicate a strong implicit message to its reader through the symbology of the 'golden apple'. To take the former position, the notion that this account is unadorned fact is supported by the existence of various banal details about this banner's capture. According to various accounts, Robert of Normandy purchased the banner – complete with its golden apple – after the battle for twenty marks and donated it to the church of the Holy Sepulchre (such coincidental details often suggest validity).[59] Clearly it was a very memorable banner because Albert of Aachen also reports its capture although he doesn't mention a golden apple.[60] To take a more sceptical position, 'golden apples' were potent symbols with strong inherent meanings; a point which raises the possibility that this description formed part of the author's interpretative framing of his Fatimid enemy. In the German empire a golden apple was carried by the emperor as a symbol of authority.[61] In ancient Greek literature it was the prize given to the most beautiful Olympian goddess (Aphrodite).[62] According to a much later legend Melchior (one of the three Magi) offered the baby Jesus a golden apple as his gift.[63] The notion of the 'apple' also calls to mind the sinfulness of Adam and Eve. Any of these attached meanings may have been intended, including the association with Aphrodite, who in the Byzantine tradition was said to have been reverenced by the pre-Islamic 'Saracens' (and Anna Comnena writing in the twelfth century described them as 'slaves' to Aphrodite).[64] Or perhaps he was simply baldly describing a

---

[58] *GF*, p. 95.

[59] RM, p. 108. See also: AA, p. 468.

[60] AA, p. 468.

[61] M. Stroll, *Symbols as power: The papacy following the Investiture Contest*, Brill's Studies in Intellectual History XXIV (Leiden: Brill, 1991), p. 67.

[62] M. S. Cyrino, *Aphrodite*, Gods and heroes of the ancient world (Abingdon: Routledge, 2010), pp. 83–84.

[63] Tolan, *Europe and the Islamic world*, p. 182. For discussion on the place of the Magi within the medieval thought world see: B. Hamilton, 'Prester John and the three kings of Cologne', *Studies in medieval history presented to R.H.C. Davis*, ed. H. Mayr-Harting and R. I. Moore (London: Hambledon, 1985), pp. 177–192.

[64] John of Damascus, 'On heresy', p. 153; AC, p. 276. See also G. Hoyland, *Seeing Islam as others saw it: a survey and evaluation of Christian, Jewish and Zoroastrian writings on early Islam* (Princeton, NJ: Darwin Press, 1997), p. 106. Curiously this is not the last time that a Muslim army is shown marching beneath a golden apple. Centuries later in 1480 during the siege of Rhodes, the Ottoman attackers are said to have bourne a similar banner, although in this case, as with the above instance, the significance of this symbol is not explained. Whether there is any kind of link connecting them is unclear, but it is interesting that the theme reoccurs. Ademar Dupuis, 'Le siège du Rhodes', *Hospitaller piety and crusader propaganda: Guillaume Caoursin's description of the Ottoman siege of Rhodes, 1480*, ed. T. Vann and D. Kagay (Aldershot: Ashgate, 2015), p. 272.

physical banner (or both). In such cases, dividing reality from representation becomes a case of balancing probabilities, or even admitting – in the postmodern sense – that some symbols cannot be satisfactorily unravelled.

What is being described here is not a structured 'methodology,' rather a general stance. This approach is characterised by (1) a willingness to at least consider the possibility that some even of the crusaders' wildest stories bear some relation to historical reality and (2) a readiness to focus closely on the relationships between sources from multiple civilisations.

1   Predicates

Latin Christendom on the Eve of the Crusades:
Historical Background

During all that time, the Muslims were gaining control over the largest
part of the high sea [the Mediterranean]. Their fleets kept coming and
going, and the Muslim armies crossed the sea in ships from Sicily
to the great mainland opposite Sicily on the Northern shore. They
fell upon the European Christian rulers and made massacres in their
realms... The Christian nations withdrew their fleets to the north-
eastern side of the Mediterranean, to the coastal regions inhabited by
the European Christians and the Slavs, and to the Aegean islands, and
did not go beyond them. The Muslim fleet had pounced upon them as
eagerly as lions upon their prey. They covered most of the surface of
the Mediterranean with their equipment and numbers and travelled its
lanes (on missions both) peaceful and warlike. Not a single Christian
board floated on it.[1]

Ibn Kaldun, The Muqaddimah

In this passage Ibn Khaldun (d. 1406) muses nostalgically on an
early-medieval world where Islamic states controlled both Sicily and
the Mediterranean. His words contain a fair degree of hyperbole, but
nonetheless they reflect the underlying balance of power that had characterised Islam's relationship with Christendom for centuries. Certainly,
between the eighth and mid-eleventh centuries, the initiative had almost
always lain with Islam in its dealings with Christendom. Muslim merchants dominated the sea lanes while Islamic fleets could prey with
impunity upon the ports and coastal regions of southern Europe.

This imbalanced relationship had developed very swiftly following the
death of Mohammed (632). Arab forces burst from the Arabian Peninsula
bringing thousands of square miles of territory across the Near East under
their control. Islam's conquest of the North African littoral progressed
with equal rapidity and by 708 much of the land between Egypt and

---

[1] Translation from Ibn Khaldun, *The Muqaddimah*, p. 210.

Tangier was under Islamic rule. In 711 their armies invaded Visigothic Spain where they soon established their authority across much of the Iberian Peninsula. Meanwhile at sea, Arab fleets made their presence felt, challenging Byzantine naval hegemony. Their first maritime raid was launched against the isle of Cyprus in 649; in 655 an Islamic fleet scored a significant victory over a Byzantine force at the Battle of the Masts; and in 674 another naval armada proved sufficiently powerful to blockade the Byzantine capital, Constantinople, for four years.[2] Following these advances, western Christendom suddenly found itself confronted by the Islamic world on two fronts: the Mediterranean seaboard and Iberia. Contemporary writers were clearly alarmed by these developments. The references to Islam found in the Venerable Bede's (*c.* 673–735) work change in tone over time becoming increasingly hostile as he grappled with the rising 'Saracen' threat.[3] In later years, Arab forces made some forays across the Pyrenees, deep into Frankish territory, raiding widely and assaulting cities such as Barcelona, Narbonne, and Carcassonne. In *c.* 732 Abd al-Rahman staged a major invasion of France during which he sacked Bordeaux, but he was later famously defeated on the road to Tours by Charles Martel at the battle of Poitiers.[4] This incursion marked the high-water mark of the Arab conquests in Europe and whilst later waves of invaders broke against the Carolingian Empire, the frontiers gradually stabilised.

In later centuries the Muslim polities situated on the shores of the Mediterranean continued to assert their maritime dominance, both in trade and war. The speed of the Islamic conquests in the mid seventh century had permitted the former administrative and governmental structures of the Byzantine and Persian empires to be captured virtually intact and these systems continued to ply wealth into their new masters' coffers, enabling them to maintain a position of supremacy. Meanwhile, Arab rulers could draw upon the expertise, intellectual achievements, and technological experience of the peoples now under their control. The result was that by the eighth century, the Islamic Empire had become a world superpower possessed of enormous political, economic, and cultural might.

The same was not true in western Christendom. The collapse of the Western Roman Empire in the fifth century had been a long drawn-out

---

[2] H. Kennedy, *The great Arab conquests: How the spread of Islam changed the world we live in* (London: Phoenix, 2008), pp. 200–224, 324–343.

[3] C. Kendall, 'Bede and Islam', *Bede and the future*, ed. P. Darby and F. Wallis (Aldershot: Ashgate, 2014), pp. 93–114.

[4] Kennedy, *The great Arab conquests*, pp. 319–323.

process. The bitter disputes between the various tribal peoples, who had migrated/invaded across its borders, destroyed much of the remaining infrastructure and commercial networks. When eventually the tempests of war subsided, the societies that emerged were a mere shadows of their classical forbears. Moreover, Europe's commerce in the Mediterranean declined as international trade routes were drawn east by the magnetic appeal of the rising Islamic empire. The Muslim world was in the ascendency while Europe was struggling to recover from a long period in decline. The few Islamic travellers who set out for Christendom were not impressed by what they saw and they were generally disdainful in their descriptions.[5] There was little that early-medieval Europe produced, which the Muslim world wanted. Writing in the ninth century, Ibn Khurradadhbih listed the valuable goods to be acquired in western lands as follows: 'eunuchs, young girls and boys, brocade, beaver pelts, marten and other furs and swords'.[6] Slaves were probably the most important of these commodities and they were required to work in the great North African olive-producing estates.[7] These slaves could be transported in large numbers and the pilgrim Bernard the Frank recalled how he had arrived in Muslim-held Taranto in 870 to find six ships carrying Christian slaves to North Africa.[8] Slaves aside, Europe was commercially marginal. Islam's real rivals at this time were Byzantium, India, and China. These were the powerful civilisations that drew the Muslim world's attention, not Christendom.

From the European perspective, the Muslim world was regarded as one foe among many. In the eighth and ninth centuries, the powerful Carolingian Empire confronted foes on almost every quarter. Their armies marched not only against Islamic forces, but also against Saxons, Vikings, Bretons, Avars, Bulgars, Slavs, and Magyars and there is little to suggest that Muslims were considered to be more dangerous than any other hostile neighbour.[9] Very few writers do more than note the presence of Islamic polities on their borders and the fact that they constituted a threat. On this latter point, however, they are very clear

---

[5] A. al-Azmeh, 'Barbarians in Arab eyes', *Past and present* 134 (1992), 7.

[6] This section and translation from Ibn Khurradādhbih's account can be found in *Ibn Fadlān and the land of darkness: Arab travellers in the far north*, trans. and intro. by P. Linde and C. Stone (London: Penguin, 2012), p. 111.

[7] Y. Lev, 'A Mediterranean encounter: The Fatimids and Europe, tenth to twelfth centuries', *Shipping, trade and Crusade in the medieval Mediterranean, studies in honour of John Pryor*, ed. R. Gertwagen and E. Jeffreys (Aldershot: Ashgate, 2012), p. 139.

[8] Bernard the Frank, 'Itinerarium', *Itinera Hierosolymitana et descriptiones Terrae Sanctae*, ed. T. Tobler and A. Molinier (Geneva, 1879), pp. 310–311.

[9] Tolan, *Europe and the Islamic World*, p. 33.

even if they are brief. In the early eighth century, when the famous missionary to Germany, Boniface of Mainz, wrote to the Abbess Bugga concerning her proposed pilgrimage to Rome, he cautioned her to wait for the threat from the Saracens to pass.[10] Clearly, news of the Islamic advance had penetrated even to the North Atlantic seaboard. The histories of this period are studded with frontier wars against Muslim forces, both in Southern France and Italy. Islam clearly remained a threat to the Carolingians, but the days of the sweeping Islamic advances were over.

Warfare, however, was not the only language of inter-civilisational discourse. There were also moments of diplomatic activity and trade. Treaties were occasionally signed between Muslim and Christian rulers. Even Charlemagne's famous attack on Spain in 778 (later commemorated in the *Chanson de Roland*), which ended disastrously with his defeat at the hands of the Basques, was provoked by a request for assistance from the Muslim ruler of Barcelona who was in rebellion against his masters in Cordoba. Arguably the most famous diplomatic exchange between the Carolingian and Islamic worlds occurred in 801 when envoys from Caliph Harun al-Rashid sent Charlemagne a series of handsome gifts including most famously an elephant.

These diplomatic dealings notwithstanding, as the ninth century progressed, the scale of the threat posed by the Islamic world to Europe steadily intensified.[11] For the most part the Christian territories of Northern Spain proved capable of handling the rising tempo of attacks, but the same was not true of Italy. Here the pressure began to mount, with the despatch of multiple Muslim naval attacks against its shores. The most symbolically significant of these sea-borne raids was the sack of St Peter's in Rome in 846; an act which struck at the heart of the Catholic Church. Southern Italy (which by this stage was sparsely populated and politically divided) offered opportunities for ambitious Muslim warriors and while some came as mercenaries, others were intent upon plunder and conquest. In the mid-to-late ninth century many cities and monastic communities were raided by Arab fleets including Bari (847), Conza (858 and 862), Ascoli (861) to name but few. For the most part these were hit-and-run affairs, but some commanders were intent on establishing their own states on Italy's shores. Among these was the emirate of Bari, which lasted from 847 to 871. Muslim attacks were launched from a number of different areas; some from North Africa, some from Iberia, and several from Sicily, which by the 840s was almost entirely under Islamic

---

[10] Boniface of Mainz, 'S. Bonifatii et Lulli epistolae', *MGHES*, vol. 1 (Berlin, 1916), p. 48.

[11] This section has drawn upon B. Kreutz, *Before the Normans: Southern Italy in the ninth and tenth centuries* (Philadelphia: University of Pennsylvania Press, 1991), *passim*.

control.[12] These attacks were not part of a formulated policy devised by the Islamic Empire as a whole but rather the initiatives of North African potentates. Nevertheless, there was little capacity among the Christians in this divided region to fend off even limited incursions. Some attempt was made by the various southern Italian polities to offer resistance and at times Christian cities banded together for mutual protection. Following the sack of Rome, a fleet was assembled under Caesar, son of the duke of Naples, which won a naval victory at the battle of Ostia in 849. Nevertheless, greater assistance was needed and by the 860s much of southern Italy was under Islamic control.

Increasingly the Carolingian rulers of Northern Italy were drawn into the wars of the south. Chief among these was Louis, great-grandson of Charlemagne (d. 875). He laboured relentlessly to retake Bari, eventually succeeding in 871. The Italian theatre entered a new phase in 876 when the Byzantines despatched a large army to this region, restaking their claim. Many cities were taken in this invasion and the Byzantines continued to strengthen their position throughout the 880s. Over the next few decades they bore the brunt of several Arab attacks. There was considerable friction between the Byzantines and the other Christian rulers of southern Italy, but at times circumstances compelled them to work together against the Arabs. In 915, for example, following an Aghlabid invasion in 902, Pope John X formed a league with the Byzantines and other Italian cities, which destroyed the major Arab base at Garigliano.

Around this time early reports began to emerge that Iberian Islamic raiders were operating out of a base in Southern France at La Garde-Freinet. This fortress would pose a serious threat to travellers in this region for decades and its garrison frequently blocked the Alpine passes between France and Italy; on one occasion its raiders are even said to have reached southern Germany. This base was only destroyed in 972 by Count William of Arles. Islamic incursions into southern Italy continued throughout the early tenth century and eventually proved sufficiently destructive to attract the attention of the Ottonian Emperors of Germany. In 982 Otto II marched into southern Italy at the head of a large imperial army. This dramatic move had been provoked by a spate of attacks from Fatimid Egypt which had caused considerable destruction. Otto eventually encountered a major Egyptian army near Stilo in Calabria where he suffered a major defeat. Following this encounter, however, such attacks upon southern Italy began to dwindle. Raids still took place well into the

---

[12] The first known Muslim raid against Sicily took place in *c.* 652. A. Metcalfe, *The Muslims of medieval Italy*, The new Edinburgh Islamic surveys (Edinburgh: Edinburgh Press, 2009), p. 5.

eleventh century – Pisa was sacked in 1004 and Salerno was besieged in 1016 – and even into the twelfth but they became more infrequent.

Although the Islamic world continued to pose a threat to Latin Christendom's southern flank throughout this period some commerce was conducted across this frontier of war, particularly between the Italian cities and Fatimid Egypt. Cities such as Amalfi and later Venice traded with Islamic ports, especially Alexandria in Egypt. They transported goods from across the Mediterranean and in many cases, the items they purchased either in Egypt or Byzantium had already been carried for great distances by sea from India or overland from China along the Silk routes.[13] These commercial connections brought prosperity to these cities, but they also rendered their loyalties suspect at times of war. When the Fatimids sent a major army to besiege Salerno in 871 the Amalfitans offered support reluctantly to their Italian allies; they are said to have been concerned that their assistance would jeopardise their relationship with Egypt.[14] This is only one example among many where the Amalfitans' commercial relations with North Africa dictated their policy. In 880 Pope John VIII excommunicated the city after it proved reluctant to play its part in a mutual defence agreement with several other Italian cities on the grounds that it did not want to sever its relations with the Islamic world.[15] Such ports walked a dangerous path, balancing the need to preserve their mercantile interests with the defensive obligation to prevent the complete collapse of southern Italy to the forces of Islam.[16] This was a relationship with tensions at both ends and clearly the presence of Amalfitans in Egypt caused disquiet within some circles because in 996 Amalfitan merchants were massacred in Cairo.[17]

Traders and diplomats were not the only travellers to cross the civilisational divide. The Holy Land may have been under Muslim control, but it was always a site of enormous spiritual potency for Christians. Many were prepared to take ship to visit the holy sites and following the conversion of Hungary some pious travellers took the arduous overland route to the east. Several accounts by these pilgrims have survived, describing their experiences, and these generally report that the Arab authorities of this region were fully accustomed to receiving such visitors. Hugeburc, abbess of Heidenheim, explained how Willibald (later raised to the

[13] A. Citarella, 'The relations of Amalfi with the Arab world before the Crusades', *Speculum* 42 (1967), 301; Lev, 'A Mediterranean encounter', pp. 140–143.

[14] Kreutz, *Before the Normans*, p. 56. [15] Kreutz, *Before the Normans*, p. 59.

[16] C. Cahen, *Orient et Occident au temps des Croisades* (Paris: Aubier Montaigne, 1983), p. 69.

[17] Kreutz, *Before the Normans*, p. 82.

office of bishop of Eichstätt) travelled to the Levant in the 720s, entering Islamic territory by sea at Tortosa. He then set out on the overland
leg of his pilgrimage, but shortly afterwards his party was imprisoned
on suspicion of spying. They were subsequently released after a Muslim
elder observed that the arrival of such pilgrims was not uncommon.[18] He
was arrested again almost immediately afterwards, but having secured a
written permit, he was able to travel freely. Later travellers seem to have
had similar experiences and Bernard the Frank was also imprisoned in
Egypt in *c.* 870, although he was later able to pay his way to freedom. He
then travelled widely and, reflecting upon his journey, commented upon
the peaceful coexistence of the local Christians and Muslims in the lands
which he visited.[19] In Jerusalem itself he noted the presence of a Latin
pilgrim hospice, which claimed was founded by Charlemagne.[20]

In most cases, pilgrims seem to have been able to travel without hin-
drance through this region. Even so, this began to change over time
and reports of attacks against both pilgrims and indigenous Christians
became steadily more prolific in the tenth and eleventh centuries.[21]
Threats could take many forms and in the eleventh century particularly there seems to have been an increase in Bedouin raids against the
Jerusalem area. These incursions prompted the Fatimid authorities to
strengthen the city's walls. The Christian community in Jerusalem also
suffered from outbreaks of persecution, the most important of which
occurred on the orders of the Caliph al-Hakim (d.1021), who destroyed
the Church of the Holy Sepulchre on 28 September 1009.[22] Hostility

---

[18] Hugeburc of Heidenheim, 'Vita Willibaldi', *MGHS*, ed. O. Holder-Egger, vol. 15.1
(Hanover, 1887), p. 94.

[19] Bernard the Frank, 'Itinerarium', pp. 312, 319; R. McKitterick, *Charlemagne: The
formation of a European identity* (Cambridge: Cambridge University Press, 2008),
p. 285.

[20] Bernard the Frank, 'Itinerarium', p. 314. For discussion on this hospice, see D. Pringle,
The churches of the crusader kingdom of Jerusalem, a corpus: Volume III, the city of Jerusalem
(Cambridge: Cambridge University Press, 2007), p. 192.

[21] A. Jotischky, 'The Christians of Jerusalem, the Holy Sepulchre and the origins of the
First Crusade', *Crusades* 7 (2008), 35–57.

[22] The question of how widely news of the destruction of the Holy Sepulchre circulated
in western Christendom has aroused considerable attention. Cahen (1954) felt that
the caliph's actions made a 'deep impression' on western Europe, but this notion was
rebutted by France (1996) who argued that they were not well known. More recently,
Morris (2005) has largely followed this view although he stresses the central importance
of Jerusalem itself in Europe's thought-world. Jean Flori (1999), however, feels that this
event was better known than France allows. In a related line of argument however,
several historians, most recently Gabriele, have argued that an encyclical purporting to
have been issued by Sergius IV in response to the destruction of the Holy Sepulchre is
genuine and not a forgery (as it often claimed). As Gabriele observes, this contests the

towards Christian minorities and pilgrims may well have been connected
to the anxiety and hysteria caused by the multiple famines that took place
during this period.[23] Year after year the Nile failed to flood between 950
and 1072 causing starvation and disease. The worst of these droughts
lasted for a total of seven years (1065–1072). The persecution of Christians seems in part to reflect the sad reality that in times of crisis, societies vent their frustrations on minorities. Meanwhile nomadic tribes
took advantage of the power vacuum left by elites in the Jerusalem area,
who found themselves unable to tax their subjects and provide adequate
defence against their depredations. As a consequence of these changes,
Jerusalem fell into decline. Its population dropped; its aqueducts ran dry;
its new wall encompassed a far smaller area; and the roads to its gates
became increasingly unsafe.[24] Even so, this was also a time when the
volume of pilgrim traffic was increasing dramatically and many western
European noblemen departed for the east. Some expeditions could be
very large, including one German group in 1064 which was said to have
been 7000 strong.[25]

Although Christendom's thoughts were steadily refocusing on its spiritual heart in the Holy Land, it is a notable feature of its engagement with
Islam that so little attempt was made to win converts from among their
ranks in these early years. The hope that Muslims might one day convert to Christianity was occasionally referenced, but few serious efforts
seem to have been made to launch missionary expeditions.[26] This stands
in stark contrast to the very vigorous contemporary evangelistic efforts

notion that this event was not well known. See C. Cahen, 'An introduction to the First
Crusade', *Past and present* 6 (1954), 7; J. France, 'The destruction of Jerusalem and the
First Crusade', *Journal of ecclesiastical history* 47 (1996), 1–17; C. Morris, *The sepulchre
of Christ and the medieval West, from the beginning to 1600* (Oxford: Oxford University
Press, 2005), pp. 135–136, 138; J. Flori, *Pierre l'Ermite et la première croisade* (Paris:
Fayard, 1999), p. 94; M. Gabriele, *An empire of memory: The legend of Charlemagne, the
Franks, and Jerusalem before the First Crusade* (Oxford: Oxford University Press, 2011),
p. 142.

[23] Although the events of 1009 are the most famous persecutions of Christians in Jerusalem
during this period, there had been anti-Christian rioting in 966, during which the
patriarch was killed and the Holy Sepulchre was sacked. Christians were also expelled
from Jerusalem in 1056 on the orders of the Fatimid caliph. *History of the patriarchs of the
Egyptian Church*, ed. and trans. A. Atiya et al., vol. 2, part 3 (Cairo, 1959), pp. 267–269.
Ellenblum has demonstrated that these were also periods of famine. R. Ellenblum, *The
collapse of the eastern Mediterranean: Climate change and the decline of the East, 950–1072*
(Cambridge: Cambridge University Press, 2012), pp. 175, 188.

[24] Ellenblum, *Collapse of the eastern Mediterranean*, pp. 28–29, 53–47, 196–197.

[25] This figure is, however, almost certainly too high. For discussion, see J. France, *Victory
in the east: A military history of the First Crusade* (Cambridge: Cambridge University
Press, 1994), p. 87; Morris, *The sepulchre of Christ*, p. 139.

[26] See, for example, Theodulf of Orleans' comments on the subject: *Poetry of the Carolingian renaissance*, ed. and trans. P. Goodman (London: Duckworth, 1985), p. 152.

made in eastern Europe and Scandinavia. The current explanation for the relative absence of missionary activity is the prohibitive effects of a ban on such activity within Islamic territory.[27]

Reflecting on the relations between Christendom and Islam at around the time of the first millennium, it is clear that for three hundred years the Muslim world had maintained a position of supremacy. Its attacks may have been sporadic and generally lacked any true desire for conquest, but they *were* sustained. Europe was a soft target and an easy source of loot. The major outcome of this imbalanced relationship was that Europe learnt to fear the 'Saracens'.[28] The menace they posed may not have been central to European life or identity, but it was consistent. Only a tiny proportion of its population would ever have seen a Muslim and their raids rarely penetrated far beyond the Mediterranean coastline. Moreover, confronted with invasion from Vikings, Slavs, and Magyars, Islam was only one enemy amongst many. Nevertheless, the *annals* histories of this period, even those written hundreds of miles from the frontier, are punctuated by reports of burning cities or pilgrims harassed as they crossed the Alps; proof that news of these acts was disseminated.[29]

During this time, Arab Muslim forces were described in much the same way as the other major threats to western Christendom. In their accounts of attacks upon Christendom, authors tended to deal with Muslim attacks in the same breath as Viking depredations or Magyar raids; little attempt was made to differentiate them from the others. Consider the following passage for the year 848 from the Annals of St Bertin:

The Slavs invading aggressively into Louis' [the German] kingdom were overcome by him in the name of Christ. Charles [the Bald] attacked a force of Northmen assailing Bordeaux and manfully defeated them. Lothar's army fighting against the Saracens holding Benevento were victorious.[30]

This reference is typical and simply lists the 'Saracens' as one of a number of different foes who encountered Carolingian forces in that year. Likewise, Richer of St Rémi, described Muslim raiders as 'barbarians' (*barbari*), which was the same term he used for Vikings and other

---

[27] B. Kedar, *Crusade and mission: European approaches toward the Muslims* (Princeton, NJ: Princeton University Press, 1988), pp. 9–14.

[28] Blanks has rightly observed that 'fear' has not received sufficient acknowledgement as a formative factor in Christendom's approach to Islam: Blanks, 'Western views of Islam', p. 38.

[29] Scarfe Beckett has demonstrated that Aelfric, abbot of Eynsham, writing at the turn of the tenth century, could write freely about 'Saracens' without feeling the need to explain who they were. She argues that this demonstrates that they were known outside elite intellectual circles. Scarfe Beckett, *Anglo-Saxon perceptions*, p. 187.

[30] *Annales de Saint-Bertin*, ed. F. Grat, J. Vielliard, S. Clémencet (Paris, 1964), p. 55.

attackers.[31] For the most part such accounts describe Muslim attacks relatively briefly, passing over the event in a single line, but there are some authors who provide a little more detail.

One such writer was Ermoldus Nigellus, whose early-ninth-century poem celebrated the life of Charlemagne's son, Louis the Pious, and provided a detailed description of Louis' capture of the Muslim-held city of Barcelona in 801. His account of this engagement draws attention in particular to the valour of the Frankish people, but it also dwells at length upon the Muslim defenders. These warriors are portrayed as cruel in their deeds and stubborn in their determination both to reject Christianity and continue to follow the 'orders of the Devil'.[32] Those Muslims who fell in battle were said to have been sent to the Underworld whilst, following the conquest of Barcelona, Louis is said to have 'cleansed' (*mundare*) the city that had formerly worshipped demons.[33] Ermoldus' approach then was both inherently hostile and placed particular stress upon the idea that this was a people who were under a demonic influence. Strikingly, however, almost exactly the same types of description can be found in accounts of Viking attacks. For example, in his tale of the defence of Paris against the Viking attack of 885, Abbo of Saint Germain-des-Prés dwelt at length upon these northern aggressors. In a similar vein to Ermoldus' descriptions of Muslims, he presented the Norsemen as the 'offspring of Satan' (*proles Satanae*), who were dreadful (*dirus*) and deadly (*funestus*).[34] Fallen Vikings, like the Muslims in Ermoldus' narrative, were said to have been despatched straight to Hell.[35] Comparing the way in which these enemies are characterised in these texts is instructive and makes the point that whilst Muslims were approached with considerable hostility, particularly at times of war, there was no specific terminology that was reserved for them alone. Moreover, fellow Christians too could be described as acting under demonic influence. Having told his tale of the Viking siege of Paris, Abbo went on to warn fellow clerics of the dangers of being drawn into the Devil's service. Thus to a contemporary eye, adherents of foreign religions may have been considered to be in the service of the Devil, but this was a threat that was common to all people, Christian or not.[36]

---

[31]   Richer of Saint-Rémi, *Histories*, ed. J. Lake, *Dumbarton Oaks Medieval Library*, 2 vols (Cambridge, MA: Harvard University Press, 2011), vol. 1, pp. 22, 26, 28, vol. 2, 224. For a similar example, see Ralph Glaber's work, in which he groups Norman and Muslim attacks under the title, '*De paganorum plagis*'. RG, p. 32.

[32]   Ermoldus Nigellus, *Poème sur Louis le Pieux*, ed. E. Faral (Paris, 1932), p. 30.

[33]   Ermoldus Nigellus, *Poème sur Louis*, pp. 34, 46.

[34]   *Bella parisiacae urbis*, pp. 38, 40.   [35]   *Bella parisiacae urbis*, pp. 34, 52, 66.

[36]   *Bella parisiacae urbis*, p. 100. For discussion on the contemporary conflation of the threat from Islam with other external threats, see T. Mastnak, *Crusading peace: Christendom, the Muslim world and western political order* (Berkeley: University of California Press, 2002),

This phase in the relationship between Catholic Christianity and Islam ended in the early eleventh century. By this stage the Abbasid Empire was in long-term decline with many regions asserting degrees of independence. In the east, the Turks were carving up swathes of its former territories, whilst the Shia Fatimid dynasty seized power in Tunisia in 909 and later transferred its rule to Egypt in 969. In the 970s the Fatimids were able to conquer much of Syria in a series of campaigns. By contrast, on the northern shores of the Mediterranean, Latin Christendom was rising quickly in strength. Its population was growing rapidly, while its missionaries were leading former enemies to Christianity. The Scandinavians converted and the Viking raids ended. The Magyars converted and their invasions also ended. Europe began to draw together; communications improved and monastic innovators and thinkers paved the way for new approaches to art and architecture. Moreover, the former Vikings who had settled in Northern France (Normans) were soon to lead Christendom's armies against Islam in the Mediterranean. Within a short space of time then, where it had formerly faced threats on many fronts, the Islamic world was rapidly becoming Europe's last remaining major opponent. True, there were always hostile tribes on Europe's eastern borders who continued to offer resistance, but the trend on this front was almost always one of expansion and conquest rather than defence. This shift did not pass unnoticed and Ralph Glaber, writing in Auxerre in the 1030s, noted that whilst the northern and western parts of the known world had become Christian, the same was not true of the lands to the south and east (the Islamic world).[37]

The conversion of Scandinavia strengthened another channel of communication between Northern Europe and the Islamic world. The Vikings had well-established trade routes between the Baltic and the Black Sea. Goods could be transported for much of the distance along rivers such as the Neva, Oder, and Dnieper, with established portage ways allowing ships and cargoes to be transported from the headwaters of one river, which ultimately emptied into the Baltic, to another which terminated in the Black Sea or Caspian Sea.[38] The objectives of these journeys were to seek glory and wealth, whether through commerce or with the sword from the Byzantine and Islamic cities to the south. Militarily the Vikings were a sufficiently powerful presence in these eastern regions to stage several attacks on Constantinople and in the tenth century the Khazar ruler voiced the belief that if he did not restrain these

pp. 96–114; J. Flori, *La Guerre Sainte: La formation de l'idee de croisade dans l'Occident chrétien* (Paris: Aubier, 2001), pp. 228–230.

[37] RG, p. 42.

[38] A. Winroth, *The conversion of Scandinavia: Vikings, merchants, and missionaries in the remaking of Northern Europe* (New Haven, CT: Yale University Press, 2012), pp. 92–93.

adventurers then they would destroy the Islamic world even as far as Baghdad.[39] The hardiest and most successful of these Norse travellers returned home bearing news, trade goods, and coins to the Baltic and Northern Europe. The scale of this traffic should not be underestimated and archaeologists have discovered over 200,000 Dirhams dating from this period in Scandinavia and a further 207,000 in Russia, Belarus, and the Ukraine.[40] Likewise, the Jewish traveller Ibrahim ibn Ya'qub noted that in the year 965 Dirhams were accepted as currency in Mainz, deep in Europe where most foreign coins would have been reminted into local currency. He was also struck by the availability of Indian spices.[41] Of course, the wide dissemination of Islamic coins and products from eastern regions does not constitute proof that detailed information was available in Scandinavia concerning the Islamic world. Nevertheless, it does show that this was one potential channel of information about Islamic territory; or 'Sarkland' as it was known.[42]

Norman bellicosity and aggression combined with Frankish arms, fortification techniques, and cavalry tactics proved a potent mix and in the eleventh century Christian armies began to drive outwards, seeking to regain the lands lost to Islam in the Mediterranean. The Normans often spearheaded these campaigns, having inherited their forefathers' thirst for travel and adventure. Some fought for the Byzantine Empire in the Varangian guard. Others arrived in southern Italy where, beginning as mercenary captains, they eventually seized control over the entire region. In time they became sufficiently powerful to attempt the re-conquest of Sicily. The island itself had been conquered by Muslim forces from the Byzantine Empire between 827 and 902. In 1038 the Byzantines made an abortive attempt at retaking the island with some Norman support, but it was only when the Normans began their own conquest in 1061 that the island was successfully restored.[43] The conquest of Sicily was not the first Christian attempt to contest control over the Mediterranean. In 1015–1016 Genoa and Pisa defended Sardinia from two Islamic invasions, in 1034 the Pisans attacked Annaba, whilst in 1087 they sacked the North African city of Mahdia.[44] These Italian cities were rising rapidly as the dominant commercial and military powers. Both Genoa in 934

[39] P. Golden, 'The peoples of the south Russian steppes', *The Cambridge history of early inner Asia*, ed. D. Sinor (Cambridge: Cambridge University Press, 1990), p. 268.

[40] Winroth, *The conversion of Scandinavia*, pp. 86, 98, 167. For coins found in the British Isles see: Scarfe Beckett, *Anglo-Saxon perceptions*, p. 56.

[41] This section from Ibrāhīm ibn Ya'qūb's account can be found in *Ibn Fadlān and the land of darkness*, pp. 162–163.

[42] Winroth, *The conversion of Scandinavia*, p. 98.

[43] The conquest of Sicily was completed in 1091.

[44] For discussion see: Metcalfe, *The Muslims of medieval Italy*, p. 75.

and Pisa in 1004 had been plundered by Muslim forces, but by the mid-eleventh century they along with Venice were firmly in the ascendency. They conducted an immensely profitable trade with all the major civilisations of the Mediterranean rim and beyond into the Black Sea. By the early twelfth century, Islamic maritime power was in steep decline in the face of these energetic city states. This process was driven in part by the collapse and splintering of the Abbasid Empire along with a series of famines and epidemics in North Africa. Muslim naval raids upon Christendom remained a threat into the twelfth century, but these were rare exceptions in a century characterised by the steady advance of European hegemony across the Mediterranean. In this changed scenario, Christendom was no longer the passive partner in this civilisational relationship. It was even able to consider retaliation against acts of aggression conducted against its co-religionists, including those in the Holy Land. The possibility has even been raised that Pope Sergius IV (1009–1012) did indeed issue a call to arms following al-Hakim's destruction of the Holy Sepulchre; a notion long doubted by historians. If this is true then it is a striking reflection of Christendom's growing confidence that such a scheme was even contemplated.[45]

The story in Iberia was roughly similar. In the ninth century, the remaining Christian territories clinging to the northern shores of the peninsula had begun to form themselves into political entities: the county of Portugal, the county of Castile, and the kingdom of Asturias. Their growing cohesion and organisation was enabled by major rebellions within the Umayyad caliphate. Increasingly, in the north-west Christian settlers began to head south, establishing outposts and cultivating the land. In 910 Christian forces under Alfonso III were able to cross the Cantabrian Mountains and found their capital in Leon. When eventually the Umayyads, under the caliph Abd al-Rahman, had recovered sufficiently from their internal problems and were ready to challenge this emerging power, they proved only partially successful in dislodging the Christians from their frontier settlements and in 939 a major Muslim

---

[45] The debate on this point hinges on the authenticity of a document apparently written by Sergius calling for a campaign to the east. For a recent strongly-argued case in favour of this encyclical's authenticity, see Gabriele, *Empire of memory*, pp. 141–143. For further discussion on this source see: H. Schaller, 'Zur Kreuzzugsenzyklika Papst Sergius' IV', *Papsttum, Kirche und Recht im Mittelalter: Festschrift für Horst Fuhrmann zum 65. Geburtstag*, ed. H. Mordek (Tübingen: Niemeyer, 1991), pp. 150–153. William Purkis has recently reflected on the debate surrounding this encyclical and its authenticity and, although he does not come down decisively on one side or the other, he seems to tend towards the notion that it was the product of the later eleventh-century. W. Purkis, 'Rewriting the history books: The First Crusade and the past', *Writing the early Crusades: Text, transmission and memory*, ed. M. Bull and D. Kempf (Woodbridge: Boydell, 2014), pp. 146–147.

army was seriously defeated during a major attack on Leon. The next major challenge to these emergent Christian powers came at the end of the tenth century when the powerful ruler al-Mansur launched multiple assaults on the north. He scored a series of major victories, sacking Barcelona in 985, Leon in 988, and Santiago de Compostela in 997. Nevertheless, the momentum he built up was not to be sustained. In the years that followed the Umayyad caliphate broke apart into rival Taifa kingdoms, whose feuding and infighting in time paved the way for a gradual Christian advance. Even against al-Mansur, the Christian armies had proved to be formidable opponents, but as the eleventh century progressed they were steadily able to take the offensive against the smaller Taifa successor states. From the middle of the eleventh century, the Christian reconquest began to gather pace and in 1085 Alfonso, king of Leon-Castile, was able to retake Toledo, the old Visigothic capital of Spain. His hold on the city remained precarious for many years in the face of determined counter-attacks. Still, by the end of the century, Latin Christendom was advancing on all fronts against the Islamic world.[46]

***

Overall, by the time of the First Crusade, western Christendom had a long history of relations with Islam. The Muslim world had proved itself to be a long-standing enemy which for centuries posed a danger in the south, just as the Magyars and Vikings had marched on Europe's northern and eastern frontiers. The 'Saracen' threat was widely and consistently referenced in sources from across Christendom and for the Christian inhabitants of southern Europe it must have been a very real source of concern. True, it was comparatively rare for these attacks to be pressed home with much determination and they were often the enterprises of individual emirs, rather than the policies of major states. Even so, the relative stability of Christendom and Islam's frontiers should not belie the fact that these powers were almost permanently at war.

Away from the frontline, writers living far to the north of the Pyrenees or Mediterranean coastline generally referenced the threat of Arab attack in their histories and even Adam of Bremen – perched on the North Sea coast – heard news about Otto II's wars with the Fatimids. Even so, such references tended to be brief.[47] Indeed, the general impression given by these authors is of a distant danger, existing on the edge of their

[46] H. Kennedy, *Muslim Spain and Portugal: A political history of al-Andalus* (London: Longman, 1996), pp. 60–153.

[47] Adam of Bremen, 'Gesta Hammaburgensis Ecclesiae Pontificum', *MGH: SRG*, vol. 2, ed. B. Schmeidler (Hanover, 1917), p. 82.

knowledge, but playing little role in their day-to-day concerns.[48] Moreover, in such texts, Muslim invaders were often described using precisely the same terminology as other non-Christian aggressors and there is little sense that they were viewed as an enemy of special significance. Certainly, when Urban launched the First Crusade, there is little to suggest that he was preaching to an audience that radiated an inherent sense of hatred towards Muslims.[49]

Still, many of Christendom's warriors came to focus their gaze on the Islamic world to the south during the eleventh century. The shift took place not because Islam was posing a steadily greater danger – in fact as shown earlier it was increasingly on the defensive – but because it was the only major enemy left. The conversion both of the Scandinavians and the Magyars in a relatively short space of time meant that Islam was Christendom's last serious remaining rival. The argument has been made that through the First Crusade, Islam became western Christendom's 'normative' enemy.[50] Nevertheless, for centuries these powers had been normative enemies and there had never been a substantial break in the fighting, only a shift in the fortunes of war. The evolution through which Islam became Christendom's sole major rival was, rather, a process of elimination, not a dramatic escalation.

The Lenses through Which Western Christendom Viewed Islam

Attempting to define how one civilisation perceives another is in some ways a flawed endeavour. Both Latin Christendom and the Islamic world were civilisations comprising of millions of individuals and thousands of communities. Within their borders lived many different ethnic groups and societies. There were differences in wealth, communications with the wider world, regional identity, and religious observance. Some societies lived in close proximity to the followers of other religions; others lived hundreds of miles from the nearest border. Some zones of interaction were fraught with conflict, others less so. An Iberian noble, for example, born and raised in a culture of resistance against Muslim al-Andalus, would not have perceived Islam in the same way as a Venetian trader with

[48] See France, 'destruction of Jerusalem', 13.
[49] J. France, *The Crusades and the expansion of Catholic Christendom, 1000–1714* (Abingdon: Routledge, 2005), p. 31.
[50] For discussion see: Mastnak, *Crusading peace*, pp. 115–117; T. Mastnak, 'Europe and the Muslims: The permanent Crusade?', *The new Crusades: Constructing the Muslim enemy*, ed. E. Qureshi and M. Sells (New York: Columbia University Press, 2003), pp. 206–207.

experience of Mediterranean commerce, or a Norman landowner on the Welsh borders. Nevertheless, this endeavour is not hopeless. Despite the disparities between western Christendom's various communities, they still had several shared characteristics which played a vital role in shaping, what could be described as a general world view.

Latin Christendom's communities were united in their shared adherence to the Catholic Religion and the traditions of the Church Fathers. The Church had long-established views about the status of non-Christian peoples that had been circulated and reinforced for centuries. This established a degree of uniformity and it is striking that clerical sources produced in England, or Southern France, or Italy reference a very similar theological approach when discussing non-Christians. This period also saw the evolution of a complex code of knightly behaviour that would later become known as chivalry. This was a shared culture common to a class of warriors who were: committed to warcraft and the exhibition of their masculinity through martial conduct; devoted to God and the pursuance of the Christian message; and endowed with (or seeking) the rule of great estates. The resultant value system placed great emphasis on the recommended approach that should be adopted towards non-believers and, given that it was disseminated widely through *chansons* and epic verse, constituted another source of inspiration and guidance in the treatment of members of other faiths. Both these structures of thought were to some degree Pan-European. That is not to say they were everywhere the same, but nonetheless they represented a common rhetoric and frame of reference which included many shared values and expectations. Discussion on these ecclesiastical and knightly recommended approaches to Muslims will be the subject of this section.

Theological

Running through the Christian sources from this period which discuss Muslims are distinctive terms and phrases, which carry clear theological associations. Many of these trace their origins back to the Bible itself and are deeply rooted in exegetical traditions. For the purposes of this present study, perhaps the most important concept is the notion of error. Muslims are described in various ways but the idea of them being at error is common to the vast majority of medieval texts which touch upon their status.

This term is used consistently through the Bible and communicates a clear meaning. It appears, for example, in the gospel of Matthew in a passage describing Jesus' teaching to his disciples on the Mount of Olives. Jesus warns them of the events to come, stressing that they must be wary of those who might lead them astray. In his description of the

Second Coming he tells them that 'false messiahs and false prophets will appear and produce great signs and omens, to lead astray [literally – into error/*in errorem*], if possible, even the elect' (Matthew 24:24).[51] A similar message is conveyed in 2 Timothy where St Paul describes the dangers of 'imposters' leading others into error (2 Timothy 3:13). Those in error then are defined in the Bible as those who are entitled to God's forgiveness and redemption and yet have been drawn away from the path to salvation and into corrupted activities and beliefs. The agents who lead such individuals away from God are depicted in various ways. Paul in his letter to Timothy, for example, warns his readers that in times to come people will be led astray by 'deceitful spirits and the teachings of demons' (1 Timothy 4:1).[52] Even in an erring state, such individuals are still fully redeemable, but it is necessary for them to reject their former ways if they are to receive salvation.

The notion of error effectively divides human beings into two groups, those that are in relationship with God and those who are in error. According to 1 John 4:6, 'We are from God. Whoever knows God listens to us, and whoever is not from God does not listen to us. From this we know the spirit of truth and the spirit of error'. This binary structure underpinned Classical and medieval theology and contextualises the individual Christian's duty to lead others out of error. This responsibility to lead erring people to the Christian faith is the fundamental duty of all Christians; a point made continually in the New Testament. The specific dividing line between these groups is the sacrament of baptism.[53] Describing the rise of the early Church, for example, Eusebius of Caesarea (d. *c.* 340) wrote:

In every city and village arose churches crowded with thousands of men, like a teeming threshing floor. Those who by hereditary succession and original error had their souls bound by the ancient disease of the superstition of idols were set free as if from fierce masters and found release from fearful bondage by the power of Christ.[54]

Likewise, in May 719 Pope Gregory II commended Boniface of Mainz's mission to convert pagans, charging him to spread the 'divine word' so that these people may no longer be 'restrained by the error of infidelity'.[55]

---

[51] Biblical quotations in modern English from *The new Oxford annotated Bible* (Oxford: Oxford University Press, 1991). Latin text is from the Vulgate.

[52] This idea was firmly embedded in medieval theology. See Gregory III's letter to the Saxons: Boniface of Mainz, 'S. Bonifatii et Lulli Epistolae', p. 35.

[53] B. Nilsson, 'Gratian on pagans and infidels: A short outline', *Cultural encounters during the Crusades*, ed. K. Jensen, K. Salonen, and H. Vogt (Odense: University Press of Southern Denmark, 2013), pp. 154–155.

[54] Translation from Eusebius, *The ecclesiastical history, books I–V*, ed. and trans. by K. Lake, Loeb classical library CLIII (Cambridge, MA: Harvard University Press, 2001), p. 115.

[55] Boniface of Mainz, 'S. Bonifatii et Lulli Epistolae', p. 17.

As is clear from these passages, the transition from a state of error into the service of Christ was often characterised metaphorically. In these cases, it is presented as a healing from sickness, or a freedom from bondage; in other sources: a liberation from slavery or a cleansing from pollution. St Augustine described his own conversion as the movement from madness to sanity.[56]

Although those in error were all deemed to share the common quality of being separated from God, medieval writers advanced the case that there were different levels of unbelief. Peter the Venerable, for example, presented Islam as the summit of unbelief, the 'sum of all heresies', placing it above the errors of other faiths.[57] This reflects the common practice of classifying non-Christian religions by the scale of their divergence from the Christian message: the greater the deviation, the greater the error.

If a medieval Christian's ongoing duty then was to lead those *in error* to a true knowledge of God, this naturally raises the question of how the faithful were guided to view those still in an erring state, who had yet to embrace the Christian message. Again, St Augustine offers some guidance on this point. In his *De Civitate Dei contra Paganos* he writes:

The man who lives by God's standards, and not by man's, must needs be a lover of the good, and it follows that he must hate what is evil. Further, since no one is evil by nature, but anyone who is evil is evil because of a perversion of nature, the man who lives by God's standards has a duty of 'perfect hatred' towards those who are evil; that is to say, he should not hate the person because of the fault, nor should he love the fault because of the person. He should hate the fault, but love the man. And when the fault has been cured there will remain only what he ought to love, nothing that he should hate.[58]

Augustine's message of 'perfect hatred' can essentially be rendered as: 'love the sinner; hate the sin' and its importance lies in the distinction it establishes between the individual and his/her sinful behaviour.[59] Following this view, the faithful are not permitted to hate, or simply denounce as inherently evil, those who adhere to other faiths because they are required to accept them as manifestations of God's creation, who still have an opportunity to turn away from their sinful behaviour. Crucially, the same, however, is not true of those beliefs or temptations that have led

---

[56] St Augustine, *Confessionum: Libri* XIII, ed. L. Verheijen, CCSL XXVII (Turnhout: Brepols, 1981), p. 137. See also *Bede's ecclesiastical history of the English people*, ed. B. Colgrave and R. Mynors, OMT (Oxford: Clarendon Press, 1998), p. 160.

[57] Translation from Iogna-Prat, *Order & Exclusion*, p. 356.

[58] Translation from St Augustine, *City of God*, trans. H. Bettenson (London: Penguin, 2003), p. 556; St Augustine, *De civitate Dei*, ed. B. Domart and A. Kalb, CCSL XLVIII, vol. 2 (Turnhout: Brepols, 1955), p. 421. Translation from St Augustine, *City of God*, trans. H. Bettenson (London: Penguin, 2003), p. 556.

[59] The idea of 'perfect hatred' is biblical in origin, appearing in Psalm 139.

these individuals astray. These are deemed to be absolutely and inherently evil.[60] It is for this reason that, as several historians have noted, depictions of Mohammed tend to be far harder than those directed at other Muslims.[61] The latter were deemed responsible only for being led into error, while the former was held up by contemporaries as being accountable for propagating this error.

The distinction between believer and belief is communicated clearly in many sources concerning medieval Islam, including the ninth century verse written by Ermoldus Nigellus. In this account he included a speech given by Charlemagne ordering an attack on Islamic-held Barcelona in which the emperor is alleged to have said: 'if this people honoured God, was pleasing to Christ, and was anointed with the oil of sacred baptism, peace would have been established between us, and that peace would have endured, for it is possible to be united by the religion of God. But for the moment it remains a cursed people; it refuses our salvation; and it follows the commands of the Devil'.[62] This blunt statement rests on a series of assumptions that come across clearly and can be reduced to the following: salvation is available to the Muslims of Barcelona should they become Christians; complete unity with other Christians is available to them should they become Christians; but whilst they continue to adhere to a non-Christian religion they remain under a demonic influence that separates them from the faithful.

This theological structure created a lens through which Classical and early-medieval Christians could view their non-Christian neighbours. Its presence can be detected in many sources, including the history written by Adam of Bremen (d. c. 1081) concerning the conversion of Northern Germany and Scandinavia. At the start of his account he offered a description of the conversion of the Saxons to Christianity in the early ninth century. He began by explaining that the Saxons had formerly been living under the 'darkness of error' and had been engaged in the worship of demons.[63] He also pointed out their hostility towards Christianity and the Church. Nevertheless, having described their conversion he wrote: 'they are hereby granted their pristine liberties and are

---

[60] Likewise, later theologians, who acquired some understanding of the Islamic religion (and recognised areas of shared belief between Christianity and Islam), often concluded that the mixing of truth with error represented an attempt to draw Christians away from their faith. Daniel, *Islam and the West*, pp. 186–219.

[61] J. Tolan, 'Veneratio Sarracenorum: shared devotion among Muslims and Christians, according to Burchard of Strasburg, envoy from Frederic Barbarossa to Saladin (c.1175)', *Sons of Ishmael: Muslims through European eyes in the Middle Ages* (Gainesville: University Press of Flordia, 2008), p. 101.

[62] Ermoldus Nigellus, *Poème sur Louis le Pieux*, p. 30.

[63] Adam of Bremen, 'Gesta Hammaburgensis Ecclesiae Pontificum', p. 9.

absolved from every payment due to us for the love of Him who accorded us victory, and are tributary and subject to him'.[64] Adam's statements here are significant. He is describing the movement of a people from error to salvation. His words also contain a series of implicit judgements; most importantly the conviction that no entry requirement besides conversion was required for their full integration within Christendom.[65] Ralph Glaber made a similar statement when speculating about the possible future conversion of the Islamic world. He wrote:

It remains an inviolable tenet of our Catholic faith that, in all places and amongst all peoples without exception, he who is regenerated by baptism and believes in the Almighty Father and His Son Jesus Christ and in the Holy Spirit, the one and only true God, and who performs some good deed through faith, will be acceptable to God.[66]

Thus – in theory at least – the only requirement for inclusion with the Christian community was spiritual conversion. In practice of course substantial difficulties could arise with the cultural and linguistic integration of an individual or community, but the Church tended to try and ease this transition.

Another author, whose work demonstrates a similar approach towards Muslims is Geoffrey of Malaterra. He wrote a history of the Normans in Italy and Sicily in c. 1098, offering a vivid account of their activities in these regions. Describing the conquest of Sicily he outlined many episodes of holy warfare against Islam and these again reveal the same approach of drawing a line between Muslim believers and the Islamic religion. As with the earlier authors, he felt that Muslims live under a demonic influence. At one point he described a naval confrontation between the Arab ruler of Syracuse and Roger I of Calabria, during which he wrote that the Muslim commander was inspired by the Devil.[67]

---

[64] Adam of Bremen, 'Gesta Hammaburgensis Ecclesiae Pontificum', p. 14. Translation from Adam of Bremen, *History of the archbishops of Hamburg-Bremen*, trans. F. Tschan (New York: Columbia University Press, 2002), p. 15.

[65] Many studies have demonstrated that countries which declared themselves Christian during the medieval period often required several centuries to be fully incorporated into Europe's dynastic and clerical networks; the practice was always messier than the theory. Even so, what Adam is pointing out is that once contemporaries were sufficiently convinced that a people-group had set out on the path to become fully Christian (often following the conversion of the ruling family), a fundamental rubicon had been crossed which entitled that territory to full inclusion within Christendom. See Winroth, *The conversion of Scandinavia*, pp. 128–129; N. Berend, *At the gate of Christendom: Jews, Muslims and 'pagans' in medieval Hungary, c.1000–c.1300* (Cambridge: Cambridge University Press, 2001).

[66] Translation from RG, p. 43.

[67] Geoffrey of Malaterra, *De Rebus Gestis Rogerii Calabriae et Siciliae Comitis et Roberti Guiscardi Ducis fratris eius*, ed. E. Pontieri, Rerum Italicarum Scriptores V part1 (Bologna, 1927), p. 86.

In this passage, along with later comments about churches being saved from the 'jaws of unbelieving heathen', he demonstrated his conviction that Islamic belief was a malign influence.[68] At an earlier point, however, in an account of the fall of Messina to the Normans, he told the story of a Muslim brother and sister who were forced to flee the city. According to his tale, the two had only travelled a short way when the sister became unable to run any further and her brother was forced to kill her to prevent her from being defiled. This story was told with considerable compassion demonstrating a strong degree of empathy on Geoffrey's part.[69] These episodes again underline this key distinction in his world view which could be summarised as follows: foreign religious beliefs are by definition evil and demonic, but their adherents are simply human beings – part of God's creation – who have the misfortune to be living in error and under an evil influence.[70] As Peter the Venerable observed when discussing the Turks and Arabs: '[they are] humans of course, but resistant to their salvation'.[71]

Geoffrey of Malaterra is even more explicit on this point in a passage describing the defence of a fort situated above the river Cerami against a large Islamic army in 1063. This siege was concluded when the garrison commander, the future Count Roger I of Sicily, sallied through the gate with a handful of knights, routing the Muslim force. In his reflection on this Islamic defeat Geoffrey wrote:

Their God was punishing them and their Lord had shut them up with nails of His wrath in the depths of their iniquity. I say "their God" not because they acknowledge him in their worship, but because, although unworthy insofar as they are ungrateful to their Maker, they are nevertheless His creatures.[72]

This passage has many qualities, but of particular interest is its insistence that 'Saracens' *must* be regarded as examples of God's own creation and, by implication, that they *must* be seen as valuable to God. The same ideas

---

[68] Geoffrey of Malaterra, *De Rebus Gestis Rogerii*, p. 90.

[69] Geoffrey of Malaterra, *De Rebus Gestis Rogerii*, p. 32. See also Baxter Wolf's comments on this topic: K. Baxter Wolf, 'Introduction', *The Deeds of Count Roger of Calabria and Sicily and of his brother Duke Robert Guiscard by Geoffrey Malaterra* (Ann Arbor, 2005), pp. 24–25.

[70] For discussion on this theme see: N. Daniel, 'The Church and Islam II: The development of the Christian attitude to Islam', *The Dublin review* 231 (1957), 292. Ducellier has demonstrated that the Byzantine author Nicetas of Byzantium took a similar stance in his attitude towards Muslims. See A. Ducellier, *Chrétiens d'Orient et Islam au Moyen Age, VIIe-XVe siècle* (Paris: Armand Colin, 1996), p. 155.

[71] *The letters of Peter the Venerable*, ed. G. Constable, vol. 1 (Cambridge, MA: Harvard University Press, 1967), p. 219.

[72] Geoffrey of Malaterra, *De Rebus Gestis Rogerii*, p. 43. Translation from Geoffrey Malaterra, *The deeds of Count Roger of Calabria and Sicily and of his brother Duke Robert Guiscard*, trans. K. Baxter Wolf (Ann Arbor: University of Michigan Press, 2005), p. 108.

appear in crusading texts including the eyewitness report *De expugnatione Lyxbonensi*, which describes of the siege of Lisbon in 1147 by forces of the Second Crusade. The author reflected on the successful outcome of the siege, commenting first that the 'bridle of error' (*frenum erroris*) had been lifted from the people of that area, before reminding his readers that they too should give thanks to God for their own freedom from this same 'bridle'.[73] His message here is important not only because it speaks both of Muslim liberation from error and of their shared humanity, but also because it reminds the Christian reader that they – or their people – had once been in the same position. Thus, all parties are presented simply as human beings, co-equal in their dependence on God for their salvation.

Overall, Christianity *requires* its adherents to view non-Christians as valued examples of God's creation. They may be perceived as misguided or malignly influenced, but they are important nonetheless and capable of winning salvation.[74] This viewpoint imposes a binding restraint on the impulse to simply hate or dehumanise 'the other'.[75] Nevertheless, the medieval Christian position towards non-Christian religions is entirely different. These are entirely alien and represent the spiritual vehicles that have drawn their adherents into this error, and the theological pressure runs in completely the opposite direction, guiding believers to view such religious systems as demonic and depraved.

The structure of thought outlined here is the starting point for this analysis and its various manifestations will be referenced in detail in later sections. This discussion generates a series of additional theological issues, which will be explored at this point. These can be condensed into three key questions: (1) How did medieval Christians view non-Christians who both persisted in rejecting the Christian faith – even when they had access to it – and who also presented a sustained military threat? (2) How much interaction was permissible between Christians and non-Christians living in the same community? (3) Were Christians prepared to identify virtues in non-Christians?

To take the first question, if all human life is deemed to be God-created and therefore precious, this naturally raises a whole array of problems for contemporaries when justifying the perimeter protection

---

[73] *De expugnatione Lyxbonensi: The conquest of Lisbon*, ed. C. Wendell David (New York: Columbia University Press, 2001), p. 182.

[74] Buc provides some interesting discussion on stereotypes – including madness and fury – often attributed by Christians throughout the Classical and medieval period to heretics and members of other religions. See P. Buc, *Holy war, martyrdom, and terror: Christianity, violence, and the West, ca. 70 c.e. to the Iraq war* (Philadelphia: University of Pennsylvania Press, 2015), pp. 121–133.

[75] See Classen's thought-provoking discussion on Wolfram von Eschenbach: Classen, 'The self, the other', pp. xxv–xxvi.

of Christendom's frontiers. Defensive military action, not to mention expansionist warfare, requires the use of lethal violence. As many studies have shown, throughout the medieval period the concept of Christian just or holy warfare went through a series of evolutions of which the crusade itself was an advanced form. This section will not delve deeply into this topic but will reflect upon the ways Christian participants in such campaigns were encouraged to view their enemies and, by extension, how theologians spliced the injunctions to value human life with the perceived need to provide military protection. As several commentators from this period observed: killing a non-believer would necessarily cut-short that person's opportunity to turn to Christ.[76] Thus the act of homicide effectively barred them from entry to heaven because they would die in a state of non-belief. This thought was not lost on the papacy and in 1074 Pope Gregory VII specifically ordered Archbishop Arnald of Acerenza to prevent Count Robert of Apulia from killing Muslims in recently-conquered Sicily so that they would have an opportunity to convert.[77]

Nevertheless, such arguments could have carried little real weight in Latin Christendom which was governed by military elites who were fully convinced of the need to provide military protection for the Christian communities in their care. There is no evidence to suggest that the general abandonment of lethal violence in frontier defence was ever seriously contemplated by any major authority. A different approach evolved – essentially a theological compromise – through which the act of killing a non-Christian was considered spiritually less reprehensible than killing a Christian. This conclusion was widely referenced and no lesser personage than Abbot Suger of St Denis (d.1151) made this point explicitly in his account of Louis VI's preparations for a battle against Emperor Henry V outside Reims. During a pre-battle council, advice was proffered that the French army should allow their enemy to penetrate deep within Frankish territory so that it would become cut off from help; only then could the Germans be 'slaughtered mercilessly, just like Saracens'.[78] He was evidently operating on the understanding that Saracens' could be killed with a clear/clearer conscience than his co-religionists.[79] Likewise, the

---

[76] Gratian, 'Decretum', *Corpus Iuris Canonici*, ed. A. Friedberg, vol. 1 (Graz, 1959: reprint of 1879–1881 edition), col. 195 (D. 50 c. 40).

[77] *The register of Pope Gregory VII, 1073–1085*, ed. and trans. H. Cowdrey (Oxford: Oxford University Press, 2002), p. 193.

[78] Suger, *Vie de Louis VI le Gros*, ed. H. Waquet, Le Classiques de l'histoire de France au Moyen Age XI (Paris: Les Belles-Lettres, 1964), p. 222. For a similar statement, see Otto of Freising, 'Gesta Friderici I. Imperatoris', *MGH: SRG*, ed. G. Waitz, vol. 46 (Hanover and Leipzig, 1912), p. 217.

[79] For further discussion, see Flori, *La Guerre Sainte*, pp. 228–229.

military orders trained their brethren for war with non-Christians, whilst demanding that they abstain from killing fellow Christians; again a line was clearly drawn between the two.

Certainly the notion that 'pagans' could be killed in the defence of Christendom and that this was deemed a good deed in its own right was widely referenced in earlier sources, often with reference to Old Testament authority. In 878 Pope John VIII responded to a question posed by a group of bishops in the Eastern Frankish realm, who had enquired whether those who died in the military defence of the Church would gain an indulgence for their sinful behaviour and be permitted to go to heaven. John answered citing the example of Manasses, king of Judah (2 Chronicles 33), whose early reign was characterised by a refusal to serve God, but who then suffered imprisonment during which he promised to be obedient to God. Manasses then expressed his recommitment to God by fortifying his kingdom and destroying idolatrous shrines. Through this exemplar, Pope John advanced the case that those who defend Latin Christendom are committing a holy and sanctifying act that will ensure their salvation.[80] Even so, John VIII was a rather unusual case and not necessarily representative of his time. For most writers, until the turn of the first millennium, killing of any kind was considered a sin for which penance was required. The major shift took place during eleventh century, particularly in the 1060s.[81] At this time, Pope Alexander II made an interesting distinction on this point when explaining how non-Christians should be treated in Iberia. He noted that those (in this case Saracens) who actively attack Christians can be killed justly, whilst those who are prepared to accept Christian rule should be unmolested.[82] Again, he seems to reference the belief that it is an enemy's hostility that qualifies them for destruction because they pose a threat to Christian communities; their adherence to a non-Christian religion alone is not in itself sufficient.[83] Orosius had made a similar point back in late antiquity, writing that anyone who is not a Christian is an 'alien' (*alienus*), but he only become a military target (*inimicus*) if he becomes hostile.[84] Even when enemies were both unbelievers and aggressors,

---

[80] 'Iohannis VIII. Papae Epistolae', *MGH: Epistolae*, vol. 7 (Berlin, 1928), pp. 126–127. For discussion, see A. L. Bysted, *The Crusade indulgence: Spiritual rewards and the theology of the Crusades, c. 1095–1216*, History of warfare CIII (Leiden: Brill, 2014), pp. 54–55.

[81] D. Bachrach, *Religion and the conduct of war, c.300–c.1215* (Woodbridge: Boydell, 2003), pp. 100–104.

[82] Pope Alexander II, 'Epistolae et Diplomata', *PL*, vol. 146 (1884), cols. 1386–1387.

[83] P. Herde, 'Christians and Saracens at the time of the Crusades: Some comments of contemporary medieval canonists', *Studia Gratiana*, 12 (1969), 365.

[84] Paulus Orosius, 'Historiarum Libri Septem', *PL*, vol. 31 (1846), col. 1147. It should be noted however that the clergy was still required to abstain from violence: Gratian,

Christian warriors were expected to approach these foes without enmity. Gratian's *Decretum* specifies that those who fought their enemies, having succumbed to feelings of hatred, had sinned and were required to perform a penance.[85] In another line of thought, which may well have classical roots, predating Christianity, some authors claimed that humans who had separated themselves from God had reverted to a beast-like state and, again, could be killed should it be necessary to prevent them from causing harm.[86] This idea was frequently referenced by Pope Gregory I who repeatedly described 'pagans' as requiring redemption from their animalistic existence.[87] Essentially these arguments represent compromises struck by a society attempting to blend its spiritual obligation to love and, in time, to win converts from its non-Christian neighbours with a fundamental conviction that warfare was a necessity for the defence of its territories and could be justified in the eyes of God.

In medieval descriptions of non-believers and their spiritual status, several personal qualities were frequently associated with the sin of unbelief. These included stubbornness, pride, and arrogance. In this context, all these vices carry a linked meaning, which is that individuals have refused to see/accept/follow God's direction even when they have access to it in person. In short, they were deemed to be 'stubborn' for having seen the truth, but then refused to acknowledge it. Orosius explains this idea as a process which runs as follows. He describes how all human beings instinctively sense the presence of God, but that those who lack news of Christian teachings will respond to that intuitive recognition by representing God in different forms and will establish their own distinct religions. This state of ignorance is accepted as entirely understandable up to the point at which such societies gain access to the Christian message. At this point they are expected to recognise the overriding truth of the gospel message and convert. Those who fail to make this transfer are in the position of having seen the truth, but then having rejected it. This necessarily places them on a pathway to sin through rebellion against God that will ultimately lead to disaster, both on earth and in

'Decretum', vol. 1, col. 179 (D. 50 c. 6); Nilsson, 'Gratian on pagans', p. 157. See also Caffaro, *Annali Genovesi di Caffaro e de' suoi continuatori*, ed. L. Belgrano, Fonti per Storia D'Italia XI (Rome, 1890), pp. 9–10. Völkl offers some interesting reflections on the crusaders' abilities to draw distinctions between enemies and 'strangers' which run along similar lines. See: M. Völkl, *Muslime – Märtyrer – Militia Christi*, pp. 161–166.

[85] Gratian, 'Decretum', vol. 1, col. 195 (D. 50 c. 40); Nilsson, 'Gratian on pagans', p. 157. See also J. Brundage, 'The hierarchy of violence in twelfth – and thirteenth-century canonists', *International History Review* 17 (1995), 670–692.

[86] This approach is much in evidence during the early/central medieval period and is referenced by many authors including Gregory I. See Pope Gregory I, 'Epistolarum libri quatuordecim', *PL*, vol. 77 (1862), cols. 692, 700.

[87] See: Pope Gregory I, 'Epistolarum libri quatuordecim', cols. 692, 700.

the afterlife.[88] This theological framework is much in evidence across the medieval period with those who are portrayed as having rejected God's commands generally being presented in this way.[89] Christians too were not immune from acquiring qualities, such as stubbornness and arrogance, and Bernard of Clairvaux described the slippery slope which might lead one of the faithful into pride. Again, this vice manifests itself as a turning away from God's path and onto a new road defined by wilful self-assertion that will ultimately end in sin and destruction.[90]

Regarding the second of the earlier questions, it is necessary to consider the zones of social interaction within which it was deemed theologically permissible for Christians to encounter unbelievers. Here the boundaries were relatively wide. Theologically, a hard line was drawn between the spiritual status of believers and unbelievers, but this same theology accepted that there could be considerable social interaction across the faith boundary. Again, this can be traced back to scripture where there is a fundamental expectation that Christians should interact with non-Christians. Pope Gregory I repeatedly emphasised Christians' obligation to live among unbelievers, drawing them to Christianity through kindness and good works; similar arguments were made by Augustine and later in Gratian's *Decretum*.[91] As Augustine pointed out, this was the example set by Christ. Cross-cultural interactions could take many forms. To some degree, there had always been trade between these two civilisations and, as western Christendom gradually reasserted its position in the Mediterranean, many Muslim communities fell under Catholic rule. Likewise, thousands of Christians lived in Muslim states. Each of these scenarios necessitated cross-cultural interactions and whilst these were not always friendly, and rarely took place on an equal playing field, the crucial point is that *in principle* during the eleventh and twelfth centuries such relations posed no fundamental theological problems for contemporary Christians. The sources contain many stories of inter-faith alliances, personal friendships, diplomacy, and in some cases a shared reverence for holy sites. To take one example, it is not surprising that the Arab nobleman Usama Ibn Munqidh included many stories in his

---

[88] Paulus Orosius, 'Historiarum Libri Septem', cols. 985–986.

[89] For wider discussion see: Kedar, *Crusade and mission*, pp. 16–17.

[90] Bernard of Clairvaux, 'De Gradibus Humilitatis et Superbiae', *Sancti Bernardi Opera*, ed. J. Leclercq and H. Rochais, vol. 3 (Rome, 1963), pp. 13–59. For context, see K. Petkov, 'The cultural career of a 'minor' vice: arrogance in the medieval treatise on sin', *Sin in medieval and early modern culture: The tradition of the seven deadly sins*, ed. R. Newhauser and S. Ridyard (Woodbridge: Boydell, 2012), pp. 43–64.

[91] Gratian, 'Decretum', vol. 1, col. 905 (C. 23 q. 4 c.17); Nilsson, 'Gratian on pagans', p. 158.

Book of Contemplation in which Frankish Christians were presented as friends. The most famous of these is his account of his trip to worship in a small mosque on the Temple Mount in Jerusalem where he described the Templars in this way.[92] He also recalled a story where he went to visit a Frankish knight, who used to refer to him as 'his brother', and who offered to take Usama's son to be educated in Europe. This latter story is a remarkable demonstration of the inter-faith relationships that could develop and many other sources furnish similar examples. Nevertheless, this latter story also sharply delineates the boundaries of such interactions. Usama may have been prepared to visit his Christian friend and to eat with him, just as his friend clearly valued him enough to make such an invitation, but Usama found the suggestion that his son should be educated in western Europe to be absurd and indisputable proof of Frankish stupidity.[93] It is not unreasonable to speculate that he may have been prepared to form friendships with Christians, but he would not have wanted to expose his son to any experience that would have challenged his fundamental Muslim identity. A similar pattern can be seen in reverse in the relationship that emerged between Richard I of England and Saladin's brother al-Adil during the Third Crusade. These men again seem to have enjoyed each other's company and to have won one another's respect, but Richard's suggestion that al-Adil should marry his sister Joanna was universally condemned by all parties, including the lady herself.[94]

These two examples help to define boundaries of interaction that were understood by both parties because they both describe moments when they were in danger of being transgressed. It seems likely that in both cases an inter-faith relationship was permissible up to, but not including, the point where the core religious identity of co-religionists might be placed in jeopardy. Any attempt to breach these social frontiers could provoke instant condemnation. These boundaries are equally clear in the crusading narrative produced by Fulcher of Chartres, a first crusader and chaplain to Baldwin of Boulogne. He described how the other Frankish settlers in the east had merged with the local population, inter-marrying with a range of different ethnic groups including Syrians, Armenians, and baptised 'Saracens'. The last of these named groups is important because again, it defines this same boundary. There was no objection to

---

[92] Usama Ibn Munqidh, *The book of contemplation: Islam and the Crusades*, trans. P. Cobb (London: Penguin, 2008), p. 147.

[93] Translation from Usama Ibn Munqidh, *The book of contemplation*, p. 144.

[94] See also R. Schwinges, *Kreuzzugsideologie und Toleranz: Studien zu Wilhelm von Tyrus* (Stuttgart: Hiersemann, 1977), p. 146.

marrying a 'Saracen', but only if he/she had become a Christian.[95] All the other people-groups mentioned were traditionally Christian.

With regard to the third question, Christians were perfectly willing to identify virtues among their non-Christian neighbours – even among bitter enemies. The theological foundation for this perspective was grounded in the notion of natural law. It was believed that all human beings, whether they accepted Christian teaching or not, had an inherent sense of morality that derived directly from their intuitive awareness of God (see Romans 2: 12–16). Isidore of Seville (d. 636) defined it as 'the instinct of nature'.[96] He pointed out that this law represents an inherent sense of morality – imparted by God – that is common to all mankind.[97] Later theologians such as Peter Abelard (d.1142) demonstrated that individuals, acting on the impulse of natural law alone, could be pleasing to God. He referenced as evidence the fact that early biblical figures such as Abel, Noah, Lot, and Melchisedech won divine favour even though they lived before the New and Old covenants. He himself defined natural law as the innate desire to love God and one's neighbour.[98] This discussion has relevance for attitudes towards medieval non-Christians because – along these lines – it was deemed entirely plausible that they could and would respond to the promptings of natural law and consequently display many virtues even without conversion to Christianity.

Speculation on natural law was not confined to ivory towers, but could play an active role in the perceptions of medieval frontiersmen. This is evident in St Boniface's (d. 754) letter to King Ethelbald (Christian king of Mercia) in 746–747. In this correspondence he expressed his concern that the king was neither married nor chaste and that he had committed several crimes of a sexual nature. Having warned him of the spiritual consequences of these sins, he described how even pagan Saxons would be appalled by his actions. He observed that whilst they do not know the law of the gospels they respect the institution of marriage because they adhere to natural law.[99] Writing in the ninth century, Rudolf of Fulda[100] made this same point and his work was later incorporated into

---

[95] FC, pp. 748–749. For thought-provoking discussion on the issue of inter-faith marriage and procreation, see L. Ramey, 'Medieval miscegenation: Hybridity and the anxiety of inheritance', *Contextualizing the Muslim other in medieval Christian discourse*, ed. J. Frakes (New York: Palgrave Macmillan, 2011), pp. 1–19.

[96] Translation from Isidore of Seville, *The etymologies*, p. 117.

[97] See also St Augustine, 'De Praedestinatione Sanctorum', *PL*, vol. 44 (1865), col. 968.

[98] Peter Abelard, *Collationes*, ed. and trans. J. Marenbon and G. Orlandi, OMT (Oxford: Clarendon Press, 2001), p. 24.

[99] Boniface of Mainz, 'S. Bonifatii et Lulli Epistolae', p. 150.

[100] Rudulf of Fulda, 'Translatio S. Alexandri', *MGHS*, ed. G. Pertz, vol. 2 (Hanover, 1829), p. 675.

the history of Adam of Bremen.[101] Clearly these frontier churchmen had no difficulty accepting Saxon/non-Christian virtue on the basis that they were responding to natural law.

One important aspect of Boniface's letter is his use of the morality of unbelievers to highlight the immorality of Christians. This was an important trope that can be found throughout the medieval period, often in sources describing Islam. It occurs, for example, in the earlier-mentioned *De expugnatione Lyxbonensi* in an almost certainly fictional conversation between the Muslim defenders of Lisbon and the Christian besiegers. In this exchange, the Muslim leader criticised the crusaders for their avarice and their lack of pure spiritual motivation.[102] It is worth pondering the implications of this tale. In essence it is an example of a Christian author describing an imagined Muslim who in turn is lecturing Christian crusaders about their sinful behaviour. Gregory VII used a similar device in his letter to the Christian faithful in 1084. He decried the sufferings of the western Christendom, claiming that Christian law was so widely ignored by its adherents that it had become an object of derision for Jews, Saracens, and Pagans. He went on to point out that whilst the non-Christian laws of unbelievers will not lead their followers to salvation, they are nonetheless followed with a diligence that was conspicuously lacking among Christians.[103] The underlying point communicated by both authors is clear and could be given as the following statement: how shameful it is that you, with the benefits and advantages of God's love and teaching, should fail and sin to such a degree that your immorality falls below the standards even of a non-Christian people?[104] Such a message seems to be founded on three expectations: (1) That non-Christians are capable of virtue through natural law; (2) that Christians are capable of conduct more depraved than that of non-Christians; (3) that typically Christians *should* maintain a higher level of morality. Broadly speaking the logic undergirding all these examples seems to be that all human beings feel the presence of God and have an intrinsic sense of morality; thus they are all capable of possessing positive qualities. Nevertheless, those who

[101] Adam of Bremen, 'Gesta Hammaburgensis Ecclesiae Pontificum', p. 8.

[102] *De expugnatione Lyxbonensi*, p. 120.

[103] *The Epistolae Vagantes of Pope Gregory VII*, ed. and trans. by H. Cowdrey, OMT (Oxford: Clarendon Press, 1972), pp. 128–134. See also *Register of Pope Gregory VII*, p. 139. For similar examples: Alcuin of York's letter to Archbishop Ethelhard of Canterbury: Alcuin of York, 'Epistolae', *MGH: Epistolae Karolini Aevi*, ed. E. Duemmler, vol. 2 (Berlin, 1895), p. 47; Gregory I, 'Epistolarum libri quatuordecim', cols. 766, 941.

[104] This structure (holding up the positive behaviour of the non-believer as a mark of shame for the faithful) is also much in evidence in Muslim sources, see IAA, vol. 1, pp. 155, 163. M. Barber, *The crusader states* (New Haven, CT: Yale University Press, 2012), pp. 101, 102. See also Tolan, *Saracens*, pp. xiii–xiv.

have accepted Jesus' teaching and have been baptised are both saved and protected by God's guidance, teaching, and forgiveness (although they like all humans are still vulnerable to sinful temptation). Non-Christians can also have innate good qualities, but that natural goodness is imperilled by their spiritual affiliations, which renders them more susceptible to the influence of the Devil.

Reflecting upon these theological issues it might be observed that whilst intellectuals may have had the time and resources to engage with ideas of this complexity, they would have been among the exalted few. Such an argument could go on to point out that theologising notions and discourses on non-Christians of this kind could have had little relevance for the rank-and-file crusader, whose intellectual horizons would generally have been far narrower. This is an important question for a study on crusading attitudes, one which will reoccur in many of the following chapters. Even so, there are two points that can be made from the outset. Firstly, the theological perspective described earlier is frequently referenced in the crusader sources for this period. True, such works were often written by churchmen so they do not constitute proof of lay religious attitudes, but many authors were clerics of intermediate rank, rather than senior clergy, and these were the very people from whom the crusaders sought guidance. Secondly, whilst the full logic underpinning this theological perspective is both complex and intellectual, its fundamental elements are simple. An individual who understands that his/her enemy is a human being, who is: beloved by God, capable of conversion, but tainted by adherence to an 'evil' religion, has already grasped its essentials. This perspective is not beyond the reach of even the simplest crusader and this may explain why it is so widely referenced.

Chansons and the Voice of Knightly Culture

> King Alderufe was very bravely bred,
> A worthy knight, a man of mighty strength –
> But he shunned God and so his soul was dead;
> He served Beelzebub, Pilate the wretch,
> And Antichrist, Bagot and Tartaren.
> And Astarut the old who dwells in Hell.
> *La Chanson de Guillaume*[105]

For an aspiring knight in Northern France, who had recently taken the cross, there were perhaps two dominant and interlinked discourses that

---

[105] Translation from 'The song of William', *Heroes of the French epic*, ed. and trans. M. Newth (Woodbridge: Boydell, 2005), p. 105. *Chanson de Guillaume*, ed. P. Bennett, vol. 2 (London: Grant and Cutler, 2000), p. 135.

would have moulded his preconceptions and foreknowledge of Islam (or more broadly hostile non-Christians). The first was the theologically approved view of 'Saracens' propounded by the Church, discussed earlier. Certainly, our knight would have had many opportunities to familiarise himself with the broad trajectory of theological thinking; perhaps through sermons, or during his education, or possibly in conversation with members of the clergy, or at second hand through his peers. If he had been particularly diligent in his studies he may even have ventured into some of the monastic chronicles that touch upon this subject. There was however another discourse in circulation – dependent in part upon the first – which may also have guided his attitudes and, later, his actions. At high days and feast days it is probable that our hypothetical knight would have attended banquets or other events at which *chansons* were performed. These *chansons* almost invariably tell tall stories of pious warriors and their mighty deeds of arms against tyrannous kings and unruly barons. They also include many stories of war conducted against non-Christians, especially Iberian and North African Muslims. Charlemagne's expedition to Spain, or more specifically the deeds of Roland at Roncesvalles, were particular sources of inspiration.

These epic poems dwell at length upon the 'Saracens' and for the most part they describe a reasonably coherent attitude towards them. Their shared approach has some parities with the theological model outlined earlier; indeed, the Church endeavoured vigorously to steer the knightly classes towards an idealised form of behaviour of its own defining. This agenda manifests itself frequently in the *chansons*, many of which were written or performed by churchmen.[106] Still, these sources are not merely dumbed-down versions of high theology. They also reflect the preferences and bellicose jocularity of the knightly classes. Moreover, they reveal a class of arms bearers who accepted the Church's guidance on their own terms and, as Kaeuper usefully puts it, 'wherever ecclesiastical restraints . . . cut into chivalric flesh, the knights simply refused to comply'.[107]

At the heart of many of these *chansons* is the classic set piece encounter between Christian knights – generally wildly outnumbered – and the 'Saracen' or 'Moorish' horde. Rather than dealing in theological niceties and biblical exegesis, the bulk of these narratives dwell upon gory swordthrusts and well-handled lances. Beautiful ladies, whether Christian or Islamic, swoon over the pious victors while enemy commanders are forced

---

[106] R. Kaeuper, *Holy warriors: The religious ideology of chivalry* (Philadelphia: University of Pennsylvania Press, 2009), pp. 52–65.

[107] Kaeuper, *Holy warriors*, p. 57.

to witness the destruction of the mighty hosts in which they had placed such faith. The stage-set then for the bulk of such sources' reflections on themes of inter-faith relations is generally the battlefield and the discourse is militant in the extreme. This then is very much the theology of war.

The Christian knights described in these *chansons* are often presented as self-consciously seeking to imitate Christ. This commitment is manifested through: their humble suffering for the defence of the faith, their ostentatious acts of piety, and their willingness to serve God – just as a knight might serve his lord or king. The worthy knights succeed in achieving these goals, whether through their victories or their martyrdom; the unworthy fall or flee in disgrace. Their contests of arms against non-Christians are given as quasi-judicial duels in which the rectitude of the faiths propounded by the two combatant parties is gauged on the field of battle. This is very literally the case in *Le Couronnement de Louis* where the pope and the Muslim king Galafré arrange a contest of arms between their champions. During the ensuing encounter William of Orange faces and exchanges retorts with the 'Saracen' champion Corsolt. They both manifest the belief that their God will grant them victory, whilst deriding the other's faith as hollow. Corsolt, for example, is given berating William and saying: 'you believe in a God who is of no use. From beyond the firmament what can he do? . . . Christianity is only for fools'.[108] Naturally, William then defeats Corsolt, symbolically disproving both his arguments and his faith, whilst proving the veracity of his own.[109] Following the encounter, King Galafré declares himself to be impressed by William's God and, following the subsequent defeat of his army, he chooses to convert. This again is very typical of this genre where martial victory and spiritual truth are presented as inextricably linked.

Such tales may seem far removed from the erudite theology of Christendom's senior churchmen, but they bear similar hallmarks. The dichotomy between believer and belief is maintained. These *chansons* consistently reference the conviction that the Saracen religion is both false and even demonic. This is stated very bluntly in the *Chanson de Roland*: 'Pagans are wrong and Christians are right'.[110] No explanation is supplied for this statement, presumably because it simply name-checked what to contemporaries would have been a self-evident fact. Nevertheless, the 'Saracen' peoples themselves are depicted very differently. Some

---

[108] Translation from 'The coronation of Louis', *Guillaume d'Orange: Four twelfth century epics*, trans. J. Ferrante (New York: Columbia University Press, 2001), p. 87. *Le Couronnement de Louis: Chanson de Geste du XIIe Siècle*, ed. E. Langlois, 2nd ed. (Paris: Honoré Champion, 1984), p. 27.

[109] *Le Couronnement de Louis*, pp. 14–40.   [110] Translation from *SR*, p. 64.

are presented as hideous malformed monsters who conduct dastardly acts of villainy. Such figures are shown performing acts of sexual depravity, extreme brutality, and evil trickery; manifestations of the belief that erroneous faith leads directly to sin. There are however other 'Saracen' knights who are depicted more favourably. They are shown as courteous, brave, valiant, and even virtuous. In the 'Saracen' king Marsile's horde, for example, the handsome, noble, and strong Balaguer ('were he a Christian'!) fights alongside the evil and ill-favoured Falsaron.[111] The 'Saracen' King Fierabras in his eponymous poem is likewise accorded almost the complete spectrum of knightly virtues, excepting of course a belief in Christ:

> If you had leisure to look at Fierabras
> You couldn't but remember how fine he was and grand.
> If only he'd believed in the Son of God and Man,
> No better knight or fighter the Christians would have had.[112]

These two very different kinds of 'Saracen' march side by side into battle against the Christians, revealing that contemporaries did not believe Muslims to be homogenous, but anticipated considerable diversity – moral and physical – within their ranks. These distinctions seemingly reflect the underlying presence of the earlier-mentioned theological model. Muslims are presented very differently to their religion. They are not given as inherently evil but are shown as human beings who have either been degenerated by their beliefs into beastlike savages or in some cases have still maintained their virtue; a belief that may distantly recall notions of natural law.[113] In many cases, those Saracens who eventually convert are often – although not always – amongst those who had previously received the greatest praise for their virtue, whilst those enemies accorded monstrous qualities are almost inevitably killed. Again there seems to be an expectation that the more virtuous Muslims will have a natural predisposition towards Christianity.[114] Thus, the *chansons* resemble works of theology in the same way that a sledge hammer resembles a surgical laser, but the similarities remain.

Depictions of the 'Saracen' religion in the *chansons* are, for the most part, simplistic and inaccurate. Islam is almost always presented as an

---

[111] Translation from *SR*, pp. 60, 72. For discussion see Akbari, *Idols in the East*, pp. 155–199.

[112] Translation from *Fierabras and Floripas: A French epic allegory*, ed. and trans. M. Newth (New York: Italica Press, 2010), p. 63. (Newth's primary text for his translation was *Fierabras: Chanson de geste*, ed. A. Kroeber and G. Servois, Les Anciens Poetes de la France (Paris, 1860), p. 20).

[113] See also Akbari, *Idols in the east*, p. 166.   [114] See: Daniel, *Heroes and Saracens*, 39.

idolatrous and polytheistic faith which reverences a range of Gods including: Apollo, Mohammed, and Tervagant.[115] Often these 'Saracen' gods
form a trinity, which was almost certainly intended to represent an 'evil
opposite' to the Christian Holy Trinity. Only rarely do the narrators of
these *chansons* provide any further detail – presumably it was not deemed
to be of interest to a knightly audience, for whom it was sufficient to
know that the enemy was enslaved to a demonic faith. Such representations in *chansons* persist throughout the twelfth and thirteenth centuries
and show little variation. From the writers' perspective, it probably was
not considered particularly important to be specific about the nature of a
serious religious error: after all, an error is an error. Indeed, in many cases
(including the *Chanson d'Antioche*) the Slavs are listed as Saracen allies,
an association which suggests that all Christendom's non-Christian foes
were deemed to be in league.[116]

With regard to wider 'Saracen' culture, these narrators generally have
little to say. Saracen buildings and cities are often portrayed, dripping
with gold and filled with bizarre curiosities, but in many cases these
authors simply filled in the blanks by assuming that their social hierarchies, religious structures, and culture were much the same as those in
western Christendom.[117] The Muslim ruler, King Aragon, in *La Prise
d'Orange* is depicted drinking wine, whilst possessing fiefs and marches.
His nobles are described as barons, while the gender norms within his
great palace are roughly comparable to those in medieval Europe.[118] In a
similar vein, 'Saracen' rulers are often presented as adhering to the same
(or similar) codes of martial conduct.[119] In *La Destruction de Rome*, for
example, when the pope is unseated from his horse whilst jousting with a
Moorish knight, his opponent permits him to escape because it would be
shameful to kill a cleric.[120] Likewise in *Fierabras* the Muslim champion
Fierabras is shown to be unwilling to fight a duel against a man of inferior
birth; again a conceit that smacks of Frankish warrior culture.[121]

[115] Leclercq, *Portraits croisés*, pp. 190–201.
[116] 'La Chanson d'Antioche', *The old French Crusade cycle: Volume IV*, ed. J. Nelson
(Tuscaloosa, AL: University of Alabama Press, 2003), pp. 65 and passim.
[117] C. Meredith Jones, 'The conventional Saracen of the songs of geste', *Speculum* 17.2
(1942), 206–210; Daniel, *Heroes and Saracens*, pp. 47–68.
[118] *Les Rédactions en vers de La Prise d'Orange*, ed. C. Régnier (Paris: Klincksieck, 1966),
passim.
[119] M. Jubb, 'Enemies in the holy war, but brothers in chivalry: the crusaders' view of their
Saracen opponents', *Aspects de l'épopee romane: Mentalités, idéologies, intertextualités*, ed.
H. van Dijk and W. Noomen (Groningen: E. Forsten, 1995), pp. 251–259.
[120] 'La Destruction de Rome: Première Branche de La Chanson de Geste de Fierabras',
ed. G. Goeber, *Romania* 2 (1873), 28.
[121] *Fierabras: chanson de geste*, p. 15.

One topic, which seems to have attracted endless attention in the *chansons*, but which hardly ever appears in theological works is 'Saracen' women. It might well be imagined – given the contemporary conviction that 'Saracen' society was riddled with impassioned sexual promiscuity conducted in opulent surroundings bedecked with gold and silk – that knights might have given more than a little thought to the character of Saracen women. Certainly the various Saracen heroines described in these tales are the very essence of knightly fantasy. For example, the Saracen Queen Orable in the *La Prise d'Orange* is described as follows:

> There is none so lovely from here to the East,
> a beautiful body, slender and fine;
> her skin is white, like a flower on a stem.

She is not, however, shown to be without defect because:

> God, what good is her body or her youth,
> She doesn't know God, our father almighty![122]

Through this presentation, Orable is situated among her fellow unbelievers, but in her physical attributes she is characterised as distinct and alien from her countrymen and family, conforming rather to Frankish ideals of beauty. A reader or listener is consequently encouraged to see her as incomplete and out of place in her 'Saracen' homeland, requiring to be saved and converted by the knightly hero William before her virtues can be fully realised. Again one might well imagine how the notion of a mysterious and beautiful Saracen woman, eager to be carried off by a worthy knight, might have played on the imaginations of a knightly elite.[123]

An area where the monastic authors and the troubadours are in full agreement, however, is in their conviction that it is possible to slay 'Saracens' with a much clearer conscience than their co-religionists.[124] Here the knightly and the theological flowed together in close accord but whilst the theologians described earlier might carefully work through the theology/philosophy underlying such conclusions, the *chansons* put this theory into practice describing, often with lavish detail, the righteous killing of non-Christian invaders. In the mid-twelfth-century *chanson Aliscans* a virtue is made of the hero's refusal either to imprison or ransom his 'pagan' enemies. His approach was always to kill them immediately. No explanation is given for this approach, although it is wreathed in

---

[122] Translation from 'The conquest of Orange', *Guillaume d'Orange: Four twelfth century epics*, trans. J. Ferrante (New York: Columbia University Press, 2001), p. 147. *La Prise d'Orange*, p. 103.
[123] See: Akbari, *Idols in the East*, pp. 173–189.   [124] Kaeuper, *Holy warriors*, p. 104.

exemplars underlining his piety, suggesting that the author believed this approach to be a self-evidently virtuous stance.[125]

One dimension where these works of epic verse differ from more theological texts is their intense curiosity about the lands of the 'Saracen', lying to the south and east. Many warriors embarking on the Crusades would have had little knowledge of Saracen territory, but they would not have been entirely ignorant. A handful of trade goods, either from the Islamic world or beyond, were available as luxury items during this time. Pepper and spices are perhaps the most famous of these and they were available in the kingdom of England from at least the eighth century.[126] Silks and other fabrics could also be obtained at exorbitant price in European markets. Clearly troubadours built upon what little they knew about 'Saracen' culture when writing their *chansons* because Muslim potentates are often described draped in silk cloth and eating eastern delicacies. Their warriors are also equipped with Damascene hauberks and mounted on Arab mares – items of sufficiently high quality that they had penetrated into the aspirational worlds of European elites. Muslim territory is also presented as fabulously wealthy; one has only to think of descriptions of Marsile's horde marching to fight Roland, dripping with gold and gems, or the palace of King Aragon, crested with gold and filled with strange beasts, exotic foods, and other wonders.[127] Again these are not solely fabricated representations. They are exaggerated certainly, but they also reflect a common geopolitical perception. By the time of the First Crusade, the Islamic world had maintained a position of economic dominance over its northern neighbours for centuries and its great metropolises dwarfed western European cities whilst the quality of its craftsmen was proverbial. Legends had long circulated in western Christendom about this extraordinary wealth including the long remembered gifts made by Harun al-Rashid to Charlemagne. It is also possible that stories of magnificent ancient civilisations from the classical period about Ancient Greece and the campaigns of Alexander the Great would have dilated this effect. Evidently, the vague awareness that somewhere to the south/south-east lay great civilisations of unimaginable wealth had been fully internalised within contemporary culture; a knowledge manifested clearly in these *chansons*.

The *chansons* were in most cases designed to entertain and propound masculine warrior ideals; relating acts of incredible bravery and prowess. Deep down within their tales there is occasionally the kernel of a genuine historic event – often dating back to the Carolingian era – but for the

---

[125] *Aliscans*, ed. C. Régnier, vol. 1 (Paris, 1990), p. 65.
[126] Scarfe Beckett, *Anglo-Saxon perceptions*, p. 61.
[127] *SR*, p. 65; *La Prise d'Orange*, pp. 111–112.

most part they are the stuff of knightly dreams. This should not obscure, however, the influence of their heroes as role models for the martial elite whose deeds many sought to emulate. These works need to be taken seriously as formative influences in knightly behaviour and expectations. This influence can be seen manifested in many instances. Usama ibn Munqidh, for example, tells the tale of a small cavalry skirmish near Apamea in 1119. During this encounter, he fought with a Frankish knight called Philip who was mounted on a black horse. Usama ended the contest when he skewered Philip with his lance, even though he was wearing double-thickness chainmail. Shortly afterwards Usama received a visit from another Frankish knight who wished to meet the Muslim warrior who had dealt Philip so vigorous a blow and he had travelled into Islamic territory specifically for this purpose.[128] This is a fascinating story which betrays a number of expectations held by both parties. The Frankish knight clearly saw no contradiction in fighting Muslims one day and then visiting them on the next to compare notes about their very bloody encounter. This conduct, which is reminiscent of the tournament field and the world of the jongleur, also reveals the knight's confidence that his non-Christian enemies would both welcome him and refrain from taking advantage of him whilst he was in their company. This incident calls to mind an episode in the epic poem *Fierabras* where Oliver (the Christian champion) and Fierabras (the Muslim champion) discuss their lineages and equipment – Oliver even assisting his opponent to arm himself – before immediately springing into bitter combat.[129] It also suggests that, in a similar vein, this knight felt that his enemy (Usama) would be willing to discuss a brutal moment of hand-to-hand combat in the spirit of shared warrior values. This was not some attempt at cross-cultural reconciliation – the knight wanted after all to discuss a mighty lance thrust inflicted in battle – but he clearly expected that his enemy would be guided by a code of conduct not dissimilar to his own; a point that mirrors the expectations of the *chansons*.

Parities between the deeds of other Frankish warriors/crusaders and behaviour typically found in *chansons* have been identified elsewhere. Loutschitskaja and Kostick have both observed that the duel between Christian and Turkish champions proposed by Peter the Hermit during his embassage to Karbugha at siege of Antioch during the First Crusade bears a marked resemblance to common set-piece contests of this kind found in the *chansons*.[130]

---

[128] Usama ibn Munqidh, *The book of contemplation*, pp. 50–52.

[129] *Fierabras: Chanson de geste*, p. 20.

[130] C. Kostick, *The social structure of the First Crusade*, The medieval Mediterranen LXXVI (Leiden: Brill, 2008), p. 127; S. Loutchitskaja, 'L'idée de conversion dans

Reviewing both the knightly and ecclesiastical sources, two linked discourses emerge. Both situate Christ and personal piety at the heart of their thought-worlds. Both view the Islamic religion as unvaryingly evil. Both view Muslims rather differently to their faith, perceiving them as God-created human beings who nonetheless will have been tainted to varying degrees through their adherence to a non-Christian religion. There are however, significant dissimilarities which reflect their specific audiences and milieu. The theological texts encapsulate the mentalities of the cloister and the ecclesiastical court. They accord closely with canon law, exemplifying the qualities of dogmatic uniformity, consistent biblical exegesis, and the traditions of the Church fathers. The *chansons* by contrast speak of the battlefield, of straight-talking fighting men, whose sincere and pragmatic faith was meshed both with their prickly sense of personal honour and their more earthy desires. Their questions and concerns were not the same as those of the Church and the Bible is only one of their points of reference. They tend to be far freer in their acceptance of killing, often communicating the idea that the value of human life – Christian or pagan – is held to be far cheaper than in theological sources. The *chansons* also tend to focus their attention almost solely on heroic characters. The hundreds of thousands of ordinary warriors who fall on all sides during their belligerent narratives are passed over in an eye-blink; what matters is the conduct of the handful of leading warriors, Christian or Muslim.

Consequently, marked dissimilarities distinguish these two discourses, clerical and knightly; reflecting the roles, views, and backgrounds of their audiences.[131] Still they should not be approached as two entirely distinct identities. The noble families which staffed the cloister and the chapterhouse also filled the ranks of the martial host. Clerics listened to *chansons* and dreamed of their Carolingian ancestors, whilst secular nobles attended sermons and supported their local religious houses. These worlds were inextricably linked and these connections manifest themselves in the sources. To take a few examples, the great monastic historian Orderic Vitalis was ready to attest the reliability of *chansons* as sources for his great *Historia Ecclesiastica*; whilst many of the judgements made in the verse-narratives bear the hallmarks of contemporary theology.[132] Many clerical-authored Crusading chronicles contain

---

les chroniques de la première croisade', *Cahiers de civilisation médiévale* 45 (2001), 39–53. Flori has similarly stressed the influence of the *chansons* on the crusaders' attitudes towards Islam: Flori, *Pierre l'Ermite*, pp. 221–225.

[131] For further discussion on the discourses emerging from western Christendom and the extent to which they were independent entities see: Akbari, *Idols in the East*, pp. 221–235.

[132] OV, vol. 3, p. 218.

set-piece dialogues between Christians and Muslims which are almost indistinguishable in their essence from those contained in *Aliscans* or *Le Couronnement de Louis*, whilst several *chansons* demand that their readers recognise them as authentic works of history, just like the monastic chronicles. These sources overlap with one another and, as we shall see, the crusading chronicles are often the very embodiment of this confluence.

Experiential Factors

It is not the purpose of this chapter to attempt to identify every pressure, trend, or guiding principle that helped to shape European Christians' attitudes towards Islam. Rather, this section seeks to identify some of the major attitudinal building blocks that would have been common to many peoples' perceptions. Thus far, the values of knightly conduct have been explored, along with the theological lens propounded by the Church. Nevertheless, human beings do not simply regurgitate wholesale the values – chivalric or religious – to which they are exposed. The earlier-mentioned theological or knightly approaches represent perhaps (drawing upon Foucault) 'a set of values and rules of action that are recommended to individuals through the intermediary of various prescriptive agencies such as the family (in one of its roles), educational institutions, churches, and so forth'.[133] Thus these may have been the 'recommended' approaches, but it was up to the individual to accept/reject these structures or at least to decide how to respond to them.

To be translated into action then, these 'recommended' approaches – theological or chivalric – had to pass through an individual's cognitive apparatus, which in turn would have been a product of their: family history, personality, experiences, and learnt knowledge etc.[134] Thus, to take an imagined example, two individuals might hear a preacher outline a theological approach towards Muslims but each might interpret it in very different ways according to their background.

This section serves primarily as a reminder that none of the authors discussed in this work were detached cold-blooded observers who perfectly reproduced any 'approved' discourse concerning Islam. They might have felt some need to signpost their adherence to such norms in their writings, but these same works often reveal a much more complex perspective which bears the hallmarks of their own distinct experience. For example, many of them had either lived through the cut and thrust of a crusading campaign or had served personally on a Latin Eastern frontier. Some

---

[133] M. Foucault, *The use of pleasure: The history of sexuality, volume 2*, trans. R. Hurley (London: Penguin, 1985), p. 25.

[134] For discussion on the influence of lived experience upon the crusaders' portrayals of Muslims see: Völkl, *Muslime – Märtyrer – Militia Christi*, pp. 15–19 and *passim*.

had suffered a personal loss at Muslim hands. William of Tyre lost a brother in battle against Saladin in 1179.[135] Walter the Chancellor was taken prisoner after witnessing the defeat of the Antiochene army at the Field of Blood in 1119. Peter Tudebode's references to the deaths of two knights called Arnald and Arvedus Tudebode seem to refer to the loss of two family members.[136] Many other writers suffered the deprivations and horrors of marching for months in a crusader column across Asia Minor. So when characterising a writer's viewpoint their theological framework needs to be spliced with the impact of their experiences.

In some cases there is an obvious tension between an individual's theology/inherited values and their personal inclinations. This is particularly apparent with the issue of hatred. The Church's general position was that while a non-Christian's beliefs might be considered as evil, unbelievers could not simply be hated because they were manifestations of God's creation and subject to natural law. Even so, several sources for this period manifest a tension between loving and hating one's enemies. As the tenth-century writer Liudprand of Cremona (d.972) shrewdly observed, 'man, formed in the likeness and image of God, conscious of the law of God, capable of reason, not only strives not to love his neighbour, but sets out vigorously to hate him'.[137] The conflict between the Christian injunction to love and the instinctive urge to hate – within the context of crusader campaigns (where these two emotions were often deeply muddled) is much in evidence throughout the sources for this period.

There is also the question of distance. Some crusading authors lived and breathed the events and milieu of the Near East, others wrote their accounts without having ever seen the Mediterranean, let alone a Muslim, but relied rather upon the reports of others. Thus their proximity to events could play a profound role in shaping their writing. With these points in mind, this analysis will proceed on no assumption beyond the broad notion that most of Christendom's Catholic inhabitants will have developed an attitude towards Islam that to varying degrees shows the hallmarks of: theological teaching, knightly role models, and the moulding power of their own instincts and experiences.

[135] WT, vol. 2, p. 1002.   [136] PT, pp. 97, 116.
[137] Liudprand of Cremona, 'Antapodosis', *Liudprandi Cremonensis Opera Omnia*, ed. P. Chiesa, CCCM CLVI (Turnhout: Brepols, 1998), p. 17.

2 The Launch of the First Crusade

"A nerve was touched of exquisite feeling; and the sensation vibrated to the heart of Europe."

Edward Gibbon, *The Decline and Fall of the Roman Empire*[1]

Historical Background

At the council of Clermont on 27 November 1095, Pope Urban II did the same thing that rulers across the Near East and Southern Asia (whether Islamic, Hindu, or Christian) had been doing for over a century: he launched a campaign against the Turks.

The Turks had long been a major force on the inner Asian steppe. The Chinese began to view them as a serious threat back in the sixth century (although fleeting references to their existence can be traced back as far as the first century CE).[2] Under the Tang dynasty (618–907) increasing Turkish pressure on the empire's western frontiers spawned an uneasy relationship between the emperors and their Turkish steppe neighbours, known to the Chinese as the 'Tujue'.[3] During the seventh and eighth centuries, periods of peace, tribute, and diplomatic marriages were punctuated by invasions and brutal confrontations. This phase of warfare and diplomacy came to an end in 744 with the collapse of the Second Turkish Kaghanate. Their place was taken by the Uighurs, again a people of Turkic origins, whose kaghanate lasted until 840 AD.[4]

Moving south, the Arabs had known about the Turks since the seventh century. Their forces encountered them after crossing the river Oxus during the rapid expansion of Islam. In later years an uneasy relationship

---

[1] Edward Gibbon, *The history of the decline and fall of the Roman Empire* (Ware, 1998), p. 918.

[2] D. Sinor, 'The establishment and dissolution of the Türk empire', *The Cambridge history of early inner Asia*, ed. D. Sinor (Cambridge: Cambridge University Press, 1990), p. 285.

[3] C. Findley, *The Turks in world history* (Oxford: Oxford University Press, 2005), p. 21.

[4] D. C. Wright, 'The northern frontier', *A military history of China* (Lexington: University Press of Kentucky, 2012), pp. 57–80.

existed between the two peoples, punctuated by wars and raids, but for the most part the Turks' military incursions were generally kept at bay. Arab travellers journeyed among the steppe peoples at times and sent home reports about the Turks and their various tribes.[5] Many Turks travelled south, occasionally as settlers, but often having been sold as military slaves intended for Arab masters.[6] Frequently, these slave soldiers '*Ghulams*' rose to positions of prominence and formed an elite core within Abbasid armies.

By the late tenth century the relatively stable frontier between the nomadic lands of Inner Asia and Islamic Persia began to collapse.[7] For decades the Turkic peoples had been in the process of migrating westwards from their homelands in Mongolia into Central Asia; a movement that brought them increasingly into contact with the Islamic world to the south. At the same time, changing climatic conditions on the Central Asian Steppe may have incited the Turks to move south, away from their frozen winter pastures. They were joined in this movement by thousands of fellow nomads, some travelling from as far afield as Tibet.[8] The threat posed by their incursions steadily increased, stretching frontline Muslim rulers to breaking point. The Iranian Samanids of Transoxiana, whose lands were already riven by famine and infighting, were the first to buckle. The Samanids' most dangerous Turkish neighbours, the Qarakhanids, came to exert an irresistible pressure on their borders that was only exacerbated by disaffection amongst their own Turkish slave soldiers. After a bitter struggle, the Samanid capital of Bukhara fell in 999 and a Turkish mamluk named Sebuktigin took power, founding the Ghaznavid

---

[5] See the account written by Ibn Fadlan: *Ibn Fadlān and the land of darkness, passim*.

[6] C. Bosworth, 'Introduction', *The Turks in the early Islamic world*, ed. C. Bosworth, The formation of the classical Islamic world IX (Aldershot: Ashgate, 2007), pp. xxxix–xli. See also R. Frye and A. Sayili, 'Turks in the Middle East before the Saljuqs', *The Turks in the early Islamic world*, ed. C. Bosworth, The formation of the classical Islamic world IX (Aldershot: Ashgate, 2007), pp. 179–212.

[7] This section has been drawn extensively upon: E. Bosworth, 'The steppe peoples in the Islamic World', *The new Cambridge history of Islam: volume 3: The eastern Islamic world, eleventh to eighteenth centuries*, ed. D. O. Morgan and A. Reid (Cambridge: Cambridge University Press, 2010), pp. 21–49; Peacock, *Early Seljūq History*.

[8] Ellenblum, *Collapse of the eastern Mediterranean*, pp. 61–62, 82. The extent to which the changing climate caused the Turks to migrate is contested. Peacock has recently cast doubt on the importance of this argument commenting that 'it usually takes more than one single factor to spark a migration': A. Peacock, *The Great Seljuk Empire*, Edinburgh history of the Islamic empires (Edinburgh: Edinburgh University Press, 2015), pp. 24–25, 288 (quote: p. 35). Ellenblum's thesis has also been reviewed by Preiser-Kapeller in: J. Preiser-Kapeller, 'A collapse of the eastern Mediterranean? New results and theories on the interplay between climate and societies in Byzantium and the Near East, ca. 1000–1200 AD'. I am indebted to Johannes Preiser-Kapeller for sending me an advanced draft of this article which will hopefully be published soon.

Empire.[9] The Qarakhanids' victories over the settled peoples to the south encouraged other Turkic groups to launch their own campaigns into the area. Among these was a tribal confederation known as the Oghuz Turks, led by the Saljuq family. They initially began to assert themselves in this region as allies of the Qarakhanids and Ghaznavids. Even so it was not long before they were acting independently and threatening their erstwhile allies. In the first decades of the eleventh century they started to drive south, encroaching on Ghaznavid territory. The Ghaznavid ruler Mas'ud marched out to meet the Saljuqs and their armies met with victory and defeat. Even so, the tide was turning against the Ghaznavids and in 1035, and again in 1040 at Dandanqan, the Saljuq Turks won two significant victories against Mas'ud and they subsequently pressed home their advantage. Soon afterwards the Ghaznavids were swept aside by the Saljuqs, who unseated them from power in much of their western territory. Freed from all restraint, the Saljuqs continued to drive west encountering only limited resistance, conquering and devastating much of Persia.[10] They discovered that many regional Arab and Kurdish potentates were all too ready to come to terms, while those who offered resistance were crushed. In 1055 the Saljuq leader Tughril seized Baghdad, assuming the title of sultan. In the decades that followed the Saljuqs continued to consolidate their control, whilst expanding west into: Iraq, the Jazira and eventually Syria and the Byzantine Empire.

Despite the defeats they received at the hands of the Saljuqs, the Ghaznavid Turks began to make substantial inroads to the east into Northern India during the eleventh century. By this stage the Ghaznavids had abandoned much of their steppe way of life and assumed many of the practices and beliefs of the agricultural societies of the south.[11] Ghaznavid raiding into Hind began in the early eleventh century and it was not long before their newly won conquests were consolidated through the erection of new settlements. By the 1030s, operating out of the city of Lahore, they were able to assert control over much of the Punjab. These advances marked the extent of the Ghaznavid conquests but in later years there

---

[9] C. Bosworth, 'The Turks in the Islamic lands up to the mid-11th century', *The Turks in the early Islamic world*, ed. C. Bosworth, The formation of the classical Islamic world IX (Aldershot: Ashgate, 2007), pp. 193–212.

[10] For discussion on this see: O. Safi, *The politics of knowledge in premodern Islam: Negotiating ideology and religious inquiry* (Chapel Hill: University of North Carolina Press, 2006), pp. 22–33.

[11] A. Wink, 'The early expansion of Islam in India', *The new Cambridge history of Islam: volume 3: The eastern Islamic world, eleventh to eighteenth centuries*, ed. D. O. Morgan and A. Reid (Cambridge: Cambridge University Press, 2010), p. 90. The point has also been made that many people groups who are generally labelled as nomadic include communities who pursue a more sedentary lifestyle. H. Kim, *The Huns, Rome and the birth of Europe* (Cambridge: Cambridge University Press, 2013), p. 42.

was considerable raiding beyond their frontiers. Their objectives in these endeavours were plunder and captives and, to this end, many important Hindu sites were looted.[12]

The Byzantines had long been aware of the Turks, who had been both allies and antagonists in earlier periods. The first major diplomatic contacts between the two occurred in 563 and later the Turks provided much needed auxiliaries for Emperor Heraclius in his struggle with the Persians.[13] The Turks' empire in Central Asia, however, fell into decline in the eighth century and, as their power waned, they lost touch with Constantinople. Byzantine writers and commentators turned their attention instead to new threats and knowledge of the Turks faded. The empire's military strategists followed suit and where Maurice's *Strategikon*, written *c.* 592–610, offered advice upon Turkish tactics and warcraft, later manuals produced in the tenth century had very little to say.[14] They were more preoccupied with the Arabs to the south or the danger of an Avar invasion and their advice focused upon these strategic priorities. On the rare occasion that the word 'Turk' was used at all, it referred to the Hungarians and not to the Turks of inner Asia.[15] The Byzantines still encountered the Turks at times on the battlefield because they often served as mercenaries or auxiliaries to the Arab armies of northern Syria.[16] Even so, the memory of Turkish tactics had evidently dwindled because when a Byzantine army suddenly encountered a large Turkish contingent supporting an Arab force invading Anatolia in July 838 they were badly defeated and John Skylitzes recalled their shock at experiencing the Turkish archery barrage that would become so familiar in later years.[17]

The Turkish incursions into the Byzantine Empire during the eleventh century dramatically reacquainted the Byzantines with the Turks. The first Turkish raid upon Byzantine Asia Minor took place in *c.*1029 and

[12] Wink, 'The early expansion of Islam in India', pp. 94–96.
[13] Golden, 'The peoples of the south Russian steppes', p. 260; Sinor, 'The establishment and dissolution of the Türk empire', p. 302. See also Nikephoros, patriarch of Constantinople, *Short history*, trans. C. Mango, Corpus Fontium Historiae Byzantinae XIII (Washington, DC: Dumbarton Oaks, 1990), p. 56; G. Leiser, 'The Turks in Anatolia before the Ottomans', *The new Cambridge history of Islam: volume 2: The Western Islamic World, eleventh to eighteenth centuries*, ed. M. Fierro (Cambridge: Cambridge University Press, 2010), pp. 301–307.
[14] *Maurice's Strategikon: Handbook of Byzantine military strategy*, trans. G. Dennis (Philadelphia, PA: University of Pennsylvania Press, 1984), pp. xvi, 23, 116.
[15] *Three Byzantine military treatises*, ed. and trans. G. Dennis (Washington, DC: Dumbarton Oaks, 1985), pp. 280, 292.
[16] The Byzantines also employed Turkish warriors and by 855 they formed an elite unit within the Third Hctaeria of the imperial bodyguard: W. Treadgold, *Byzantium and its army: 284–1081* (Stanford: Stanford University Press, 1995), p. 110.
[17] JS, pp. 78–79.

their attacks intensified in later years.[18] Their incursions during the 1050s and 1060s affected much of Eastern Anatolia and many cities were destroyed. In 1071 the Byzantine Emperor Romanus Diogenes marched out in an attempt to stem the Turkish advance but on 19 August he was heavily defeated at Manzikert. The Turkish commander, Sultan Alp Arslan, did not follow up this victory, but news of the battle, linked to political unrest within the Byzantine Empire, drew attention to the vulnerabilities of this region, encouraging multiple attacks by Turcoman tribal groups. The defeat at Manzikert also provoked the Byzantines to appeal to Rome for aid and Pope Gregory VII attempted to assemble an army to help them. Even so, the pontiff was locked in conflict with the German emperor and little was achieved.

Meanwhile, Turkish depredations were affecting the pilgrim routes to Jerusalem and the Norman chronicler William of Apulia expressed his concern about the effects of the Turkish onslaught on those wishing to reach the Holy Land.[19] He was not the only contemporary to recognise this problem and Michael the Syrian (Jacobite patriarch, d. 1199) reported that such pious visitors were often mistreated and heavily taxed; a point also noted by the Muslim writer al-Azimi and later by Bar Hebraeus.[20]

By 1095 the Byzantines' need for reinforcements remained acute. The important city of Nicaea was in Turkish hands and its loss meant that the frontier with Turkish-held territory was only 60 miles from Constantinople. Meanwhile, news of Turkish atrocities continued to proliferate across the Near East. The Armenian and Byzantine histories of this period

---

[18] Peacock, *Early Seljūq History*, p. 139.

[19] William of Apulia, 'Gesta Roberti Wiscardi', *MGHS*, ed. R. Wilmans, vol. 9 (Hanover, 1851), p. 267. See also Frutolf of Michelsberg, 'Chronicon', *MGHS*, ed. G. Waitz, vol. 6 (Hanover, 1844), p. 208. The continuator to Frutolf's chronicle – who participated in the 1101 crusade – noted that the Turks had destroyed many monasteries and other buildings around Jerusalem to provide stone for rebuilding the city walls. *FE*, p. 134. See also 'Gesta Adhemari, Episcopi Podiensis', *RHC: Oc*, vol. 5 (Paris, 1895), p. 354.

[20] MS, vol. 3, p. 182; C. Hillenbrand, *The Crusades: Islamic perspectives* (Edinburgh: Edinburgh University Press, 2006), p. 50. *The History of the patriarchs of the Egyptian Church* describing the events of 1092–1093, explains how, after an initial period of persecution, the Turks appointed a Jacobite Christian to look after Christian visitors arriving in the city, either from Egypt or from 'other countries'. Exactly what conclusion should be drawn from this statement concerning the Turks' general treatment of pilgrims is unclear, but it helps to build a more nuanced picture of their policies in the holy city: *History of the patriarchs*, p. 364. See also GN, p. 16; Caffaro, *De Liberatione Civitatum Orientis*, ed. L. Belgrano, Fonti per Storia D'Italia XI (Rome, 1890), pp. 99–100; Bar Hebraeus, *The chronography of Gregory Abû'l Faraj: The son of Aaron, the Hebrew physician commonly known as Bar Hebraeus*, trans. E. Wallis Budge, vol. 1 (Oxford: Oxford University Press, 1932), p. 234; BB, p. 5; 'Chronicon monasterii Sancti Petri Aniciensis', *Cartulaire de L'abbaye de St Chaffre du Monastier*, ed. U. Chevalier (Paris, 1891), p. 162.

are filled with accounts of Turkish attacks while Norman mercenaries returning to western Christendom likewise reported Turkish advances and Byzantine defeat.

With warfare raging in Anatolia, the Fatimid rulers of Egypt were also struggling for survival against the Turks. The Egyptians had long been accustomed to recruiting Turkish warriors in large numbers, but in the late 1060s feuding between these Turkic troops and the army's Sudanese contingents escalated into a protracted conflict that lasted for many years (1062–1073). The Fatimids themselves were in no position to stem the fighting. Egypt as a whole was in the grip of a protracted famine; the Nile failed to rise between 1065 and 1072 with massive socio-economic repercussions. The Fatimids' inability to pay their troops had been one of the major factors in sparking this confrontation.[21] This disruption became so serious that it posed an existential threat to the dynasty. These internal problems were soon exacerbated by the arrival of Turcoman forces under Atsiz into Syria from the east. They had originally been called in as Fatimid allies against Bedouin depredations but any notion of co-operation was soon dispelled and their objectives swiftly morphed into regional conquest. Jerusalem fell to the Turks in June/July 1073, and Tyre and Damascus in 1075.[22] Vast swaths of Fatimid territory were lost, but some semblance of control was restored by the commander Badr al-Jamali (Fatimid vizier from 1073) who firmly reimposed order and defeated the rebellious Turks. He later defeated an invasion force led by Atsiz outside the gates of Cairo in February 1077. Soon afterwards Badr attempted to retake Syria, whose inhabitants were sufficiently encouraged by his progress to rise against their Turkish overlords. Jerusalem was briefly retaken, but Badr was unable to restore Fatimid control to Damascus. The struggle between the Fatimids and Turks rumbled on up to the time of the First Crusade with neither party gaining ascendency. When the Franks reached this area in early 1099 they found that the Turks ruled the inland areas, operating out of Aleppo and Damascus, whilst many of the coastal cities were still under Arab rule and maintained some connection with the Fatimids.[23]

This history of the Turkish conquests of the eleventh century places Urban's call for a crusade in a broad historical context. By recruiting

---

[21] Ellenblum, *Collapse of the eastern Mediterranean*, pp. 151–153.

[22] AST, pp. 172, 190; M. Gil, *A history of Palestine, 634–1099*, trans. by E. Broido (Cambridge: Cambridge University Press, 1992), pp. 409–410. This date is disputed see: S. Gat, 'The Seljuks in Jerusalem', *Towns and material culture in the medieval Middle East*, ed. Y. Lev (Leiden: Brill, 2002), 5–6.

[23] L. al-Imad, *The Fatimid vizierate*, Islamkundliche Untersuchungen CXXXIII (Berlin: Schwarz, 1990), pp. 99–119.

forces to combat this threat he was very far from unique; rather he was acting in precisely the same way as almost every other major civilisation within striking distance of the Eurasian steppe. This is an important point because the First Crusade is often treated as a unique phenomenon; a classic case study for the conflict between east and west. From this perspective, however, the First Crusade was simply the latest in a long line of counter-offenses launched against Turkic groups by multiple civilisations whether Islamic, Christian, or Hindu from across Eurasia and Northern Africa. It was perhaps the most successful of these ventures, but it had only a localised impact on the Saljuq sultanate, which showed little interest in its arrival, and several later Muslim authors of Turkish histories did not bother to report the fact that either the First Crusade or the subsequent Frankish settlement had ever taken place.[24]

Objectives

Having established the major predicates for our discussion, we now turn to our main issue: the first crusaders' attitude towards Islam. Here we immediately enter deep water. The First Crusade can be constructed in many different ways. Even the question of whether it was conceived as an *offensive* or a *defensive* campaign raises many problems.[25] On this issue, arguments might be raised to support a variety of conclusions. To take the *offensive* position in this debate, it might be pointed out that the crusade set out to conquer much of the Levantine littoral and, most importantly, the holy city of Jerusalem. These were frontier regions contested between the Saljuq Turks and the Fatimid rulers of Egypt, which posed no immediate threat to western Europe; so their actions here were *by definition* offensive, not retaliatory. Jerusalem itself had not been in Christian hands since 638AD – over four hundred years previously – so the crusade was hardly a knee-jerk reaction to its loss. Likewise, if the crusade had been intended as a defensive response to the centuries of Islamic aggression against Europe (described in Chapter 1) then Spain or North Africa would have been more appropriate targets. The counter-argument could be made that the crusade set out to defend Byzantium from the

---

[24] *The history of the Seljuq state: A translation with commentary of the Akhbār al-dawla al-saljūquiyya*, trans. C. Bosworth, RSIT (Abingdon: Routledge, 2011); *The History of the Seljuq Turks*, ed. C. Bosworth, trans. K. Luther (Richmond: Curzon, 2001). S. Mecit, *The Rum Seljuqs: Evolution of a dynasty*, RSIT (Abingdon: Routledge, 2014), p. 140; W. Montgomery Watt, *The influence of Islam on medieval Europe* (Edinburgh: Edinburgh University Press, 1972), p. 57; Peacock, *The great Seljuk Empire*, pp. 82–83.

[25] See also Asbridge, *The Crusades*, pp. 26–29.

Turks but this point could be headed off by pointing out that, especially in the latter stages of the crusade, the pilgrims showed little interest in providing protection for Greeks against Turkish attack. On these grounds then the crusade could be constructed as a war of aggression.[26]

To take the *defensive* position, others might argue that Urban could not possibly have anticipated the huge response that – in the event – he provoked through his call for a crusade and that all he and Alexius had ever really expected was to raise a force of knights to defend Byzantium.[27] If true, then the crusade was initially conceived as a small and entirely defensive expedition against the Turks, who were a new, not an old threat. Even if a grander scheme had been intended, recent Turkish attacks on pilgrims travelling to the east and their treatment of the local Christian populace provide a defensive explanation for crusaders' later acts and choice of targets (especially Jerusalem). Thus they were guided by the *defensive* desire to protect pilgrims, eastern Christians, and the holy places of the east. In addition, viewed from a wider perspective, having suffered centuries of Muslim aggression, the crusade could be seen as part of a general counter-offensive against Islam including campaigns such as the reconquest of Sicily and Toledo. Consequently, the crusade was a defensive – or at least a retaliatory – action.

Alternatively, it is plausible to advance the idea that the crusade was neither. According to this line of thought, some of its participants may have been armed, but theirs was fundamentally a pilgrimage; an act of penitential devotion that was all but irrelevant to the cut and thrust of Christian and Islamic frontier politics. The participants were consumed by an overriding desire to reach the holy city and were not particularly interested in who defended it. Moreover, the papacy had launched the campaign to provide western Christendom's military elites with a spiritual line of escape from a sinful life of disruptive infighting. The fact that so many returned to western Christendom having reached Jerusalem in 1099 demonstrates that these returnees at least were more concerned with their own spirituality than conquering land from the 'gentiles'. From this perspective, the crusade was neither offensive nor defensive, but was focused solely on Jerusalem and did not define itself in relation to the Islamic world. The enemies they encountered were merely obstacles on a spiritual journey to the east.

---

[26] To an older school of thought, the Crusades were perceived as an act of colonisation. See, for example: N. Daniel, *The Arabs and mediaeval Europe* (London: Longman, 1975), p. 138.

[27] For discussion on Urban and Alexius' expectations see: France, 'The First Crusade and Islam', 247; S. Runciman, *A history of the Crusades*, vol. 1 (Cambridge: Cambridge University Press, 1951), pp. 116–117; Cahen, *Orient et Occident*, pp. 57–58.

This issue of offense or defence is a significant question in its own right, but it is also the issue that underpins the question of the first crusaders' initial approach towards Islam. The crusaders' objectives and the significance of their Turkish opponents within those intentions contextualise the question of the crusaders' attitudes towards their opponents. Were the crusaders recruited in an environment of hate-filled anti-Islamic rhetoric, determined to seize or retake what they saw as their own? Did they set out on a war of conquest, determined to expand the frontiers of Christendom against the 'infidel'? Or did they take the cross with their minds focused squarely on Jerusalem and with barely a thought for the enemy they would meet along the way? These are important questions and this section will draw upon the materials produced in advance of the crusade to define the role played by Turks/Arabs/Muslims within the crusade's initial objectives.

Urban II

Over the past nine centuries, commentators of every kind have speculated about Pope Urban II's motives in launching the First Crusade. For historians in the twenty-first century (particularly those lecturers who set this topic as an essay question) there is a well-worn portfolio of factors that can be attributed to the pontiff's decision to instigate the campaign. These include: the determination to respond to the Turkish threat; the desire to seek reconciliation with the Byzantine Church; and an attempt to end infighting amongst Frankish knightly families. Some also cite the crusade's relevance to the struggle between papacy and empire. These themes have been discussed so exhaustively elsewhere that there is little need to advance a new thesis consisting of a slightly-different flavoured cocktail of motives. It will only be noted that doubtlessly many of these considerations were at the front of the pope's mind when he stood to give his address at Clermont. What is of greater interest here however is the question of what Pope Urban sent the crusade out to achieve. This will be the focus of this present section because it is of the first importance for this present study to ascertain both the role played by the Turks/Arabs/Muslims within these initial intentions and the way in which Urban presented them to his audiences.

Sources

One of the great temptations when investigating Urban II's ambitions for the crusade is to draw upon the accounts of his Clermont sermon, which were written up in crusade narratives produced in the expedition's aftermath. The vehement and electric rhetoric found in these chronicles' accounts is emotive and highly quotable. As has been pointed out, several of these accounts were written by eyewitnesses who were present at Clermont and the argument is often made that (making allowance for the fact that they were written many years later) they probably convey at least the gist of Urban's original message. In a similar vein, it has also long been claimed that because there are themes common to the various versions of Urban's address that these ideas must at least have been referenced in his original sermon, even if the author may not have remembered the exact wording of the actual oration.[28] Marcus Bull, however, has cast doubt on this approach, describing it as 'methodological naivety'.[29] Bull stresses that it cannot be guaranteed that authors were self-consciously attempting to recreate Urban's actual words and therefore it is not possible simply to cross-reference common topics. He convincingly argues instead that their descriptions of Clermont, 'amount to analyses of the crusaders' ideas and motivations, chronologically positioned before the event as a matter of narrative cohesion'.[30] Thus these accounts better reflect the internalised memory and experience of their authors and are not reliable as genuine attempts at reconstruction.

It is not the purpose of this discussion to pronounce judgement on the general trustworthiness of the different versions of Urban's address, rather to consider their value as a guide to the way that Urban presented his Turkish/Islamic enemies. On this point, Bull offers the thesis that some elements of Urban's original message can be wrung from these narratives via an innovative methodology (even though their authors may not have intended to recreate the exact wording of the original address). His thesis can be reduced to the following logical argumentative progression:

- At Clermont, Urban presented his audience with a powerful and emotive message, which was uniquely relevant to their thought-world.
- This message was then internalised by each member of the audience, passing through their interpretative apparatus.

---

[28] D. Munro, 'The speech of Pope Urban II. at Clermont, 1095', *The American historical review*, 11.2 (1906), 231–242. For further discussion see: P. Cole, *The preaching of the Crusades to the Holy Land, 1095–1270* (Cambridge, MA: Medieval Academy of America, 1991), pp. 2–3; T. Asbridge, *The First Crusade: A new history* (Oxford: Oxford University Press, 2004), p. 32; Flori, *Pierre l'Ermite*, p. 159.

[29] M. Bull, 'Views of Muslims and of Jerusalem in miracle stories, *c.*1000–*c.*1200: reflections on the study of the first crusaders' motivations', *The experience of crusading: Volume one, western approaches*, ed. M. Bull and N. Housley (Cambridge: Cambridge University Press, 2003), p. 22.

[30] Bull, 'Views of Muslims', pp. 22–23.

- Many listeners were profoundly affected by the pope's descriptions of the crusade's enemies and absorbed his chosen motifs into their thought-world.
- The various crusade writers then produced their versions of Urban's speech, using it as a device for advancing their own ideas and motivations rather than self-consciously attempting to reproduce Urban's exact words.
- Nevertheless, because their ideas surrounding the crusade had been moulded by Urban's original address and their perceptions still bore the impact-craters created by his words, they still, to some extent, reproduced the ideas in later texts that he had originally advanced.[31]

Consequently, Bull recognises that these sources still retain some value for historians seeking to understand and recreate elements of Urban's actual message (and its description of the crusade's enemies).

There is however a problem with his analysis in so far as it relates to the pope's presentation of the campaign's enemy. If we accept Bull's premise that the various accounts of Urban's sermon reflect the crusaders' ideas and are not genuine attempts to reproduce the pontiff's language, then it is necessary to incorporate into this analysis the indisputable fact that the crusaders' attitudes towards their enemies had not remained static in the years between Clermont and the moment when they committed their memories to writing following the campaign. In the intervening period, participants encountered Turks and Arabs at first hand whether through: battle, imprisonment, the reports of others, trade, diplomacy, or torture. These often traumatic experiences will presumably have played a decisive role in shaping their views; possibly altering them altogether. Even those authors who are thought to have attended Clermont and yet did not take part in the crusade will have been influenced by the reports carried home by returning pilgrims. Thus, when these authors came to back-project their ideas concerning Arabs/Turks onto their versions of the Clermont address, it is stretching credulity to believe that their viewpoints will still have carried the identifiable hallmarks of Urban's words given the powerful experiences they had undergone in the meantime. To take one example, many of these narrative accounts of the Clermont sermon report Urban's condemnation of Turkish atrocities in Asia Minor. If we were to follow the earlier methodology, then some of the pope's emotive ideas communicated at Clermont may have found their way into the crusade narratives because of the impact they had on their listener. Even so, the crusaders had passed through this region themselves and witnessed at first-hand what had taken place. Presumably their lived-experience would

---

[31] Bull, 'Views of Muslims', pp. 22–25.

have moulded their post-crusade perceptions in a way that Urban's words could never have achieved. Bull is correct to note that some of the themes used in these later narratives occur in the more contemporary sources for Urban's preaching, nevertheless, as shall be shown in the next section, there are also substantial discrepancies.

More reliable are the group of papal letters written between 1096 and 1097 which touch upon the crusade.[32] These are briefer than the chroniclers' accounts of the pontiff's sermon at Clermont, but they have the advantage of being both contemporary and the product either of Urban himself or his curia.[33] In addition, there are other sources produced in these years (1095–1097) which are also of value.[34] The most numerous of these are the charters, written by or for participants. These charters take different forms, but frequently they are legal documents detailing transactions concluded between a crusader busying himself with his imminent departure and a religious institution. They concern matters ranging from the sale of land to raise money for the campaign, to the purchase of mules. They generally open with a brief statement of the individual's objectives for taking part and a small minority of such texts then describe the enemy they intended to face. These documents can supply an insight into the way that Urban presented the campaign's enemy because many of them were produced in monastic houses that the pontiff had either visited in person during his four-month preaching tour or which lay close to his route. Riley-Smith has demonstrated that many of the ideas and phrases used in such documents reflect themes that were propounded in papal crusading propaganda and so it seems reasonable to suggest that they would have followed his nomenclature when describing the campaign's enemy.[35]

---

[32] Bysted has similarly concluded that the letters are a better guide to Urban's ideas than the other post-crusade sources: Bysted, *Crusade indulgence*, p. 50. For later reports of the decrees promulgated at the Council of Clermont, see: R. Somerville, *The councils of Urban II* (Amsterdam: Adolf M. Hakkert, 1972), pp. 74, 108, 124.

[33] These consist of letters written to: a group of Catalonian counts (*Papsturkunden in Spanien: Vorarbeiten zur Hispania Pontificia: I Katalanien*, ed. P. Kehr (Berlin, 1926), pp. 287–288), the congregation of Vallombrosa ('Papsturkunden in Florenz', *Nachrichten von der Gesellschaft der Wissenschaften zu Göttingen philologisch-historische klasse*, ed. Wiederhold (Göttingen, 1901), pp. 313–314), the people of Flanders (*Kb*, pp. 136–137); the people of Bologna (*Kb*, pp. 137–138), Bishop Peter of Huesca (Pope Urban II, 'Epistolae et Privilegia', *PL*, vol. 151 (1853), col. 504), and the abbey of St Gilles, (Pope Urban II,'Epistolae et Privilegia', cols. 477–478).

[34] These include: a short chronicle written by Count Fulk Le Réchin of Anjou, 'Fragmentum historiae Andegavensis', *Chroniques des comtes d'Anjou et des seigneurs d'Amboise*, ed. L. Halphen and R. Poupardin (Paris, 1913), pp. 233–238 and a letter written by the Countess Clemence of Flanders in 1097, *Kb*, pp. 142–143.

[35] Riley-Smith has noted that whilst the charters reference many themes employed in the papal preaching, there were some that do not seem to have resonated with his audience.

Who Was the Crusade Launched Against?

Drawing upon this source-base, it is necessary first to identify who Urban II named as the crusade's opponent. The most striking finding on this question is that not one of the earlier sources – papal letters, chronicles, charters – produced before 1098 mentions the 'Turks'. Of the three papal letters to name any enemy, two describe that enemy as 'Saracens'[36] and a third speaks more broadly of a 'barbaric rage' (*barbarica rabies*) destroying the churches of the east.[37] It is only in 1098, with the crusade armies already en route to Jerusalem, that the 'Turks' were specifically identified in papal correspondence.[38] The chronicles and charters follow a similar pattern. Count Fulk Le Réchin's chronicle, written in 1096, includes an account of Urban's attempt to raise support for the crusade in Angers. Here, the pontiff incited them to set out for Jerusalem and to defeat the machinations of the 'gentiles' who had seized Christian land.[39] Bernold, a monk at All Saints in Schaffhausen, likewise described how Alexius' envoys arrived at the council of Piacenza requesting aid against the 'pagans'.[40]

The charters are equally vague in their terminology. From a group of sixty-nine charters that were produced in advance of the campaign, fourteen (20%) name an enemy of some kind.[41] To take one example, Guy and Geoffrey of Signes stated their intention of 'seeking Jerusalem, both for the grace of pilgrimage and to destroy, with God's protection, the

He points out that the idea of 'fraternal love', which was found in the preaching, was not referenced in the charters. J. Riley-Smith, *The first crusaders, 1095–1131* (Cambridge: Cambridge University Press, 1997), pp. 61–66; J. Riley-Smith, 'The idea of crusading in the charters of the early Crusaders, 1095–1102', *Le Concile de Clermont de 1095 et l'Appel à la Croisade* (Rome: Ecole française de Rome, Palais Farnèse, 1997), pp. 155–166.

[36] *Papsturkunden in Spanien*, pp. 287–288; 'Papsturkunden in Florenz', p. 313.

[37] *Kb*, p. 136. See also Gabriele, *Empire of memory*, p. 152. Incidentally, he may be borrowing here from Ammianus Marcellinus who uses this same phrase to describe troubles occurring in Africa at the time of Valentinian: *Ammianus Marcellinus*, ed. and trans. J. C. Rolfe, vol. 3, Loeb Classical Library CCCXXXI (Cambridge, MA: Harvard University Press, 1939), p. 56 (book/chapter ref.: xxvii, 9, 1).

[38] Pope Urban II, 'Epistolae et Privilegia', col. 504.

[39] 'Fragmentum historiae Andegavensis', p. 238.

[40] 'Bernoldi chronicon', *MGHS*, ed. G. Pertz, vol. 5 (Hanover, 1844), p. 462.

[41] This group of sources has been formed by drawing together all identified First Crusade charters (the vast majority of which were drawn from the appendices of Riley-Smith's *The first crusaders*) and then working through them in an attempt to identify which were written in advance of the campaign and which were produced subsequently. Such a division was generally possible because many charters state that they were written by a crusader who was either on the point of departure or when he had just returned. Charters have only been considered here if individuals almost certainly took part in the crusade. As Riley-Smith points out, there are many charters which *seem* to indicate that an individual took part, but which are not entirely clear. See: Riley-Smith, *The first crusaders*, appendix I.

Table 1. *Terms used to define the First Crusade's opponents found in charters produced in advance of the campaign*

Name	Frequency
Pagans	8
Saracens	2
Barbarians (or variants on this theme)	3
Wild Peoples	1
Enemies of Christianity	1

Please note that although only fourteen charters name an enemy, there are fifteen entries here because one charter describes the intention of fighting 'pagans and Saracens'.

pollution of the pagans and the excessive madness through which already countless Christian people have been oppressed, taken captive and killed with barbaric fury'.[42]

Describing the crusade's enemy as 'pagans' was by far the most common term utilised in these documents as demonstrated in Table 1.

Moreover, 'pagans' appear in many of the charters that were produced in the religious houses which Urban II visited in person during his preaching tour; a point that raises the possibility that they were guided by him in their choice of language. The abbey of Marmoutier, for example, where Urban stayed in March 1096, issued three documents for the crusade which identified the expedition's enemy as 'pagans'.[43] Among these, Stephen of Blois declared his wish 'to go to Jerusalem with the Christian army, advancing against the pagans by the order of the Roman Pope, namely Urban II'.[44] Given the frequent reference made to 'pagans' in the charters and their authors' proximity to Urban himself it is likely that this name was favoured in papal propaganda. Certainly, a chronicle written in the monastery of Chaize-le-Vicomte also speaks of the pope preaching the crusade against 'pagans'.[45] Synthesising the earlier information, it is probable that the papacy defined the crusade's opponents using a range of different terms. Of these, the name 'Saracens' appears with the greatest frequency in the papal letters; the term 'pagans' in the charters.

---

[42] *Cartulaire de l'abbaye de Saint-Victor de Marseille*, ed. M. Guérard, vol. 1 (Paris, 1857), no. 143.

[43] *Cartulaire de Marmoutier pour le Dunois*, ed. E. Mabille (Châteaudun, 1874), nos. 64, 92, 151.

[44] *Cartulaire de Marmoutier pour le Dunois*, no. 92.

[45] G. Beech, 'The abbey of Saint-Florent of Saumur, and the First Crusade', *Autour de la Première Croisade: Actes du Colloque de la Society for the Study of the Crusades and the Latin East*, ed. M. Balard (Paris: Publications de la Sorbonne, 1996), p. 61.

Urban II's use of such rather general and imprecise terminology is significant; nevertheless, it is in complete accord with the language employed by both his pontifical predecessors and successors in their efforts to raise forces against the Turks in the east. The surviving papal letters, which describe Gregory VII's failed attempt to recruit an army for the east, following the Turkish victory at Manzikert in 1071, use similar terms. The vast majority describe the depredations of 'pagans', while one speaks of 'Saracens'; others speak more generally of the Devil being at work.[46] Similar terminology appears in Eugenius III's bull *Quantum Praedecessores* (issued in 1145/6). Here, the crusade encyclical states its opposition to 'pagans', 'enemies of the cross of Christ' and 'infidels'.[47] Likewise, the Third Crusade bull *Audita Tremendi* (issued in 1187) speaks of 'barbarians' and 'pagans'.[48] In each of these campaigns, the papacy was fully aware that the Turks were the crusade's primary enemy. Gregory VII launched his campaign against the Turks in Asia Minor; Eugenius III instigated the Second Crusade following the fall of the city of Edessa (1144) to the Turkish ruler Zangi; and the Third Crusade was instigated after the battle of Hattin against the largely Turkish forces under Kurdish (Saladin's) command (1187). We can be equally sure that when Urban used the earlier-mentioned terms that he was referring to the Turks, even if he did not name them explicitly. In many of his letters he spoke of the wide-scale destruction taking place in the east; references which can only apply to the advancing Turks.

Thus it is probable that Urban II, like other pontiffs, was adhering to a topological norm in his preaching. The most striking aspect of all these descriptors is that they are all spiritual classifications. Of these, the most general is 'pagans'. In contemporary parlance, it can be translated as 'non-Christians' or 'unbaptised'.[49] In the sources from the tenth and eleventh centuries it was applied regularly to a huge variety of neighbouring peoples, including Normans, Hungarians, Vikings (before their conversion), and Muslims. The only quality these peoples had in common was their adherence to a different religion. Thus, it seems likely that the papacy was accustomed to classifying its opponents by belief

---

[46] *Register of Pope Gregory VII*, pp. 50–51, 54–55, 94–95, 122–124, 128; *Epistolae Vagantes*, p. 12.

[47] Eugenius III, 'Epistolae et privilegia', *PL*, vol. 180 (1855), cols. 1064–6.

[48] Gregory VIII, 'Epistolae et privilegia', *PL*, vol. 202 (1855), cols. 1539–1542.

[49] For discussion see: M. Campopiano, 'La culture pisane et le monde arabo-musulman: entre connaissance réelle et héritage livresque', *Bien Dire et Bien Aprandre: Revue de Médiévistique, Un exotisme littéraire médiéval?*, ed. C. Gaullier-Bougassas, Actes du colloque du Centre d'Études Médiévales et Dialectales de Lille III (Lille: Université Lille, 2008), pp. 88–89. Nilsson points out that Christians could also be described as pagans if they failed in their obedience to God and the Church: Nilsson, 'Gratian on pagans', pp. 154, 160.

and not by using specifically ethnonyms, such as Turk. As mentioned earlier, there was one letter in 1098 in which the papacy *did* allude to Turks. This was in a letter to Bishop Peter of Huesca where he described how God was fighting through the Christians against the 'Turks in Asia and the Moors in Europe'. He then went on to describe how Huesca needed to be freed from the 'Saracens'.[50] In this correspondence, however, Urban was alluding to the threats posed by various groups from within Islam and he appears to have used the name 'Turks' simply to distinguish one sub-group from another. Drawing these points together, it is reasonable to conclude that when Urban II launched the crusade, his *intended* enemy may have been the Turks, but his *stated* enemy was given either as 'Saracens' or as a 'non-Christian people' (pagans/gentiles). His lack of consistency on this point implies that the specific religious identity of his enemy was hardly important beyond the plain fact that they were non-Christian.

Incidentally, the terms used both by Urban in his letters and by participants in their charters underscore the earlier-mentioned problems involved in using the First Crusade chroniclers' narrative accounts of Urban's Clermont sermon. The most commonly discussed versions of Urban's speech are those written by Robert the Monk, Fulcher of Chartres, Guibert of Nogent, and Baldric of Bourgueil. They describe their intended opponents as: 'a race from the kingdom of the Persians' (Robert the Monk),[51] 'Turks, a Persian people' (Fulcher of Chartres),[52] 'gentiles' and 'paganism' (Guibert of Nogent),[53] and 'Turks', 'gentiles', 'Saracens', and 'pagans' (Baldric of Bourgueil, bishop of Dol).[54] As shown earlier, the name 'Turk' does not appear in any context pre-1098 and we shall see the name 'Persians' appears only once in a letter written by the countess of Flanders.[55] The terms used by these chroniclers reflects rather the terminology that the crusaders learnt to use during the campaign itself (much of which derived from a Byzantine origin – see later) and bears little relation to the language employed during its recruitment phase. The name 'gentile' occurs only in one narrative contemporary to the crusade's recruitment.[56] Only Guibert of Nogent and Baldric of Bourgueil use terms that *were* employed routinely in papal sources and the crusade charters pre-1098, but these are mixed among names which did not proliferate until much later. Thus, there are substantial differences in nomenclature between the contemporary materials for the launch of the crusade and later narratives. These findings

---

[50] Pope Urban II, 'Epistolae et Privilegia', col. 504.   [51] RM, p.5.
[52] FC, p. 133.   [53] GN, pp. 112, 114.   [54] BB, pp. 6–10.
[55] *Kb*, p. 142–143.   [56] 'Fragmentum historiae Andegavensis', p. 238.

cast further doubt on even the most nuanced attempts to identify how Urban actually described the campaign's foe using these later narrative sources.

Having established how Urban defined his foe, it is necessary to consider what he sought to achieve through the crusade (and his enemies' role within these objectives).

What Was the Stated Purpose of the Campaign?

The argument has been advanced that Urban could not have anticipated the huge response he provoked through his call for a crusade. It is more reasonable to conclude that he anticipated raising a smaller professional force with the limited goal of supplementing the Byzantine army. *Prima facie* this argument has the ring of truth to it because it stretches credulity to believe that Urban could genuinely have foreseen that he would muster a horde strong enough to: cross much of Europe; carve a path across over a 1000 miles of enemy territory; and then take and hold a city without immediate access to maritime supply routes. On so many grounds, it seems fair to reject the notion that such goals could ever have been seriously contemplated.

And yet, the papal letters issued during the preparations for the crusade are entirely consistent on this point. Among those written before the departure of the main armies, all but one gives Jerusalem as at least one of the main goals. For example, in October 1096 Urban wrote to the monks of Vallombrosa, in an attempt to dissuade any of the monks from taking part:

We have heard that some of you want to set out with the knights who are making for Jerusalem with the good intention of liberating Christianity. This is the right kind of sacrifice, but is planned by the wrong kind of person. For we were stimulating the minds of knights to go on this expedition, since they might be able to restrain the savagery of the Saracens by their arms and restore the Christians to their former freedom: we do not want those who have abandoned the world and vowed themselves to spiritual warfare either to bear arms or to go on this journey.[57]

Whilst this letter was intended to prevent these monks from taking part, it laid out clearly the campaign's objectives: the need to offer resistance to those who threaten Christianity; the desire to free the Christians of the Near East; and in particular the determination to regain Jerusalem.

---

[57] 'Papsturkunden in Florenz', p. 313. Translation from L. and J. Riley-Smith (eds and trans), *The Crusades: idea and reality, 1095–1274* (London: Edward Arnold, 1981), p. 39.

Two of the other letters – to the people of Flanders and Bologna – are largely consistent on each of these objectives. In each case they speak of: Jerusalem, the desire to secure the 'liberation' (*liberatio*) of the Christians and churches of the east, and the need to offer some defence against their persecutors.[58] A further letter is more concise. It confirms Count Raymond of Toulouse's renunciation of his rights to the abbey of Saint-Gilles during the council of Nimes. It mentions the crusade only in passing, referencing that the count was about to go on the 'expedition to Jerusalem'.[59] Clearly, in this passage Urban reduced the campaign to its barest essentials and it is significant to note that it is Jerusalem itself, rather than any other motive, that he selected to define the campaign. In this case, the Turks, 'Saracens', 'pagans' were not even mentioned. The prioritisation of this objective above the others is also communicated through the various ecclesiastical sources purporting to enumerate the Clermont degrees. Of these, three mention the crusade and each identified the liberation of Jerusalem as at least one of its objectives. Only one names another goal, which is to liberate the churches of Asia from the 'Saracens'.[60]

Consequently, it is necessary to reaffirm that Urban felt that a campaign to Jerusalem was a plausible and realisable ambition.[61] The boldness of this decision is astonishing and highly suggestive. The fact that the crusade *did* capture Jerusalem should not belie the fact that, at the outset, such a goal was implausible in the extreme; the military

---

[58] Riley-Smith, *The First Crusade and the idea of crusading*, pp. 18, 22–23. *Kb*, pp. 136–138.

[59] Pope Urban II, 'Epistolae et Privilegia', col. 478.

[60] Somerville, *The councils of Urban II*, pp. 74, 108, 124.

[61] For a sample of the discussion on the centrality of Jerusalem as the objective for the crusade see: J. Riley-Smith, *The First Crusade and the idea of crusading*, pp. 20–25; Morris, *The sepulchre of Christ*, p. 177; A. Jotischky, 'Pilgrimage, procession and ritual encounters between Christians and Muslims in the Crusader States', *Cultural encounters during the Crusades*, ed. K. Jensen, K. Salonen and H. Vogt (Odense: University Press of Southern Denmark, 2013), p. 245; Riley-Smith, 'The idea of crusading', p. 156; S. Schein, *Gateway to the heavenly city: Crusader Jerusalem and the Catholic west (1099–1187)*, Church, faith and culture in the medieval west (Aldershot: Ashgate, 2005), pp. 9–20; J. Flori, 'Première croisades et conversion des <<païens>>', *Migrations et Diasporas Méditerranéennes (Xe–XVIe siècles)*, ed. M. Balard and A. Ducellier (Paris: Publications de la Sorbonne, 2002), p. 449; B. McGinn, '*Iter Sancti Sepulchri*: the piety of the first crusaders', *The Walter Prescott Webb lectures: Essays in medieval civilization*, ed. R. Sullivan (Austin: University of Texas Press, 1978), p. 44; Flori, *Pierre l'Ermit*, p. 165. The older orthodoxy that the crusade was launched in defence of eastern Christians advanced by Erdmann has now been widely discredited. See: France, 'destruction of Jerusalem', 2. More recently Berend has commented, using Fulcher of Chartres' chronicle as evidence 'the possibility remains, however, that Jerusalem did not feature as a significant part of Urban's message'. Nevertheless, the above evidence and the contemporary charters (see later) are consistent on this point. Berend, 'The concept of Christendom', 58.

objections were formidable. The risks involved in launching the crusade for the pope himself would have been compounded by the fact that his own position was precarious. In 1095 he was confronted by both an anti-pope and his ongoing struggle with the German emperor; a failure on this scale would have cost him dearly. The only possibility that remains is that Urban was driven by a sense of spiritual purpose so overwhelming that it could overcome all objections.

He may have had other ends in mind. Frankopan has recently drawn attention to the close interaction between Urban and Emperor Alexius on the eve of the crusade and stressed the importance of the expedition for Latin/Greek relations.[62] By extension, Urban would presumably have been aware that the successful outcome of the crusade would have strengthened the papacy's position across the board. Even so, his primary *stated* goal was Jerusalem.[63] Liberating eastern Christians from 'pagans' and 'Saracens' was clearly important, but within the papacy's published goals it emerges as a distinctly secondary initiative.

How did Urban Present His Enemy?

Having discussed the terminology Urban used to identify his Turkish enemies and the significance of those foes (or lack of it) in his wider objectives, it is necessary to explore the wider language he used to describe the Turks' general character and their actions in Anatolia.

The sources which have been discussed with the greatest frequency on this point are the accounts of Urban's speech at Clermont which were produced by crusade chroniclers following the conquest of Jerusalem. These contain lengthy denunciations of the Turks, drawing especial attention to their depredations in Anatolia. Fulcher of Chartres, for example, describes how:

The Turks, a Persian people ... have seized more and more of the lands of the Christians, have defeated them in seven times as many battles, killed or captured many people, have destroyed churches and have devastated the kingdom of God.[64]

---

[62] P. Frankopan, *The First Crusade: The call from the East* (London: Bodley Head, 2012), *passim*.

[63] Mayer offers a contrasting view, arguing that Jerusalem was not the crusade's initial stated aim, but that it became so in the years following Clermont. H. Mayer, *The Crusades*, trans. J. Gillingham, 2nd ed. (Oxford: Oxford University Press, 1990), pp. 9–10. MacEvitt challenges the notion that there was a 'single goal' that represented the 'essence' of Urban's plan: C. MacEvitt, *The Crusades and the Christian world of the East: Rough tolerance* (Philadelphia: University of Pennsylvania Press, 2008), p. 48.

[64] Translation from *Chronicles of the First Crusade: 1096–1099*, ed. C. Tyerman (London: Penguin, 2012), pp. 9–10. FC, pp. 133–134.

For the reasons given earlier, it is difficult to trust that these narrative accounts can provide any real guidance on Urban's actual words at Clermont. Even so, it is not unlikely that Urban described the Turks' destructive wars of Anatolia with considerable enmity. In three of his letters (produced between 1095 and 1097), he denounced the savagery, barbaric fury, and tyranny of his foe and it seems reasonable to speculate that he touched on this point in his sermons.

Contemplating the aggressive character that Urban II ascribed to the Turks it is tempting to conclude that his words were mere propaganda; simply emotive language designed to enrage the crowds and drive recruitment. Viewed from one perspective, it is not especially important whether Urban delivered an exaggerated or fabricated account of the Turks' deeds. Factual or not, his audience was still informed that a cruel and barbaric enemy awaited them in the east. Even so, in a discussion on Urban's objectives and general posture this issue acquires greater significance. There is a considerable difference in stance between a pope acting vigorously to protect co-religionists in the east who were *actually* suffering intensely and a pontiff cynically constructing unfounded tales of cruelty and slaughter in a premeditated effort to incite hatred. If the former scenario is the more accurate then the pope may simply have been acting as a leader diligently intent on protecting his fellow Christians; if the latter, then he was deliberately constructing horrific accusations in an attempt to provoke a sense of fury among his co-religionists. The only way to determine which of these two interpretations is the more likely is to turn to the actual events which took place in Asia Minor during this period. Certainly Urban would have been aware of the real state of affairs in that region through the reports of papal embassies, Byzantine envoys, returning pilgrims, and warriors.

The destructiveness of the Turkish conquest of Anatolia during the eleventh century is a theme that contemporary authors from a wide range of ethnic and religious backgrounds dwelt upon at length.[65] Accounts of this invasion were produced by Arab Muslims and Christians, Armenians, Georgians, Byzantines, and Latins. In many cases they interpreted the event very differently. In the *Akhbār al-dawla al-saljūquiyya* the Turkish incursions into Anatolia are offered as a potent example of the Turks' role in securing a significant advance for the Islamic

---

[65] There has been considerable discussion on the impact of the Turkish invasions. For a recent survey which tends to play down their overall impact see: Peacock, *Early Seljūq History*, pp. 128–164. Nevertheless, Ellenblum paints a rather darker picture of Turkish forces ranging across wide regions having been forced south by climatic changes. Ellenblum, *Collapse of the eastern Mediterranean, passim.*

religion.[66] For the Armenian monk, Matthew of Edessa, their arrival was presented as a tragic but inevitable period of suffering in a chain of events that would ultimately culminate with the apocalypse.[67] The Frankish monk, Guillermus, mentioned Turkish depredations only as a preface to a tale explaining how he managed to gain possession of an important relic – the head of Saint James the Persian – during his sojourn in Byzantine service.[68] St Christodoulos (d.1093) mentioned their incursions in the early sections of the monastic rule he wrote in 1091 for the monastery of St John the Theologian on Patmos; an institution founded in 1088 with financial assistance from Emperor Alexius.[69] The agendas advanced by each of these authors add a distinct flavour to their versions of events but on one point there is a general consensus: that the Turkish conquest was an exceptionally destructive process. Anna Comnena, eldest daughter of Alexius I (d. c. 1153) describes it as follows:

Since the accession of Diogenes, the barbarians had invaded the Roman Empire, at which point he had taken the first step to deal with them by launching a disastrous expedition against them. From that time until the reign of my father [Emperor Alexius], the barbarian terror had gone unchecked: swords and spears had been sharpened against the Christians; there had been battles and wars and massacres. Towns were wiped out, lands ravaged, all the territories of Rome stained with Christian blood. Some died miserably, pierced by arrow or lance; others were driven from their homes and carried off as prisoners of war to the towns of Persia.[70]

Tales of this kind abound in many surviving sources. The Aleppan chronicler Kamal al-Din (d. 1262), speaking of Turkish depredations in Northern Syria in the 1070s, said that they were the worst the region had ever encountered (and, as Zakkar points out, he was writing following the Mongol invasions).[71] Other reports speak of the flight of Anatolian refugees away from the fighting, seeking refuge in Constantinople, the

---

[66] *The history of the Seljuq state*, pp. 34–35. See also C. Hillenbrand, *Turkish myth and Muslim symbol: The battle of Manzikert* (Edinburgh: Edinburgh University Press, 2007), pp. 52–58.

[67] C. MacEvitt, 'The chronicle of Matthew of Edessa: apocalypse, the First Crusade, and the Armenian diaspora', *Dumbarton Oaks papers* 61 (2007), 158.

[68] J. Shepard, '>>How St James the Persian's head was brought to Cormery<<. A relic collector around the time of the First Crusade', *Zwischen Polis, Provinz und Peripherie: Beiträge zur byzantinischen Geschichte und Kultur*, ed. L. Hoffmann (Wiesbaden: Harrassowitz, 2005), p. 298.

[69] 'Christodoulos: rule, testament and codicil of Christodoulos for the monastery of St. John the Theologian on Patmos', *Byzantine monastic foundation documents*, ed. J. Thomas and A. Hero, trans. P. Karlin-Hayter, vol. 2 (Washington, DC: Dumbarton Oaks Research Library, 2000), pp. 579–580.

[70] Translation taken from AC, p. 463.

[71] S. Zakkar, *The emirate of Aleppo, 1004–1094* (Beirut: Dar Al-Amanah & El-Risalah Publishing House, 1971), p. 200. See also Gil, *A History of Palestine*, p. 420.

Aegean or the western tip of Asia Minor.[72] To take one example, the monastic community at Mt Latmus was forced to flee to the coastal city of Strobilos, but even there they did not feel safe because shortly afterwards they withdrew to the isle of Cos.[73]

More recently archaeological studies have been able to add extra layers of detail to this picture. The ongoing investigations into the city of Amorium have revealed a settlement that: was destroyed in 838 by an Arab invasion; recovered steadily during the tenth and early eleventh centuries; and then went into steep decline following the Turkish advance.[74] This is merely one of a large number of Anatolian cities that was sacked or destroyed by the Turks during this period and Vryonis has assembled a long and sobering list of settlements which met this fate at around this time.[75]

Naturally, such devastation would have had a significant effect on the rural economy and agriculture and this is revealed in analyses of pollen data drawn from samples of lake sediment taken from a selection of Anatolian lakes. Using such palynological analyses it is possible to chart the changing vegetation of the area surrounding the lakes in question and recent studies have shown that there was a marked decline in cereal pollen in several key regions during the late eleventh century; a clear indicator of a rapid fall in organised agriculture.[76] It is only in the late twelfth century that the pollen data shows that cereal agriculture staged a slight recovery.[77] This would chime with the image of a society suffering the turmoil of relentless raiding and dislocation evoked so clearly by the late-eleventh-century Armenian writer Aristakes, although it may also have been exacerbated by changing regional climatic conditions.[78] The

---

[72] S. Vryonis, *The decline of medieval hellenism in Asia Minor and the process of Islamization from the eleventh through the fifteenth century* (Berkeley: University of California Press, 1971), p. 169.

[73] C. Foss, 'Strobilos and related sites', *Anatolian studies* 38 (1998), 149. Jotischky has similarly concluded that the destructiveness of the Saljuq invasions into Anatolia needs to be taken seriously. He draws heavily upon accounts produced by local Christians during the late eleventh-century: Jotischky, 'The Christians of Jerusalem', 47–48.

[74] C. Lightfoot and E. Ivison, 'The Amorium project: The 1995 excavation season', *Dumbarton Oaks papers* 51 (1997), 300.

[75] Vryonis, *The decline of medieval hellenism*, pp. 166–167.

[76] For discussion see: A. Izdebski, 'The changing landscapes of Byzantine Anatolia', *Archaeologia Bulgarica* 16.1 (2012), 59.

[77] W. Eastwood et al., 'Integrating palaeoecological and archaeo-historical records: Land use and landscape change in Cappadocia (central Turkey) since late Antiquity', *Archaeology of the countryside in medieval Anatolia*, ed. T. Vorderstrasse and J. Roodenberg (Leiden: Nederlands Instituut voor het Nabije Oosten, 2009), p. 58.

[78] *Aristakēs Lastivertc 'I's history*, trans. R. Bedrosian (New York: Sources of the Armenian Tradition, 1985), pp. 121–122; Ellenblum, *Collapse of the eastern Mediterranean*, passim. Preiser-Kapeller certainly underlines the importance of a wider array of factors (including climatic issues) beyond simply Turkish attacks. He also offers a useful survey

Georgian chronicle *History of David, King of Kings* explains this problem clearly:

Such affliction for the Christians continued long. For in the springtime the Turks would come and carry out (depredations) like those first ones. In the winter they would leave. In those times there was neither sowing nor harvest. The land was ruined and turned into forest; in place of men, beasts and animals of the field made their dwelling there.[79]

Likewise, Michael Attaleiates made explicit reference to shortages in various foodstuffs experienced in Constantinople during the 1070s as well as the crowds of refugees seeking shelter in the capital from the Turks.[80] In addition to the decline of rural agriculture in parts of Eastern Anatolia, many commercial cities either went into decline or were destroyed. In 1049, for example, Artze – a major terminus for goods from Persia, India, and Asia – was sacked, again a major blow to the Anatolian economy.[81]

Still the picture of collapse is not universal. The palynological analyses are not consistent but reveal a decline of cereal pollen (and therefore local agriculture) in some areas but not in others.[82] Some international commerce evidently survived Turkish occupation. The Venetians and Amalfitans are both known to have continued trading in Antioch following its fall to the Turks in 1084. In 1087, they were apparently still able to purchase high-value goods there, such as gems, silk, and carpets.[83] Even so, merchants from Bari had a rather different experience. When they attempted to reach Antioch in the same year, they put in at Myra (s. coast Anatolia) and were dissuaded from continuing to their destination on the strength of reports that the Turks had devastated that area.[84] Consequently, although the invading Turks clearly caused considerable disruption, it is necessary to note that their impact could vary considerably across different regional zones.

---

of the palynological surveys conducted to date, see: Preiser-Kapeller, 'A collapse of the eastern Mediterranean?'

[79] Translation from 'The history of David', p. 311.   [80] MA, p. 384.

[81] A. Laiou, 'Economic and noneconomic exchange', *The economic history of Byzantium*, ed. A. Laiou, vol. 2, Dumbarton Oaks studies XXXIX (Washington, DC: Dumbarton Oaks Research Library, 2002), p. 748.

[82] See: Preiser-Kapeller, 'A collapse of the eastern Mediterranean?'

[83] D. Jacoby, 'Venetian commercial expansion in the eastern Mediterranean, 8th–11th centuries', *Byzantine trade, 4th–12th centuries: the archaeology of local, regional and international exchange*, ed. M. M. Mango, Studies for the promotion of Byzantine studies XIV (Aldershot: Ashgate, 2009), p. 388; M. Carr, 'Between Byzantium, Egypt and the Holy Land: the Italian maritime republics and the First Crusade', *Jerusalem the golden: The origins and impact of the First Crusade*, ed. S. Edgington and L. García-Guijarro, Outremer: studies in the Crusades and the Latin East III (Turnhout: Brepols, 2014), pp. 76–77.

[84] Hugh of Fleury, 'Liber qui modernorum regum Francorum continet actus', *MGHS*, vol. 9 (Hanover, 1851), p. 392.

Another group of sources that bear upon this matter are the accounts of Urban's speech at Clermont produced following the crusade. As shown earlier, these provide a poor guide for Urban's actual words at Clermont, but on this present subject (the actual impact of the Turkish invasions into Anatolia) they are of value. This study – following Marcus Bull – will approach them as the manifestations of their authors' own ideas and lived experience, rather than genuine attempts at reconstructing the pope's sermon. On this basis, their descriptions of the Turks' behaviour in Anatolia are relevant to this discussion.[85]

These authors had either crossed Asia Minor in person or they were at least drawing upon the accounts of those who had. The crusaders had passed through many devastated regions and, to take one example, when the crusaders fought their famous battle at Dorylaeum (1 July 1097), they did so next to the abandoned ruins of this once great city which had been destroyed by the Turks in c. 1080.[86] Stephen of Blois commented in a letter to his wife that the army had passed the city of Nicomedia, which had been looted by the Turks.[87] The continuator of Frutolf's chronicle (participant in the 1101 crusade) described his horror at the damage inflicted upon the chapels in Asia Minor and in particular the desecration of images of Jesus, the Virgin Mary, and the saints. He observed in particular that it was their appendages, noses, ears, hands, or feet that had been violated.[88] Having visited these sites in person, this writer's description is plausible, but even the nature of these described assaults provides further corroboration. The Turks are widely reported to have shamed their victims (whether human or in this case depictions of religious figures) by deforming their noses or ears. They are said to have acted in this way by Albert of Aachen in assaults against Armenian women in Tarsus, while a poem by Solomon ha-Kohen describing the Turks' wars in the Levant in the 1070s also bears witness to this same practice.[89] Alexius I's general Tatikios was famously said to have had his nose cut off.[90]

---

[85] Asbridge, by contrast, argues that accusations of this kind had 'little or no basis in fact': Asbridge, The First Crusade, p. 34.

[86] *Deeds of John and Manuel Comnenus by John Kinnamos*, trans. C. Brand (New York: Columbia University Press, 1976), p. 220. The Byzantines did not return to Dorylaeum until 1175 when Manuel Comnenus reconquered the area.

[87] *Kb*, p. 139.   [88] *FE*, p. 134.

[89] AA, p. 158; Gil, *A History of Palestine*, p. 416. J. H. Greenstone, 'The Turkoman defeat at Cairo by Solomon ben Joseph Ha-Kohen', *The American journal of semitic languages and literatures* 22:2 (1906), 165.

[90] For an example, see MA, p. 278. See also J. Haldon, 'Humour and the everyday in Byzantium', *Humour, history and politics in Late Antiquity and the Early Middle Ages*, ed. G. Halsall (Cambridge: Cambridge University Press, 2004), pp. 65–66. The crusaders also acted in this way at times (see: AA, p. 458; 'Anonymous Syriac chronicle', trans.

Consequently, statements about the nature of these invasions made either by the crusaders themselves or based on information received from returning pilgrims (albeit back-projected into their versions of Urban's speech) should not be so lightly laid aside. Jotischky has recently shown that the charge contained in Baldric of Bourgueil's version of Urban's speech, concerning goods stolen by the Turks from the Holy Sepulchre, seems to derive from either a pilgrim account or a Greek source and not from his imagination.[91] To take another example, let us look at the allegations made by Robert the Monk in his version of Urban's speech. His accusations against the Turks can be reduced to the following charges: the destruction and conversion of churches, widespread destruction of property, slave-taking, the forcible circumcision of Christians and the torture and, by implication, rape of Christians. He also claims that the Turks executed Christians by tying them to stakes and shooting them with arrows.[92] Often these are presented by historians as hostile representations and certainly Robert imbues his descriptions with a gruelling level of detail clearly intended to provoke a powerful emotional reaction from his audience. Yet there is nothing implausible about many of his basic charges.[93] Slave-taking, forced conversion / circumcision and the destruction of churches are widely referenced by sources, including Muslim and Georgian chronicles.[94] Ibn al-Athir reports that during the 1048–1049 Turkish attack upon Anatolia, the invaders took 100,000 prisoners

A. Tritton, *Journal of the Royal Asiatic Society* 65 (1933), 85.) and such practices were not entirely unknown in western Christendom. See, for example, H. Cowdrey, 'New dimensions of reform: war as a path to salvation', *Jerusalem the golden: the origins and impact of the First Crusade*, ed. S. Edgington and L. García-Guijarro, Outremer: studies in the Crusades and the Latin East III (Turnhout: Brepols, 2014), p. 14. See also J. Frembgen, 'Honour, shame, and bodily mutilation: Cutting off the nose among tribal societies in Pakistan', *Journal of the Royal Asiatic Society* 16 (2006), 243–260.

[91] In this article Jotischky also begins to consider whether the accusations levelled against the Turks in other chronicles have some basis in reality: Jotischky, 'The Christians of Jerusalem', 49–52.

[92] RM, p. 5.

[93] Housley, 'The Crusades and Islam', 201. For further discussion on the question of reality/representation in Robert's account of these acts see: B. Catlos, *Infidel kings and unholy warriors: Faith, power and violence in the age of Crusade and Jihad* (New York: Farrar, Straus and Giroux, 2014), p. 244; Völkl, *Muslime – Märtyrer – Militia Christi*, pp. 164–165, 181–84.

[94] Raymond of Aguilers' chronicle includes accounts of Christian communities near Tyre being subjected to forced circumcision. He also seemingly describes forced conversions taking place after the Turks' conquest of Antioch. See: RA, pp. 64, 129. A Georgian chronicle makes the same charge: 'The history of David', p. 311. Ellenblum has also drawn attention to references to forced conversion in the *Danishmendnameh*, which describes the deeds of the Danishmendeds in Anatolia and the Jazira during the late eleventh century. This account also describes the destruction of churches. Ellenblum, *The Decline of the eastern Mediterranean*, pp. 245–246. See also A. Beihammer, 'Defection across the border of Islam and Christianity: apostasy and cross-cultural interaction

along with a vast haul of plunder.[95] This figure is presumably inflated, but it is clear that large numbers were taken into captivity. Widespread raiding across many parts of Byzantine Anatolia is also well attested in the texts discussed earlier, including Ibn al-Athir's chronicle.[96] Likewise, the tenth-century Iranian author Ibn Faqih al-Hamadhani described how the Turks were accustomed to launch slave-taking expeditions, searching particularly for women and children.[97] In a similar vein, the *Akhbār al-dawla al-saljūquiyya* recalls the destruction of churches in towns near to Ani (which fell in 1064) and their replacement with mosques.[98] Michael the Syrian also described the transformation of the church of Cassianus in Antioch into a mosque by Suleiman ibn Qutalmish following its conquest in 1084. The crusaders later observed that the Turks had covered the church's statues of the saints with cement.[99]

The suggestion that the Turks executed their victims by shooting them with arrows is also referenced in both Armenian and other Frankish sources. Orderic Vitalis describes the Turkish ruler Balak executing his prisoners in this way. Walter the Chancellor's history contains similar reports describing the treatment of prisoners held in Aleppo by Il-ghazi.[100] In addition, Gervase of Bazoches, ruler of Tiberias, met a similar fate in 1108 at the hands of the Damascene ruler Tughtegin. Having been taken captive and with the failure of ransom negotiations, Tughtegin took him to the centre of Damascus and executed him by this means. His scalp was then cut off and his skull was turned into a cup.[101] Moreover,

in Byzantine-Seljuk relations', *Speculum* 86 (2011), 616. See also A. Mallett, *Popular Muslim reactions to the Franks in the Levant, 1097–1291* (Aldershot: Ashgate, 2014), pp. 72–74.

[95] AST, p. 68 (see also pp. 153–155). References to slave taking abound in the sources for this period. See: 'Anonymous Syriac chronicle', 71.

[96] AST, p. 178.   [97] Ibn Faqih al-Hamadhani, 'On the Turks and their lands', p. 50.

[98] *The history of the Seljuq state*, p. 31. See also ME, p. 104.

[99] MS, vol. 3, p. 173; AA, p. 338; *HAI*, p. 61. This church under crusader rule became the cathedral of St Peter, see: H. Kennedy, 'Medieval Antioch', *The city in late antiquity*, ed. J. Rich (London: Routledge, 1992), p. 188.

[100] OV, vol. 6, p. 112; Walter the Chancellor, *Bella Antiochena*, ed. H. Hagenmeyer (Innsbruck, 1896), p. 110.

[101] AA, p. 770. GN, p. 350. It may be relevant to note that Aristakēs reports prisoners being shot for target practice: *Aristakēs Lastivertc 'I's History*, p. 138. Peter Tudebode and Guibert also observe that the Turks executed their victims in this way during the First Crusade, see: PT, p. 35; GN, p. 126. William of Malmesbury tells a similar story about the execution of a captive by the Fatimids: WM, vol. 1, p. 466. See also WT, vol. 1, 570. Walter the Chancellor also reports Tughtakin of Damascus ordering Robert Fitz-Fulk's decapitated head to be turned into a goblet: Walter the Chancellor, *Bella Antiochena*, pp. 108–109. For further discussion on this episode see: C. Hillenbrand, 'What's in a name? Tughtegin – the 'minister of the Antichrist'?', *Fortresses of the intellect: Ismaili and other Islamic studies in honour of Farhad Daftary*, ed. Omar Ali-de-Onzaga

ritual and judicial actions involving bows, bowstrings, and arrows were certainly commonplace in Turkish culture; for example, rulers were often assassinated by strangulation with a bowstring.[102] Bar Hebraeus likewise described how Sultan Alp Arslan once planned to kill a rebel leader by tying him to posts and shooting him. According to this tale the rebel protested that he deserved a more noble death and so Alp Arslan freed him, tried to shoot him, missed, and was then fatally wounded by this vengeful rebel.[103]

In this way, Robert's account needs to be taken seriously, not perhaps as an accurate rendition of Urban's oration, but as a piece of highly emotionally-charged reportage based on eye witness accounts concerning Turkish practices during the Anatolian wars.[104]

Overall, the conquest of Asia Minor was a prolonged affair that took many decades to complete. It was also uneven in its impact. Some regions were thoroughly despoiled whilst others were relatively lightly affected. Even so, the textual and non-textual sources tell the story of a Byzantine society in full retreat. They report abandoned settlements, sacked cities, widespread raiding and plundering, and refugees fleeing to the west; classic hallmarks of steppe invasions throughout history. Thus, it is not difficult to imagine the anxiety and concern that the reports of refugees and emissaries would have provoked in Rome as the papacy became aware of the full extent of the chaos engulfing the region. Placed within this context, Urban's calls for a campaign to the east take on a new character. It seems very unlikely that his deep hostility towards the Turks was merely a fabricated expression of a long-standing hatred towards the Muslim 'other'.[105] Instead the terminology in his letters communicates a genuine sense of alarm at the actions of a fundamentally new enemy.

(London: I.B. Tauris, 2011), pp. 463–475; O. Turan, 'The ideal of world domination among the medieval Turks', *Studia Islamica* 4 (1955), 78.

[102] For an example see: AC, p. 178. See also Bar Hebraeus, *The chronography*, vol. 1, p. 201. For wider discussion see: C. Cahen, *Pre-Ottoman Turkey: A general survey of the material and spiritual culture and history c.1071–1330*, trans. J. Jones-Williams (London: Sidgwick & Jackson, 1968), p. 36; C. Bosworth, 'The origins of the Seljuqs', *The Seljuqs: politics, society and culture*, ed. C. Lange and S. Mecit (Edinburgh: Edinburgh University Press, 2011), p. 18; A. Başan, *The great Seljuqs: A history*, RSIT (Abingdon: Routledge, 2010); Peacock, *The great Seljuk empire*, p. 126. They were not the only steppe people to use arrow-based symbology. The Avars, for example, buried their warriors with arrows; see: S. Szádeczky-Kardoss, 'The Avars', *The Cambridge history of early inner Asia* (Cambridge: Cambridge University Press, 1990), p. 226.

[103] Bar Hebraeus, *The chronography*, vol. 1, p. 224.

[104] Frankopan has performed a similar analysis on the accusations levelled against the Turks in a letter which purports to have been sent form the Emperor Alexius to Count Robert of Flanders prior to the crusade. Frankopan, *The First Crusade*, pp. 60–61.

[105] A view advanced by Mastnak: Mastnak, *Crusading peace*, pp. 115–117.

Participants: Intentions

For Urban, seated at Christendom's helm and possessed of detailed information from across the Mediterranean, the need to buttress Byzantium was an obvious priority. The same cannot be said, however, for the knightly families he approached for support. These were communities with far more restricted horizons whose knowledge of the tumultuous events taking place in Anatolia would, for the most part, have been limited.[106] By appealing to this audience Urban faced the challenge of persuading warriors to leave their homes and families for a prolonged period and to risk their lives in a war that – hitherto – may have been entirely unknown to them. Urban was evidently successful in this aim, but it is necessary to identify which components of his preaching motivated his audience to take the cross. It is especially significant to establish the importance participants attached to the idea of fighting pagans. This is a fundamental question because it helps to contextualise the crusaders' initial posture towards their future foe.

In some cases, Urban was highly successful in communicating his message. Writing in 1096, Count Fulk Le Réchin, who had attended Urban's sermon at Angers, recalled that the pontiff had incited his audience to take part in an expedition that was intended to: (a) reach Jerusalem, (b) protect the Christians in that region, and (c) defeat the invaders who threatened the Christian people.[107] These objectives tally exactly with those enumerated in Urban's letters, suggesting that Fulk had fully understood what Urban was trying to achieve. Many of the charters demonstrate a similar correlation. For example, in December 1095 Urban wrote to the people of Flanders, writing:

Your brotherhood, we believe, has long since learned from many accounts that a barbaric fury has deplorably afflicted and laid waste the churches of God in the regions of the Orient. More than this, blasphemous to say, it has even grasped in intolerable servitude its churches and the holy city of Christ, glorified by his Passion and Resurrection. Grieving with pious concern at this calamity, we visited the regions of Gaul and devoted ourselves largely to urging the princes of the land and their subjects to free the churches of the east.[108]

---

[106] As John France commented, 'the papacy of the eleventh century had a wide view of the world a remarkable grasp of history which differentiated its outlook sharply from that of the generality of the European elites'. J. France, 'Byzantium in western chronicles before the First Crusade', *Knighthoods of Christ: Essays on the history of the Crusades and the Knights Templar presented to Malcolm Barber* (Aldershot: Ashgate, 2007), p. 8.

[107] 'Fragmentum historiae Andegavensis', pp. 233–238.

[108] Translation from 'Urban to the faithful in Flanders, December 1095' in: *Chronicles of the First Crusade*, pp. 24–25; *Kb*, p. 136; *Papsturkunden in Spanien*, pp. 287–288; 'Papsturkunden in Florenz', p. 313.

The following year in October 1096, Count Robert II of Flanders, when on the point of setting out for the east, made the following declaration in a document settling local affairs in Flanders:

I, therefore, by the inspiration of divine admonition, promulgated by the authority of the apostolic seat, travelling to Jerusalem for the liberation of the church of God, which is continually oppressed by wild peoples . . . have determined on this decree.[109]

This charter resonates with the language of Urban's letter: referencing the same goals; speaking of the campaign as a 'liberation' and describing the savagery of the campaign's enemy.[110] Consequently, in Robert's case at least, Urban's ambitions and objectives had been received, internalised, and translated into action with little blurring. As Riley-Smith has shown, other charters mirrored Urban's language, using terms that reflect the penitential nature of this journey and its status as a pilgrimage.[111]

In many cases, the participants seem to have understood and retained the main messages communicated through Urban's propaganda. Even so, whilst the charters reference the pope's major objectives and language, there is a change in emphasis. For Urban, the desire to reach Jerusalem appears to have been his main goal, but it was listed among a number of stated aims which included: defending fellow Christians and fighting the 'Saracens'/'pagans'. For the crusaders, by contrast, the desire to reach Jerusalem is overwhelming. It appears with an almost 100 per cent consistency across all the charters and the centrality of this desire is accentuated by the fact that many participants referred to themselves explicitly as 'Jerusalemites'.[112] Other objectives are referenced only sporadically. The desire to protect eastern Christians appears very rarely whilst the intention of confronting any enemy appears in only 20 per cent of these documents.[113] Given that these charters were produced in a range of institutions – for the most part spread across the kingdom of France – their unanimity in defining solely the holy city (or a least the Holy

---

[109] *Actes des comtes de Flandre, 1071–1128*, ed. F. Vercauteren (Brussels, 1938), no. 20.

[110] Riley-Smith, *The first crusaders*, p. 62; Riley-Smith, 'The idea of crusading', p. 156.

[111] Riley-Smith, *The first crusaders*, pp. 61–66.

[112] Godfrey of Bouillon even had coins minted for himself before his departure which seem to have borne the inscription 'Ierosolimitanus', see: V. Tourneur, 'Un Denier de Godefroid de Bouillon Frappé en 1096', *Revue Belge de Numismatique* 83 (1931), pp. 27–30.

[113] Charters that reference this objective include: *Cartulaire de l'abbaye de Saint-Victor de Marseille*, no. 143; *Cartulaire de Sauxillanges*, ed. M. Doniol (Clermont, 1864), no. 697. See also J. Riley-Smith, *The First Crusade and the idea of crusading*, p. 22. G. Constable, 'Medieval charters as a source for the history of the Crusades', *Crusaders and crusading in the twelfth century* (Aldershot: Ashgate, 2008), p. 112.

Sepulchre) as the goal of the campaign demands serious attention. Evidently, it was this objective more than any other which inspired individuals to take the cross. The charter evidence chimes well both with wider sources and the later events of the crusade, which similarly confirm an intense desire to reach the holy city. The mere presence of noncombatants on the campaign shows that for them their involvement in the crusade was primarily spiritual and – by definition – not military. Following the siege of Antioch, several chroniclers report the pressure placed upon the expedition's leaders to proceed immediately to Jerusalem – again confirming its overriding importance. Moreover, with only a handful of exceptions – the most significant being the conquest of Nicaea the bulk of the crusader army did not purposefully seek out the strongpoints of Turkish authority (as one would expect had their ambition been to destroy Turkish hegemony in Anatolia and Syria). Indeed, Aleppo and Damascus were purposefully avoided precisely because they possessed significant Turkish garrisons.[114] As Barber notes, 'Urban's wish to rescue the eastern Christians from infidel oppression had never inspired the crusaders in the way that his call for an armed pilgrimage to liberate Jerusalem had done'.[115]

Overall, the sources build a picture of a pope besieged by tidings of defeat in the east, yet aware of a widely felt longing for the holy city, who then spliced these various imperatives into an overall call for holy war. His message was then received by an audience which had only a limited understanding of the tactical situation in Anatolia, but which had heard tales of Jerusalem from birth. Some nobles, such as the count of Flanders, who had strong links to the Byzantine court, would have understood the imperative to defend Asia Minor, but for the vast majority it was Jerusalem itself that defined their participation in the crusade. The incredible unanimity across the charters makes the point that among the various messages propounded by Urban it was this notion more than any other that penetrated furthest into his audience's minds. This is important for this present analysis because it suggests that, for the majority, fighting 'pagans' or 'Saracens' was a decidedly secondary endeavour; indeed these foes may only ever have been perceived as little more than hurdles straddling the road to their main objective: Jerusalem.[116]

---

[114] AA, p. 394.   [115] Barber, *The Crusader states*, p. 24.
[116] For discussion on this and related points see: N. Housley, *Fighting for the cross: Crusading to the Holy Land* (Yale: Yale University Press, 2008), p. 221; Housley, 'The Crusades and Islam', 195.

Participants: Foreknowledge of the Turks

Whatever the crusaders' initial intentions may have been, the Turks lay directly on their line of march. They were not a long-standing enemy, either of Byzantium or western Christendom, and had only begun to make their presence felt in the Near East at around the turn of the first millennium. As shown earlier, the Greeks and Arabs had long been aware of the Turks as a group of nomadic peoples migrating across the Eurasian steppe. The rapid Turkish advance, however, was a new phenomenon; one that redefined their relationship. Their first foray into Byzantine lands occurred in *c.* 1029, yet by 1090 much of Anatolia was in their hands.[117] For the Arabs too the Saljuq invasions were as unwelcome as they were unprecedented and in the late eleventh and early twelfth centuries, many leading Arab dynasties across Syria fell beneath the rising tide of Turkish dominance. By contrast, western Christendom was insulated to some degree from these upheavals. It was separated from the conflict in Syria and Asia Minor by the intervening bulk of the Byzantine Empire and the wide expanse of the Mediterranean. Thus, as an enemy that was both distant and new, it is likely that many crusaders would never have heard of the Turks. This lack of knowledge was not alleviated by papal preaching which, as noted earlier, did not name them explicitly. Urban indicated only that the pilgrims would encounter a 'pagan' (or in some cases 'Saracen') enemy of barbaric character in Asia Minor.

It is unclear precisely how widely information about the Turks had disseminated across western Europe before 1095.[118] One source of information, which *prima facie* seems to suggest a widespread ignorance of this people group, is the crusade charters. There is no reference to 'Turks' in any of these documents. Certainly, their unanimity is striking, but these documents alone are not incontrovertible proof on this point. The possibility has to be entertained that, as shown earlier, the charters' authors were merely mimicking the terminology used in papal preaching and correspondence (which also did not name the Turks). Thus their choice of such imprecise language may also not mark the extent of their knowledge. Moreover, in one case at least we can be sure that a religious house which named 'pagans' in its charters had direct access to specific and recent

---

[117] Peacock, *Early Seljūq History*, p. 139.

[118] For my early study on this subject see: N. Morton, 'Encountering the Turks: The first crusaders' foreknowledge of their enemy: some preliminary findings', *Crusading and warfare in the Middle Ages: Realities and representations. Essays in honour of John France*, ed. S. John and N. Morton, Crusades subsidia VII (Aldershot: Ashgate, 2014), pp. 47–68.

information concerning the Turks. This was the abbey of Marmoutier. In
c. 1090, a monk named Goibertus returned to Marmoutier after a period
of service with Emperor Alexius. He later appears in Marmoutier charters
as the prior of Saint-Martin de Chamars (the earliest reference occurring
in 1092). Goibertus is significant for this present matter because, having spent time in Constantinople in the late eleventh century, he would
surely have understood the threat posed by the Turks.[119] Even so, when
Stephen of Blois made a donation to Marmoutier during his preparations
for crusade – a gift which Goibertus had personally encouraged him to
make – he still described his enemy as 'pagans'. Clearly Goibertus was
present and possessed more precise information, yet the more generic
term 'pagans' was still employed.[120] This example serves as a warning
against using the terminology in the charters as a gauge of the author's
knowledge. It seems likely instead that their usage derived from stylistic
norms and the imperative to imitate papal preaching. This conclusion
is only confirmed by the fact that the charters produced for crusaders
between 1099 and the time of the Second Crusade continue to define
their enemies as either 'pagans' or 'Saracens' rather than Turks. By this
stage or course – with the return of the first crusaders – the Turks would
have been widely known across Christendom and yet they are still not
mentioned in any charter. The only identified western European charter
to reference the Turks in any context during this period is not specifically
concerned with crusading. It is a charter defining a donation made to
the abbey of Charroux, which was dated to the second year after the
conquest of Jerusalem from the 'Turks and pagans'.[121]

A stronger indication that the Turks were not well known in 1095–1097
is the paucity of information available upon them in western Christendom's archives at this time. 'Turks' make only infrequent appearances in
sources produced in Christendom before the First Crusade. Some Classical Roman authors may possibly have heard of them and Pomponius
Mela (first century) identified *Turcae* living in forests bordering Amazon
territory, while Pliny the Elder (d. 79 CE) located them near the Sea of
Azov.[122] After this point, the Turks seem to have largely dropped below

---

[119] Shepard, 'How St James the Persian's head was brought to Cormery', pp. 298, 314–
317.

[120] *Cartulaire de Marmoutier pour le Dunois*, no. 92.

[121] *Chartes et Documents pour servir à l'histoire de l'abbaye de Charroux*, ed. P. de Monsabert,
Archives Historiques du Poitou XXXIX (Poitiers, 1910), no. 22; Constable, 'Medieval
charters', p. 114.

[122] Bosworth, 'Introduction', p. xiv; *Pomponius Mela's description of the world*, ed. and trans.
F. Romer (Ann Arbor: University of Michigan Press, 2001), pp. 66–67; Pliny (the
Elder), *Natural history II, Libri III-VII*, ed. H. Rackham, vol. 2 (London: Heinemann,
1942), p. 350.

the knowledge horizon for nearly a millennium, only to be revived following the First Crusade. The sources produced in the intervening period are *almost* silent.

Among the few texts that do refer to 'Turks' in any context is the seventh-century *Chronicle of Fredegar*, which contains references to people called the 'Turks' (*Turchi/gens Turquorum*).[123] These 'Turks' appear in a legend describing the origins of the Frankish people. Fredegar explains how the Frankish people began as refugees fleeing from the fall of Troy who, after long wandering, found themselves on the banks of the Danube. At this point they broke into two parties with one setting out west (later establishing the Frankish kingdom) and the other remaining where they were and electing a king called Torcoth, who gave his name to his people: the 'Turks'.[124] The question of how widely this story had circulated by the time of the First Crusade and whether it played a role in shaping medieval approaches to the Turks has attracted a fair amount of attention.[125] At the centre of this debate is a statement made by the *Gesta Francorum*'s author that he had encountered some Turks who had claimed that they shared a common descent with the Franks.[126] Exactly what can be inferred from this statement has been the subject of much debate.

Runciman's view was that the *Gesta*'s author was clearly aware of the Fredegar legend. He argues that whilst Fredegar's tale had been forgotten in western Christendom, it had long been remembered in Iceland. He then suggests that the story may have been carried south by Vikings serving in the Byzantine Varangian guard, who might then have been captured by the Turks, who might then have told their Turkish captors, who might then have told the crusaders.[127] Runciman's argument consists of

---

[123] 'Fredegarii et aliorum chronica', *MGH: Scriptores rerum Merovingicarum*, ed. B. Krusch, vol. 2 (Hanover, 1888), pp. 46, 93.

[124] 'Fredegarii et aliorum chronica' Several historians have attempted to identify Fredegar's *Turchi*. Meserve discusses the historiography surrounding this question, concluding that it is difficult to draw any firm conclusions on this point. M. Meserve, *Empires of Islam in Renaissance historical thought* (Cambridge, MA: Harvard University Press, 2008), p. 50. Kim has more recently drawn the conclusion, following Cahen, that Fredegar was describing the Torcilingi 'a Turkic-speaking tribe under Hunnic rule'. Kim, *The Huns, Rome and the Birth of Europe*, pp. 100–102.

[125] For discussion on the inclusion of this episode from Fredegar's chronicle in later chronicles see, Meserve, *Empires of Islam*, p. 51.

[126] *GF*, p. 21.

[127] S. Runciman, 'Teucri and Turci', *Medieval and Middle Eastern studies: In honor of Aziz Suryal Atiya*, ed. S. Hanna (Leiden: Brill, 1972), pp. 347–348. Snorri Sturluson is the main source for Runciman's assertion. He wrote many decades after the crusade, but Runciman points out that his work was based on earlier traditions. Snorri Sturluson, *Edda*, trans. A. Faulkes (London: J.M Dent, 2004), pp. 64–65. Jubb, 'The Crusaders' Perceptions of their Opponents', p. 234.

a rather speculative chain of transmission which, as Murray points out, 'strains credulity'. Murray suggests instead that whilst it is not impossible that the *Gesta*'s author knew of the legend from the Western tradition, it is more probable that his conviction that there was a relationship between their peoples was based rather on their shared competence in war.[128] Meserve has drawn a similar conclusion.[129]

On this point it is impossible to be sure. All the aforementioned authors agree that the Fredegar legend of a Turkish-Frankish common ancestry is absent from the western tradition in the centuries between the completion of Fredegar's chronicle and the eleventh century and yet, as Meserve points out, it does seem to reappear soon after the time of the First Crusade. Hugh of St Victor reproduced this legend in his *Priorum Excerptionum libri decem* (wr.c. 1130), noting immediately afterwards that 'today' the Turks are known as '*Turci*', thereby recognising a link between Fredegar's legend and contemporary Turks.[130] His was not an isolated reference and this legend would reappear in later centuries.[131] Evidently, it remained known in some circles.

There is another possible explanation for the *Gesta Francorum*'s report which warrants attention. In the late-medieval period, the Mamluk historian Badr al-Din Mahmud (d. 1451) – drawing upon far earlier sources – traced the racial origins of mankind back to the time of Noah (and ultimately Adam). He made the point that all the world's peoples are descended from Noah's sons Shem, Ham, and Japheth. Crucially, he explained that the Turks and the Franks share a common descent from Japheth's eldest son Gomer. Gomer himself fathered three further sons, Riphath (father of the Franks), Ashikiyan (father of the Slavs), and Togarmah (father of the Turks).[132] Consequently, according to this narrative, and following an entirely different explanatory pathway to the Latin tradition, the Turks may also have believed that they were ultimately related

[128] A. Murray, 'William of Tyre and the origin of the Turks: observations on possible sources of the *Gesta orientalium principum*', Dei Gesta per Francos: Etudes sur *les croisades dédiés à Jean Richard: Crusade studies in honour of Jean Richard*, ed. M. Balard, B. Kedar and J. Riley-Smith (Aldershot: Ashgate, 2001), pp. 223–224.

[129] Meserve, *Empires of Islam*, p. 56.

[130] Hugh of St Victor, 'Priorum Excerptionum libri decem', *PL*, vol. 177 (1854), cols. 275–276; Meserve, *Empires of Islam*, p. 51.

[131] This connection persisted into the early modern period where this connection between the Turks and Trojans came under sustained criticism. Meserve, *Empires of Islam*, pp. 22–64.

[132] Badr al-Din Mahmud (al-Ayni), 'Genealogy and tribal division', *The turkic peoples in medieval Arabic writings*, trans. Y. Frenkel, RSIT (Abingdon: Routledge, 2015), p. 67. Naturally it had long been believed that the Turks were descended from Japheth and Gomer, but this is the earliest reference I have seen which identifies the Franks as descending from this common root.

to the Franks. Whether it was this link that lay behind the *Gesta Francorum*'s report that some Anatolian Turks claimed a relationship with the crusaders is unknowable; still it opens up the possibility that the answer to this question lies in the Turkic, rather than the Latin, tradition.

Whilst Fredegar's account raises many questions, it also provides one of the very few references to the 'Turks' in western European sources written before the tenth century. Among the handful of other works to name them is the *Cosmography of Aethicus Ister*. This is a rather bizarre text, produced in the early eighth century, in which the unknown author, posing as St Jerome, sets out to edit and reflect upon a much earlier work by an Istrian pagan philosopher called Aethicus Ister. This 'pagan' source discusses Aethicus' philosophy and gives an account of his journeys ranging from *Taprobane* (Sri Lanka) to the Orkneys. He describes lands populated by strange phenomena and mythical beasts, which lie side by side with more accurate observations corroborated by other sources. Within this colourful account, the Turks receive a lengthy treatment. The author comments that they are largely unknown by contemporaries and he proceeds to make amends for this deficit.[133] He situates them among a group of peoples including the Huns, Danes, and Alans in 'Germania', a land he locates between the Rhine and the Meotic marshes. For him the Turks were among the unclean peoples and monstrous northern races, descendants of Gog and Magog, who Alexander the Great had attempted to trap behind the Caspian gates until the end of days and the coming of the Antichrist. He presents them as dirty, debauched, idolatrous worshippers of Saturn who were ready to eat the most unclean of meats (including aborted human foetuses).

Some parts of his lurid descriptions may well have been the product of his evidently powerful imagination; nevertheless, several of his ideas find their echo in eastern Christian eschatological sources. Of these, the *Apocalypse* written in Syriac by Pseudo Methodius (writing *c.* 691) seems to have been particularly influential. It presents a broad overview of world history from the formation of the earth to the Second Coming of Christ. Its most significant feature is the incorporation within this chronology of an account of the rise and ultimate fall of Islam. Most importantly for this present analysis, the *Apocalypse* offers a description of the foetus-eating peoples of Gog and Magog trapped to the north of the Caspian

---

[133] *The cosmography of Aethicus Ister*, ed. and trans. by M. Herren, Publication of the journal of medieval Latin VIII (Turnhout: Brepols, 2011), pp. 28–32. Meserve has suggested that the Turks described in this work may have been Turkic Khazars: M. Meserve, 'Medieval sources for Renaissance theories on the origins of the Ottoman Turks', *Europa und die Türken in der Renaissance*, ed. B. Guthmüller and W. Kühlmann (Tübingen: Niemeyer, 2000), p. 424.

gates.[134] These details tally closely with the description of the Turks given in the *cosmography*. Nevertheless, the *cosmography* does not seem to have been drawing upon the *Apocalypse* directly. Pseudo-Methodius may attribute these qualities to the peoples of the north but his work does not include the Turks among these northern peoples.[135] It supplies a list of different names. The inclusion of the Turks among races of Gog and Magog occurred many years later. The first author to establish this link may possibly have been Jacob of Edessa, who was writing shortly after Pseudo-Methodius.[136] Subsequently, many eastern Christian authors associated the Turks to varying degrees with these peoples. For example, the Georgian *Primary History of K'art'Li* describes the Turks as a people of Gog and Magog (it also mentions their supposedly unpleasant diet).[137] Moreover both this work and the *cosmography* contain the story that Alexander the Great attempted to conquer the Turks but was then forced to withdraw – a story not contained in Pseudo-Methodius' *Apocalypse*.[138] Thus these works describe the Turks in similar terms; raising the likelihood that the *cosmography*'s author was drawing in some way upon eastern Christian sources based ultimately on Pseudo-Methodian tradition.[139] It is also possible that this information was connected in some form to Islamic traditions and some tenth-century Arab writers claimed that some pre-Islamic Turks ate fell meats, including dead bodies, and reverenced Saturn.[140] Another example of cross-cultural borrowing occurred in the 870s when the papal librarian Anastasius Bibliothecarius copied the *Chronographia* of Theophanes into

---

[134] Pseudo-Methodius, *Apocalypse*, ed. and trans. B. Garstad, Dumbarton Oaks Medieval Library (Cambridge, MA: Harvard University Press, 2012), pp. 23, 97.

[135] The Turks are mentioned at one point briefly in this work, but in a very different context: Pseudo-Methodius, *Apocalypse*, p. 37.

[136] M. Dickens, 'Turkāyē: Turkic peoples in Syriac literature prior to the Seljuks', unpublished PhD thesis, University of Cambridge (2008), pp. 72–75. Dickens observes that it is difficult to identify which parts of Jacob of Edessa's text are his own and which are additions by later redactors. The first Syriac author to unambiguously make this connection between Magog and the Turks was Michael the Syrian. M. Dickens, 'The sons of Magog: The Turks in Michael's chronicle', *Parole de l'Orient* 30 (2005), 436.

[137] S. H. Rapp, *Studies in medieval Georgian historiography: Early texts and Eurasian contexts*, Corpus Scriptorum Christianorum Orientalium: Subsidia CXIII (Louvain: Peeters, 2003), p. 257.

[138] *The cosmography of Aethicus Ister*, pp. 32–34.

[139] Dickens also points out that the *cosmography* describes the gates of the north as the 'breasts of the north'. Again this is a convention found in Syriac sources from the seventh century. See: Dickens, 'Turkāyē: turkic peoples', p. 128.

[140] Ibn Faqih al-Hamadhani, 'On the Turks and their lands', pp. 51–52; Abu Dulaf, 'Pseudo-travel', *The turkic peoples in medieval Arabic writings*, trans. Y. Frenkel, RSIT (Abingdon: Routledge, 2015), pp. 55, 57.

Latin; thereby making available a work which contains some references to Byzantium's early dealings with the Turks.[141]

When the name 'Turk' next resurfaced in the work of Liutprand of Cremona (d. 972), it did so in a rather different form. In his chronicle *Antapodosis* he used the name 'Turks' as a synonym for the Hungarians. During Liutprand's lifetime the Hungarians were still pagan so they appear in his narrative as the entrenched opponents of Christendom. To take one example, Liutprand described the battle fought between King Louis IV 'The Child' of East Francia at Lech in 910 using the terms *Hungarii* and *Turci* interchangeably.[142] He discussed *Turci* subsequently in a poem, which touched upon their depredations, using standard terminology reserved for pagan attackers: presenting them as an 'evil race' and 'enemies of God'.[143]

Nevertheless, the identification of Hungarians as 'Turks' was not common practice in western Christendom, nor was it strictly accurate.[144] There were some later authors who drew upon the connection he created (as we shall see) but they were few. The Hungarians themselves are of Finno-Ugric extraction; although admittedly having lived for many centuries on the steppe they had picked up some elements of Turkish culture and language.[145] European authors, both contemporary and in later centuries, tended instead to describe the Hungarians as *Hungrii* or Huns.[146] Liutprand's inspiration for using this ethnonym seems rather to derive from the Byzantine tradition, which frequently conflated

---

[141] Meserve, 'Medieval sources for Renaissance theories', p. 430.

[142] Liudprand of Cremona, 'Antapodosis', pp. 36–37.

[143] Liudprand of Cremona, 'Antapodosis', p. 47.

[144] Although it was rare for later Western authors to describe the Hungarians in this way there were a few occasions where Hungarians were named as 'Turks'. In the thirteenth-century one reader of Otto of Freising's *History of Two Cities* added a marginal note to a passage describing the conversion of 'Garda' king of the Huns at the time of the Emperor Justinian. He commented that his contemporaries call the Huns 'Turks' and that the western Huns were commonly called 'Hungarians' or 'Avars'. This is however an isolated case and there is little to suggest that the crusaders perceived an association between these two peoples. Otto of Freising, 'Chronica sive Historia de Duabus Civitatibus', *Monumenta Germaniae Historica: SRG*, ed. A. Hofmeister, vol. 45 (Hanover, 1912), p. 233.

[145] P. Golden, 'The peoples of the Russian forest belt', *The Cambridge history of early inner Asia*, ed. D. Sinor (Cambridge: Cambridge University Press, 1990), p. 243; P. Engel, *The realm of St. Stephen: A history of medieval Hungary: 895–1526* (London: I.B. Tauris, 2005), pp. 8–10.

[146] For the characterisation of Hungarians as 'Huns' see: A. Sager, 'Hungarians as *vremde* in medieval Germany', *Meeting the foreign in the Middle Ages*, ed. A. Classen (New York: Routledge, 2002), pp. 27–44; Berend, *At the gate of Christendom*, p. 204; Engel, *The realm of St. Stephen*, pp. 8–9. The Hungarians do not seem to have described themselves in this way, see: A. Róna-Tas, *Hungarians and Europe in the early Middle Ages* (Budapest: Central European University Press, 1999), pp. 275–282.

Turks and Hungarians. This practice occurs widely in Byzantine sources for this period including the histories of John Skylitzes and various texts attributed to Constantine VII Porphyrogenitus (d.959).[147] In his work on court protocol, Constantine outlined the correct modes of address to be used when dealing with foreign dignitaries, explaining that the Hungarian leaders were to be described as the 'archons of the Turks'.[148] Indeed, the Hungarians were referred to as 'Turks' by the Byzantines even in an inscription on a crown sent from Constantinople to the Hungarians in the late eleventh century.[149] Liudprand's employment of this distinctively Byzantine terminology is hardly surprising. He travelled to Constantinople on several occasions and learned Greek there in 949–950. *Antapodosis* itself is studded with Greek phrases and references.

The first clear reference to the Turks' activities in Anatolia in western European sources occurs in the chronicle of Amatus of Montecassino (written *c.* 1080). Within his account of the Normans' wars in southern Italy and Sicily, he included a brief report of the defeat of the Byzantine army at Manzikert in 1071 and the role played by the Norman commander Roussel de Bailleul during the battle. He described: Roussel's subsequent captivity; his honourable treatment at the hands of the Turkish sultan; and his later deeds.[150] Several other Norman sources discuss the involvement of warriors from western Christendom in the eleventh-century defence of Asia Minor and these also mention the Turks, although – Amatus aside – they were all written either during or after the First Crusade and consequently are an uncertain guide when attempting to establish how much was known in advance of the campaign.[151] It seems likely that Amatus' information on this topic derived from Normans returning from Byzantine service. Certainly he was well placed

[147] JS, pp. 170–171, 215, 220, 223, 231, 265, 276; *Constantine Porphyrogenitus: De Administrando Imperio*, ed. G. Moravcsik, trans. R. Jenkins (Washington, DC: Dumbarton Oaks Center for Byzantine Studies, 1967), *passim*. See also Nicholas I, patriarch of Constantinople, *letters*, trans. R. Jenkins and L. Westerink (Washington, DC: Dumbarton Oaks Center for Byzantine Studies, 1973), p. 159.

[148] Translaiton taken from: Constantine Porphyrogenitus, *The book of ceremonies*, trans. by A. Moffatt and M. Tall, vol. 2 (Canberra: Australian Association for Byzantine Studies, 2012), p. 691.

[149] Róna-Tas, *Hungarians and Europe*, p. 277.

[150] Amatus of Montecassino, *Storia de' Normanni*, ed. V. de Bartholomaeis, Fonti per la Storia d'Italia LXXVI (Rome, 1935), pp. 18–20.

[151] William of Apulia, 'Gesta Roberti Wiscardi', *passim*. An anonymous source from the British Isles written around the time of the First Crusade, which also describes Turkish depredations in Syria and Asia Minor, may also have been produced by returning warriors. See: *The life of King Edward who rests at Westminster*, ed. F. Barker, OMT, 2nd ed. (Oxford: Clarendon Press, 1992), p. 108.

to interview such warriors, who represent one possible route by which news of the Turks might have reached western Christendom before the First Crusade.

The above references complete the survey of pre-crusade references to 'Turks' (at least in the Western tradition). Evidently only a very small number of authors were aware of them. Still, there were some lines of communication from the east which may have conveyed further news. As Amatus of Montecassino's chronicle suggests, for example, it is likely that mercenaries returning from service with the Byzantines in Anatolia would have been substantially better informed. These forces hailed from many regions and in the 1090s one particularly large contingent was despatched to this frontier by Count Robert I of Flanders. Robert sent these troops on the explicit request of Emperor Alexius, who he visited in 1089 whilst on his return journey from a pilgrimage to Jerusalem.[152] Robert seems to have acted swiftly upon this matter because his knights arrived the following year and were sent to support the defenders of Nicomedia.[153] The link between the house of Flanders and Constantinople could have served as another conduit by which news from Byzantium could reach the west.

There was evidently a strong relationship between the counts of Flanders and Byzantium and it is even possible that Alexius wrote to Robert I of Flanders shortly afterwards encouraging him to send further aid. Several First Crusade chronicles report that Byzantine emissaries arrived with just such an appeal and thirty-six manuscripts of Robert the Monk's chronicle include a copy of a document purporting to be the actual letter of appeal.[154] Guibert of Nogent's chronicle also includes an *epitome* of this letter.[155]

The authenticity of this letter however has been widely disputed and multiple arguments have been advanced about its reliability. For some historians it is a fabrication (either partial or total) created in western Christendom for propaganda purposes after the crusade (possibly connected to Bohemond's subsequent crusade against Byzantium); for others it was a heavily-redacted Latin version of a Byzantine original; the possibility has even been raised that it was written by a Frank living

---

[152] AC, p. 199.

[153] P. Adair, 'Flemish comital family and the Crusades', *The Crusades: Other experiences, alternative perspectives*, ed. K. Semaan (Binghampton: Global Academic Publishing, 2003), pp. 101–112.

[154] E. Joranson, 'The problem of the spurious letter of Emperor Alexius to the court of Flanders', *The American historical review* 55.4 (1950), 811–832.

[155] GN, pp. 100–104.

in Constantinople.[156] Without further data it is difficult to pass judgement on this point, beyond noting that there is nothing implausible about renewed Byzantine appeals for aid to the counts of Flanders. Certainly, those who were in communication with Constantinople or who had recently travelled on pilgrimage to the east represent another route by which news of the Turks might have reached western Europe.

This transmission of information concerning the Turks from Byzantium to western Christendom via the house of Flanders is evident in a letter written by Countess Clemence to the Christian faithful in 1097 concerning the early stage of her husband's crusade. In this document she reports: Count Robert's acquisition of relics whilst passing through Italy enroute for the Holy Land; his decision to send them to her; and then her subsequent actions with them. Although her correspondence was primarily concerned with these artefacts, her opening remarks described briefly her husband's reasons for setting out on crusade. Here she mentioned the depredations of the Turks, naming them as 'Persians' (*Persae*).[157] None of the handful of earlier references to the Turks in western European sources describe the Turks as 'Persians' but this was frequently the case in Byzantium. Archaic terms, such as 'Persians' were often applied to contemporary neighbours by Byzantine authors including many chroniclers writing in the eleventh century such as Michael Psellus and Michael Attaleiates.[158] Thus Clemence's choice of terminology seems to reflect this Byzantine influence.

Count Robert I of Flanders was among the most important pilgrims to have travelled to the east before the First Crusade. Pilgrimage to the Holy Land had always been important to Christians in western Europe, but during the eleventh century pious individuals and groups set out for the east in ever increasing numbers. Some of the parties were very large and in 1064 a substantial expedition set out under the leadership of the archbishop of Mainz and a group of German bishops. Until *c.* 1070 these expeditions would have reached the Levant to find it under Fatimid control, but in later years the region became a frontline in their war with the

---

[156] For discussion see: C. Sweetenham, *Robert the Monk's history of the First Crusade: Historia Iherosolimitana*, Crusade texts in translation XI (Aldershot: Asgate, 2005), pp. 215–218; Frankopan, *The First Crusade*, pp. 60–62; Joranson, 'The problem of the spurious letter', 811–832; Flori, *Pierre l'Ermite*, pp. 105–108.

[157] *Kb*, p. 142.

[158] Michael Psellus, *Fourteen Byzantine rulers*, trans. E. Sewter (London: Penguin, 1966), pp. 351–355; MA, pp. 190, 192, 270. K. Durak, 'Defining the 'Turk': mechanisms of establishing contemporary meaning in the archaizing language of the Byzantines', *Jahrbuch der österreichischen Byzantinistik* 59 (2009), 65–78. Western Europeans would continue to describe the Turks in this way well into the early modern period see: Meserve, *Empires of Islam*, p. 1. For more discussion see Chapter 5.

Turks. Between 1073 and 1098, control of Jerusalem was repeatedly contested by these two powers and European visitors would necessarily have
encountered the Turks and therefore have brought back tidings. Unfor-
tunately, no account written before the crusade has survived in which
these pious travellers described their experiences with Turks.[159] It can
only be assumed therefore that, following their return to the west, they
would have discussed their perceptions of this recently-arrived people.[160]

One pilgrim journey that is particularly relevant to this discussion is
Peter the Hermit's visit to Jerusalem in *c.* 1085. The crusade chronicler
Albert of Aachen gives an account of his experiences explaining how,
after his arrival in Turkish-held Jerusalem, Peter was horrified by the
Turks' treatment of the local Christians and holy places. He then met
with Symeon II, patriarch of Jerusalem, and promised him that he would
return with help. Shortly afterwards, whilst at prayer, Peter fell asleep
and saw a vision of Jesus, who instructed him to tell his countrymen
of the suffering of the eastern Christians and to bring aid. Peter duly
did – the First Crusade.[161] Exactly what should be made of this story
is unclear, but the notion that Peter *did* visit Jerusalem and *did* meet
with the patriarch needs to be taken seriously. Following the capture
of Jerusalem in 1099 the local Christians are said to have given him a
hero's welcome, apparently recognising that he had fulfilled his promise
to them.[162] Consequently, Peter himself is likely to have been a first-hand
source of information on the Turks for those taking part in the campaign.
This is important given his role in the preaching for the First Crusade.
Even so, a lack of contemporary material on his activities renders it
impossible to ascertain the extent to which he disseminated information
on the Turks.

Another source of information on the Turks would have been merchants conducting commerce in the eastern Mediterranean. Several Italian cities conducted a brisk trade with both Levantine and Egyptian ports

---

[159] Morris, *The sepulchre of Christ*, p. 139.

[160] For discussion on earlier pilgrim journeys to the east (1070–1098) see: Jotischky, 'The
Christians of Jerusalem'. 35–58.

[161] AA, pp. 2–6. For discussion on Peter's role in the launch of the First Crusade see:
Flori, *Pierre l'Ermite, passim.*

[162] WT, vol. 1, pp. 415–416; C. Kostick, *The siege of Jerusalem: Crusade and conquest in 1099*
(London: Continuum, 2009), p. 133; Jotischky, 'The Christians of Jerusalem', 37, 54.
Jotischky has pointed out that there were precedents for eastern Christians seeking
aid from western Europe. It has also been noted that Peter's journey to Jerusalem is
also reported in a separate source: 'Annales Sancti Rudberti Salisburgenses', *MGHS*,
ed. G. Pertz, vol. 9 (Hanover, 1851), p. 774. See also Morris, *The sepulchre of Christ*,
p. 176. By contrast in an earlier article, Cahen (1954) stated that it is an 'established
fact that non-Greek Christians sent no appeal to the West, not even to the papacy'.
See: Cahen, 'An introduction', 13.

and their seafarers would presumably have learnt news of the Turkish advances. The Amalfitans were especially active in this region and
a nobleman from this city established hospitals in Jerusalem and Antioch in *c*. 1070s.[163] Residents at these institutions, like other merchants
in the east, would presumably have been acutely aware of the Turks.
One commercial expedition that certainly returned home with news of
the Turks was a group of merchants from Bari who were en-route for
Antioch but having reached Myra they were dissuaded from going any
further having received reports of Turkish advances.[164] Tales of Turkish activity could have been conveyed along multiple trading arteries to
western Christendom and not solely those spanning the Mediterranean.
The Scandinavians had long established links with many Central Asian
societies and, as shown earlier, they dealt directly both with Byzantium
and the Abbasid caliphate. They too may have carried back reports about
the Turks.[165]

Western travellers, however, were not the only source of news on the
Turks. Throughout the early and central Middle Ages, the Byzantines
themselves maintained strong connections with many secular and ecclesiastical authorities across Europe, keeping them up to date with recent
developments. Towards the end of the eleventh century, appeals for aid
against the Turks were despatched both to Rome and to other leading
magnates. In 1073–1074, Pope Gregory VII responded by planning his
famous expedition that would march to assist Byzantium and then continue beyond to the Holy Sepulchre. In the 1090s several further letters
and embassies seem to have been sent; the most famous of which was the
party that met the pope at Piacenza in March 1095.[166] Moving from the
diplomatic to the military sphere, it is even possible that some Europeans
may formerly have encountered Turks fighting in Byzantine service. It
was common practice for Byzantine armies to recruit auxiliaries from
its neighbours and Turks are frequently reported fighting in Italy, Sicily,
and Western Greece during the tenth and eleventh centuries. Turkish
contingents are numbered among the forces that took part in the 935
campaign in Italy, the 1027 invasion of Sicily, and Alexius' campaign

[163] Amatus of Montecassino, *Storia de' Normanni*, p. 342.
[164] Hugh of Fleury, 'Liber qui modernorum regum Francorum continet actus', p. 392.
[165] The suggestion has been made that ninth-century Frankish merchants may have
       encountered Turkish traders in Slavic territory: E. Goldberg, *Struggle for empire: King-
       ship and conflict under Louis the German, 817–876* (Ithaca, NY: Cornell University Press,
       2006), p. 121.
[166] The continuator of Frutolf of Michelsberg's chronicle speaks of letters being sent by
       Alexius to Pope Urban II. See: *FE*, p. 136.

against Robert Guiscard in 1081.[167] As France has pointed out, Bohemond may have acquired experience of fighting Turks serving under Alexius whilst campaigning in Greece with his father.[168]

In the foregoing discussion it has been necessary to fall back upon an investigation into the possible routes by which contemporaries in western Christendom might have learnt of the Turks primarily because explicit references are so scarce. Before the first millennium the Turks seem to have been almost entirely unknown to most contemporaries in the west and the sources contain only the odd glimpse of their activities in the east. During the eleventh century, it is likely that, with the Turkish advance into the Near East, many more Europeans would have encountered the Turks. Normans serving in Anatolia and Italians conducting their business in the Levant would presumably have shared news of the Turkish conquests with their fellows. Thus it seems reasonable to suggest that those living in the major Mediterranean commercial ports and their dependent commercial arteries would have been amongst the best informed. Scandinavians, trading along the rivers of eastern Europe, also had some interaction with Turkic peoples. Nevertheless, the knightly families of France and northern Germany would have had far fewer sources of information. Some might have met a pilgrim returning from Jerusalem, others may have been connected in some way to warriors serving in the Byzantine army, but for many their links to the east would have been tenuous at best. The well-informed crusade chronicler Guibert of Nogent seems to imply at the opening of his chronicle that he had not previously heard of the Turks.[169] It is possible that Peter the Hermit might have named them in his preaching, but it is equally clear that the papacy did not. Consequently, in forming a judgement on how well known the Turks were amongst those who took the cross, it is reasonable to conclude that despite some regional variations they were largely unknown.[170] This

---

[167] Constantine Porphyrogenitus, *The book of ceremonies*, p. 661; Lupus Protospatarius, 'Annales', *MGHS*, ed. G. Pertz, vol. 5 (Hanover, 1844), p. 62; AC, p. 15. There is always the possibility that these references to Turks in Byzantine service pertain rather to Hungarians, who were also often identified as 'Turks'. AA, p. 842.

[168] J. France, 'The Normans and crusading', *The Normans and their adversaries at war: Essays in memory of C. Warren Hollister*, ed. R. Abels and B. Bachrach (Woodbridge: Boydell, 2001), p. 94.

[169] GN, pp. 82, 83, 352.

[170] Frankopan, by contrast advances the case that the Turks were well known through Byzantine appeals. It is not impossible that some learnt of the Turks through this route, but it is not clear that these appeals circulated widely: Frankopan, *The First Crusade*, pp. 60, 89. Cahen also describes a Europe which at the time of the crusade was well accustomed to viewing the Turks as oppressors of Christians. See: Cahen, *Orient et Occident*, p. 26.

deduction is admittedly an argument *ex silencio*, but when the absence of references pre-crusade is contrasted against the enormous quantity of material written about the Turks post-crusade, this creates a dichotomy that is too pronounced to be overlooked. One point, however, that comes across clearly from the foregoing analysis is that the little information that *was* available concerning the Turks had been gathered from eastern Christian sources.

3 The First Crusade and the Conquest of Jerusalem

Encountering the Turks

Having crossed the Bosporus, the crusaders were finally in a position to experience the Turks at first hand. The earliest crusading contingents to reach Constantinople were led by Peter the Hermit who reached the capital in August 1095. His pilgrims were then swiftly transported to Civitos in Northern Anatolia. They made some attempt to strike inland but were swiftly defeated and massacred by the Turks in October of the same year.[1] The survivors later joined with the various armies raised by Christendom's princes that were converging on Constantinople.

In the months that followed, as the first crusaders fought their way from Nicaea to Antioch and from there to Jerusalem, they had ample opportunity to temper their preconceptions of the Turks with their own experience. Their encounters with the Turks were not confined simply to the battlefield, but could take many forms. The crusaders took Turkish prisoners, who could presumably have offered information about the affairs of the east. One of these is said to have converted to Christianity, taking the name Bohemond.[2] This Turkish Bohemond would later work closely with the crusading army, offering invaluable assistance during the siege of Antioch.[3] The crusaders also: formed a series of treaties with various Turkish rulers; received Turkish converts; negotiated with their envoys; suffered imprisonment at their hands; gathered news about them from their Byzantine and Armenian allies; and, on some occasions, fought

---

[1] France, *Victory in the east*, pp. 93–95.

[2] AA, p. 234. For another reference this Turkish Bohemond see: RA, pp. 158–159. Incidentally, there seems to have been quite a trend for converted Turks/Muslims to take the name of their Christian sponsor. Roger of Sicily, for example, gave his name to a Sicilian convert called Ahmad. Baldwin I of Jerusalem gave his name to another Muslim convert. See: Kedar, *Crusade and mission*, pp. 50. 62, 75. For discussion on the crusaders' intelligence gathering see: S. Edgington, 'Espionage and military intelligence during the First Crusade, 1095–99', *Crusading and warfare in the Middle Ages: Realities and representations: Essays in honour of John France*, ed. S. John and N. Morton, Crusades subsidia VII (Aldershot: Ashgate, 2014), pp. 75–86.

[3] AA, p. 270.

alongside them. A few, among the Sicilian Normans, could even speak Arabic and thus consult Arabic-speaking authorities.[4] Perhaps one of the most remarkable sources of information was a knight named Hugh Bonel from Normandy. He appeared suddenly in the crusader camp having spent the last twenty years in the east following his murder of Countess Mabel of Bellême. During this time he had become an expert in local customs and languages.[5]

The many crusading chronicles produced by participants, along with several letters and charters, record the pilgrims' impressions of the Turks and these materials will form the basis for this chapter. The authors of the main narratives are: Fulcher of Chartres, chaplain to Baldwin of Boulogne, Raymond of Aguilers, chaplain to Raymond of Saint-Gilles, Peter Tudebode, and the anonymously-authored text known as the *Gesta Francorum*. Also relevant is the continuator of Frutolf of Michelsberg's chronicle, who also participated in the later crusade of 1101 and therefore acquired first-hand knowledge of the Turks.[6] The many other chronicles produced later by authors in western Europe will be only sparsely referenced in this section. Their works seem to include some reports carried home by returning crusaders but they also reflect the process of theological contextualisation that characterises many of the later attempts to place the events of the crusade in a broader theological framework.[7]

---

[4] K. Tuley, 'A century of communication and acclimatization: interpreters and intermediaries in the kingdom of Jerusalem', *East meets west in the Middle Ages and early modern times: Transcultural experiences in the pre-modern world*, ed. A. Classen, Fundamentals of medieval and early modern Culture XIV (Berlin: De Gruyter, 2013), pp. 312–319.

[5] OV, vol. 5, pp. 156–158. For discussion on this incident see: M. Chibnall, *The world of Orderic Vitalis: Norman monks and Norman knights* (Woodbridge: Boydell, 1984), pp. 14–41 (esp. 24).

[6] It used to be thought that this chronicle's continuator was Ekkehard of Aura. Nevertheless, the evidence which had formerly been used to identify Ekkehard as the author of this narrative and therefore a participant in the 1101 crusade has recently been challenged by McCarthy. He argues that the evidence connecting Ekkehard to this work is slight and that the textual similarities between Ekkehard's other works and this chronicle are not as great as has been previously supposed. He has also problematised the notion that Ekkehard ever resided at the monastery of Michelsberg (where the chronicle was produced). Thus this present work – following McCarthy – will simply describe the author of this piece as the continuator of Frutolf's chronicle. For a full discussion see: McCarthy, '*Introduction*', Chronicles of the Investiture Contest: Frutolf of Michelsberg and his continuators (Manchester: Manchester University Press, 2014), pp. 44–48, 73–74. Another key debate centres on the relationship between the *Gesta Francorum* and Peter Tudebode's chronicle. For recent discussion see: M. Bull, 'The relationship between the *Gesta Francorum* and Peter Tudebode's *Historia de Hierosolymitana*: the evidence of a hitherto unexamined manuscript', *Crusades* 11 (2012), 1–18. There have been several excellent overviews outlining the background and inter-relationships between the crusade chronicles, see for example: Lapina, *Warfare and the miraculous*, pp. 8–14; Kostick, *Social structure*, pp. 9–50.

[7] Riley-Smith, *The First Crusade and the idea of Crusading*, p. 135.

Their attitudes and perceptions are subtly different and will be discussed in the following chapter. The only exception to this division is the history produced by Albert of Aachen. His is the longest and most detailed of all the crusading chronicles and is largely independent of the other narratives, many of which are connected in some way to the *Gesta Francorum* tradition.[8] He did not participate in the campaign, but the sheer quantity of precise data provided in Albert's work demonstrates the author's close reliance upon eye-witnesses, who were themselves shrewd observers.[9] Thus, his chronicle will be discussed in this section.[10]

Military Confrontations

The chroniclers reveal a close interest in their Turkish antagonists and their narratives are full of their reflections. The topic which ubiquitously receives their greatest attention is the Turks' conduct in war. All the chroniclers discuss the challenges posed by their skirmishes with waves of mounted Turkish archers and for some it was the Turks' skill as bowmen more than any other cultural characteristic that defined them as a people group. Fulcher of Chartres, for example, summed up the 'Eastern Turks' describing them simply as 'extremely accurate archers with the bow'.[11] In the tales of battle found in these narratives there are frequent references to relentless showers of arrows and many writers drew explicit attention to the fact that Turkish forces could be comprised entirely from archers. Describing the Turkish forces at the battle of Dorylaeum, Fulcher of Chartres, for example, commented: 'they were calculated to number 360,000 warriors, specifically archers, for it is their custom to use arms of this kind'.[12]

The crusaders were curious about the Turks' weapons and chroniclers offered descriptions of their arms, observing that their bows were made from layers of bone and horn.[13] They swiftly learnt that these weapons had their vulnerabilities, in particular that Turkish bowstrings lost their

---

[8] For discussion on the question of the relationship of Albert's *Historia* to other crusading chronicles see: J. Rubenstein, 'Guibert of Nogent, Albert of Aachen and Fulcher of Chartres: three crusade chronicles intersect', *Writing the early crusades: Text transmission and memory*, ed. M. Bull and D. Kempf (Woodbridge: Boydell, 2014), pp. 24–37.

[9] For discussion see: S. Edgington, 'Albert of Aachen reappraised', *From Clermont to Jerusalem: The Crusades and crusader societies, 1095–1500*, ed. A. Murray (Turnhout: Brepols, 1998), pp. 55–67; S. Edgington, 'Albert of Aachen and the *Chansons de Geste*', in *The Crusades and their sources: Essays presented to Bernard Hamilton*, ed. J. France and W. Zajac (Aldershot: Ashgate, 1998), pp. 23–37; Riley-Smith, *The first crusaders*, p. 1; Flori, *Pierre l'Ermite*, pp. 51–70.

[10] France similarly feels that Albert's history deserves to be treated with the same seriousness as an 'eyewitness' narrative. France, *Victory in the east*, p. 381.

[11] FC, pp. 179–180.   [12] FC, p. 193.   [13] AA, pp. 34, 322, 602.

tension in the rain.[14] Clearly the rain could become a serious problem for the Turks and one commentator noted that the glue holding together the various layers of bone and horn was water-soluble, rendering the bows useless in such conditions.[15] The crusaders' decision to march by night across some parts of Anatolia may also have been driven by a desire to negate Turkish archery.[16]

There are only a few references to Turkish body armour, which – if worn at all – is likely to have been light. Turkish horses were not raised to bear great loads and they tended to be smaller than crusader mounts. Moreover, one Byzantine account observed that their horses could be unshod, in which case they could only be lightly burdened.[17] Historically, the Turks seem to have known how to manufacture iron-gear and there are indications from the sixth century that they had some aptitude with metallurgy.[18] In addition, by 1098 the Turks had conquered many agricultural regions in the Near East and had access to metal armour, either from their subjects or through the spoils of war.[19] Even so, such items were sufficiently scarce to be prized and when Ibn al-Athir listed the plunder taken during a Turkish raid against Asia Minor in 1048–1049 he specifically mentioned their seizure of chainmail jackets, suggesting that especial importance was attached to metal war gear.[20] Nevertheless, Turkish warcraft was characterised by movement and flexibility and it is not surprising that there are only sporadic references to Turks wearing hauberks or helmets.[21]

An exception to this trend is the cavalry formation in Karbugha's army at the battle of Antioch, which the crusaders described as '*Agulani*'.[22] They are said to have numbered 3000 and to have been heavily armoured; both horse and rider were apparently covered in iron mail. These '*Agulani*' were *Ghulams* (elite slave soldiers). The Saljuqs had been employing these forces since the 1060s and in 1071 Alp Arslan had deployed a large contingent at Manzikert.[23] Exactly how the crusaders

[14] AA, p. 236.   [15] FC, p. 342.

[16] B. Bachrach and D. Bachrach, 'Ralph of Caen as a military historian', *Crusading and warfare in the Middle Ages*, ed. S. John and N. Morton, Crusades subsidia VII (Aldershot: Ashgate, 2014), p. 94.

[17] JS, p. 423. Even so the hardiness of Turkish horses' hooves impressed the eleventh-century writer Aristakes of Lastivert who described them as 'solid as rock'. *Aristakēs Lastivertc 'I's History*, p. 64.

[18] Sinor, 'The establishment and dissolution of the Türk empire', pp. 295–296.

[19] For an explicit reference to the Turks acquiring arms from their foes during their early Persian wars see: *The History of the Seljuq Turks*, p. 35.

[20] AST, p. 68.   [21] AA, p. 106.   [22] *GF*, pp. 20, 45, 49.

[23] Peacock, *Early Seljūq History*, pp. 94–98; Peacock, *The great Seljuk empire*, pp. 225–228; M. Bennett, 'First crusaders' images of Muslims: the influence of vernacular poetry', *Forum for Modern Language Studies* 22 (1986), 109; S. Loutchitskaja, 'Barbarae

learnt to identify this force is unclear, but they were quite correct that these were amongst the Turks' most heavily armoured warriors. The *Ghulams* are also said to have fought solely with a sword; another point differentiating them from the vast majority of the Turkish army. There are occasional references to the Turks bearing shields; these are reported to have been small and crescent shaped (*peltae*).[24] Some chroniclers also describe the Turks using swords or lances, but Raymond of Aguilers observed that the Turks generally preferred to rely on their ballistic superiority and were not practiced in close-combat.[25]

The extreme mobility of the Turkish forces posed additional problems for the crusaders, challenging them to adapt their practices.[26] Many writers described the Turks' preference for surrounding their foes, even when they were themselves outnumbered.[27] In some encounters the Turks' ability to withdraw from battlefield with incredible speed also attracted attention. In most cases, the Turks were content to harass their foes, rather than seeking to confront and defeat them in a single encounter. The crusade's leaders explained this approach to war in a letter to Pope Urban in September 1098, writing: 'In their usual fashion they split up into groups, occupying the hills and making for the roads wherever they could in order to encircle us, because they thought that they would be able to kill us all that way'.[28] The most famous Turkish manoeuvre, however, was to feign flight during battle.[29] This manoeuvre involves giving the impression of a panicked retreat in order to lead a pursing opponent into a trap. Alexius warned the crusade commanders specifically about this tactic.[30] The fundamental purpose of the Turkish tactics of harassment and encirclement seems to have been to slow/halt an enemy and then to corral them in a single space, wearing them down until they either

Nationes: Les peuples musulmans dans les chroniques de la Première Croisade', *Autour de la Première Croisade: Actes du Colloque de la Society for the Study of the Crusades and the Latin East*, ed. M Balard (Paris: Publications de la Sorbonne, 1996), p. 103.

[24] RC, p. 28.   [25] RA, pp. 50–52.

[26] The Turks' ability to respond to various strategic threats would only have been enhanced by their use of carrier pigeons; a practice observed by the crusaders, see: AA, 348. For discussion see: S. Edgington, 'The doves of war: the part played by carrier pigeons in the Crusades', *Autour de la Première Croisade: Actes du Colloque de la Society for the Study of the Crusades and the Latin East*, ed. M. Balard (Paris: Publications de la Sorbonne, 1996), pp. 167–175.

[27] RA, p. 52; *Kb*, p. 157.

[28] Translation from *Letters from the east: Crusaders, pilgrims, and settlers in the 12th–13th centuries*, ed. and trans. M. Barber and K. Bate, *Crusade texts in translation XVIII* (Aldershot: Ashgate, 2010), p. 32. *Kb*, p. 163.

[29] See for example: Nicéphore Bryennios, *Historiarum Libri Quattuor*, ed. P. Gautier, Corpus Fontium Historiae Byzantinae IX (Brussels, 1975), p. 111.

[30] AC, p. 292.

fled or surrendered. Such an approach hinged on their ability to inspire a sense of fear in an opponent. This was achieved in many ways and, to take one example, many authors frequently describe the Turks attacking them whilst shouting war cries.[31]

Reflecting upon these encounters, Albert of Aachen frequently characterised the crusading army as a flock of sheep beset by wolves. He drew upon this image repeatedly, for example, when narrating: the collapse of Peter the Hermit's force in Anatolia; the destruction of a foraging party led by Louis of Toul during the siege of Antioch; and Bohemond's experiences during the Battle of Antioch.[32] In the last of these examples, this analogy was intended to capture the sense of isolation and vulnerability created by Turkish encirclement:

Since they were overwhelmed, indeed, by the forces of so many and the cunning enemy's trick, Bohemond's surrounded troops were forced into a wretched and worried flock, like sheep about to be killed by wolves, and they could no longer resist, but were on the point of dying surrounded on all sides by troops of infidels.[33]

Similarly, Fulcher of Chartres described the Turks 'howling' (*ululantes)* during the battle of Dorylaeum and in his early history of the kingdom of Jerusalem he explicitly characterised a Turkish force as 'howling *like wolves*'.[34] Not only did the wolves/sheep analogy capture the demoralising effect of Turkish tactics upon the crusaders, but – spiritually – it calls to mind the biblical metaphor of the True Shepherd which describes the Christian community as a flock beset by wolves. Ralph of Caen employed a similar device styling the crusaders as a boar surrounded by dogs.[35]

In their characterisation of the Turks as 'wolves' the crusaders may have been acting independently, devising this comparison by drawing upon their own traditions, but it is equally possible that they were being guided to use these metaphors by eastern Christians. Both Armenian and Byzantine authors employed precisely the same imagery, depicting the Turks as wolves preying upon the Christian flock, and, to take one example, the Armenian writer Aristakes described the sufferings of his people

---

[31] PT, p. 74; AA, pp. 41, 599, 602; MA, pp. 149, 285; ME, 235; WM, vol. 1, p. 630; *GF*, p. 40; FC, p. 194. Völkl, *Muslime – Märtyrer – Militia Christi*, p. 249. There are also references to the Turks using trumpets and horns in battle, AA, p. 150.

[32] AA, pp. 24, 222, 328.   [33] Translation from AA, p. 329.

[34] FC, pp. 194, 362. See also BB, p. 15.

[35] RC, p. 30. For discussion on the links drawn between wolves and Muslims in the eleventh century see: C. Lauranson-Rosaz, 'Le Velay et la Croisade', *Le Concile de Clermont de 1095 et l'Appel à la Croisade* (Rome: Ecole française de Rome, Palais Farnèse, 1997), p. 43.

at the hands of the Turks, characterising them as 'ravenous wolves'.[36] Likewise Greek authors including both Anna Comnena[37] and Michael Attaleiates (d. c. 1085) presented the Turks in this way. Attaleiates named the Turks 'wild wolves' in a chapter outlining the rise of the Saljuqs in the mid eleventh century.[38] He drew this comparison explicitly because of the Turks' propensity for raiding and plundering. These parities in the polemical labels applied to the Turks raises the possibility that the crusaders adopted them whilst passing through eastern Christian territory. Certainly this seems to have been the case for the earlier-mentioned monk Guillermus. He travelled to Byzantium some years before the crusade and later served with the Byzantine army. In his later description of his acquisition of relics from the town of Nicomedia he spoke of the Turks as 'ravening wolves' (*lupi rapaces*).[39] His choice of imagery compares closely with Byzantine norms.[40]

An alternative explanation is that all these groups were originally influenced by the Turks themselves. Wolves featured prominently in Turkish folklore and symbology.[41] It is possible that they promoted an image of themselves as wolves to give themselves a more fearsome aspect in battle.

While the Turks certainly aroused strong feelings of fear within the crusading army, the Franks were often impressed by the Turks' proficiency in battle and whilst they often derided Byzantine or Fatimid warriors,

---

[36] *Aristakēs Lastivertc 'I's History*, pp. 64, 122. See also ME, p. 97. For further discussion on his use of animal imagery see: S. La Porta, 'Conflicted coexistence: Christian-Muslim interaction and its representation in medieval Armenia', *Contextualizing the Muslim other in medieval Christian discourse*, ed. J. Frakes (New York: Palgrave Macmillan, 2011), pp. 107, 110.

[37] AC, p. 444.

[38] MA, p. 81. A. Papageorgiou, 'οἱ δὲ λύκοι ὡς Πέρσαι: the image of the "Turks" in the reign of John II Comnenus (1118–1143)', *Byzantinoslavica* (2011), 149–161. For descriptions of Turks as wolves in the Syriac tradition, see: Dickens, 'Turkāyē: turkic peoples', pp. 122–125; A. Beihammer, 'Die Ethnogenese der Seldschukischen Türken im Urteil Christlicher Geschichtsschreiber des 11. und 12. Jahrhunderts', *Byzantinische Zeitschrift* 102.2 (2009), 600.

[39] Shepard, 'How St James the Persian's head was brought to Cormery', pp. 298.

[40] Notably wolves had long played an important role in Turkic mythology: Papageorgiou, 'The image of the "Turks"', 152; Peacock, *The great Seljuk empire*, p. 129.

[41] The extent to which the Turks drew upon lupine imagery in their culture and symbology during this period has been the subject of some debate. Clauson has argued that this association lay primarily in the eyes of outsiders and that the Turks did not draw heavily upon such imagery themselves. Stepanov however has reaffirmed this connection. See: T. Stepanov, *The Bulgars and the steppe empire in the early Middle Ages: The problem of the others*, trans. T. Stefanova and T. Stepanov (Leiden: Brill, 2010), pp. 55–56; G. Clauson, 'Turks and wolves', *Studia Orientalia* 28.2 (1964), 20. Clearly some eastern Christian authors came to learn of the Turks' associations with wolves in their origin myths because this connection appears albeit in a garbled form, in the *Chronography* of Bar Hebraeus and *Chronicle* of Michael the Syrian. See: Dickens, 'The Sons of Magog', 441–442. See also Golden, 'Religion among the Qıpčaqs of Medieval Eurasia', 186–189.

they could be lavish in their praise of Turkish prowess.[42] Statements of this kind appear in many crusading narratives and the author of the *Gesta Francorum* felt so strongly about the Turks' marshal competence that he endorsed the notion that they must be related to the Franks.[43] This was no mean compliment. In the eleventh century western Christendom notions of divine ordination and providence were thickly entwined in the warp of Frankish identity and the term 'Franks' had – in the eyes of many Frankish authors – almost become almost a synonym for *populus christianus*.[44] The author's astonishing willingness therefore to link the Turks so directly to his own people-group (and the willingness of the *Gesta*'s later redactors to repeat this association) reflects a profound sense of respect and there is no reason to doubt the author's sincerity when he lamented that the Turks were not Christian. Expressions of respect and admiration, however, are not universal across the crusade chronicles. Some authors were less impressed and the continuator of Frutolf's chronicle, coming to terms with the destruction of the 1101 crusade, compared the Turks' tactics to those of robbers, although he also noted their proficiency.[45]

Overall, in their encounters with the Turks, the western knights confronted an enemy that was fundamentally new.[46] Alexius' advice aside, when the crusaders crossed into Asia Minor they had virtually no prior-knowledge of their enemy's warcraft. It is possible that some Normans or Anglo-Saxons may have encountered the Turks previously whilst serving in Anatolia. There is also a chance that some crusaders from the German Empire or eastern Europe might have been able to draw upon tales of earlier wars against the Hungarians. Certainly there were marked similarities between Turkish and Magyar tactics. Regino of Prüm (d. 915) described how Magyars fought with bows of horn and 'know nothing about fighting hand-to-hand in formation or taking besieged cities. They fight by charging forward and turning back on their horses, often indeed simulating flight'.[47] Even so, whether there was a small pool of

---

[42] C. Kostick, 'Courage and cowardice on the First Crusade, 1096–1099', *War in History*, 20.1 (2013), 47–48.

[43] *GF*, 21. For other statements of admiration for the Turks' valour see: AA, pp. 36, 173; *Kb*, p. 139.

[44] Gabriele, *Empire of memory*, pp. 102, 154–157 and *passim*.   [45] *FE*, p. 168.

[46] J. France, 'Warfare in the Mediterranean region in the age of the Crusades, 1095–1291: A clash of contrasts', *The Crusades and the Near East: Cultural histories*, ed. C. Kostick (Abingdon: Routledge, 2011), pp. 1–26. See Anna Comnena's comments on the distinctive nature of Turkish warcraft: AC, p. 439.

[47] Translation from *History and politics in late Carolingian and Ottonian Europe: The chronicle of Regino of Prüm and Adalbert of Magdeburg*, trans. S. Maclean (Manchester: Manchester

experience among the crusader ranks or not, in their correspondence, the crusade commanders declared themselves to have been unprepared for Turkish tactics, which had taken them by surprise.[48] Likewise, Fulcher of Chartres, brooding upon the scattered corpses of Peter the Hermit's army, explained their defeat writing that they were 'unaware and new to the use of the arrow'.[49] Confronted with this fundamentally new style of war, the crusaders had to adapt. Their armoured cavalrymen and infantry squadrons were poorly equipped to defeat a fast-moving enemy that was content to harass them from a distance. The Turks, for their part, learnt to fear the crusaders' cavalry charge and this was instrumental in many of their defeats. They had experienced such charges before in their Anatolian encounters with Frankish mercenaries in the eleventh century, but such a manoeuvre could still prove decisive if launched at the right moment.[50] Still, the highly-mobile Turks were well suited for evading any enemy whilst the lumbering crusaders had little answer to a cycle of Turkish attacks withering their marching columns. Moreover, once broken, fleeing Frankish forces – particularly infantry – were exceptionally vulnerable against pursuing Turkish riders. Thus, the onus was on the Franks to adjust their tactics.

The crusaders' battlefield encounters with Turks form the rump of most of the crusade narratives. The cut and thrust of the raids, massacres, and skirmishes instigated by both sides constitute a substantial proportion of each chronicle and it is almost always within accounts of such confrontations that chroniclers offer further details of the Turks' character, clothing, beliefs etc. This point is important because it is necessary to recognise that the crusaders' experiences of their enemies occurred in an environment in which the Turks were *seeking* to provoke a sense of fear. Their battlefield tactics were predicated on causing panic and dread among their enemies. Recalling their memories of the Turks, the crusade chroniclers were quite plainly not studying this people group with any sense of detachment, let alone presenting their cold-bloodied theological assessment of 'Islam', but rather were recalling moments when, huddled together with their fellows and harassed by Turkish forces, they felt quite literally like lambs to the slaughter. It

---

University Press, 2009), p. 205; Regino of Prüm, 'Chronicon', *MGH: SRG*, ed. F. Kurze, vol. 50 (Hanover, 1890), p. 133. See also C. R. Bowlus, *The battle of Lechfeld and its aftermath: The end of the age of migrations in the Latin West* (Aldershot: Asghate, 2006), pp. 19–44, 73–95.

[48] *Kb*, p. 163.   [49] FC, p. 180.

[50] Michael Attaleiates described Roussel de Bailleul's earlier success with heavy cavalry against the Turks, see: MA, p. 332, 334.

is within this unique and violent context then that the crusaders' perceptions of their Turkish opponents need to be placed if they are to be understood and interpreted.[51]

Hierarchies, Culture, and Religion

The crusaders displayed some inquisitiveness about the Turks that extended beyond simply their martial qualities. At times their works include discussion on their social hierarchies and leadership. The *Gesta Francorum*, among others, showed an awareness of the offices of the caliph and the sultan as well as the title of 'emir'.[52] Likewise, the names (and in some cases genealogies) of several Turkish rulers are identified with a degree of accuracy (if garbled).[53] All the chronicles name Karbugha of Mosul (*Curbaram, Corbagath* et al.)[54] and some also name other Turkish leaders, including: Yaghi Siyan, governor of Antioch (*Cassianus, Darsianus, Gitcianus*),[55] Balak ibn Bahram (*Balas*),[56] Balduk of Samosata (*Balduc*),[57] Ridwan of Aleppo (*Brodohan de Halapia*),[58] and Suqman ibn Artuq (*Socomannus*).[59] Both Albert of Aachen and the *Gesta Francorum* correctly identified that Yaghi Siyan had a son called Shams ad-Dawla (*Sensadolus, Sansadonias*).[60] Naturally some of these renditions of Turkish names bear a closer resemblance to their originals than others and there are some errors and moments of confusion; for example, in certain places the term 'emir' is offered as first name rather than a title.[61] There also seem to have been moments when these authors' choice of names were guided by rather different considerations. As Sweetenham has observed, Robert the Monk named the Fatimid general at Ascalon

---

[51] Other historians to raise this point include: Hill, 'The Christian view of Muslims at the time of the First Crusade', p. 1. Völkl also discusses moulding power of the crusaders' experiences: Völkl, *Muslime – Märtyrer – Militia Christi, passim*.

[52] *GF*, pp. 44, 52.

[53] Housley, *Fighting for the cross*, p. 225. See also A. Beihammer, 'Christian views of Islam in early Seljuq Anatolia: perceptions and reactions', *Islam and Christianity in medieval Anatolia*, ed. A. Peacock, B. de Nicola and S. Nur Yildiz (Aldershot: Ashgate, 2015), p. 69.

[54] *GF*, p. 49; FC, p. 242.

[55] RA, p. 60; AA, p. 194; *GF*, p. 47. The *Gesta Francorum*'s rendition of Yaghi Siyan's name as *Cassianus* is rather curious given that there was a major church in Antioch called the church of Cassianus. Whether there is a deeper meaning in his conflation of these two names or whether the *Gesta*'s author simply confused the two is unclear.

[56] AA, p. 176.   [57] AA, p. 170.   [58] AA, p. 328.

[59] AA, p. 444.   [60] *GF*, p. 50; AA, p. 196.

[61] AA, p. 230. Fulcher knew that the term 'emir' was a title, although he also used a variant as the first name of a Turkish leader: FC, pp. 249, 253.

'Clemens' and it might not be entirely coincidental that Pope Urban II's challenger to the papal throne also bore that name![62]

The crusaders tended to explain Turkish hierarchies to their readers by locating equivalent positions in their own communities, filling in any gaps by assuming that the Turks would organise their society in much the same way as western Christians.[63] This is evident in the *Gesta Francorum* within a fabricated letter which purports to have been written by the Turkish general Karbugha to the caliph of Baghdad. This begins: 'To the caliph, our pope, and to our king, the lord sultan'.[64] In this opening the author has placed Turkish and western European titles side by side very probably so that contemporaries in western Christendom will be able to understand the broad significance of roles, which to them would otherwise have been entirely foreign. The expectation that Turkish society was similar to that in western Christendom appears in other places. Chroniclers describe Turkish rulers as 'kings' or 'dukes', who communicate with one another through letters secured by 'seals',[65] and who in one case issues a 'royal summons'[66] to their levies of nobles and knights.[67] Peter Tudebode's assertion that the defenders of Jerusalem bore a spear surmounted by a covered depiction of Mohammed along the walls of Jerusalem – which of course cannot be true – probably reveals the same expectation that Turks would select images to adorn their banners on the same basis as the Franks themselves.[68] It might also indicate the influence of ideas drawn from the *chansons*, where 'Saracen' armies are occasionally said to have carried such standards.[69] Other parallels occur throughout these works, including descriptions of religious buildings and Albert of Aachen depicts Mawdud of Mosul at prayer in his 'oratory' (*oratorium*).[70] In short, the Franks anticipated that Turkish hierarchies, institutions, and social structures would be fundamentally be the same as their own in form, if not in religious allegiance, and they projected this expectation into their chronicles.[71]

It could be concluded from this approach that the Franks were purposefully depicting their foes' society so as to fabricate an evil mirror

---

[62] C. Sweetenham, 'Crusaders in a hall of mirrors: the portrayal of Saracens in Robert the Monks' Historia Iherosolimitana', Languages of love and hate: Conflict, communication, and identity in the medieval Mediterranean, ed. S. Lambert and H. Nicholson, International Medieval Research XV (Turnhout: Brepols, 2012), pp. 59–61.

[63] Köhler, *Alliances and treaties*, p. 32.   [64] *GF*, p. 52.

[65] AA, p. 252; RA, p. 135.   [66] Translation from AA, p. 260.

[67] *GF*, p. 52; AA, p. 252.   [68] PT, p. 137.

[69] Daniel, *Heroes and Saracens*, 149.   [70] AA, p. 852.

[71] See: Akbari, *Idols in the east*, pp. 206–208; Völkl, *Muslime – Märtyrer – Militia Christi*, pp. 226–227, 230.

image of their own. Thus the caliph is presented as the Turkish 'pope' in deliberate juxtaposition to the Christian 'pope', emphasising a sense of binary opposition between the two (good pope-vs-evil pope). Nevertheless, the passages presenting Turkish rulers as 'kings' using 'seals' and leading armies of 'knights' are rarely couched in hostile language. Even the references to the caliph as the 'pope of the Turks' (*papa Turcorum*) generally seem more explanatory in purpose than polemical.[72] It is more likely that the crusaders were simply trying to locate the Turks within their own frame of reference – based on their societal backgrounds. Incidentally, the same process can be found in reverse with Muslim writers explaining the significance of Christian rulers by drawing parallels to leaders in their own society; Ibn Wasil, for example, identified the pope was the 'caliph of Christ'.[73]

The participant narratives also reveal that by the end of the campaign their authors had acquired some knowledge concerning the Turks' ethnic identity and their prehistory. The Turks themselves are identified with a number of descriptors. The most frequent is *Turci* (Turks), but there were variants on this term; many of which betray a Byzantine influence. A possible example of this can be found in Fulcher of Chartres' description of the crusaders' arrival at Nicaea where he identifies their foes as '*Turci Orientales*' (Eastern Turks).[74] This reference may simply have been intended to mean 'Turks from the East' and certainly this was the position taken by Ryan in her translation of his chronicle.[75] Nevertheless, this phrase may have a far more specific meaning. Several civilisations, including the Byzantines, had long been accustomed to dividing the Turkish peoples into 'Eastern' and 'Western' groups.[76] In these cases, this distinction served to differentiate the earlier Turkish tribes, operating out of central Asia, or 'Eastern Turks', from the Hungarians who were identified as 'Western Turks'.[77] John Skylitzes, for example, referred frequently to 'Turks' in the earlier part of his chronicle exclusively with reference to the

---

[72] RA, p. 110.

[73] Translation from O. Latiff, 'Qur'anic imagery, Jesus and the creation of a pious-warrior ethos in the Muslim poetry of the anti-Frankish Jihad', *Cultural encounters during the Crusades*, ed. K. Jensen, K. Salonen and H. Vogt (Odense: University Press of Southern Denmark, 2013), pp. 135–151. For another example see the work of Yaqūt al-Rūmī (d. 1229) who explained the role of the pope by comparing him to the 'Commander of the Faithful'. His account can be found in: *Ibn Fadlān and the land of darkness*, p. 187.

[74] FC, p. 179.

[75] F. Ryan, *Fulcher of Chartres: a history of the expedition to Jerusalem, 1095–1127* (New York: W.W. Norton, 1973), p. 80.

[76] See: Nicholas I, *Letters*, p. 158; *The chronicle of Theophanes Confessor: Byzantine and near eastern history, AD284–813*, trans. C. Mango and R. Scott (Oxford: Clarendon Press, 1997), p. 446. In this case, Theophanes was referring to the Khazars.

[77] Sinor, 'The establishment and dissolution of the Türk empire', p. 289.

Hungarians, but then used the term 'Eastern Turks' when his narrative turned to the movement of the Saljuqs into Persia – clearly he wanted his readers to be aware of the distinction.[78] Emperor Constantine VII Porphyrogenitus (d. 959) provided an explanation for this division of the Turkish people in his *De Administrando Imperio*. He explained that originally there were seven Turkish tribes who lived near the Khazars, but following a defeat at the hands of the Pechenegs they broke into two groups, one heading west and the other east towards Persia.[79] Fulcher's use of this term may betray his assimilation of this Byzantine practice and evidently many Greek authors were aware that the Saljuqs derived from the 'Eastern Turks'.

A Byzantine influence is also evident in other ethnonyms used to describe the Turks. Many of the participant narratives and the crusade letters refer at times to the Turks as 'Persians' while the sultan of Baghdad was often named as the king or sultan of Persia.[80] Again this reflects standard practice in Byzantine texts, which often applied archaic names to contemporary peoples. As Durak's study has shown, it was common for Byzantines to identify the Turks in this way and the term 'Persians' served to distinguish them from Arab Muslims, who were identified as 'Saracens'. The term 'Persians' however was not simply a generic descriptor applicable to all Turks, at least in the eleventh century, but rather it was used by Byzantine authors to refer specifically to Turks who actually lived in Persia. Thus this ethnonym pertained to one specific group of Turks, rather than the people group as a whole.[81] The crusaders seem to have adopted elements of this practice. Certainly, they too described the Turks as 'Persians', and these references do *tend* to pertain to Turks who have travelled to the Levant from lands further to the east, but they do not show the same clear-cut geographical division as the Byzantine authors.[82] Thus the sultan of Baghdad is ubiquitously referred to as the ruler of Persia and Karbugha's army (which many authors believed to have been sent by the sultan) is reported to have included Persians. Nevertheless, forces made up of Anatolian Turks are also occasionally

---

[78] JS, p. 315 (for his reference to 'Eastern Turks') 170–171, 215, 220, 223, 231, 265, 276 (for his references to Hungarians as Turks). See also *Three Byzantine military treatises*, p. 148.

[79] Constantine Porphyrogenitus, *De Administrando Imperio*, pp. 170–172.

[80] For example: *GF*, p. 49 (although such references are found widely across most First Crusade narratives). William of Apulia, whose work discusses Turkish advances into Anatolia, also describes the Turks as 'Persians'. Again, he is an author with clear links to Byzantium. William of Apulia, 'Gesta Roberti Wiscardi', pp. 265–267.

[81] Durak, 'Defining the "Turk", 65–78; Beihammer, "Die Ethnogenese"', 608–610.

[82] Loutchitskaja, 'Barbarae Nationes', p. 102.

described as 'Persians', both at the siege of Nicaea and at Dorylaeum.[83] Thus they do not entirely conform to the standard Byzantine schema. It seems likely that the Franks adopted some elements of common Byzantine parlance and applied it as they saw fit.

A local influence is also apparent in the chroniclers' knowledge of the Saljuqs' early history and religious beliefs. Several accounts take an interest in this subject and speak of them emerging from the land of 'Khurasan' (in the *Gesta 'Corosanum', 'Corrozanam'*).[84] According to Peter Tudebode, Khurasan was ruled by the caliph and was situated far to the east. Many other chroniclers speak of Turkish reinforcements emerging from these lands and captives being led off to Khurasan into slavery. Albert of Aachen even ventured a description of its terrain presenting it as 'so enclosed by mountains and watery marshes on all sides that anyone who is once captured and enters there is unable to come out again'.[85] He supplied this information in a passage describing the Turks' enslavement of captured crusaders.[86] He also mentions a town called '*Sanmarthan*' which Murray plausibly suggests is a garbled reference to Samarkand.[87] These references clearly pertain to Persia and the Caliphate of Baghdad (Khurasan is a province in Persia), which the Turks had conquered several decades previously.[88] Their identification of this land specifically as 'Khurasan' mirrors common practice among Muslim, Armenian, Coptic, and Byzantine writers, who all routinely use this same toponym to identify the Turkish heartlands and in much the same contexts.[89] This is not surprising. Khurasan was a major centre of

---

[83] Examples: *GF*, pp. 21, 49, 70; PT, pp. 54, 89; FC, pp. 133, 193, 220, 242.

[84] *GF*, pp. 4, 5, 15, 39.   [85] Translation from AA, p. 613. See also RA, p. 87.

[86] A curious point worth mentioning is that when the Byzantines described 'barbarian' territory they often described the landscape itself as being hostile and forbidding. In 1294, for example, Theodore Metochites presented the lands beyond the Byzantine frontier as 'blind marsh, or Scythian cold'. Naturally this is a very late example, but it is worth considering the possibility that Albert has inherited (probably at second or third hand) a description of Turkish territory derived ultimately from Byzantine polemics. Quotation and discussion from D. Korobeinikov, *Byzantium and the Turks in the thirteenth century*, Oxford Studies in Byzantium (Oxford: Oxford University Prss, 2014), p. 98.

[87] A. Murray, '*Coroscane*: homeland of the Saracens in the *chansons de geste* and the historiography of the Crusades', *Aspects de l'épopee romane: Mentalités, idéologies, intertextualités*, ed. H. van Dijk and W. Noomen (Groningen: E. Forsten, 1995), p. 178.

[88] Murray, '*Coroscane*: homeland of the Saracens', p. 177. Albert of Aachen also speaks of Baghdad as the capital of Khurasan; a reference that reinforces the idea that it was perceived by the heart of the Turkish sultanate: AA, p. 594 (see also Murray, '*Coroscane*: homeland of the Saracens', p. 178).

[89] See: ME, p. 135; *History of the Patriarchs of the Egyptian Church*, vol. 2, part 2, p. 311; *The History of the Seljuq Turks*, p. 31, *passim*; AC, pp. 179–180, 306, 318, 321, 410, 450; JS, pp. 72, 420. For an earlier reference see: *The chronicle of Theophanes Confessor*, pp. 512, 587, 661, 665.

power for the Turks and many of their administrators and cultural traditions derived from this area. Peacock has even observed that the Saljuq empire was 'in some respects as much a Khurasani empire as a Turkish one'.[90] The crusaders had evidently learnt to identify this region through the peoples they encountered.

There may however be another dimension to this toponym. The various participant narratives treat Khurasan simply as a place name, following the practice of other eastern authors. Most subsequent authors, such as Baldric of Bourgueil, simply transliterated this name without making any alterations.[91] Still, Robert the Monk seems to have seen an opportunity to imbue this term with additional eschatological meaning.[92] When Robert the Monk wrote his account of the crusade, drawing on the *Gesta*, he amended its spelling from *'Corosanum'* to *'Chorozaim'*.[93] This is a significant shift. *'Chorozaim'* is the name of a Galilean town mentioned in the New Testament in Matthew 11: 20–24 and Luke 10: 13–15. In these verses Christ upbraids three towns (Chorazin, Bethsaida, and Capernaum) for refusing to hear his teaching and he prophesies their doom. These same verses were subsequently remoulded in the later apocalyptic work of Pseudo-Methodius who depicted Chorazin as the birth place of the Antichrist.[94] Pseudo-Methodius' work was later used by the tenth-century author Adso, abbot of Montier-en-Der, in his own widely circulated work on the Antichrist, although here Chorazin was given as the place where the Antichrist would grow up.[95] What seems to have happened here is that Robert theologically redacted the purely geographic term 'Corosanum' (Khurasan) to give it eschatological overtones, effectively positioning the Turks within the homelands of the Antichrist.

Peter Tudebode and the *Gesta Francorum* offer some further speculation about the Turks' more distant origins in their versions of the earlier-mentioned letter which purports to have been sent by Karbugha to the caliph of Baghdad. This source presents Karbugha eagerly anticipating battle with the Franks, stating that he will either be victorious or he will be driven beyond the 'rivers of the Amazons' (*Amazonia*

---

[90] Peacock, *The great Seljuk empire*, p. 9.   [91] BB, pp. 61, 63.

[92] For previous discussion on the usage of this term and its potential eschatological connotations see: Murray, *'Coroscane*: homeland of the Saracens', pp. 177–184; Tolan, *Saracens*, p. 112. Sweetenham has specifically drawn attention to the way that Robert realigned this name, see: C. Sweetenham, '"Hoc enim non fuit humanum opus, sed Divinum": Robert the Monk's use of the Bible in the *Historia Iherosolimitana*', *The uses of the Bible in crusading sources*, ed. E. Lapina and N. Morton (forthcoming). Carole has kindly permitted me to reference this article before publication.

[93] RM, p. 59.   [94] Pseudo-Methodius, *Apocalypse*, p. 63.

[95] Murray, *'Coroscane*: homeland of the Saracens', pp. 182–184.

flumina) and even into 'upper India' (*India superior*).[96] Exactly what information these statements were based upon is unclear. One explanation is that these references to Amazons and India were intended to denote nothing more than simply: faraway places beyond the horizons of knowledge. It is also plausible, however, that his identification of the Amazons and India was not coincidental. Michael Attaleiates stated that the Turks had first invaded Persia from across the Ganges, which he reported to be a river that is four and a half miles wide.[97] This is seemingly a garbled reference to the campaigns of the Ghaznavids. Perhaps these authors had also picked up a rumour of Turkish activity in this region. The references to Amazons are also thought-provoking because back in the first century, Pomponius Mela had also described a Turkish homeland bordering the Amazons.[98] The Syriac tradition likewise situated the Turks near to Amazon territory. This is shown explicitly in the *Ecclesiastical History of Pseudo-Zachariah* (written 555 AD).[99] These similarities may be sheer coincidence, but they may also reflect Peter's dependency upon classical and/or eastern Christian authorities. This is not to suggest that they actually read *Pseudo-Zachariah*; rather that this kind of association may have been in circulation in eastern Christian circles at this time. Likewise, there was nothing unusual about a medieval traveller seeking guidance from classical and early-medieval texts when attempting to understand the world of central Asia; Friar William of Rubruck in the thirteenth century consulted Solinus and Isidore of Seville before his journey across Asia.[100]

The crusaders' grasp of Turkish history for the period between their conquest of Persia and the time of the First Crusade was far stronger. They recognised that the Turkish conquests in Anatolia and Syria were recent occurrences. Fulcher of Chartres noted that they had crossed the Euphrates around half a century previously and had then set about conquering vast swathes of Byzantine Asia Minor. In a similar vein, Raymond of Aguilers correctly dated the Turkish capture of Antioch to 1084; fourteen years before the crusaders' conquest of the city.[101] The most detailed history of the Turkish attacks into Syria and their confrontations with the Fatimids can be found in Albert of Aachen's chronicle.

---

[96] *GF*, p. 51; PT, p. 92.
[97] MA, p. 76. For discussion on the Byzantine understanding of the Turks' pre-history and their sources of information see: Beihammer, 'Die Ethnogenese', 589–614.
[98] *Pomponius Mela's description of the world*, pp. 66–67. See also Pliny (the Elder), *Natural History*, vol. 2, p. 350.
[99] Dickens, 'Turkāyē: turkic peoples', pp. 19–21.
[100] *The mission of Friar William of Rubruck*, trans. P. Jackson, Hakluyt Society: Second Series CLXXIII (London: Hakluyt Society, 1990), p. 4.
[101] RA, p. 64.

He narrated how the Turks had taken Jerusalem from the Egyptians with a force apparently numbering 300 warriors, which had then extracted a considerable tribute from both 'Saracen' and Christian travellers seeking entry into the holy city.[102] He then explained how the city had been retaken by the Egyptians shortly before the crusaders' arrival and he was aware that the Turks had been commanded by a Turkish prince called '*Socomannus*' (Suqman ibn Artuq). According to this narrative, Suqman then sought shelter with his brother in Damascus (This is a reference to Duqaq, who in fact was not Suqman's brother).[103] Such references demonstrate that it was well known that the Turks were comparatively recent invaders, who had stirred up considerable resentment amongst the peoples of the Near East.[104] Accounts of the suffering they inflicted on the Armenians appear with particular regularity in many accounts and Raymond of Aguilers reports that the collapse of Turkish resistance in the forts and towns around Antioch (in the face of the crusaders' advance) owed much to the hostility of the local populace.[105] The effect of the crusaders' arrival upon the Armenian population is confirmed in the Muslim sources and Ibn al-Qalanisi likewise reports that many towns in the vicinity of Antioch ejected their Turkish garrisons upon news of the Christians' approach.[106]

Considered as a corpus, the general impression given by the crusade narratives is one of intense interest concerning any detail about the Turks that might give them a tactical or strategic advantage. The Turks' prior history and the resentment they had stirred up among the peoples they had conquered were both themes of significance because they had military applications. Even so, there are very few references to wider cultural factors, such as the Turks' manners or way of life. In one brief passage, which mourns the enslavement of Christian women by the Turks, one author imagines the captives being carried away by Turks with partially shaved heads and untrimmed beards.[107] Whether these Turkish hairstyles

---

[102] AA, p. 442. For recent discussion on the impact of the Seljuk conquest see: Gat, 'The Seljuks in Jerusalem', pp. 1–39.

[103] AA, pp. 442–445.   [104] FE, p. 152.

[105] RA, p. 48. See also GF, p. 41; Kamal al-Din, 'Extraits de la Chronique d'Alep', pp. 578–579.

[106] Ibn al-Qalanisi, *The Damascus chronicle of the Crusades*, ed. and trans. H. Gibb (Mineola, NY: Dover, 2002), pp. 42–43.

[107] Describing the pre-crusade period, Matthew of Edessa observed that the Turks tended to have long hair 'like women'. ME, pp. 44, 83. For discussion on steppe hairstyles during this period see: Stepanov, *The Bulgars and the Steppe Empire*, pp. 49–50. For further Frankish commentary on Turkish and Arab beards see: *HAI*, p. 48; AA, p. 612; GN, pp. 84, 339. It is interesting to note that the Turks historically had not always been bearded. Travelling among the shamanistic Turks in the early tenth century, the envoy Ibn Fadlan noted that the Turks tended to pluck their beards (although they retained

have any basis in reality or were merely the product of the author's imagination is unclear.[108]

The crusaders' showed fractionally more interest in the Turks' religious beliefs, but even on this point their curiosity was uneven. One aspect – omnipresent through every crusade narrative, whether it was written by a participant or not – is the basic fact that the Turks adhered to a non-Christian religion. Each author leaves his readers in no doubt on this point, using terms such 'pagans', 'heathens', and 'gentiles'. Cumulatively, these names convey little information beyond the plain fact that the Turks were not Christian. The repeated use of such labels embeds the idea that religious difference was a fundamental notion which informed the crusaders' world view and was of particular importance in their perception of the Turks. A connected theme, which again appears with considerable regularity in these narratives, is the attribution of 'evil' characteristics to the Turks' religion. Several chronicles include references to mosques (*machomaria*) and the *Gesta Francorum* refers them on two occasions using deeply-hostile language presenting them as 'the hall of the Devil' (*diabolicum atrium*) and the 'house of the Devil' (*domus diabolica*).[109] The Turks, by extension, are referred to with linked terms such as 'unbelieving' (*increduli*), or 'enemies of God' (*inimici Dei*).[110] Terminology of this kind is present – to varying degrees – in all the chronicles for the crusade and each relates directly to the Turks' spirituality.

Still, none of this language conveys any real knowledge of the Turks' religion and certainly many of their descriptions of the Turks' 'paganism' drew upon long-standing tropes that had long been applied to Christendom's non-Christian enemies. Albert of Aachen demonstrated this practice where he described the Turkish 'king of Khurasan' seeking advice from 'magicians, prophets and soothsayers' (*magi, arioli, aruspices*).[111] Naturally, the identification of these spiritual advisors offers no accurate information about the Islamic religion and this allusion seems to derive from the Old Testament where these same mystics appear in the Book of Daniel in the entourage of Nebuchadnezzar.[112] Perhaps Albert thought it appropriate to present the king of Khurasan in the same way as the biblical king of Babylon. More likely, this was simply a standard way among medieval writers of describing the spiritual leaders of other

their moustaches). Even so, the sources seem to agree that the Turks confronting the crusaders were bearded. This may be a sign of their movement towards Islam: *Ibn Fadlān and the land of darkness*, p. 19. Guibert of Nogent also points out that the crusaders were instructed by the Adhemar of Le Puy to shave so that they would not be mistaken for Turks. GN, p. 206. See also Leclercq, *Portraits croisés*, pp. 118–119.

[108] AA, p. 612.   [109] GF, pp. 42, 75. See also PT, p. 77.

[110] GF, pp. 20, 32, 62; AA, p. 234.

[111] Translation from AA, p. 259. See also RM, p. 63.   [112] Daniel 2:27.

faiths. Notably, Cosmas of Prague (d.1125) in his history of Bohemia described how Duke Bretislav expelled this same trio in 1092 from his land when he sought to rid himself of paganism.[113] In a similar vein, Adam of Bremen included references to magicians (*magi*), soothsayers (*augures*), and necromancers (*nigromantici*) in his descriptions of Scandinavian paganism.[114] Thus it was not only Muslims who were said to look to magicians and soothsayers, rather they were deemed to be omnipresent among non-Christian peoples.

Having identified the Turks as a hostile non-Christian enemy, the chroniclers' interest in their religion largely evaporates.[115] They showed some awareness of the fact that Arabs and Turks adhered to linked religious traditions through their very occasional application of the term 'Saracen' to both peoples – although they were also aware that the Turks' spiritual beliefs were closely enmeshed with their ethnic identity (see later). Some crusaders were broadly aware of the Sunni/Shia divisions within Islam and there are a few references to Mohammed. They were less clear about Mohammed's status within Islam. Fulcher described Mohammed as the Turks' 'advocate' (*advocatus*).[116] Peter Tudebode less accurately referred to Muslims worshipping Mohammed and 'other Gods' (*alii dii*), advancing the idea that they were polytheists (interestingly, the same accusation was sometimes levelled at Christians by Muslim writers).[117] Albert of Aachen makes a similar claim.[118] In sum, it seems likely that these authors neither knew, nor wanted to know, much about their enemies' beliefs beyond what was of immediate military utility.

The crusaders' lack of interest in the Islamic religion and its tenants of faith is not surprising.[119] For centuries Christendom had been launching evangelical campaigns across its eastern borders into eastern Europe

---

[113] 'Die Chronik der Böhmen des Cosmas von Prag', *MGH: SRGNS*, ed. B. Bretholz, vol. 2 (Berlin, 1923), p. 161.

[114] Adam of Bremen, 'Gesta Hammaburgensis Ecclesiae Pontificum', p. 244.

[115] Housley, 'The Crusades and Islam', 197; Meserve, *Empires of Islam*, p. 157; Tolan, *Saracens*, p. 110; Irwin, *For the lust of knowing*, p. 21; Leclercq, *Portraits* croisés, p. 229. This uninterest seems in some cases to have been mirrored by Muslim authors. See for example, Micheau's study on Ibn al-Athir: F. Micheau, 'Ibn al-Athīr', *Medieval Muslim historians and the Franks in the Levant*, ed. A. Mallett (Leiden: Brill, 2014), p. 73.

[116] FC, p. 220.

[117] PT, p. 80; *The history of the Seljuq state*, p. 37. For discussion see: Latiff, 'Qur'anic Imagery', p. 144; Hill, 'The Christian view of Muslims', p. 3; N. Christie, 'Ibn al-Qalānisī', *Medieval Muslim historians and the Franks in the Levant*, ed. A. Mallett (Leiden: Brill, 2014), p. 16.

[118] AA, p. 258.

[119] Discussing the Anglo-Saxon sources for the period before the First Crusade, Scarfe Beckett has drawn a similar conclusion. Scarfe Beckett, *Anglo-Saxon perceptions*, p. 8. See also Campopiano, 'La culture pisane', p. 89; Daniel, *Islam and the West*, p. 16.

and the Baltic, but whilst many sources celebrate the deeds of leading missionaries, they contain few details about the religious beliefs held by those they were seeking to convert.[120] Up to the eleventh century at least, it seems that converting non-Christians was considered interesting and important, while the beliefs from which these people were being converted was not. Even Archbishop William of Tyre who spent decades in the east, took a lively interest in his Muslim neighbours, and was an intelligent and inquisitive observer, betrays only a marginally greater knowledge of this faith.[121]

One curious aspect of the crusaders' convictions concerning the 'Saracen' religion was their belief that Muslims were idolaters.[122] This is repeated in many chronicles and among these several authors claimed that the crusaders actually discovered a statue of Mohammed in the Dome of the Rock/*Templum Domini* in Jerusalem shortly after its conquest. This report is made in Fulcher of Chartres' chronicle (although he was not actually there) and it later appears in the *Gesta Tancredi* (whose author was also not there), which speaks of a silver idol of Mohammed, enthroned and covered in jewels.[123] Naturally, the belief that Muslims were idolaters had a substantial pedigree in western Christendom that long predated the First Crusade; thus, the repeated identification of Muslims in this way was not new.[124] Nor were western Christians alone

---

[120] See: R. Fletcher, *The barbarian conversion: from Paganism to Christianity* (Berkeley, CA: University of California Press, 1999), pp. 3–4; H. Mayr-Harting, *The coming of Christianity to Anglo-Saxon England*, 3rd ed. (London: Batsford, 1991), p. 22.

[121] N. Morton, 'William of Tyre's attitude towards Islam: some historiographical reflections', *Deeds done beyond the Sea: essays on William of Tyre, Cyprus and the military orders presented to Peter Edbury*, ed. S. Edgington and H. Nicholson, Crusades subsidia VI (Farnham: Ashgate, 2014), p. 16.

[122] Again this accusation was also made by Muslim authors about the Franks. The poet Mu'izzi, for example, wrote of a time when 'Those miserable idolaters will become the sport of lions, those accursed pig-eaters will become food for pigs'. G. Tetley, *The Ghaznavid and Seljuk Turks: Poetry as a source for Iranian history*, RSIT (Abingdon: Routledge, 2009), p. 143.

[123] FC, p. 290; RC, p. 107. William of Malmesbury mentions this idol, following Fulcher of Chartres: WM, vol. 1, p. 642. The *Hystoria Antiochiae atque Ierusolymarum* also refers to it following the *Gesta Tancredi*, see: *HAI*, pp. 123–124. The *Hystoria Antiochiae atque Ierusolymarum* claims that the Turks erected three 'shrines to the Devil' in the church of St Peter's in Antioch. One of these in particular is reported to have been very ornate. *HAI*, p. 61.

[124] For an example see: Hrotsvit of Gandersheim's *Pelagius* ('Passio Sancti Pelagii Pretiosissimi Martiris', in 'Hrotsvithae Opera', *MGH: SRG*, ed. P. de Winterfeld, vol. 34 (Berlin, 1902), pp. 53–58). Other crusade narratives also reported idols of Mohammed: 'Passio Thiemonis Archiepiscopi', *MGHS*, vol. 11 (1854), pp. 60–61; BB, p. 7. Bartolf of Nangis speaks of idols in Caesarea: see, Bartolf of Nangis, 'Gesta Francorum Expugnantium Iherusalem', *RHC: Oc*, vol. 3 (Paris, 1866), p. 527. On the genesis of this identification see: Scarfe Beckett, *Anglo-Saxon perceptions*, pp. 104–109, 212–217; J. Flori, 'Tares et défauts de L'Orient dans les sources relatives a la première croisade',

in this conviction; the Byzantines had also long described the Islamic religion in these terms.[125] Norman Daniel is almost certainly correct that an influential train of thought that led contemporaries to this conclusion can be reduced to the following progression: (1) the Muslims are deemed to worship God falsely, (2) therefore they worship a false God. (3) If they worship a false God then by definition they worship an idol.[126] As Gregory VII pointed out to the clergy of Constance in 1075, in discussion upon 1 Samuel, all resistance to the will of God is idolatry.[127] Thus many contemporaries probably would not have seen much utility in drawing distinctions between non-Christian religions because they were all perceived as the idolatrous work of demons. John of Würzburg spelled out this reasoning when explaining why the reverence shown by Muslims' for the *Templum Domini* was not theologically acceptable. Drawing upon Augustine, he stated that idolatry is anything that 'differs from the faith of Christ'.[128] This theological background may explain how contemporaries could view Islam as idolatrous, even if they would have searched in vain for any actual Muslim statues.

Nevertheless, Fulcher and Ralph of Caen's chronicle do not simply label Islam as idolatry, they specifically claimed that an *actual* idol of Mohammed was discovered in the Dome of the Rock. Their reports warrant closer attention. The first point to make is that the crusaders did not find a statue of Mohammed on the Temple mount. This would have been emphatically against Islamic law and Albert of Aachen, who

Monde Oriental et Monte Occidental dans la culture médiévale (Greifwald, 1997), pp. 45–56; Schwinges, *Kreuzzugsideologie*, p. 88.

[125] For further discussion see: Tolan, *Saracens*, p. 118; Kedar, *Crusade and mission*, p. 21; Daniel, *Islam and the West*, pp. 338–343; Akbari, *Idols in the east*, pp. 204–205, 243–245.

[126] Daniel, *The Arabs and mediaeval Europe*, p. 31. See also Daniel, *Islam and the West*, p. 343; Daniel, *Heroes and Saracens*, p. 145; Ducellier, *Chrétiens d'Orient*, pp. 32, 161–162. Although it should be pointed out that the early twelfth-century author Petrus Alfonsi described Islam as idolatrous on different grounds. He claimed that Muslims worshipped idols originally dedicated to Saturn and Mars in Mecca. See: Petrus Alfonsi, *Dialogue against the Jews*, trans. I. Resnick (Washington, DC: Catholic University of America Press, 2006), p. 158.

[127] *Epistolae Vagantes*, p. 27. Pope Gregory made a similar point in his *Moralia* (later included in Gratian's *Decretum*). See: Nilsson, 'Gratian on pagans', p. 160. Flori argues that the crusaders' allegations that Muslims were idolaters are rooted in the traditions of the *chansons de geste* where such claims are frequently made. It is not impossible that they were influenced by such ideas, which certainly do appear in the *chansons*, but even so these sources were themselves manifestations of the long-standing belief that almost all non-Christian religions are idolatrous. Flori, 'Première croisades et conversion', p. 452.

[128] 'John of Würzburg', *Peregrinationes Tres*, ed. R. Huygens, CCCM CXXXIX (Turnhout: Brepols, 1994), p. 94. For a similar statement see: *Bede's Ecclesiastical History*, p. 168. In the 1160s Benjamin of Tudela noted that the Franks were particularly concerned to keep the *Templum Domini* empty of any image or statue: 'The travels of Rabbi Benjamin of Tudela', *Early travels in Palestine*, ed. T. Wright (London, 1848), p. 68.

lists the contents of the building in some detail, does not mention any idol.[129] The descriptions of an idol of Mohammed seem rather to have been symbolic and can perhaps be explained with reference to a parallel example. In his recent study on the conversion of Scandinavia, Winroth has demonstrated that the famous pagan Temple of Uppsala in Sweden, described by Adam of Bremen in some detail, may in fact never have existed. Despite Adam's lengthy explanation of its lurid practices, archaeologists can find no trace of it. Winroth's suggestion, rooted in local politics, is that Uppsala was a figment of Adam of Bremen's imagination; he located the temple at Uppsala because the local Christian rulers had not subordinated themselves to the archbishop of Hamburg-Bremen.[130] Yet there may be something more here too. Adam used the fictional Uppsala as a symbolic focal point for local paganism which, with its destruction, opened up the area to Christianity. It seems that Fulcher and Ralph's reference to a statue of Mohammed should be understood in the same context; an imagined item symbolising the focal point of an idolatrous belief, which was being set up simply so that it could be cast down in ruin.[131] Schwinges may also be right that this idol was introduced into these texts as an allusion to 2 Thessalonians 2,4. This verse prophecies that in the end times the son of perdition will take up residence in the Temple of God, and will pose as God before being cast down. This same notion is mirrored closely in the Pseudo-Methodian apocalyptic tradition.[132]

Overall, reflecting upon these points, what makes the first crusaders' experiences of the Turks so distinctive is the fact that they were

---

[129] AA, p. 448. Muratova has raised the possibility that this 'statue' may have been a missidentified Roman statue of Jupiter (Folda follows her in this: J. Folda, *The art of the Crusaders in the Holy Land, 1098–1187* (Cambridge: Cambridge University Press, 1995), p. 44). Still, as Bennett and Loutchitskaja observe, it seems unlikely that a statue to a Roman god would have remained upon the Temple mount while it was under Muslim rule. X. Muratova, 'Western chronicles of the First Crusade as sources for the history of art in the Holy Land', *Crusader art in the twelfth century*, ed. J. Folda (Oxford: British School of Archaeology in Jerusalem, 1982), p. 55; Bennett, 'First crusaders' images of Muslims', 102; S. Loutchitskaja, 'L'image des musulmans dans les chroniques des croisades', *Le Moyen Âge* 105 (1999), 727–728.

[130] Winroth, *The conversion of Scandinavia*, p. 148.

[131] For further discussion on this theme see: Bennett, 'First crusaders' images of Muslims', 104.

[132] Schwinges, *Kreuzzugsideologie*, p. 123. See also Muratova, 'Western chronicles of the First Crusade', pp. 53–57; Pseudo-Methodius, *Apocalypse*, pp. 67–69, 137. Another piece of evidence that warrants attention is the claim made by al-Muqaddasi (tenth century) that the Dome of the Rock was constructed to outcompete the Holy Sepulchre. Had this tradition become known to the crusaders it might help to account for the specific symbolic importance they attached to its capture. *Pringle, churches of the crusader kingdom: Volume III*, p. 399; al-Muqaddasi, *The best divisions for knowledge of the regions*, trans. A. Collins (Reading: Garnet, 1994), p. 153.

encountering a people about whom they previously knew virtually nothing aside from the fact that they were hostile and non-Christian. True, some may previously have heard tales about the Saljuqs carried by returning pilgrims and mercenaries; others might have learnt something from the Byzantines. The crusaders' skirmishes with the imperial turcopoles during their march to Constantinople might also have provided a source of reflection. Turcopoles are mentioned in several sources and Raymond of Aguilers explains that they were either Turks who had migrated to Byzantium or were the sons of mixed marriages between Turks and Greeks.[133] Even so, only a tiny minority of crusaders would have had any prior personal experience before their first meeting in Asia Minor. Consequently, the First Crusade chronicles and letters serve as a case-study for how medieval Europeans approached a new, but hostile, people. These works describe their authors' efforts to locate the Turks within their world view and lived experience and their narratives represent a synthesis of curiosity, shrewd military observation, and theological interpretation.

As shown earlier, on many subjects their information frequently betrays eastern Christian hallmarks, suggesting that the crusaders recognised that their co-religionists were a natural source of knowledge. Western Christians had long relied upon their Eastern cousins for guidance on a whole range of topics. From Charlemagne proudly displaying a Byzantine water-clock at Aachen through to William the Conqueror using Byzantine ship designs and naval signalling techniques during his conquest of England, there was a long deferential tradition of drawing upon Byzantine authorities.[134] Earlier pilgrim groups had likewise returned to the west bearing gifts, goods, and ideas from Byzantium. Among these was Bishop Gunther of Bamberg, who was buried in a silk Byzantine tapestry in 1065 whilst returning from Jerusalem.[135] Clearly, the first crusaders were no different. In one place Raymond of Aguilers explicitly stated that he was supplying the Greek name for one of the hills on which Antioch was built; a point which demonstrates his dependency on Greek-mediated information.[136] Descriptions of some of the other people groups encountered by the Franks reveals a similar influence. To take an example,

---

[133] RA, p. 55.

[134] B. Bachrach, 'On the origins of William the Conqueror's horse transports', *Transport and culture* 26.3 (1985), 505–531. See also K. Ciggaar, 'Byzantine marginalia to the Norman Conquest', *Anglo-Norman Studies IX*, ed. R. Allen Brown (Woodbridge: Boydell, 1986), pp. 43–63.

[135] D. Jacoby, 'Bishop Gunther of Bamberg: Byzantine and Christian pilgrimage to the Holy Land in the eleventh century', *Zwischen Polis, Provinz und Peripherie: Beiträge zur byzantinischen Geschichte und Kultur*, ed. L. Hoffmann (Wiesbaden: Harrassowitz, 2005), pp. 267–285.

[136] RA, p. 48.

several crusaders noted that there were 'Azymites' (*Azimitae*) and 'Publicans' (*Publicani*) among the ranks of their enemies.[137] These are both predominantly Byzantine terms.[138] 'Azymites' is a polemical name used by the Greeks with reference to those who use unleavened bread (*azymus*) in the Eucharist. In this case it seems to refer to Armenians fighting with the Turks. Naturally, the term 'azymus' was present in western Christendom's lexicon, but 'Azymites' (those who use unleavened bread) seems to have been borrowed. The issue of leavened/unleavened bread was an important topic in eleventh-century Byzantium and the use of unleavened bread was deemed to be an erroneous Judaizing influence that was to be condemned.[139] Ironically the Franks themselves were often labelled as 'Azymites' by Greek authors because they too used unleavened bread, but neither of the Frankish authors to use this term shows any awareness of this fact. It seems more likely that they simply picked up a Greek term of abuse for Armenians and applied it to those serving with the Turks without fully understanding its implications.

The second term *Publicani* refers to Paulicians, who were dualists and therefore deemed heretics. Paulicians were not well known in western Europe and lived for the most part in isolated communities spread across Asia Minor.[140] Again it is unlikely, although not impossible, that the crusaders could have identified them without Byzantine, or at least Armenian, assistance.[141] In a similar vein the mysterious group of crusaders known as Tafurs seem to have adopted a name with either Armenian or Arabic roots (historians are divided on its precise etymology, but it clearly has an eastern origin).[142] It might also be relevant to point out that the

---

[137] *GF*, pp. 45, 49, 83; PT, pp. 84, 89, 147; AA, pp. 456. 462, 464, 468. Peter located them among the Egyptian forces and Albert of Aachen noted the presence of 'Publicans' (*gens Publicanorum*) in the Fatimid army at Ascalon. The *Gesta* claimed that there were 'Publicans' at Arqa.

[138] Loutchitskaja, 'Barbarae Nationes', pp. 104–105.

[139] T. Kolbaba, 'Byzantine perceptions of Latin religious "errors": themes and changes from 850 to 1350', *The Crusades from the perspective of Byzantium and the Muslim world*, ed. A. Laiou and R. Mottahedeh (Washington, DC: Dumbarton Oaks, 2001), pp. 121–126.

[140] The Paulicians had in earlier centuries allied with the Arabs against the Byzantines. Their support for the Turks may have been offered in a similar context. See: S. Dadoyan, *The Armenians in the medieval Islamic world, paradigms of interaction, seventh to fourteenth centuries, volume 1: The Arab period in Armīnyah, seventh to eleventh century* (New Brunswick, NJ: Transaction Publishers, 2011), pp. 45, 100; Z. Pogossian, 'The frontier existence of the Paulician heretics', *Annual of medieval studies at CEU*, vol. 6, ed. K. Szende and M. Sebők (Budapest: Central European University, 2000), pp. 203–206.

[141] J. Hamilton and B. Hamilton, *Christian dualist heresies in the Byzantine world, c.650–c.1450* (Manchester: Manchester University Press, 1998), pp. 22–24.

[142] C. Sweetenham, 'The count and the cannibals: the old French crusade cycle as a drama of salvation', *Jerusalem the golden: The origins and impact of the First Crusade*,

warrior saints who in a letter written by both Greek and Latin prelates (also in several chronicles) were reported to have come to the crusaders' aid in their battle against Karbugha at Antioch (SS. George, Theodore, Demetrius, Mercurius and Blaise) were all Greek warrior saints; another possible indication of cross-cultural influence.[143] Such examples help to identify the process by which the crusaders gathered information about the peoples they encountered, demonstrating their sustained reliance on Greek guidance.[144] Incidentally this discussion strengthens John France's argument that relations between the Franks and Greeks may have been more cordial than has been imagined hitherto.[145]

Encountering the Arabs and Fatimids

The crusaders' relations with Arab Muslims contrast sharply from their dealings with the Turks. Unlike the Turks, the Arabs were better known across western Christendom which for centuries had traded with, and defended against, the Muslim polities along the southern and eastern shores of the Mediterranean. Aspiring crusader knights may initially have anticipated that they would be confronting the Arabs in the east during the crusade. After all, the Turks were not mentioned in the crusade preaching and Urban's repeated use of the term 'Saracen' may have led some to conclude that they were marching to face the long-standing opponent that had raided Christendom's seaboard for centuries.

ed. S. Edgington and L. García-Guijarro, Outremer: studies in the Crusades and the Latin East III (Turnhout: Brepols, 2014), pp. 326–328.

[143] Riley-Smith, *The First Crusade and the idea of Crusading*, p. 105; *Kb*, p. 147. It might be added that different authors reported slightly different groups of saints coming to the crusaders' assistance. The *Gesta Francorum* named SS. George, Mercurius and Demetrius. *GF*, p. 68. For further discussion: Jotischky, 'The Christians of Jerusalem', 47–50; C. Walter, *The warrior saints in Byzantine art and tradition* (Aldershot: Ashgate, 2003). Lapina has demonstrated that the Normans in particular, during their many interactions with the Byzantine Empire in earlier decades, had learned to reverence these saints. Notably, she advances the case that references to these saints in crusading sources indicate an authorial desire to demonstrate that the saints had abandoned the Byzantines and were now fighting for the Franks. Thus it was a form of 'aggressive borrowing'. E. Lapina, *Warfare and the miraculous*, pp. 54–74. For an example of the centrality of these saints in the Byzantine thought world see the Greek epic *Digenis Akritis* where George, both Theodores and Demetrius (along with Basil) are presented from the outset as the defenders of Byzantium against the Muslims. *Digenis Akritis: The Grottaferrata and Escorial versions*, ed. E. Jeffreys, Cambridge medieval classics VII (Cambridge: Cambridge University Press, 1998), p. 4. Also Leo the Deacon describes how a knight on a white horse supported a Byzantine army in battle against the Rus in 971. See: *The history of Leo the Deacon: Byzantine military expansion in the tenth century*, trans. A.-M. Talbot and D. Sullivan (Washington, DC: Dumbarton Oaks, 2005), p. 197.

[144] Loutchitskaja, 'Barbarae Nationes', pp. 99–107.

[145] France, 'Byzantium in western chronicles', pp. 3–16.

Strictly speaking, the first pilgrims to encounter Muslims of any ethnicity during the crusade were those who took the cross whilst surrounded by large numbers of friendly Muslim forces. One of these was Bohemond of Taranto. He originally joined the crusade during the siege of Amalfi in 1096. This city had rebelled against his half-brother's (Roger Borsa, duke of Apulia) authority and they were both engaged in quelling the unrest. When the city was on the point of surrender, Bohemond suddenly declared his intention of taking part in the crusade and induced so many other warriors to follow his example that Roger Borsa was apparently forced to lift the siege.[146] A significant aspect of this episode is that Roger Borsa's army at Amalfi was supported by a large force of 'Saracen' warriors. This was not unusual for the Normans of southern Italy and Sicily whose armies often included large Muslim contingents.[147] In this case Geoffrey of Malaterra suggests that they numbered twenty thousand – surely an exaggeration – but it is necessary to take seriously the notion that they formed a sizeable company.[148] Thus, when Bohemond joined the crusade, he did so surrounded by the encampments of many thousands of allied Muslim warriors. It is not stretching credulity too far to speculate that some Muslims may even have marched with his crusading army. Bohemond is said to have recruited extensively from the besiegers and it is entirely possible that there may have been some Muslims within the households of the departing Norman knights; they may also have been among his paid retainers.[149] The Norman rulers of this region would have seen nothing contradictory in marching to fight the 'Saracens' whilst supported by 'Saracen' allies. In 1113, when Adelaide of Salerno (widow of Roger I of Sicily) set out for the east to marry King Baldwin I of Jerusalem, she was accompanied by a troop of Saracen archers, whose skill with the bow was much admired – again there is no suggestion that this was problematic in any way.[150]

The crusaders' first encounter with the Arab Muslims in the Near East was more hostile and occurred during their crossing of Asia Minor.

---

[146] Geoffrey of Malaterra, *De Rebus Gestis Rogerii*, p. 102.

[147] Catlos, *Infidel kings*, p. 145.   [148] Lupus Protospatarius, 'Annales', p. 62.

[149] In her article on intelligence gathering during the First Crusade, Edgington noted that some of Bohemond's scouts could communicate with the local peoples. She argues that he must have recruited Greek and Arabic speakers. Reflecting on her article, it is not stretching credulity too much to imagine that some of these could have been Muslim. Edgington, 'Espionage and military intelligence', pp. 75–86. For discussion on the financial relations between Bohemond and his company see: C. Tyerman, 'Paid crusaders: "pro honoris vel pecunie"; "stipendiarii contra paganos"; money and incentives on crusade', *The practices of crusading: Image and action from the eleventh to the sixteenth centuries*, Variorum collected studies series (Aldershot: Ashgate, 2013), pp. 35–37 (article XIV).

[150] AA, pp. 842–844.

Several accounts note that there were 'Arabs' amongst the Turkish forces which resisted the crusader advance, particularly during the battle of Dorylaeum (1 July 1097). The author of the *Gesta Francorum* identifies the enemy forces as being made up of 'Turks, Arabs and Saracens' along with others who he did not know.[151] It is tempting to question whether the author of the *Gesta Francorum* had identified his foe correctly. After all, the battle was fought in formerly Byzantine territory against the forces of Qilij Arslan, the Turkish ruler of Rum; a long way from the major centres of Arab settlement. It is possible that he included this reference to 'Arabs' simply to bulk out a list of the foes arrayed against them. Nevertheless, shortly afterwards, he made a specific point of emphasising the sheer size of the Arab contingent present at the battle writing: 'of whose number, no-one except God alone knows', suggesting that their inclusion among the enemy's ranks was not simply rhetorical.[152] This is not entirely implausible and there are known to have been some Arab communities in Asia Minor prior to the Turkish invasions of the eleventh century.[153]

Subsequently, the Arabs are listed as auxiliaries within the Turkish-led armies encountered by the crusaders, although they are never given prominence; they are almost always simply one name in a list of foes rather than the central enemy. During the siege of Antioch several chroniclers noted their presence among the city's defenders and also within the relieving armies despatched to raise the siege by Duqaq of Damascus and later Karbugha of Mosul.[154]

As the crusade headed south into Syria, the pilgrims came to realise that they were passing out of Greek/Armenian territory and into lands populated predominantly by Arabic-speaking peoples. This change is discernible in accounts of the siege of Antioch. Several authors, describing crusader incursions to the south, speak of them leaving ethnically Greek or Armenian territory and entering the 'land of the Saracens' (*terra Saracenorum*). This phrase was first used to describe the region raided by Bohemond of Taranto and Robert II of Flanders during their expedition into the Orontes valley where they later defeated the forces of Damascus.[155] This term demonstrates these authors' awareness that the raiders had crossed an ethnic frontier (certainly this could not be a political frontier because, before the arrival of the First Crusade, all these lands were ruled by the Turks); notably, the earlier pilgrim Richard of St Vanne, who visited the east in 1026–1027, is also said to have

---

[151] *GF*, p. 19; PT, p. 35.   [152] *GF*, p. 20.

[153] See: Korobeinikov, *Byzantium and the Turks*, p. 94.

[154] *GF*, pp. 26, 30, 47, 49; AA, p. 190; RA, p. 52.

[155] *GF*, p. 30; AA, p. 217. See also PT, p. 65; France, *Victory in the east*, pp. 237–238.

entered 'Saracen' territory south of Antioch.[156] The crusaders evidently perceived 'Saracen' lands to be more dangerous than Christian areas because the *Gesta Francorum* reported that no one was prepared to cross into Saracen territory without a strong force.[157]

Raymond of Aguilers also recognised these changes in the underlying demography and he too used different terminology when discussing these areas. Like other chroniclers he felt that Bohemond and Robert's expedition had crossed an ethnic border, but he described these new lands distinctively as '*Hispania*'.[158] Marching with the Provencal forces, and serving as chaplain to Raymond of Toulouse, whose territories lay close to Spain, it seems likely that for him the notion of *Hispania* was synonymous with the identification of ethnically-Muslim territory.[159] This idea is confirmed by the fact that at a later point he described the Arabs of Tripoli as 'Moors' *(Mauri)*.[160]

Whilst the *terra Saracenorum* might have been viewed as a dangerous environment, the crusaders were also conscious of the fact that relations were strained between the Turks and the Arabs. As shown earlier, they knew the Turkish conquest of Syria and Anatolia to be a recent event and several described how the Turks had 'terrified' (*terrere*) the Arabs and other peoples of the region during the process.[161] They were aware that the Turks' incursions had provoked the enmity of the Arab peoples and there are reports of moments of conflict between these two groups both during, and shortly after, the crusade. One of these is described by Albert of Aachen in an account of events which occurred shortly after Baldwin of Boulogne took power in Edessa. He explained how a neighbouring Turkish ruler named Balak ibn Bahram sought Baldwin's assistance in suppressing a rebellion instigated by 'Saracens' in nearby Sororgia, who were refusing to pay him tribute.[162] It seems probable that news of the mounting Turkish defeats suffered at the hands of the crusaders may have encouraged them to rebel.

This same tension appears at a later point in Albert's chronicle in a description of Baldwin of Boulogne's journey south from Edessa along

---

[156] Although in this instance it is possible that he was describing a political frontier as well as an ethnic one. After 969 Antioch was under Byzantine control. It did not fall to the Turks until 1084. 'Chronicon Hugonis monachi Virdunensis et Divionensis', *MGHS*, ed. G. Pertz, vol. 8 (Hanover, 1848), p. 394.

[157] *GF*, p. 30; PT, p. 65.

[158] RA, pp. 50, 53. The continuator of Frutolf's chronicle includes a letter that purports to have been written by Robert of Flanders. This letter also uses this term. See: *FE*, 152.

[159] France, 'The First Crusade and Islam', 249. The letter written by Daimbert of Pisa (along with several further crusader commanders) also used this term. See: *Kb*, p. 170.

[160] RA, p. 125.   [161] *GF*, p. 21; PT, p. 55; RA, pp. 109–110.   [162] AA, p. 178.

the Levantine littoral to become king of Jerusalem in 1100. Albert explained how a mixed force of Arabs ('Saracens') and Turks sought to waylay Baldwin near Dog River. He then presented an imagined conversation that took place between the Turkish leaders on the eve of the battle. According to his narrative, the Turkish ruler of Homs suggested that they should stage a night attack upon the Franks, but the Turkish ruler of Damascus refused. He was concerned 'lest we should suddenly be surrounded and killed by the Saracens, who have always hated us'.[163] Here he identifies the Arab-Turkish enmity explicitly. Admittedly, it seems unlikely that Albert would have had first-hand information about this conversation, thus it is probably a product of his imagination. Still he reveals an acute awareness of Arab hostility towards the Turkish invader.

In a similar vein, the crusaders seem to have been aware that their sustained advance into Anatolia and the Levant was causing the Turks to become concerned that their Arab subjects might choose this moment to rebel. Raymond of Aguilers, for example, reports that following the defeat of Peter the Hermit's army, the Turks sent captured weapons and captives to 'Saracen' leaders to assure them of their victory whilst deriding the Franks' competence in war.[164] Whether this is factually true or not, the pilgrims had evidently grasped the idea that the Turks felt the need to impress their authority upon the subjugated populace when threatened by Frankish invasion. More importantly, several chronicles include an account of a conversation – again probably entirely fictional – between Qilij Arslan (named by many chroniclers as 'Suleiman' – his father's name)[165] and the leader of a force of Arabs following the battle of Dorylaeum. The story runs as follows: having just been defeated, this Turkish commander is shown to be in despair and in full retreat. The Arab leader then accosted him and asked why he was fleeing and he explained that he had just suffered a disastrous reverse. The Arab commander is then said to have been so moved by this account that his force immediately scattered. The Turks are then said to have changed their story, telling everyone they met that they had defeated the Franks.[166] This is a rather garbled tale, but it does communicate one idea clearly: the crusaders understood that their victories were troubling the Turks and were having a disruptive effect upon Saljuq dominance over the subjugated Arab population.[167] A better known example of Islamic (non-Turkish) rulers taking the military initiative following these Turkish reverses was the

---

[163] Translation from AA, p. 535.   [164] RA, p. 45.

[165] Beihammer discusses Fulcher's account which describes Qilij as Suleiman, son of Suleiman. He suggests that this reflects common Islamic usage. See: Beihammer, 'Christian views of Islam', p. 67.

[166] GF, pp. 22–23; PT, p. 56.   [167] See also RA, p. 101.

reconquest of Jerusalem by the Fatimids in August 1098. Raymond of Aguilers recognised that this Fatimid assault had been stimulated by a growing aura of Turkish defeat generated by the crusaders' advances because he explained that the Christian conquest of Antioch gave them the confidence necessary to attack the holy city.[168] He also pointed out that the defeat of Karbugha had such an effect on the 'Saracen' cities to the south that if the crusaders had attacked south immediately there was no one [from Antioch] to Jerusalem who would have thrown so much as a rock at them.[169]

The crusade chroniclers were not wrong in their identification of these Turkish/Arabic tensions. It is clear from the various Muslim and eastern Christian accounts that the crusaders' victories did indeed have a substantial effect on the Arab Muslim population of the Middle East. To take one example, Ibn al-Athir agrees with the crusader accounts that Arab contingents were among Karbugha's army, when he marched to the relieve Antioch.[170] Kamal ad-Din however adds the detail that arguments broke out between the Arabs and Turks, causing the Arabs to leave the army.[171] He later reported how in 1100 forces from the Banu Kilab tribe (the Arab rulers of Aleppo before the Turkish invasion) then raided Aleppan territory.[172] Certainly, the Arabs seem to have resented the Turks who they had long viewed as drunken and uncouth barbarians.[173] Other chroniclers likewise report the sense of shock that spread across the Levantine region following this catalogue of Turkish defeats. Michael the Syrian describes how in the period following the crusade, the Arabs 'lifted their head' and began to make war on the Turks.[174] The aura of Turkish weakness would only have been compounded by the fact that Alexius' forces under John Doukas capitalised on the crusaders' advances to retake many major cities in Western Anatolia.[175] The crusaders' awareness that Turkish power was hanging in the balance was rooted in observed fact

---

[168] RA, p. 110. A similar statement was made by Ibn al-Athir: IAA, vol. 1, p. 21.
[169] RA, p. 84.   [170] IAA, vol. 1, p. 16.
[171] Kamal al-Din, 'Extraits de la Chronique d'Alep', pp. 582–583.
[172] Kamal al-Din, 'Extraits de la Chronique d'Alep', p. 586.
[173] Hillenbrand, 'What's in a Name?', p. 464; Safi, *Politics of Knowledge*, pp. 11–12; C. Hillenbrand, 'Ibn al-Adīm's biography of the Seljuq sultan, Alp Arslan', *Actas XVI Congreso Union Européene des Arabisants et Islamisants* (Salamanca, 1995), pp. 237–242. For Persian reactions to the Turks see: Tetley, *The Ghaznavid and Seljuk Turks*, *passim*.
[174] MS, vol. 3, p. 192. As Mallett observes, the Turks are often said to have been drunk on fermented mares' milk; a drink that recalls the Turks' steppe background. Mallett, *Popular Muslim Reactions*, p. 58. For more detailed analysis on this phenomenon see: N. Morton and J. France, 'Arab Muslim reactions to Turkish authority in northern Syria, 1085–1128', *Warfare, crusade and conquest in the Middle Ages*, Variorum collected studies series (Farnham: Ashgate, 2014), XV (1–38).
[175] Frankopan, *The First Crusade*, pp. 145–146.

and demonstrates their close attention to the evolving political affairs of the east. Consequently the pilgrims created enough disruption to allow dissenters – whether Armenian, Arab, or even Turkish – to contemplate resistance to Saljuq authority.

Although the Syrian Arabs' resistance to the Turks was recognised by the pilgrims, the crusaders were aware that the Fatimid rulers of Egypt represented the heart of local opposition to the Turks. Albert of Aachen, for example, described the mutual 'hatred' (*odium*) between the two, which had arisen through the Turks' former incursions into the Near East and especially their conquests of Jerusalem in 1073/8.[176] Raymond of Aguilers makes a similar point, explaining how the Turks had conquered vast swaths of Fatimid territory only a few decades previously.[177]

When historians have discussed the Saljuq/Fatimid conflict previously, they have tended to couch the confrontation between these two peoples in religious terms. Having covered events such as the Fatimid recovery of Jerusalem from the Turks in 1098, it is typical for historians to step in and explain this conflict on sectarian grounds pointing out that the Turks were Sunni Muslims, whilst the Fatimids were Shia. This distinction is true enough, as far as it goes, but the prioritisation of religious difference as the main cause of hostility is not without its problems. In particular, the crusaders seem to have understood the conflict between these two powers to be a struggle between two rival ethnicities at least as much as it was a war of religions. As shown earlier, the crusaders were broadly aware of the difference between Sunni and Shia Islam, although no author dwelt upon this issue. Raymond of Aguilers observed that the Egyptians revere Ali, 'who is from the family of Mohammed'.[178]

Still, Raymond does not present sectarian divisions as the main reason for the Saljuq/Fatimid conflict. Describing the diplomatic negotiations between the Fatimids and crusaders at Arqa, he reports that, having suffered a series of defeats at the hands of the crusaders, the Turks had offered to convert to Shia Islam in order to secure Fatimid assistance; a statement which carries the implication that the Turks were prepared to sacrifice their religious identify in favour of political expediency.[179] *Prima facie* Raymond's claim sounds absurd because historians have long considered the Turks to have been steadfast adherents to Sunni Islam, who would never have compromised their piety in this way.[180] Even so, his account is not without its merits.[181] Many of the key Muslim sources for

---

[176] AA, p. 230 (see also p. 442).   [177] RA, p. 129.
[178] RA, p. 110.   [179] RA, p. 110.
[180] See, for example: Gil, *A History of Palestine*, p. 409; Cahen, *Pre-Ottoman Turkey*, pp. 42–43.
[181] Köhler also feels that this report is 'credible': Köhler, *Alliances and Treaties*, p. 46.

this period were written (or compiled) many decades/centuries after these events at a time when the Turks had indeed become vigorous advocates of Sunni Islam. They were written by authors who were keen to show that piously-observed Sunni Hanafi religiosity had characterised Saljuq policies from the moment of their conversion.[182]

Nevertheless, they may have overstated this point. As Peacock has demonstrated, the Turks' adoption of Islam seems to have been a slower process (particularly at a tribal level) than these authors either hoped or imagined. In many cases their Sunni adherence may have been rather nominal, while many Turks retained their shamanistic beliefs, and others seem to have been drawn towards Shia Islam.[183] The Turks in Asia Minor – ruling over a large eastern Christian population – even seem to have adopted some Christian practices in their religious ritual and there is a Byzantine document from the twelfth century that suggests that many Turkish Muslims were accustomed to receiving a baptism from a Christian priest shortly after their birth. Apparently some Turks believed that baptism was a kind of medicine that would immunise them from the attacks of demons.[184] The blurred and transitional nature of the Turks' religious alignments at this time is reflected clearly in a tale told about the siege of Antioch. According to the *Gesta Francorum*, on the day following a major skirmish, a group of Turks departed from the city to collect their dead. They then buried them at a mosque, which lay just outside the walls. The crusaders subsequently seized the mosque, despoiled the graves, and decapitated the corpses. Their motives for such aggressive behaviour are immediately apparent: these Turkish corpses had been buried with valuable grave goods. The *Gesta* notes the presence of cloaks, money, bows, arrows, and other items.[185] This incident is important because it supplies details about Turkish funerary practices. The fact that they buried them outside a mosque shows that this building held an important spiritual meaning for them – a sign of their movement

---

[182] Safi, *Politics of knowledge*, pp. 1–42.

[183] Peacock, *Early Seljūq History*, pp. 99–127. See also Hillenbrand, 'What's in a Name?', p. 464; Başan, *The great Seljuqs*, pp. 172–174, 187 and *passim*. In addition, it has been noted that steppe peoples tended to convert for political purposes. See: Stepanov, *The Bulgars and the steppe empire*, p. 64. Michael the Syrian provides some interesting insights into their motives, see: MS, vol. 3, pp. 156–157 (on Michael see also Dickens, 'The Sons of Magog', p. 443).

[184] For detailed discussion on this evidence and – more broadly – Christian/Muslim identity among Anatolian Saljuq elites see: R. Shukurov, 'Harem Christianity: The Byzantine identity of Seljuk princes', *The Seljuks of Anatolia: court and society in the medieval Middle East*, ed. Peacock, and Sara Nur Yıldız, (London: I.B. Tauris, 2013), pp. 115–150; M. Brand, 'The Turkish element in Byzantium, eleventh–twelfth centuries', *Dumbarton Oaks papers* 43 (1989), 16; Korobeinikov, *Byzantium and the Turks*, *passim*.

[185] GF, p. 42.

towards Islam. Nevertheless, the interment of the dead with grave goods speaks rather of long-established pre-Islamic steppe practices. Travelling among the shamanistic Turks in the early tenth century, the Arab envoy Ibn Fadlān had observed this custom closely. He saw how deceased Turks were interred with their clothes, a bow, their horses, food, and a wooden cup. They believed that these items would serve the dead in the afterlife.[186]

Other reports similarly cast doubt on the notion that when the Turks did convert that they sided decisively with Sunni Islam. Peacock draws attention to a moment in 1062–1063 when Sultan Tughril touted the possibility of his conversion to Shia Islam when the caliph in Baghdad attempted to prevent him from marrying his daughter.[187] Clearly he was prepared to compromise his religious adherence if it served his dynastic purposes. It might be added that Ridwan, ruler of Aleppo (d. 1113), entered into an alliance with Fatimid Egypt in 1097 which resulted in him ordering the Fatimid caliph to be named in the *khutbah* (the Friday sermon) across his lands. The fact that he was later persuaded to revoke this agreement does not detract from his readiness to trade his religious adherence for political advantage. Likewise, it is worth noting that some among later sultans of Rum raised the possibility of converting to Christianity when it was in their interests to do so in both the late twelfth and early thirteenth centuries. Qilij Arslan II (d/1192) seems to have made this offer in his dealings with both the Emperor Frederick I and Pope Alexander III.[188] Kay-Kusraw I (d.1211) is even said to have been

---

[186] Ibn Fadlān and the land of darkness, p. 18. Leclercq, Portraits croisés, pp. 144–145. In a similar vein it has been noted that Turkish tombs found in Anatolia (tekkes) retained many features common with steppe practices. See: J. Freely, *Storm on horseback: The Seljuk warriors of Turkey* (London: I.B. Tauris, 2008), p. 141; C. Emilie Haspels, The highlands of Phrygia: sites and monuments, vol. 1 (Princeton, NJ: Princeton University Press, 1971), pp. 264–267. There are many other examples of the Turks retaining their earlier steppe practices. The mid-twelfth-century Persian treatise Sea of Precious virtues reports that the Turks firmly believed in the spiritual properties of various types of stone, a custom observed in the pre-Islamic Turks. See: The sea of precious virtues (Baḥr al-Favā'id): a medieval mirror for princes, trans. J. S. Meisami (Salt Lake City: University of Utah Press, 1991), p. 281; Ibn Faqih al-Hamadhani, 'On the Turks and their lands', pp. 46–48.

Likewise, See also S. Vryonis, 'Evidence on human sacrifice among the early Ottoman Turks', *Journal of Asian history* 5 (1971), 140–146. See also Golden, 'Religion among the Qıpčaqs', 202–203.

[187] Peacock, Early Seljūq History, pp. 120–121. Tor has recently restated the case for a strong sense of religiosity at least among the early Turkish sultans: D. Tor, '"Sovereign and pious": The religious life of the great Seljuq sultans', *The Seljuqs: politics, society and culture*, ed. C. Lange and S. Mecit (Edinburgh: Edinburgh University Press, 2011), pp. 39–62.

[188] We know of Qilij Arslan II's offer to the papacy from Pope Alexander III's reply: 'Instructio fidei Catholicae ad soldanum Iconii missa', PL, vol. 207 (1904), cols. 1069–1078. Another account of this letter suggests that the sultan was actually baptised, see:

baptised.[189] With this background, Raymond's claim that the Turks dangled the possibility of their conversion to Shia Islam in their negotiations with the Fatimids becomes less outlandish. If the Turks' Sunni adherence was more nominal than has previously been thought then sectarian tensions between the two can only supply a partial explanation for the animosity between the Fatimids and Saljuqs. Ethnic hostility, however, provides a stronger answer.

On this point, it is significant that when the crusaders described the main religious and secular authorities in Baghdad they often portrayed them in distinctively racial terms. The sultan and caliph, for example, were not presented as 'Saracen' leaders who – incidentally – derived from a Turkish background, but rather Turks advancing their own ethic group. Both Raymond of Aguilers and the *Gesta Francorum* described the Abbasid caliph as the 'pope of the Turks'. Raymond also speaks of Turks as those who 'walk in Khurasan and worship the God of the Turks'.[190] In a later section, which deals with the sufferings of the Christian population near to Tyre under Turkish rule, he explained that these Christians had been compelled to be 'turkified' (*turcandum*).[191] Anselm of Ribemont likewise, in his letter to Manasses, archbishop of Reims, described Karbugha's determination to assail the crusaders until they had 'denied Christ and professed the law of the Persians' (synonym for Turks).[192] Describing the siege of Antioch, the *Gesta Francorum* likewise reports Karbugha demanding to Peter the Hermit that the crusaders give up

Matthew Paris, Chronica Majora, ed. H. R. Luard, Rolls Series LVII, vol. 2 (London, 1874), pp. 250–260. For the sultan's offer to Frederick I (to convert in return for a marriage alliance) see: 'Ottonis de Sancto Blasio Chronica', MGH: SRG, ed. A. Hofmeister, vol. 47 (Hanover, 1912), p. 37.

[189] George Akropolites, *The history: introduction, translation and commentary*, ed. R. Macrides, Oxford Studies in Byzantium (Oxford: Oxford University Press, 2007), p. 124; Robert of Clari, La Conquête de Constantinople, ed. P. Noble, *British Rencesvals Publications III* (Edinburgh: British Rencesvals Publications, 2005), p. 66; Oliver of Paderborn, 'Historia Damiatina', Die Schriften des Kölner Domscholasters, Späteren Bishofs von Paderborn und Kardinal-Bischofs von S. Sabina, Bibliothek des Litterarischen Vereins in Stuttgart, CCII (Tübingen, 1894), p. 235. For discussion see: See: Korobeinikov, Byzantium and the Turks, pp. 115–126.

[190] RA, p. 87. Völkl offers some interesting discussion on related themes: Völkl, Muslime – Märtyrer – Militia Christi, pp. 238–240.

[191] RA, p. 129. A similar verb appeared in an earlier passage see: RA, p. 64. See also RC, p. 81. Even into the fourteenth century a similar formulation was used by European authors to describe inclusion into Turkish society. Ramon Muntaner described how sons born to a Turkish mother and a Greek Christian mother were circumcised and became Turks. See: Ramon Muntaner, *The Catalan expedition to the east: From the chronicle of Ramon Muntaner*, trans. R. Hughes and J. Hillgarth (Woodbridge: Boydell, 2006), p. 46.

[192] *Kb*, p. 160. Phrases such as 'law of the Saracens' or 'law of Mohammed' were often used to denote the Islamic religion during this period.

their God and become 'Turks'.[193] In each of these pieces of evidence, the Turks' ethnicity is stressed while their religious adherence is subsumed within this racial identity. Thus, these authors link the Turks' religious leaders and beliefs directly to their ethnicity and not to any concept of a pan-Islamic/'Saracen' community. As shown earlier, the crusaders *were* aware that the Turks were 'Saracens' (Muslims) and yet these passages demonstrate that the Turks had also impressed the pilgrims with the notion that their policies and religion were specific to their people group. In this context, Raymond's suggestion that the Turks were prepared to renegotiate their religious identity with the Fatimids gains further credibility. Overall, the crusaders seem to have surmised that the Turks were ultimately concerned with the advancement of their people's interests. This seems to have been their defining objective and it was this purpose that presumably had originally brought them into conflict with the Fatimids. Their religious identity was part of this agenda, but it was seemingly open to compromise and adaptation if such a shift would serve the advancement of Turkish interests.

As might be expected, the crusaders attempted to exploit these ethnic and sectarian divisions. Their initial policy was to seek an alliance with the Fatimids against the Saljuqs and to this end they embarked upon a protracted period of diplomacy with the representatives of the Egyptian caliphate.[194] Their first embassy to Cairo seems to have been despatched during the siege of Nicaea in the summer of 1097 on the advice of Emperor Alexius. The Byzantines had long considered the possibility of an alliance with the Fatimids against the Turks so such a suggestion would have been entirely in accordance with existing policy.[195] The legation was led by Hugh of Bellafayre, Bertrand of Scabrica and his chaplain Peter of Picca.[196] Fatimid envoys later arrived in the crusader camp during the siege of Antioch to discuss a treaty. Clearly the crusaders saw no objection to establishing treaties with a Muslim power and no contemporary author felt the need to provide any kind of justification – theological or otherwise – for such an accord. Indeed, they report the crusaders working strenuously to win favour with the Egyptian envoys. Following the

---

[193] *GF*, p. 67.
[194] Incidentally, Ibn al-Athir suggests that the crusaders had actually been invited to invade the Near East by the Fatimids: IAA, vol. 1, p. 14.
[195] A. Hamdani, 'Byzantine-Fātimid relations before the battle of Manzikert', *Byzantine Studies* 1–2 (1974), 69–79.
[196] 'Historia peregrinorum euntium Jerusolymam', *RHC Oc.*, vol. 3 (Paris, 1866), p. 181; *HAI*, p. 28. For discussion on these sources see: J. France, 'The use of the Anonymous *Gesta Francorum* in the early twelfth-century sources for the First Crusade', *From Clermont to Jerusalem: The Crusades and crusader societies, 1095–1500*, ed. A. Murray (Turnhout: Brepols, 1998), pp. 33–39.

crusaders' victory over the army of Ridwan of Aleppo on 9 February 1098, the Fatimid envoys were presented with a selection of decapitated Turkish heads.[197] This grisly choice of gift (which was repeated shortly afterwards) was presumably intended both to demonstrate the crusaders' prowess and to assure the Fatimids of their vehement and mutual opposition to the Turks.[198] The outcome of these negotiations is unclear, although a letter from Stephen of Blois may imply that a treaty had been established and that Frankish envoys had been despatched to Egypt.[199]

The next phase in these diplomatic negotiations began with the arrival of a new deputation from Egypt during the crusaders' siege of Arqa in May 1099. The Fatimid envoys brought with them the Frankish ambassadors who by this stage had been held in Egypt for over a year. In the intervening period the crusader armies had marched south without meeting significant opposition. The Arab princes of this region, presumably torn between their desire to resist the Turks and the uncertainties of allying themselves with the powerful, but brutal, and largely unknown crusaders, had generally been anxious to speed the Christian armies on their way whilst offering very little resistance (for further discussion see later). When negotiations reopened at Arqa, the crusaders found that the Fatimids' position had changed in a number of ways. Firstly, by this stage the Turks had suffered multiple defeats and were prepared to offer substantial concessions to secure a peace treaty with the Fatimids (thus the Egyptians now had the choice of an alliance with either the Franks or the Turks). Secondly, the Fatimids themselves had seized Jerusalem from the Turks and were determined to retain control of the city. Thirdly, Alexius I is said to have written to the Egyptians telling him that the Franks had lost much of their manpower. The crusaders for their part were not prepared to sign any treaty that did not give them control of Jerusalem; their best offer was that they would take control of the holy city but would assist the Fatimids to regain their other former territories in Syria.[200]

Viewed from a Fatimid perspective, given that the Turks now posed less of a threat and the crusaders were absolutely determined to retake the holy city, which the Egyptians were equally determined to keep,

---

[197] *GF*, p. 37. Albert of Aachen suggests that the Egyptians participated in the battle (AA, p. 236). Both sides seem to have indulged in displaying their foes' decapitated heads. For discussion see: Leclercq, *Portraits croisés*, p. 123.

[198] *GF*, p. 42.

[199] RA, p. 58; *Kb*, p. 151. Albert of Aachen also states that a treaty was agreed because he later accused the Egyptians of breaching it during the siege of Jerusalem (AA, p. 402). France, *Victory in the east*, p. 251.

[200] RA, pp. 109–110.

the incentives for a treaty with the crusaders were substantially reduced.[201] Thus Raymond reports that the Fatimids were uncertain whether to ally themselves with the Franks or the Turks.[202] In the event, these negotiations came to nothing and the crusaders continued their march south, ultimately besieging Fatimid-controlled Jerusalem. Nevertheless, the conflict between the two should be seen as a last resort that occurred only after sustained diplomatic activity.[203]

In general, the crusaders seem to have viewed the Arabs in a very different way to the Turks.[204] The Arabs were hardly ever described as 'barbarians' (barbari). In many of the texts, it is the Turks alone who are assigned labels such as 'barbarous', 'barbaric', 'barbarian'.[205] In the Gesta Francorum, for example, this term was exclusively reserved for Turks (although there are moments when Turkish armies, which included Arab companies, are presented in this way). The crusaders were not alone in describing the Turks with such terminology. The Byzantines, Arabs and Armenians all held similar opinions about the Turks' 'barbarism'; a shared response which presumably encapsulates the standard reactions of complex agricultural societies to their aggressive nomadic neighbours.[206] A sample of this hostility can be found in the work of the eleventh-century Baghdadi writer Ghars al-Ni'ma who described the rise of the Saljuqs and their Khurasani supporters as follows:

---

[201] France, *Victory in the east*, p. 326. [202] RA, p. 110. [203] RA, p. 110.

[204] See also Meserve, *Empires of Islam*, p. 156. The Byzantines also drew clear distinctions between Turks and Arabs, see: Beihammer, 'Christian views of Islam', p. 55.

[205] See, for example, references in the following texts: *GF*, pp. 20, 29, 31, 73; FC, p. 136. In the first six books of his work, which concern the First Crusade, Albert uses the term slightly more broadly, at times to encapsulate all the enemies confronted by the crusaders, and also to describe some of the 'Ethiopian' troops serving the Fatimid caliphate. See: AA, pp. 258, 290, 308, 322, 342, 448, 456, 474, 480. The Turks were considered to be barbarians long into the early-modern period; see: Meserve, *Empires of Islam*, pp. 65–116. This point should nuance Jubb's argument that for the crusaders, 'barbarians' were 'those who are distinct from the Latin (western) crusaders, most notably in language and customs'. Clearly their frame of reference was more sophisticated and focused. Jubb, 'The Crusaders' Perceptions of their Opponents', p. 226. For further discussion on this term in crusade texts see: A. Holt, 'Crusading against barbarians: Muslims as barbarians in Crusades era sources', *East meets west in the Middle Ages and early modern times: Transcultural experiences in the pre-modern world*, ed. A. Classen, Fundamentals of medieval and early modern culture XIV (Berlin: De Gruyter, 2013), pp. 443–456.

[206] See for example: A. G. Savvides, 'Byzantines and the Oghuz (Ghuzz): some observations on nomenclature', *Byzantinoslavica* 54 (1993), 147–155; E. van Donzel and A. Schmidt, *Gog and Magog in early Christian and Islamic sources: Sallam's quest for Alexander's wall*, Brill's Inner Asian Library XXII (Leiden: Brill, 2010), pp. 82–96. Beihammer has demonstrated that the Byzantines also viewed the Turks and Arabs differently. See: A. Beihammer, 'Orthodoxy and religious antagonism in Byzantine perceptions of the Seljuk Turks (eleventh and twelfth Centuries)', *Al-Masōq* 23.1 (2011), 18–19.

The chiefs of the land and its elites were not happy with this dynasty when it emerged. They despised it, and disassociated themselves from it. As a result they were destroyed, ruined and perished. The rabble, low life and scum followed [the Saljuq dynasty], and were promoted and raised high.[207]

The crusade authors also adopted a far softer tone in their presentation of the Fatimids. It was not forgotten that the Fatimids had long acted as protectors of pilgrims wishing to visit Jerusalem.[208] The *Gesta Francorum* for example reports an emir fleeing from the Franks after the battle of Ascalon (12 August 1099), lamenting his misfortune and commenting that the Egyptians used to give alms to Franks visiting the Holy Land. Placing such a remark in the mouth of a defeated Muslim potentate may even indicate a slight sense of guilt on the author's part that they were attacking those who had formerly offered pilgrims assistance.[209] Another important distinction concerns the Fatimids' competence in war. Unlike the Turks, they did not impress Raymond of Aguilers with their martial prowess. He described them as 'more cowardly than deer and more harmless than sheep'.[210] In this passage it is possible that he may not have been making a specific judgement about the Fatimid's warlike abilities, but rather making the spiritual point that their attempt to withstand the followers of Christianity was inherently doomed to failure. Even so, the notion of Egyptian military incompetence reoccurs in later sources.[211]

Although many writers who travelled on crusade were rather more favourable in their expressed opinions concerning native Muslims than they were towards the Turks, there is one author who diverges from this pattern. The continuator to Frutolf's chronicle, who participated in the 1101 crusade, wrote that the 'Saracens' are 'a more disgraceful people than many Turks'.[212] This statement occurs in his account of the earlier conquest of Jerusalem by Atsiz in 1073. The author does not deem it necessary to explain himself at this point; perhaps he assumed that this distinction would be obvious to his intended readership. It is therefore left to the reader to ponder his rationale. One possibility is that he, like the author of the *Gesta Francorum*, was referring to the supposed kinship that existed between the Turks and the Franks.[213] This might have led him to be more sympathetic to the Turks than to the 'Saracens'. This suggestion is not impossible, but it is not likely. Such a link is not referenced in any other part of the text, not does it seem to have been well known at this time. Another explanation that can be rejected is any notion the

---

[207] Translation taken (with only one minor modification: the rendering of the name 'Seljuk') from Peacock, *The great Seljuk empire*, p. 201.

[208] RA, p. 58; PT, p. 147.   [209] GF, p. 96; PT, p. 147.   [210] RA, p. 157.

[211] See for example: WT, vol. 2, pp. 898, 915.   [212] FE, p. 134.   [213] GF, p. 21.

Turks were perceived to be less brutal than the 'Saracens' (this reference occurs in a detailed description of the Turks despoiling the holy sites in Jerusalem).[214] A more likely explanation is that the author felt that the Turks, as newcomers to the region, might never have had any prior experience of the Christian religion and were therefore less culpable for their ignorance of Christianity than the native Muslims who had long known of the faith and yet had failed to convert.[215]

Overall, up to the siege of Jerusalem, the crusaders' treatment of Arab Muslims was ambiguous. They recognised them to be adherents of a rival religion and they encountered them in battle on occasion as Turkish auxiliaries. Still, the crusaders seem to have harboured no especial dislike of the Arabs. Bohemond evidently saw no contradiction in taking the cross whilst surrounded by Muslim troops at the siege of Amalfi. Moreover, having reached the east, pilgrims seem to have learnt of the tensions between the Arabs and Turks at a relatively early stage in the campaign and, by extension, the usefulness of this antipathy for their own endeavours. They knew the Arabs were the resentful subjects of the Turks and were consequently potential allies to be courted, rather than purely 'Saracen' foes. The crusade commanders were perfectly prepared to deal with Fatimid envoys, along with several other Arab dynasties in Syria, and they instigated these negotiations freely and on their own volition.

These rather mixed relations between Franks and Arabs permit a number of wider conclusions to be drawn concerning the crusaders' general attitudes towards Muslims. Firstly, the crusaders' determination to try and reach a diplomatic solution with the Fatimids and the Arab princes of the Near East suggests that they did not consider 'Saracens' *en bloc* to be their major enemy. They perceived their religion to be an evil doctrine, but they were generally prepared to deal peaceably with its adherents provided that they posed no obstacle to their progress. Moreover, their behaviour towards the Turks was very different from their dealings with the Arabs; demonstrating that they drew clear distinctions between these two ethnic groups and did not approach them both purely as an undifferentiated group.

It is particularly noteworthy that the crusaders made their first diplomatic approach to the Fatimids while they were at Nicaea. This was an early stage in the crusade and – aside from the defeat of Peter the Hermit – the crusaders had yet to experience a serious setback. Thus,

---

[214] *FE*, pp. 134–136.

[215] There were Christians in Central Asia and the Byzantines had long sent out missionaries to the Eurasian steppe, but this was not well known in western Christendom. Such an interpretation however is not entirely unproblematic however because the author of the *Gesta Francorum* seemed to believe that the Turks were formerly Christian. *GF*, 21.

their decision to seek an alliance was made while they were in a position of strength and was not driven by force of circumstances. Historians have often suggested or implied that the crusaders entered the Near East impelled by zeal for holy war, but were eventually compelled by the exigencies of the journey to compromise their fervour and make alliances with non-Christians. This interpretation is problematic. The crusaders were exploring diplomatic solutions from the outset and there is little to suggest that they perceived alliances or treaties with Muslims to be theologically/spiritually reprehensible.[216]

How Important Were the Turks and Arabs to the Crusaders?

Every crusade narrative, whether it was written by a participant or not, provides exhaustively detailed accounts of warfare with the Turks. Descriptions of the crusaders' encounters with this foe fill page after page. Clearly these encounters were vitally important to the crusaders' recollections and, having reflected upon this corpus of material, many historians have concluded that this was a war in which the crusaders considered themselves to be locked in binary opposition against a bitter foe – good Christian crusaders versus bad Muslims.[217] Viewed from this perspective, the defeat of Islam was central to the crusaders' purposes and they measured their righteousness against the tyranny of the Muslim 'other'. Evidence can be found to support such an argument, but it will be shown here that such a thesis does not bring the crusaders' objectives and beliefs fully into focus. This section will deal will the issue of binary opposition, considering the role Turks and Arabs played in the crusaders' thought-world and objectives.

An important predicate in this discussion is the near ubiquitous conviction – found across the First Crusade sources – that the campaign bore marked similarities with the wars of the Old Testament. For some, the battles of Judas Maccabaeus, King David, Moses and Joshua, were a source of simile and imagery; for others, the crusade was depicted as a continuation or even a reincarnation of these ancient wars. The centrality of this idea to the crusaders' identity is revealed throughout the crusade.

---

[216] Kristin Skottki has also challenged the frequently-propounded narrative that the first crusaders entered the Near East as fanatics who then moderated their views as they acclimatised themselves to local conditions. See: K. Skottki, 'Of 'pious traitors', and dangerous encounters: historiographical notions of inter-culturality in the principality of Antioch', *Journal of transcultural medieval studies* 1 (2014), 104.

[217] For discussion on this theme see: Rubenstein, *Armies of Heaven*, pp. 119–120; Loutchitskaja, 'L'image des musulmans', 721; Völkl, *Muslime – Märtyrer – Militia Christi*, pp. 167, 255 and *passim*.

The fact that during the siege of Jerusalem the army marched around the holy city in a symbolic re-enactment of Joshua's conquest of Jericho, demonstrates how deeply this notion was embedded in their sense of purpose. Later commentators were struck by this idea with equal force and Green has demonstrated that an epic German poem (c. 1120), known as the *Millstätter Exodus*, based on the first chapters of the book of Exodus, used language resonant with crusading terminology in its presentation of the events of the Exodus, effectively conflating the two.[218]

Certainly the book of Exodus seems to have been a particular source of inspiration. This is not surprising. It describes the long arduous march of God's chosen people to the Promised Land. The crusaders saw their expedition in the same way and endlessly elaborated upon this theme. Albert of Aachen, for example, described a vision experienced by a knight called Hecelo from Kinzweiler, near Aachen. In his sleep he dreamt that he had been brought to the place on Mount Sinai where Moses had received instruction from God. Then, standing on the mountain's peak, he saw Godfrey of Bouillon blessed and divinely appointed as the leader of the Christian people by two figures dressed as bishops, just as Moses had before him. He then woke up. Reflecting on this vision, Albert described Godfrey as a new Moses, ordained by God to lead His people on a journey to the Promised Land.[219]

In a similar vein to the tribulations described in the Old Testament, the problems the crusaders encountered on the road to Jerusalem were presented as challenges designed to test their faith in God. These 'tests' took many forms: cold, hunger, enemy attack, exhaustion etc. This overarching theme is present throughout the crusade narratives. A case in point is Raymond of Aguilers' report of a skirmish that took place during the siege of Antioch between Raymond of Toulouse's forces and the Turkish garrison. This engagement was precipitated by the departure of a Frankish raiding party from the crusader lines. Their absence incited the Turks to launch an attack on the diminished camp. Raymond explains that the Franks fought off this assault and compelled the Turks to flee. A company of footsoldiers then set out in pursuit, while a group of knights competed with one another to gain possession of a runaway horse. Both Frankish parties then fell prey to a Turkish counterattack and many fled, dropping their weapons and impeding one another in their flight. Raymond interpreted these events spiritually, showing how the sinfulness of these warriors had caused God to punish them and to demand their

---

[218] D. Green, *The Millstätter Exodus: A crusading epic* (Cambridge: Cambridge University Press, 1966), *passim*.

[219] AA, pp. 446–448.

repentance. These were then juxtaposed against the victorious warriors who had gone out on the raiding campaign who – presumably because of their virtue – were blessed with victory.[220] This is merely one of a number of scenarios where God is depicted using the battlefield as a challenge or tutorial device, punishing the sinful and rewarding the faithful. Raymond speaks of these challenges as divine corrections intended to draw 'His children' to penance.[221] Fulcher likewise, described the extremes of temperature and hunger experienced by his fellows explaining that they were being purified by God, like gold being passed repeatedly through furnace fires.[222] The message communicated by these authors is clear and closely parallels the message of the Old Testament: only the faithful will be able to reach Jerusalem.

The assaults of the Turks form part of this interpretive structure because they are depicted acting as the instrument of God's discipline upon the crusaders.[223] Fulcher of Chartres, for example, presents the arrival of Karbugha's army outside Antioch as a punishment for the crusaders' liaisons with prostitutes after their capture of the city.[224] In this scenario, enemy attacks are not depicted as diabolical activity, or even the consequence of unfolding political/military events, but rather God-inspired punishments and tests designed ultimately to guide His people into righteous behaviour. A similar message is evident in a report of Peter Bartholomew's vision of St Andrew following Karbugha's defeat. Through this vision St Andrew issued a warning to Count Raymond of Toulouse. He admonished him that if he does not follow the Lord's commands then he will never reach Jerusalem and, moreover, 'infidels' will be used as an instrument of God's vengeance against him, retaking those lands which the crusaders had already seized.[225] Again, in this case, the enemy is not set up in binary opposition to the crusaders – as an 'evil' counterweight to the Franks' godly virtue. Rather, the Turks are shown as divine scourges used to correct the crusaders' sinfulness, failings, and evil behaviour. Daimbert of Pisa made a similar point in his letter to the pope, written in September 1099, claiming that the siege of Antioch was a test through which the crusading army was humbled and stripped of its pride (*superbia*).[226]

---

[220] See also Riley-Smith, *The First Crusade and the idea of crusading*, pp. 112–113.
[221] RA, pp. 50–54 (quote 54).   [222] FC, p. 226.
[223] Incidentally, the idea that non-Christian enemies could serve as a form of divine punishment is widely referenced in medieval sources. Bede presents the arrival of the Saxons in early-medieval England in much the same way: *Bede's Ecclesiastical History*, p. 52. For further discussion see: S. Kangas, 'Deus vult: violence and suffering as a means of salvation during the First Crusade', *Medieval history writing and crusading ideology*, ed. T. Lehtonen, K. Jensen et al. (Helsinki: Finnish Literature Society, 2005), pp. 169–170.
[224] FC, p. 243.   [225] RA, p. 87.   [226] Kb, p. 169.

Naturally the connection between faithfulness to God and victory in war was not unique to the crusade, but was widely referenced throughout the medieval period. Charlemagne's counsellor Alcuin explained this connection succinctly when he connected personal (interior) sin with military (external) failure, writing: 'external enemies have power because of interior enemies'.[227] The crusade narratives manifest the same conviction, with the distinction that the crusade itself is described as a process of spiritual instruction – of which the Turks are part–whose culmination was Jerusalem.

The crusaders' ability to continue their advance through the Levant was understood to be the product of an ongoing spiritual conversation between the pilgrims and God. Intercessors such as St Andrew, the Virgin Mary, and – following his death – Ademar of Le Puy are described as appearing in visions whilst Jesus Himself is said to have visited Peter Bartholomew. Faithfulness and virtue were deemed to bring them one step closer to the holy city, whilst sinfulness and vice blocked their path. This paradigm was a close match for the experiences of the Jews on their journey to the Promised Land, as outlined in the Old Testament. This dialogue between man and God was given as the sole reason for the campaign's success, overriding all strategic, tactical, and diplomatic considerations. Turks and other enemies were understood simply as obstacles set up intentionally by God to test their faith.

This point is vital because it helps to identify the main 'other' for the crusade. The crusaders did not measure their conduct self-confidently against that of the Turks, but negatively against the Christian ideal, being fully aware of their own failings when set against the example of Christ. They rarely stressed their own virtue over Turkish vice, but tended rather to underline how little their conduct reflected the moral exemplars found in scripture. Thus their 'other' was neither the Turks nor Arabs, but God Himself; a 'positive other' whose example they aspired to reach, rather than a 'negative other' whose vice served to underline their virtues. Raymond of Aguilers, in particular, does not spare either himself or his fellows when he describes their sinfulness and failings. Even the sins committed by his master, Count Raymond of Toulouse, are discussed in detail.[228] It was presumably for this reason that he referred to the crusaders as 'His beggars' (pauperes).[229]

The same structure is apparent in the biblical accounts of the Jewish people's journey to the Promised Land. They too fought many wars against the peoples they encountered but these foes were not presented as their evil 'other'. The Old Testament rarely does more than mention

---

[227] Alcuin of York, 'Epistolae', p. 55.
[228] For an example see: RA, p. 91.   [229] RA, p. 102.

their existence and certainly it does not dwell upon hostile representations.

If the crusade was transposed into a theatrical performance there would be two main groups of protagonists: the crusaders and God. They would dominate both the stage and script. All other characters would play roles that were dependent on this relationship. St Andrew and the other heavenly figures who appeared to the crusaders would form part of God's communication with the Franks while prayers, fasting, and processions were the channels by which the crusaders appealed to God. The Turks and Arabs, along with the various topographical/climatic problems encountered by the crusaders, were the challenges and punishments meted out to the pilgrims by God. In this way, when attempting to frame the crusaders' attitude towards their enemies, it is important to note that they played only an auxiliary role in their thought-world. They were in large part a side-effect or consequence of their wider relationship with God.

Conversion, Evil, and the Problem of Hatred

> Baligant sees his banner fall
> And Mohammed's standard abandoned;
> It begins to dawn on the emir
> that he is wrong and Charlemagne is right.
> Silence falls on the pagans of Arabia.
> *Chanson de Roland*[230]

It was well known among the Franks that back in the fifth century their people had originally converted to Christianity following a closely fought battle against the Alemans. The renowned Gregory of Tours described how the Frankish King Clovis cried out to God during this conflict, imploring Him for aid and offering Him his spiritual allegiance in return. Having defeated his foe, Clovis later fulfilled his promise by being baptised; an act that – so the story goes – swiftly led to the conversion of his people.[231] By the eleventh century this tale had become deeply embedded in Frankish culture as a foundation myth for their people, one that was central to their collective identity. This legend is important for this present discussion because it establishes a connection between combat and voluntary conversion. In this case, military victory was understood by

---

[230] Translation from *SR*, p. 153.
[231] Gregory of Tours, 'Decem Libri Historiarum', *MGH: Scriptores rerum Merovingicarum*, ed. B. Krusch (Hanover, 1951), pp. 74–76.

Clovis' Franks to be indisputable proof of the rectitude of the Christian religion; sufficient to bring about their conversion.

This conviction that voluntary conversion can be brought about through warfare is significant because many later authors projected a similar expectation upon other non-Christian peoples, including Muslims. Especially in *chansons* and epic verse, authors concocted colourful stories in which 'Saracen' or Slavic foes initially march proudly against Christendom, boasting of their own gods and deriding Christianity. Nevertheless, as they suffer defeat after defeat, they increasingly come to question the efficacy of their own faith and slowly acknowledge the validity of Christianity. Such tales inevitably conclude with either the death or conversion of their leaders.

In these sources, warfare is presented as an evangelical tool, leading unbelievers to Christianity through a process that could be described as voluntary-conversion-through-force. To take one example, the *chanson* '*Fierabras*', within a tale of Charlemagne's wars against Islam, contains a lengthy description of a duel between Oliver (the Christian champion) and the 'Saracen' king Fierabras. This duel is not simply a contest of arms but is presented as a test of the veracity of the two religions and when Oliver finds himself on the back foot he cries out:

> As truly noble Lord, as I believe and heed You
> And everything I've said about You, I beseech you
> To help me end the pride of this deriding heathen,
> So *he* can see Your love and Your love can redeem him.[232]

The outcome of the contest then is accepted as clinching confirmation of the victor's faith.[233] Consequently, when Oliver wins the battle, Fierabras immediately sees the error of his own faith, which had not supported him in this contest, and requests baptism. The early *chansons* contain many tales of this kind; frequently referencing the expectation that Muslims will interpret their defeats as proof of the hollowness of their own religion and, in some cases, the truth of Christianity.

This concept of voluntary-conversion-through-force is important because it manifests itself frequently in chronicles of the First Crusade and in some places this conviction is stated very baldly.[234] It is

---

[232] Translation from *Fierabras and Floripas*, p. 71. (Newth's primary text for his translation was: *Fierabras: chanson de geste*, p. 30). For further discussion on the impact of *chansons* on the ideas of the first crusaders see: Bennett, 'First crusaders' images of Muslims', 101–117; Meredith Jones, 'The conventional Saracen', 222; Daniel, *Heroes and Saracens*, 244.

[233] Daniel, *Heroes and Saracens*, 167–173, 211.

[234] In an excellent article, Loutchitskaja has already drawn some strong links between the crusaders' approach to conversion and the *chansons de geste*, focusing specifically

referenced for example in an account of Raymond of Toulouse's troubled crossing of Slavonia in February 1097. In an attempt to find anything good to say about this journey, during which the crusading army came under repeated attack, Raymond of Aguilers wrote that it was 'for the cause, I suppose, that the Lord wanted His army to pass through Slavonia so that the brutish people, who are ignorant of God, would recognise the virtue and long suffering of His warriors, and either recover hereafter from savagery or as unrepentant reprobates be cast down to God's judgement'.[235] Thus, Raymond presents the crusaders' virtuous conduct in battle as a quasi-evangelical activity, which some Slavs would recognise as proof of the truth of the Christian message.

Albert of Aachen made a similar point describing the events surrounding the battle of Ascalon (12 August 1099). He explained how the governor of Ramla had struck a treaty with Godfrey of Bouillon soon after Jerusalem's fall. Albert then explained how this leader had offered Godfrey advice on the Fatimids' warcraft before joining the Franks in the ensuing battle. Albert then reports the rumour that 'after he [the governor of Ramla] had seen the strength and triumph of the Christians he received the favour of baptism'.[236] In this case at least, the connection is clear: the valour and victory of Christian crusaders was deemed proof in its own right of the rectitude of the Christian religion.[237]

---

upon the reports of Peter the Hermit's embassage to Karbugha and (their rival offers of conversion) and the tales of the conversion of 'Firuz'. Loutchitskaja, 'L'idée de conversion', 39–53. See also Leclercq, *Portraits* croisés, pp. 472–488. Flori similarly stresses the influence of the *chansons* upon the crusaders' general approach to Muslims see: Flori, *Pierre l'Hermite*, pp. 221–225. More recently, in a similar vein to this present argument, he has stressed that the crusaders sought to demonstrate to unbelievers the falsity of their faith through victory in arms, see: J. Flori, 'Jérusalem terrestre, celeste et spirituelle: Trois facteurs de sacralisation de la première croisade', *Jerusalem the golden: The origins and impact of the First Crusade*, ed. S. Edgington and L. García-Guijarro, *Outremer: Studies in the Crusades and the Latin East III* (Turnhout: Brepols, 2014), pp. 44–49. For analysis on the use of 'compulsion' within Christian conversion, including discussion on Clovis' conversion see: L. G. Duggan, '"For force is not of God"? compulsion and conversion from Yahweh to Charlemagne', *Varieties of religious conversion in the Middle Ages*, ed. J. Muldoon (Gainesville: University Press of Florida, 1997), pp. 49–62; Buc, *Holy War*, pp. 220–234. Throop discusses instances in later sources where the outcome of battle was perceived as an evangelical tool: S. Throop, 'Combat and conversion: inter-faith dialogue in twelfth-century crusading narratives', *Medieval encounters* 13 (2007), 318–319, 322. See also S. Kangas, 'First in prowess and faith: the great encounter in twelfth century crusader narratives', *Cultural encounters during the Crusades*, ed. K. Jensen, K. Salonen and H. Vogt (Odense: University Press of Southern Denmark, 2013), pp. 119–134.

[235] RA, p. 37.   [236] Translation taken from AA, p. 461.

[237] For another example see RM, p. 107: Similarly, the continuator of Frutolf's chronicle described the First Crusade's purpose with reference to Luke 15:4 (the parable of the lost sheep). In this context the crusaders are presented, like the biblical shepherd, to be attempting to bring a lost sheep (the peoples of the east) back into the fold. See: FE,

In other cases, this conversion process is explained by crusading authors at greater length and in more detail, often within passages containing imagined debates between the Turkish leaders. To take one example, the *Gesta Francorum* contains a sub-plot which charts the growing realisation among the Turks that the Christians have the full support of the true God. The storyline runs as follows: messengers arrive in Khurasan from the Turks in Antioch, reporting the crusaders' early victories. The Turkish general Karbugha receives this news and then decides to confront the Christians. He assembles a great army. When this force draws near to Antioch, Karbugha appoints an emir (Ahmed ibn Marwan)[238] to command the citadel in Antioch. Hearing of the Christians' weakness, Karbugha mocks them but is rebuked by his mother who warns him that the Christian God will fight decisively for His people. She prophetically foretells his defeat, but he ignores her advice and persists in seeking a confrontation.[239] Having arrived at Antioch, Peter the Hermit and a translator then seek an audience with Karbugha during which they offer to baptise him. He refuses scornfully and says that they should renounce their own faith and become Turks. In the subsequent battle Karbugha becomes fearful and his troops flee in terror. He dies shortly afterwards. Karbugha's emir, Ahmed ibn Marwan, commanding the Antiochene garrison, having witnessed these acts, then converts freely along with several of his fellows.[240] The message communicated by this chain of events is plain. It suggests that a dawning awareness was spreading among the Turks that, on one hand, the crusaders had the full support of God who would grant them victory while, on the other, the trust they placed in their own beliefs was unfounded and would render them no aid.[241] As this realisation took root among the Turks, it was anticipated that some would acknowledge it to be the truth (e.g. Karbugha's mother) and convert (e.g. the commander of the citadel) while others (e.g. Karbugha) would persist in their defiance and be scattered or destroyed.

132. For discussion upon similar ideas in the *chansons de geste* see: J. Tolan, 'The dream of conversion: baptizing pagan kings in the crusade epics', *Sons of Ishmael: Muslims through European eyes in the Middle Ages* (Gainesville, FL: University Press of Florida, 2008), pp. 66–74.

[238] Kamal al-Din, 'Extraits de la Chronique d'Alep', p. 582.

[239] For some interesting discussion on medieval Christian representations of Muslims foretelling their own defeat see: Leclercq, *Portraits croisés*, pp. 449–456.

[240] *GF*, pp. 49–56, 66–70. Kamal al-Din reports that his name was Ahmed ibn Marwan and that he was subsequently escorted to Aleppan territory. Kamal al-Din, 'Extraits de la Chronique d'Alep', pp. 582–583. As Tolan points out, in later verse histories describing Karbugha, he is also said to have converted. Tolan, 'The dream of conversion', pp. 66–74.

[241] See also Leclercq, *Portraits croisés*, pp. 456–464.

The essential features of the *Gesta Francorum*'s story are replicated in other accounts. Albert of Aachen's chronicle (which had little or no connection to the *Gesta* tradition) contains a similar tale. He describes the despair of Qilij Arslan, ruler of Nicaea, and Yaghi Siyan, ruler of Antioch, at the crusaders' early advances. Yaghi Siyan then requests help from the 'king of Khurasan'. This king ignores their warning about Christian valour and sends Karbugha to confront the crusade. Karbugha is repeatedly warned by Qilij Arslan that the Christians are extremely dangerous enemies, but Karbugha ignores his advice and places his trust in his own deity and the advice of soothsayers. As he gathers his army, Albert describes how his troops treat him like a god. Having reached Antioch, Peter the Hermit gives him the option to convert but he refuses. Later, after battle is joined between the Turks and Crusaders, Karbugha is rendered motionless by God and his consequent failure to direct his forces leads to his defeat.[242]

Albert's account is not as explicit as the *Gesta* and it does not conclude with any conversions. Even so, his message is similar. He communicates the idea that the falsity of the Turks' beliefs was laid bare by the Christian valour. Again, Karbugha is said to have ignored the warnings both of his peers and Peter the Hermit and to have demanded instead that they become Turks. The spiritual significance of his actions is underlined by the adjectives that are applied to him. He is shown in these and other accounts to have been filled with 'stubbornness' (*contumax*) and 'pride' (*superbia*).[243] These are spiritually loaded words, appearing frequently in the Bible. In the Old Testament book of Samuel, King Saul was described as 'stubborn' for his refusal to carry out the will of God (Samuel 15: 23). Psalm 104, likewise, describes how pride creates a distance between man and God. These then are terms used to describe those who refuse God's commands and persist in following their own designs.

Fulcher of Chartres stated this plainly when he explained how Karbugha was put to flight following the defeat of his great army writing, 'because he endeavoured to make war against God. The Lord perceiving this from afar destroyed utterly his pomp and power'.[244] In general, the crusade emerges through these stories as an evangelical enterprise, whose conspicuous successes are presented as an unambiguous statement of transcendental fact, disproving the beliefs of their foes and underlining the truth of Christianity.[245]

---

[242] AA, pp. 102, 136, 194, 258–267, 318, 330–332.
[243] AA, pp. 254, 258, 330, 320; *GF*, 66.   [244] FC, pp. 256.
[245] Discussing Fulcher's chronicle, Cole has interpreted Fulcher's presentation of Karbugha's continued resistance to the crusade as evidence that he was arguing for the

The inclusion of these sub-plots should not imply that the crusaders initially embarked upon their campaign with missionary intent. They could not have foreseen from the outset either that they would be so vigorously resisted or that they would win victories in battle against such insurmountable odds.[246] Moreover, the charters and letters produced during the crusade's recruitment phase do not list conversion among its objectives. During the campaign there was only a scattering of localised attempts to win converts directly; either through preaching, persuasion, or force.[247] It is more likely that, following the crusade, the survivors began to ponder the enormity of their victories and the effect they imagined these would have upon their enemies. These stories, which are very similar in nature, even though the texts themselves are largely unrelated, seem to represent the crusaders' shared hope that the Turks (and in some cases Fatimids) would come to see their own defeats as evidence of the falsity of their own religion. Certainly, as shown earlier, this kind of speculation would have been entirely in accordance with the long-standing conviction that the outcome of battle is decided by God and constituted proof of the Christian message.[248] Time would prove of course that the Turks did not convert en-masse, but these stories suggest that in the heady days following the fall of Jerusalem this end was in sight. Such a conviction would only have been enhanced by the repeated promises

'indiscriminate extermination of the pagan enemy' on the grounds that Karbugha symbolised an obstinate refusal to yield Antioch and acknowledge Christian supremacy. P. Cole, "'O God, the heathen have come into your inheritance" (Ps. 78.1) The theme of religious pollution in crusade documents, 1095–1188', *Crusaders and Muslims in twelfth century Syria*, ed. M. Shazmiller, The medieval Mediterranean I (Leiden: Brill, 1993), pp. 88–89.

[246] As Riley-Smith has shown, the crusaders' confidence in both divine support and their spiritual interpretation of their victories seems to have grown over time. Riley-Smith, *The First Crusade and the idea of crusading*, p. 99.

[247] Historians have taken slightly different stances on the crusaders' approaches to what might be called 'direct' conversion. For discussion on this subject see: Riley-Smith, *The First Crusade and the idea of Crusading*, 109–111; Kedar, *Crusade and mission*, pp. 57–65; A. Cutler, 'The First Crusade and the idea of "conversion"', *The Muslim World* 58 (1968), 57–71; Flori, 'Première croisades et conversion', pp. 449–451; B. Kedar, 'Multidirectional conversion in the Frankish Levant', *Varieties of religious conversion in the Middle Ages*, ed. J. Muldoon (Gainesville: University of Florida Press, 1997), pp. 190–199. Mastnak has advanced the view that the crusade was not concerned with conversion, Mastnak, *Crusading peace*, p. 122. For further discussion on the Christian accounts of the reported conversion of the Turkish traitor who helped to the crusaders to gain access into Antioch see: Skottki, 'Of 'Pious Traitors', 80–94. For a summary of the general consensus on the question of the crusaders' approach to conversion see: Loutchitskaja, 'L'idée de conversion', 40.

[248] Flori makes a similar point observing that the crusaders may have hoped that their victories would bring about a sweeping, or at least a partial, conversion of the Muslims. He also stresses the importance of the *Chansons de Geste* in forming this conviction. See: Flori, 'Première croisades et conversion', pp. 449–455.

made in the spring of 1099 by the Muslim rulers of many Levantine coastal cities that if the Franks should take Jerusalem then they would either serve them faithfully or even convert to Christianity.[249] In addition, the mere fact of the crusaders' conquest of Jerusalem was perceived by participants as undisputable proof of the falsity of paganism; one which – so they believed – all unbelievers could not fail to recognise. Incidentally, the growing realisation in later decades that *in fact* the Turks had not converted may explain why later authors such as William of Tyre, who drew heavily upon the First Crusade narratives, did not include these imagined conversations between Turkish leaders in their chronicles – they knew that this was an aspiration that would not reach its fulfilment.

Although some elements of these stories (in particular the reported conversations between Turkish leaders in distant lands) must be sheer fantasy, these tales should not be dismissed too lightly as purely figments of the crusaders' imaginations. There is a foundation of fact here that is widely referenced in the sources of many cultures. Drawing upon these materials it is not disputed that Yaghi-Siyan *did* appeal for aid. Karbugha *did* respond by raising a large army. Peter the Hermit *did* visit Karbugha before the battle and the Turks *were* subsequently defeated against all the odds. Even the crusaders' reports of Karbugha's haughty response to Peter the Hermit's offer of conversation may contain a grain of truth.[250] Ultimately, the crusaders seem to have formed their narratives through the following process: they studied their enemies and their behaviour; they then interpreted the Turks' actions through the lens of their own spiritual ideas and evangelical expectations; and finally – when producing their chronicles – they filled in any gaps with imagined scenarios that explicated their interpretation of events for their audience.

This discussion on conversion is important because it establishes a fundamental aspect of the crusaders' approach towards their Turkish opponents. If we remain focused on the earlier-mentioned stories reported in the *Gesta Francorum* and Albert of Aachen's *Historia*, it can be seen that the Turks described in these tales can be divided roughly into two groups. The members of the first group are typified by Karbugha but also include other leaders such as the 'king of Khurasan' and are described

---

[249] See later in this chapter.

[250] Turan has argued that Karbugha's counter-proposal at his meeting with Peter the Hermit (that the crusaders cast off their religion, become Turkish warriors and be richly rewarded or alternatively be dragged away in chains) bears close relation to standard contemporary Turkish assertions of their right to world dominance. If this was the case then the *Gesta Francorum*'s account of Karbugha's words may have some basis in reality. Turan, 'The ideal of world domination', 87–88; *GF*, 67. Nevertheless, Mecit challenges the notion that the Turks still maintained a concept of world domination by this stage in their history. Mecit, *The Rum Seljuqs*, p. 5.

with the utmost scorn and hostility. They are the pantomime villains of these accounts and all kinds of dastardly behaviour are ascribed to them; for example, the manufacture of chains with which to lead the Christians into captivity.[251] The second group is presented very differently. This includes Karbugha's mother, who is said to have warned her son about the inevitable victory of the Christian God, and Qilij Arslan, who likewise advised him about the potency of the Christian army. These individuals are presented in a far more sympathetic manner. Albert describes Qilij Arslan as 'magnificent' (*magnificus*), 'a man of marvellous and great diligence', 'a very noble man, but of gentile beliefs', who also felt a deep sense of grief at the defeat of his men.[252] The *Gesta* describes Karbugha's mother as a wise, diligent, and loving woman.[253] Also included in this group is Ahmed ibn Marwan who was given command over the citadel of Antioch and who later converted to Christianity. The *Gesta* presents him as 'truthful, gentle and peaceful' (*verax, mitis, pacificus*); a highly positive profile.[254] Naturally, these descriptions – positive or negative – are imagined and not based on personal experience. It is unlikely that these authors had any personal experience of these individuals – except possibly Ahmed – and the only known crusaders to have met Karbugha were Peter the Hermit and his interpreter Herluin.[255] It is far more likely that these Turkish characters exist rather as 'types' within the crusaders' thought-world.

The differences between these two groups are revealed in both texts through the fact that they are opposed to one another. Qilij Arslan and Karbugha's mother are both said to have realised that there was a special significance to the crusaders' victories that needed to be recognised and, by extension, to have attempted to restrain Karbugha. Karbugha, on the other hand, is shown to have batted away their advice and to have suffered defeat as a consequence. There is a typology at work here in which these various individuals are playing well established roles. Their differing responses to the victories are reminiscent in some ways of the New Testament parable of the sower (Matthew: 13, 1–9). This parable is generally understood to describe the receptiveness of human beings to the word of God, through the analogy of a sower spreading seed upon various types of ground. Some seeds fall in good soil and thrive, while other seeds either do not take root at all, or grow a little before being

---

[251] AA, p. 258.   [252] AA, pp. 32, 94, 136, 254.

[253] *GF*, pp. 53–55.   [254] *GF*, p. 51.

[255] The Antiochene emir who converted to Christianity is an exception here. He evidently interacted closely with several crusaders although this does not guarantee that the chroniclers themselves ever met him. For discussion on Karbugha's mother see the Introduction.

either choked by weeds or scorched by the sun. The message is clear: some will respond to the word of God and others will not. The described responses of these Turkish elites fall into very similar categories. Some (Karbugha's mother and Ahmed ibn Marwan) are shown to understand the full significance of the crusaders' victories and recognise it as proof of the truth of the Christian religion; Ahmed ibn Marwan even converts (in some later *chansons* retelling the crusade, Karbugha's mother also converts).[256] Qilij Arslan does not convert and there is absolutely no doubt in either chronicle that he remained the crusade's enemy, yet he is said to have recognised the power and valour of the Christians. The positive personal qualities ascribed to these individuals are in direct correlation to their acknowledgement of the crusade's spiritual significance. The opposite is naturally the case with Karbugha himself whose dominant characteristic, ascribed by these narrators, is his dogged refusal to accept this truth and to reject the sage warnings of those closest to him.

These typological tales establish the theological lens through which the authors of the crusade narrative viewed their Turkish opponents. They were viewed as a non-Christian people who had suddenly been confronted with unassailable proof of the validity of Christianity. The crusaders expected some among their ranks to recognise this truth, whilst others would inevitably persist in their unbelief. Thus the campaign was perceived in hindsight as a ground-breaking, if belligerent, evangelical enterprise, introducing a new people to the Christian message.[257]

This theological viewpoint is important because it carries an array of attached expectations. Firstly, as the earlier characterisations of Qilij Arslan and Ahmed ibn Marwan demonstrate, these authors were prepared to project positive – albeit imagined – personal qualities onto their enemies. Whilst these characterisations were, as shown earlier, component parts in the earlier-mentioned typographical morality tales, they still demonstrate the crusaders' readiness to accept the principle that non-Christians could possess praiseworthy virtues.[258] Secondly, these tales reveal the crusaders' recognition that the Turks were human beings

---

[256] His conversion is also mentioned in the crusaders' letter to Pope Urban II, written in September 1098 (*Kb*, p. 164). C. Sweetenham, 'What really happened to Eurvin de Créel's donkey? Anecdotes in sources for the First Crusade', *Writing the early Crusades: Text, transmission and memory*, ed. M. Bull and D. Kempf (Woodbridge: Boydell, 2014), p. 87. For discussion on the descriptions of Karbugha and his relationship with his mother in the later *chansons* (as well as tales of both Karbugha and his mother converting) see: Leclercq, *Portraits croisés*, pp. 492–513.

[257] Riley-Smith has discussed the notion that crusading could be viewed as a way of loving one's enemies, drawing upon the Augustinian notion of parents disciplining their children. Riley-Smith, *The First Crusade and the idea of Crusading*, p. 27.

[258] Schwinges by contrast argues that the crusaders generally only recognised military virtues in their enemies. Schwinges, *Kreuzzugsideologie*, pp. 143–144; R.C. Schwinges,

and manifestations of God's creation.[259] This is shown plainly through the earlier discussion. If they were not viewed in this way then they would not have been deemed capable of conversion or, by extension, of responding to God's teaching (as understood by the crusaders). Moreover, the Turks' and Franks' shared humanity is emphasised repeatedly, both explicitly and implicitly. At one point in the *Gesta Francorum* the author affirmed the idea that these two peoples were related, stating that only the Turks' adherence to a foreign religion separated them from their Frankish cousins.[260] Later in the fictional conversation between Karbugha and his mother, Karbugha asks whether Bohemond and Tancred are 'gods of the Franks' (*Francorum dii*), but his mother responds that they are mortal 'like all other people' (*sicut alii omnes*).[261] This passage was clearly designed both as a moment of comedy and to praise Bohemond and Tancred, but it is also a statement founded on an assumption of shared humanity. The difference she identifies between these Christian warriors and the Turks is their religious adherence and, by extension, the support granted to them by God.[262]

If the crusaders were prepared to accept both the Turks' shared humanity and their personal virtues, the same was not true of their religion. They believed them to be living under the profoundly malign influence of a non-Christian religion.[263] The various terms applied to the Turks, such as: 'unbelieving' (*incredulus*),[264] 'blasphemous' (*prophanus*),[265] 'excommunicated' (*excommunicatus*),[266] 'erring religion' (*ritus erroris*),[267] or 'accursed' (*execratus*)[268] carry a similar message. They all describe a group who, either by compulsion or mistaken choice, had aligned

---

'William of Tyre, the Muslim enemy and the problem of tolerance', *Tolerance and intolerance: Social conflict in the age of the Crusades*, ed. M. Gervers and J. Powell (Syracuse, NY: Syracuse University Press, 2001), p. 127. He does however note some exceptions, see: Schwinges, *Kreuzzugsideologie*, p. 152.

[259] For a contrasting view which argues that the crusaders sought to dehumanise their enemy see: Cole, 'O God, the Heathen have come into your inheritance', p. 89.

[260] *GF*, p. 21.   [261] *GF*, pp. 55–56.

[262] Incidentally, this passage from the *Gesta Francorum* closely parallels part of an inscription found in Bohemond's mausoleum which reads as follows: 'I can't call him a man; I won't call him a God'. The evident similarities between these two texts supplies another indicator that the *Gesta*'s author was prepared to relay the laudatory discourse propounded by the prince and his immediate circle. For the inscription see: A. Epstein, 'The date and significance of the cathedral of Canosa in Apulia, South Italy', *Dumbarton Oaks papers* 37 (1983), 86.

[263] See also Sweetenham, 'Crusaders in a hall of mirrors', p. 56.

[264] *GF*, pp. 20, 88.   [265] *GF*, p. 62; RA, p. 157.

[266] *GF*, p. 19. In this context, 'excommunicated' seems to mean that this group was literally cut off from communion with the Church. For wider discussion see: Nilsson, 'Gratian on pagans', p. 156.

[267] AA, p. 434.   [268] PT, p. 108; *GF*, p. 66.

themselves with an 'evil' belief system. This impression is confirmed by the descriptions of mosques where they are presented as houses of the Devil, which underline the far harder attitude taken towards the Islamic religion.[269] Again, the widely-understood distinction made by contemporaries (see chapter 1) between non-Christian peoples and their beliefs is much in evidence. Furthermore, whilst non-Christian Turks and Arabs were evidently deemed capable of virtuous behaviour, their beliefs were also presented as leaving them dangerously exposed to demonic suggestion and sinful temptation. This idea is communicated clearly in the *Hystoria Antiochiae atque Ierusolymarum* which speaks of a bearded old Turkish warrior who was captured by the crusaders and then promised to convert. The crusaders duly permitted him to join them, giving him the name *Hilarius*. Nevertheless, the author explains that because his race is 'impious' (*impius*) and 'unbelieving' (*infidelis*) the Devil was able to enter his heart the moment he had doubts about the crusading army and convince him to flee to Turkish-held Aleppo.[270] This fascinating story speaks of the authors' conviction that the sinfulness of the Turkish race as a whole rendered this individual acutely vulnerable to demonic influence, even after his – admittedly very recent – conversion.[271]

Likewise, the conviction that non-Christian beliefs could leave their adherents vulnerable to bodily temptations is also much in evidence.[272] This was a long-standing view, present in both Eastern and western Christian traditions, whose proponents had long advanced the idea that 'Saracens' were unrestrained in their enjoyment of bodily pleasures. Scarfe Beckett has shown that this belief may date back to Jerome's association of the 'Saracens' with the worship of Venus.[273] This theme emerges both in the *Gesta Francorum* and Peter Tudebode's chronicle, which contain a letter purporting to have been written by Karbugha to the

---

[269] PT, p. 77; *GF*, p. 42, 75.

[270] *HAI*, p. 48. For recent discussion on this source see: L. Russo, 'The Monte Cassino tradition of the First Crusade: from the *Chronica Monasterii Casinensis* to the *Hystoria de Via et Recuperatione Antiochiae atque Ierusolymarum*', *Writing the early Crusades: Text, transmission and memory*, ed. M. Bull and D. Kempf (Woodbridge: Boydell, 2014), pp. 53–62.

[271] Orderic Vitalis tells a similar story about a 'Saracen' convert, although in other places he gives examples of Muslims who have converted successfully and become devout Christians. See: OV, vol. 4, p. 22; (vol. 5), p. 158.

[272] Daniel, *Islam and the West*, pp. 158–185.

[273] Scarfe Beckett, Anglo-*Saxon perceptions*, pp. 1, 212–217; Ducellier, *Chrétiens d'Orient*, pp. 160–161. This was to become a long-standing association but it is worth noting that Muslim authors also connected their co-religionists with the planet Venus seemingly because they worshipped on a Friday (the day of Venus). M. Ryan, *A kingdom of stargazers: Astrology and authority in the late medieval crown of Aragon* (Ithaca, NY: Cornell University Press, 2011), p. 170. See also Petrus Alfonsi, *Dialogue against the Jews*, p. 156.

caliph, sultan and knights of 'Khurasan'. Following the salutation he cel-
ebrates with his addressees their shared love of gluttony, wanton luxury,
and destruction. The implication of this passage is that the unbelieving
Turks revelled in their sinful and ungodly passions.[274] A similar message
is communicated within accounts of Peter the Hermit's diplomatic mission to Karbugha outside the walls of Antioch. Having demanded that the
Turks convert and withdraw, Karbugha is said to have made a counter-
proposal. He offered land, titles, and wives to any crusader who was
prepared to deny his faith; thus the adoption of a non-Christian religion
is equated with the allure of material riches and the satiation of earthly
desires.[275] The perceived link between non-Christian religious adherence
and increased vulnerability to sinful living is clear through both examples.
Likewise, Turks who die in a state of unbelief are described as passing
straight to Hell.[276]

* * *

Changing ground slightly, a factor contextualising the crusaders' attitudes towards Muslims is their readiness to create treaties and alliances
with a variety of Turkish and Arab leaders.[277] As shown earlier, while the
Turks were viewed as an obstacle to the crusade's progress, their total
military defeat was not its main object. On many occasions the crusaders
attempted to secure their passage through Arab or Turkish territory
peacefully, by treaty, and without bloodshed. At other times co-operative
agreements were established voluntarily by both sides. These détentes
are listed in Table 2. Some of these relationships broke down, leading
to mistrust and hostility; a case in point being Baldwin of Boulogne's
agreements with Turkish rulers in the vicinity of Edessa (see Table 2).
Nevertheless, this was not always the outcome and, to take one example,
after the conquest of Antioch, Godfrey of Bouillon formed an alliance
with the Omar, ruler of Azaz; later fending-off an attack by Ridwan of
Aleppo against the town.[278]

An important aspect of these agreements is that the crusaders generally
made them entirely voluntarily and not necessarily through force of circumstances. There were clearly some cities which they were determined
to seize (Nicaea, Antioch, and Jerusalem), and some of the crusade's
leaders attempted to carve out principalities for themselves, but often

---

[274] PT, p. 92.
[275] PT, p. 109; Tolan, *Saracens*, p. 113. For another example see Peter Tudebode's account
of the captivity and execution of Rainald Porchet, PT, p. 80.
[276] *GF*, p. 40.
[277] The major work on this subject is: Köhler, *Alliances and treaties, passim*.
[278] RA, pp. 88–89; AA, pp. 344–354.

Table 2 *Agreements and treaties formed between crusaders and Muslims, 1097–1099 (excluding negotiations concerning the surrender of towns and castles) This table includes only those agreements which are mentioned in participant narratives*

Date	Agreement	Main Source
May/June 1097 – May 1099	Fatimids For detailed discussion on the Franks negotiations with the Fatimids see earlier.	See earlier
Spring-Summer 1098	Balak and Balduk Shortly after Baldwin of Boulogne became count of Edessa, the local Turkish ruler Balduk offered both to sell the town of Samosata to the Franks for 10,000 bezants and to enter Baldwin's service. Baldwin originally refused but was later persuaded to agree to these terms. Baldwin also asked Balduk for hostages, but he prevaricated in handing them over. Subsequently, another neighbouring Turkish ruler Balak ibn Bahram approached Baldwin suggesting that they should both attack a 'Saracen' town that was refusing to pay him tribute. Baldwin agreed and prepared for an attack but Balak attempted to play both sides and suggested to the townspeople that they ask Balduk for aid. Balduk duly arrived but the citizens were so horrified by the sight of the approaching Frankish army that they decided to flee. Balduk then fled back to Baldwin pretending that he had never intended any disloyalty and Baldwin accepted his excuses. Both warriors later joined Karbugha's army. After the defeat of Karbugha's army, Balak offered to serve Baldwin and to hand over the fortress of *'Amacha'*, but Albert claims that this offer was only made in an attempt to lure Baldwin into an ambush. Balduk also attempted to re-ingratiate himself with Baldwin but was executed.	AA, pp. 176–178, 260, 360–362. See also: Köhler, *Alliances and treaties*, pp. 37–38.
Summer 1098	Omar of Azaz Omar of Azaz was in rebellion against Ridwan of Aleppo, who was moving to besiege him in Azaz. Omar sought support from Godfrey of Bouillon who later came to his aid along with several other crusade commanders, who drove Ridwan away after suffering some casualties in a surprise attack upon the army's rear.	RA, pp. 88–89; AA, pp. 344–354; Kamal al-Din, 'Extraits de la Chronique d'Alep', p. 586.
January 1099	Banu Munqidh of Shaizar While the crusaders were besieging Ma'arra they were approached by the Munqidhs of Shaizar. Their envoys offered the crusaders safe	GF, pp. 81–82; RA, p. 103.

Table 2 (*cont.*)

Date	Agreement	Main Source
	passage along with financial support. They also promised to sell the crusaders food and horses. Ali ibn Munqidh was subsequently able to manage the crusaders' transit through his lands reasonably effectively.	
February 1099	Jana ad-Daulah of Homs	*GF*, p. 82; RA,
	Jana ad-Daulah sent messengers to the crusaders, who made an agreement on his behalf. He promised that he would do them no harm and offered them horses and gold. They in turn promised to respect his lands and interests.	pp. 103, 107.
Early 1099	The emir of Maraclea	*GF*, p. 84
	Observing the sustained crusader advance, the emir of Maraclea made a treaty with the Franks, permitting them entry into the town. He also raised their banner over his ramparts.	
March 1099	Jabala	*GF*, p. 84; RA,
	The crusaders began to besiege Jabala but having received news from Raymond of Tripoli that a relief force would arrive imminently to attack the main army in their encampment outside Arqa they made a treaty with the emir in which he granted them gold and horses in return for their withdrawal from his walls. Albert of Aachen claimed that Raymond of Tripoli had knowingly issued a false warning about this relief force having been paid a large sum of money by the inhabitants of Jabala.	p. 111; AA, pp. 380–383.[279]
May 1099	Banu Ammar of Tripoli	*GF*, pp. 83, 86; RA,
	Fakhr al-Mulk of Tripoli approached the crusaders at roughly the same time as Jana ad-Daulah. He gave the crusaders ten horses and four mules along with some gold, but (according to the *Gesta Francorum*) Raymond of Toulouse said that he would not form an agreement with the Tripolitarians unless they converted to Christianity. Raymond then laid siege of Arqa, but failed to capture the fortress.	pp. 107, 111, 125; AA, pp. 386–390.

(cont.)

---

[279] John France believes that Albert's allegation against Raymond may be probably spurious given his general hostility towards the count, see: J. France, 'Moving to the goal, June 1098-July 1099', *Jerusalem the golden: The origins and impact of the First Crusade*, ed. S. Edgington and L. García-Guijarro, Outremer: studies in the Crusades and the Latin East III (Turnhout: Brepols, 2014), p. 134. Ibn al-Athir states that the ruler spread several rumours about incoming relief armies, although he also describes these rumours to have been ineffective in their objective of compelling the Franks to lift the siege: IAA, vol. 1, pp. 38–39.

Table 2 (*cont.*)

Date	Agreement	Main Source
	Raymond of Aguilers gives a slightly different account of events explaining that Count Raymond formed an agreement with the men of Tripoli but later attacked Arqa so that he could extort more money.	
	Having laid siege of Arqa, negotiations with Tripoli continued and the crusaders were initially careful not to damage their crops. Nevertheless, there were some skirmishes with warriors from the city. Eventually, the crusaders decided to press on to Jerusalem and they formed an agreement with the Banu Ammar. According to the *Gesta*, the Banu Ammar agreed to: (1) release 300 prisoners (2) grant the crusaders 15,000 bezants (3) and 15 valuable horses. The Tripolitarians also sold the crusaders further mounts, pack animals and food. Fakhr al-Mulk also promised to become a Christian if the crusaders managed to defeat the Fatimids and capture Jerusalem. According to Raymond of Aguilers, the Banu Ammar agreed to: (1) give the crusaders 15,000 gold pieces (2) horses (3) mules (4) clothing (5) foods. He would also provide a market and release his Christian captives.	
May 1099	Beirut	AA, p. 390.
	The citizens of Beirut are said to have given the crusaders gifts in exchange for their peaceful passage past Beirut and its environs. They also promised to serve them if they should successfully capture Jerusalem. The crusaders agreed to these terms.	
May 1099	Acre	RA, p. 135.
	Fearing a siege, the ruler of Acre promised that he would grant Acre to the crusaders if they either: successfully captured Jerusalem; remained in Judaea for 20 days; or defeated the Fatimids. The crusaders duly departed.	
July–August 1099	Ramla	AA, pp. 458–460.
	Prior to the battle of Ascalon the governor of Ramla made a treaty with Godfrey of Bouillon. He explained some of the tactics that the Fatimids were likely to use in their advance upon the crusader forces in newly-conquered Jerusalem. He then joined them in the ensuing battle and may have been baptised.	

they were content to travel through a region fairly peacefully or even to achieve some of their military goals with the support of Muslim allies. Some individuals even visited Arab and Turkish ruled cities. The priest Eberhard was in Tripoli while the crusaders were besieging Antioch, while others travelled to Caesarea and Turkish-held Homs to buy horses.[280] Certainly some of these treaties will have been viewed as temporary measures driven by force of circumstances, but there is no suggestion that this was deemed to be controversial by any of the parties involved.

When defining the nature of the crusaders' overall policy towards the non-Christian rulers of the Near East, it is helpful to recall a rather blunt passage from Orosius in his account of the Gothic and Hunnic attacks on the Roman Empire at the time of the emperor Valens (d. 378). Reflecting upon these attacks he wrote 'whatever name any person may shield himself with, if he is not associated with her [The Church], he is alien; if he attacks her, he is an enemy'.[281] Orosius' approach closely matches the crusaders' perspectives. Hostile or not, the Turks and Arabs were considered to be *alieni* but this factor alone did not generally qualify them to become a military target. It was only when they opposed the crusaders that they were viewed in this way.[282] This structure seems to hold true for much of the crusade, particularly once the pilgrims had fallen out of favour with the Emperor Alexius and no-longer felt under any compulsion to support his re-conquest of Asia Minor.

These factors contextualise an important aspect of the crusaders' attitudes towards Muslims: the issue of hatred. Many historians have concluded that the crusaders harboured a deep-seated hatred for Muslims. The language used in the crusading chronicles and the massacres committed during the course of the campaign are generally submitted as proof for this contention. Nevertheless, on closer inspection this issue is not clear-cut. Certainly, the crusaders undoubtedly harboured a passionate enmity towards all non-Christian *religions*. This conviction is ubiquitous across the chronicles which describe the Turks' and Arabs' faith in hostile and demonic terms. Such an approach had the full weight of medieval European theology behind it, and both Islam and many non-Christian religions had long been presented in this way.[283]

The adherents of other religions, however, as shown earlier, were viewed differently. They were characterised as manifestations of God's

---

[280] RA, pp. 117, 103.   [281] Orosius, 'Historiarum Libri Septem', col. 1147.

[282] See also Völkl, *Muslime – Märtyrer – Militia Christi*, pp. 161–166.

[283] For similar statements concerning Slavic paganism see: Adam of Bremen, 'Gesta Hammaburgensis Ecclesiae Pontificum', p. 78. For similar statements concerning Islam in the centuries before the First Crusade see: Ermoldus Nigellus, *Poème sur Louis*, p. 46.

creation, who were living under an evil influence. Here the theological pressure was very different, steering medieval Christians to: accept their foes' status as God made beings acknowledge that they could still possess virtues; and be prepared to accept these peoples into the faith should they choose to convert. This approach may well have acted as a halter on any inclination to hate their enemies and certainly their earlier-mentioned ability both to form agreements with their enemies and to project virtues onto their leaders chimes well with this conclusion.

Even so, whilst this spiritual frame of reference appears in various forms throughout these chronicles, the crusaders' attitudes towards their Turkish opponents were not formed through theology alone. During the course of the crusade, these authors witnessed, suffered, and perpetrated many brutal acts and lived through a catalogue of horrific experiences. At times, their angry reactions to these events seem to have chaffed against the theological demands to view their enemies as human beings and led them instead to take a darker view. Fulcher of Chartres very occasionally used stronger terms in his chronicle to describe the Turks such as 'degenerate' (*degener*), which may imply a condemnation of them as an ethnic group rather than simply their beliefs.[284] Moreover, his rather grudging acknowledgement at a later stage that some Turks could be permitted to be baptised may suggest that his theology was in tension with a more personal enmity.[285] Still, even in these instances, Fulcher's remarks conform closely with long-standing tropes which make it difficult to know if he was giving voice to a personal enmity or simply namechecking an established idea. The idea of 'barbarian' peoples being degenerate in the eyes of Western authors predates both the crusade and Christianity itself. Describing the Macedonian rulers of the Near East following the conquests of Alexander the Great, Titus Livy explained that they had 'degenerated' from Macedonians into Syrians, Parthians, and Egyptians. It is possible that Fulcher was simply referencing this presumption.[286] Alternatively, he could have been citing the more spiritual conviction that races which had not accepted Christ were more susceptible to vice and therefore to moral degeneration.[287] Thus it is difficult to gauge the extent of his enmity from his language alone, which may simply be referencing long-standing discourses.

Moreover, there are tonal differences between the various contemporary writers in their presentation of Turks and Arabs which have been

[284] FC, p. 135. For the use of this term in connection to sin see: Alcuin of York, 'Epistolae', pp. 55, 57, 88. See also Robert the Monks' use of the term: RM, p. 29.
[285] FC, pp. 227–228.
[286] Livy, *History of Rome*, trans. E. T. Sage, Loeb classical library CCCXIII, vol. 11 (Cambridge, MA: Harvard University Press, 1936), p. 58.
[287] See earlier.

noted by several historians. The observation has been made that Raymond of Aguilers' language is somewhat stronger than that of the other writers; France states that his words reflect the 'pristine hatred' of the 'rank and file'.[288] Even so, caution should be exercised before concluding that the language used by the crusaders betrays a sense of 'hatred'. The phrases which have often been cited as proof of this enmity are terms such as 'enemies of God' (*inimici Dei*).[289] Comparable language is found in all the crusading chronicles and it is undoubtedly strong in tone; nevertheless reflection is required before accepting it too swiftly as evidence of hatred. The crusaders did not devise this terminology themselves; it had a long pedigree. Christendom's authors had described their foes in this way for centuries.[290] The famous Carolingian scholar Alcuin of York (d. 804) wrote a poem reflecting upon the attacks of the Norsemen in which he contemplated the destruction of great cities and civilisations. Within this work he presented both the Islamic wars in Asia and the Gothic invasions of the Roman Empire as acts committed by enemies who were 'hostile to God'.[291] In the eleventh century, Adam of Bremen described the Wends in precisely the same way.[292] Thietmar of Merseburg (d. 1018) labelled the Muslim forces who attacked Luna in 1016 as 'enemies of Christ' (*inimici Christi*) who lived in hatred of God.[293] The Benedictine canoness Hrotsvit of Gandersheim (d.1002) had similarly described Muslims as being slaves of demons.[294] Likewise, the crusaders' descriptions of mosques are comparable to earlier Christian accounts of pagan shrines. Whilst narrating the martyrdom of St Alban, the Venerable Bede spoke of pagans as 'persecutors of the Christian faith', who were making sacrifices on the 'Devil's altars'.[295] Even Christians could be described in similar terms. Benzo of Alba, an advocate of Emperor Henry IV writing during the Investiture controversy, described Pope Gregory VII as an 'idol' (*hydolum*), 'sorcerer' (*magus*), and 'stranger to the Catholic faith' (*alienus a fide catholica*) among other

---

[288] France, 'The First Crusade and Islam', 250–251.   [289] *GF*, p. 62.

[290] Menache, 'Emotions in the Service of Politics', pp. 252–253. For further discussion on how the First Crusade altered the terminology used to describe Muslims see: Schwinges, *Kreuzzugsideologie*, pp. 100–107.

[291] Alcuin of York, 'Carmina', *MGH: Poetae Latini, Aevi Carolini*, ed. E. Duemmler, vol. 1 (Berlin, 1881), pp. 230–231. See also Alcuin of York, 'Epistolae', p. 347.

[292] Adam of Bremen, 'Gesta Hammaburgensis Ecclesiae Pontificum', p. 126.

[293] Thietmar of Merseburg, 'Chronicon', *MGH: SRGNS*, ed. R. Holtzmann, vol. 9 (Berlin, 1935), p. 452. For similarly hostile terminology that predates the crusades see: Ademar of Chabannes, *Chronicon: Ademari Cabannensis Opera Omnia Pars I*, ed. P. Bourgain and R. Landes, G. Pon, CCCM CXXIX (Turnhout: Brepols, 1999), p. 63.

[294] 'Passio Sancti Pelagii Pretiosissimi Martiris', p. 58.

[295] *Bede's Ecclesiastical History*, p. 30 (see also pp. 108, 122, 148).

things.[296] The language he used is at least as strong as that employed by the first crusaders concerning Muslims and is of a similar ilk.[297] With this long-standing literary tradition behind them, the authorial intent stimulating the inclusion of such phrases is ambiguous. They could have been employed as nothing more than standard topoi, referenced as a dispassionate acknowledgement of long-standing traditions. Alternatively, they could have been selected because they gave voice precisely to the writer's deep-felt sense of enmity. Either could be true, but certainly it is not possible to make the assumption that these were simply the textual manifestations of the crusaders' heart-felt sense of hatred. A conclusion that *can* be drawn from these stock phrases is that these authors rarely felt the need to go beyond the established toolbox of terminology. Standard language alone seems to have been deemed sufficient to communicate their attitudes concerning their enemies. Thus, their presentation of the Turks was generally derivative not innovative. This is not surprising; this was, after all, the long-standing practice of monastic historicism. In many ways the terminology of the crusading chronicles is analogous to the portrayals of Franks given in Islamic sources. As Hillenbrand points out, Muslim authors frequently contextualised their descriptions of Latins with stock phrases such as 'May God curse them' or 'May God send them to perdition'.[298] Even writers such as Usama Ibn Munqidh (an author often held-up as a paragon of inter-cultural discourse) used such terminology.[299] In such cases, as with the crusaders' repeated portrayal of Muslims as 'enemies of God', it is unclear whether the inclusion of these terms was antagonistic and emotive or whether it was simply formulaic and routine.[300]

Another important point that bears on this discussion on hatred is that whilst the chroniclers clearly deemed the Turks and Arabs to be particularly susceptible to demonic influences, they were not alone in this condition. The crusaders perceived some within their own ranks to

---

[296] Benzo of Alba, 'Ad Heinricum IV. Imperatorem libri VII', *MGH: SRG*, ed. H. Seyffert, vol. 65 (Hanover, 1996), p. 596, 598, 602, 604. For discussion on the development of papal rhetoric towards papal enemies under Gregory VII see: Flori, *Pierre l'Ermite*, pp. 143–144.

[297] Several historians have noted that deeply hostile attitudes towards the 'Saracen' religion long predated the First Crusade. See for example: Scarfe Beckett, *Anglo-Saxon perceptions*, p. 1; Völkl, *Muslime – Märtyrer – Militia Christi*, pp. 178–181, 214; Flori, *La Guerre Sainte*, pp. 238–260.

[298] Hillenbrand, *The Crusades*, p. 303. For similar discussion on the *chansons* see: Daniel, *Heroes and Saracens*, pp. 107–110.

[299] Usama Ibn Munqidh, *The book of contemplation*, p. 160.

[300] Hillenbrand, *The Crusades*, p. 303. See also N. Christie, 'The origins of suffixed invocations of God's curse on the Franks in Muslim sources for the Crusades', *Arabica* 48 (2001), 254–266.

be instruments of evil. This theme is frequently referenced in all the chronicles, but a clear example can be found in Raymond of Aguilers' account of the visions experienced by crusaders during the siege of Arqa. In one of these, Peter Bartholomew was visited by Jesus along with three other figures including the apostles Peter and Andrew. Jesus then divided the crusader army into five ranks, explaining that the first three ranks consisted of those who served God, while the remaining two represented those who had turned away from Him. The members of fourth rank were likened to those who advocated Christ's crucifixion, whilst those in the final rank were compared to Judas or Pontius Pilate.[301] Evidentially, some within the crusader host were deemed to have served Christ faithfully whilst others rejected or even persecuted Him. They were certainly not all considered to be faithful heroes, but were presented instead as fallible human beings who were vulnerable to sin. Later in this conversation Jesus is said to have explained the serious consequences that befall the 'unbelieving' among the Christian pilgrims.[302] Shortly afterwards Raymond of Aguilers again underlined the threat posed by 'unbelievers' among their fellow Christians in his report of a vision that appeared to a priest named Bertrand of Le Puy.[303] Thus, religious error and terms such as 'unbeliever' were accusations that were not universally levelled at Turks and 'Saracens', but could also be applied to the crusaders' co-religionists. In a similar vein, Albert of Aachen described how the crusaders had only been saved from their former 'error' by the crucifixion; a statement which naturally accepts that they too had once been in the same state of unbelief as the Turks and Arabs.[304]

During the siege of Antioch, the crusaders went to enormous lengths to secure divine assistance through the avoidance of sin. Tight regulations were imposed on the pilgrims' behaviour and women were segregated from the men.[305] Their concern was to expel anything that might lead them into sinful behaviour. Clearly they regarded sinfulness and demonic influence as omnipresent and certainly not the sole preserve of the crusaders' opponents. Even the landscape was described as having evil intent at times. The *Gesta Francorum*, describing the mountainous region south of Coxon, presented the range as 'devilish' (*diabolicus*), whilst Fulcher of Chartres recalled how several pilgrims had been drowned in a river known as the 'river of the Demon' (*Daemonis flumen*).[306] Consequently, whilst the Turks were undoubtedly the crusaders' most powerful military foe, their attacks were given as only one of the routes by which the Devil

[301] RA, pp. 113–114. See Buc's discussion on this point: Buc, *Holy War*, pp. 167–173.
[302] RA, pp. 96, 115.   [303] RA, p. 119.   [304] AA, p. 460.
[305] Riley-Smith, *The First Crusade and the idea of crusading*, p. 88.
[306] *GF*, p. 27; FC, p. 172.

could challenge the crusade and prevent it from reaching Jerusalem. As shown earlier, the campaign itself was understood as a divine test; one which would assess the participants' worthiness to reach the holy city. In this endeavour they believed themselves to have been besieged at every point in the journey by the Devil, to whom they were themselves vulnerable through their sin. Satan manifested his opposition through: the challenges of the landscape, the threat from their enemies, the frailty of their fellows, and their own weaknesses. In this way the crusaders may have perceived their enemies to be an operating under an evil influence and to have felt hostility towards them as a result; yet they were equally aware that evil assailed them through the landscape, their fellows, and even their own misdemeanors.

* * *

Another dimension to this issue of 'hatred' is the pilgrims' treatment of the towns and cities which they captured. At Antioch, Ma'arra, Albara, and Jerusalem the crusaders' entry into the city was followed by a general massacre of the populace. Their conduct could be savage in the extreme and Raymond of Aguilers described how the fall of Ma'arra was accompanied by looting, widespread killing, and torture. By the time the crusaders left, the town it was in ruins.[307] The brutality of these actions was fully acknowledged by all the chroniclers, whose reactions varied from celebration to anxiety and pragmatic acceptance. Likewise, in the years following the conquest of Jerusalem, the populations of several coastal cities were treated in a similar manner including Haifa in 1100 and Caesarea in 1101.

Among these massacres, it is the conquest of Jerusalem in particular that has understandably attracted the most attention. The city fell on 15 July 1099 and, having broken through the outer walls, the crusaders slaughtered the populace before, three days later, massacring many of those who remained. The loss of life was not total and some inhabitants survived the siege. There are tales of members of the Jewish community being held to ransom while those who took refuge in the citadel along with some other Muslim citizens seem to have survived; nevertheless, there is no doubt that many people lost their lives.[308]

Probably the most debated questions raised by this massacre are the fundamental issues of: how many people were killed? and why was it

---

[307] RA, pp. 94–102.

[308] For examples of survivors see: S. A. Mourad and J. E. Lindsay, *The intensification and reorientation of Sunni Jihad ideology in the crusader period* (Leiden: Brill, 2013), pp. 38–40. See also S. Goitein, *A Mediterranean society: The Jewish communities of the Arab world as portrayed in the documents of the Cairo Geniza, volume V the individual* (Berkeley: University of California Press, 1988), pp. 375–376.

carried out? Regarding the first question, Jerusalem had been in steep demographic decline for many decades prior to the crusade. It had been fought over repeatedly by the Fatimids and Turks so estimates of tens of thousands of casualties are almost certainly exaggerations. The number advanced by the contemporary Andalusian writer Ibn al-'Arabi of 3000 dead feels plausible.[309] Still it is not without it problems. Hirschler has raised two objections to this figure, noting firstly Ibn al-'Arabi's general lack of statistical accuracy and secondly the fact that he suspiciously supplied precisely the same figure when describing the earlier conquest of the city by the Turkish warlord Atsiz (perhaps indicating that he conflated the two incidents).[310]

Hirschler has recently raised another pertinent factor in this discussion, examining the Arabic accounts of the Jerusalem massacre produced in the decades after 1099. He notes that they report the incident briefly, supplying little information and conveying little to suggest that this was unlike any other successful siege. Just as importantly these writers do not characterise the siege as a Christian/Frankish-Islamic religious conflict but saw it as an encounter involving different ethnic/regional groups. Ibn al-Qalanisi is a case in point, writing:

[The Franks] attacked the town and took possession of it. Some of the inhabitants withdrew to David's Tower and many were killed. The Jews assembled in the synagogue and they burned it over their heads. They took possession of David's Tower under safe conduct on 22 Sha'bān [14 July] of this year. They destroyed the shrines and the tomb of Abraham.[311]

Hirscher's conclusion is that because such authors passed over the siege and its massacre so briefly, making little remark about its scale or intensity, this implies that the Franks' behaviour at Jerusalem was not perceived to be any different from the 'usual practice of medieval warfare'.[312] This reasoning is thought-provoking, not least when it is coupled with the fact that Muslim chroniclers (including Ibn al-Qalanisi) felt that it was the crusaders' treatment of the Jewish community (rather than the Muslim population) that was particularly worthy of note. He goes on to argue that the much more gory accounts of Jerusalem's conquest written by Muslim

---

[309] It has been claimed previously that some Muslim survivors managed to reach Damascus, but this has recently been disproved. For discussion on this point and a sample of the debate on the total number killed during the siege see: B. Kedar, 'The Jerusalem massacre of July 1099 in the western historiography of the Crusades', *Crusades* 3 (2004), 56–75; France, *Victory in the east*, p. 355; Housley, *Fighting for the cross*, p. 218.

[310] K. Hirschler, 'The Jerusalem conquest of 492/1099 in the medieval Arabic historiography of the Crusades: From regional plurality to Islamic narrative', *Crusades* 13 (2014), 50–51.

[311] Translation from Hirschler, 'The Jerusalem conquest', 42–43.

[312] Hirschler, 'The Jerusalem conquest', 74.

authors in the late-twelfth/early-thirteenth century such as Ibn al-Jawzi
and Ibn al-Athir (including casualty figures of 70,000 dead) reflect the
changed political agenda of their time of writing rather than the actual
events of the late-eleventh century.[313]

The significance of Hirschler's arguments cannot be understated. He
is essentially contesting the long-standing belief that the Jerusalem massacre was a bloodbath of colossal proportions. To some extent his arguments serve as a valuable warning against exaggerating the crusaders'
actions during the city's fall. Certainly these early Muslim writers lack
the horror that one would expect should there have been an unprecedented outpouring of violence (although this is in part an argument *ex
silencio*). The inflated figures of later centuries can certainly be dismissed.
It is also entirely plausible that the crusader-conquest was not perceived
as Christian vs. Muslim struggle by contemporary Muslims. This again
tallies with many of the findings offered earlier, which underline how
differently the various ethnic groups of the Near East responded to the
Frankish incursion. Still, it is instructive to consult – alongside the Arabic
histories – the accounts written by other cultures.

The best-known of these are naturally the Frankish accounts, particularly those written by eyewitnesses (or those based on their accounts).
These tell a very different story, depicting a Christian army cutting a
path through blood soaked streets in a welter of violence. The classic
account here is that offered by the *Gesta Francorum* where the massacring-
crusaders are famously portrayed in the Jerusalem Temple wading up to
their ankles in enemy blood.[314] Other writers offer a similar account
of extreme violence including those with little/no textual relation to the
Gesta tradition. For example, Albert of Aachen depicts indiscriminate
killing and a cityscape strewn with corpses. Likewise, the letter written
to the faithful by Daimbert of Pisa again speaks of horsemen wading
through blood.[315] Thus, multiple Frankish authors, writing in different
contexts, each portrayed the city's sack in profoundly exceptional terms
(a marked contrast to the Arabic sources).[316]

Changing ground to the (non-Arabic) eastern Christian sources,
authors such as Anna Comnena, Michael the Syrian, and Matthew of
Edessa also described the conquest. Naturally each of these individuals
was writing with their own agenda and within the context of their own
theological/cultural framework, yet each draws their readers' attention to

---

[313] Hirschler, 'The Jerusalem conquest', 37–76.   [314] *GF*, p. 91.

[315] AA, p. 442; *kb*, 171. For discussion on Albert of Aachen's relationship to other chronicles see: Rubenstein, 'Three crusade chronicles intersect', pp. 24–37.

[316] For Hirschler's discussion on this disparity see: Hirschler, 'The Jerusalem conquest',
74–75.

the fact that a significant massacre took place in Jerusalem. Their allusions are often brief, but they leave their audience in no doubt that a brutal slaughter took place. Patriarch Michael speaks of the city being full of bodies.[317] He also corroborates the Frankish sources when he describes how the dead were taken from the city and burnt.[318] Anna Comnena describes the siege as follows: 'the walls were encircled and repeatedly attacked, and after a siege of one lunar month it fell. Many Saracens and Jews in the city were massacred'.[319] Her narrative is brief, but among the few details she chose to include it is the massacre that is foregrounded. Matthew of Edessa is more detailed, giving a death toll of 65,000.[320] Again, this is a different narrative from the early Arabic sources.

Reconciling these very different narratives poses many challenges. It is highly unusual to have a situation where the perpetrator – rather then the victim – foregrounds the extent of their own slaughter. As a first stage in this process it is worth raising two contextual points. Firstly, Jerusalem was a site of considerable importance within all these authors' thought-worlds and the possibility has to be considered that their descriptions of slaughter were, at least partially, symbolic rather than serious attempts to report lived experience. Raymond of Aguilers employed imagery drawn from the book of Revelation (see 14:20) in his descriptions of the pilgrims' horses wading through blood, presumably in an attempt to set the crusade in an epic or eschatological mould rather than self-consciously reporting lived events.[321] Other chroniclers may similarly have been borrowing apocalyptic-type imagery to amplify the significance of the event. Matthew of Edessa's account was guided by the parallels he drew to Vespasian's conquest of Jerusalem in 70 CE. In both cases one might enquire whether they were reporting an orgy of violence because this is what actually happened, or whether they were drawing upon an established repertoire of imagery to underline the spiritual magnitude of the event? On this point it is impossible to know although it may be useful to recall once again Adam of Bremen's description of the pagan temple Uppsala. As shown earlier, this temple may never have existed and yet its destruction played the important narrative role in his history, symbolising the regional overthrow of paganism.[322] It is possible in a similar vein that the

---

[317] MS, vol. 3, p. 185.   [318] GF, p. 92.

[319] Translation from AC, p. 315.   [320] ME, p. 173.

[321] For discussion on whether these descriptions should be viewed as biblical analogy (not designed to be taken as a serious piece of reportage) or factual observation see: Kedar, 'The Jerusalem massacre', 65; T. Madden, 'Rivers of blood: an analysis of one aspect of the crusader conquest of Jerusalem in 1099', *Revista Chilena de Estudios Medievales* 1 (2012), 25–37.

[322] See earlier.

lurid accounts of crusader violence in Jerusalem were offered to provide
suitable context for their authors' vision of the epic spiritual overthrow
of the 'Saracen religion' and may not have been intended to reflect the
more mundane events that actually took place.

The second contextual point is that Jerusalem itself had changed hands
repeatedly during the late eleventh century. Prior to the arrival of the First
Crusade it was conquered on at least three – possibly four – occasions by
Turks, Fatimids, and local factions.[323] The 1077 conquest in particular
seems to have been very bloody.[324] Perhaps the brevity of the early Arabic
chronicles simply reflects a hardened familiarity with an ongoing cycle of
conquests of this period. The crusade was not the only bitter campaign
waged in the Levantine region during the eleventh century. There had
been Turcoman depredations, Bedouin attacks, infighting among Arab
tribes, and dynastic squabbles between the Turks. Most of the cities taken
by the crusaders in the Holy Land had fallen to at least one other power at
some point within two decades of the Franks' arrival. Perhaps their rather
terse descriptions of Jerusalem's fall in 1099 should guide us not to dial
down the intensity of the crusader conquest, but to dial up the intensity
of the Fatimid-Seljuk-Turcoman-Bedouin-Arab conflicts of the previous
half century; creating an environment in which *yet another massacre* did
not stand out as an exceptional event.

Synthesising the above, the line-of-best-fit here seems to be as follows. Most importantly, the crusaders did indeed commit a substantial
and bitter series of massacres which began immediately after they broke
through the wall on 15 July 1099. The correlation on this point between
the Frankish and eastern Christian sources cannot be overlooked. Moreover, as Kedar has observed, these massacres were of such intensity that
the crusaders surprised even themselves; the participant authors presented the intensity of the slaughter as 'totally unprecedented' and their
exceptionality is revealed by the fact that their authors felt the need to
justify them.[325] He also draws attention to the fact that when Fulcher of
Chartres entered the city in December 1099 the piles of bodies, carried
out from the city after its conquest, were still unburied and decompos-
ing. There must therefore have been a very great number of cadavers.
These are all valid points.[326] This does not mean that we should necessarily believe the crusaders to have been literally wading in blood, yet the

---

[323] For discussion on Jerusalem's history during this period: Gat, 'The Seljuks in
Jerusalem', pp. 5–6.

[324] Although as Kedar observes, it probably did not reach the same level of intensity as
the 1099 sack: Kedar, 'The Jerusalem massacre', 69–70.

[325] Kedar, 'The Jerusaelm massacre', 68.

[326] Kedar, 'The Jerusaelm massacre', 17, 68.

fact that they conducted two, possibly three, massacres in the hours/days following the city's fall reveals the extraordinary nature of the event.[327] The total number of killed, however (thus the scale of the massacre as opposed to its intensity), was not even nearly as great as later authors might claim. Jerusalem was a marginal, declining city, which had been repeatedly conquered. The smallness of Jerusalem's population might go some way to explaining why the Arabic chroniclers paid the siege scant attention, although this must be coupled with the fact that they were living through an age long-accustomed to slaughter. After all, when the crusaders entered the Levant in 1097 they were not intruding upon a utopia, but stepping into a long-standing warzone.

Discussing the scale and intensity of the conquest provides vital context when assessing the crusaders' intentions – and the role of hatred within them – towards Jerusalem's population. Here again there are various schools of thought. For some, the Jerusalem massacre was simply a manifestation of standard military practice employed against Christians and non-Christians alike. France, for example, observes that William the Conqueror's capture of Mantes in 1087 and his harrying of the North were accompanied by atrocities that were almost as brutal as crusaders' actions in Jerusalem.[328] Applying such notions to the question of hatred, the crusaders' behaviour could be explained away as straightforward martial practice, not indicative of any particular anti-Islamic hatred.

In some respects this explanation feels reasonable. Certainly the crusaders followed the same procedure when assaulting Jerusalem that they had employed at Albara (Sept 1098) and Ma'arra (27 Nov–12 Dec 1098).[329] In all cases they: offered surrender terms; these terms were refused (although at Albara and Ma'arra there is some ambiguity about the agreements that may or may not have been made); the crusaders then took the city by storm. In this sense then the crusaders' actions could be interpreted as 'customary' and not suggestive of any particular hatred. Even the third massacre which took place on the third day after

---

[327] For discussion on the number of massacres perpetrated see: Kedar, 'The Jerusalem massacre', 16–18, 22–23, 61.

[328] France, *Victory in the east*, pp. 355–356. See also J. France, Western warfare in the age of the Crusades: 1000–1300 (Ithaca, NY: Cornell University Press, 1999), p. 227. Kedar disputes the idea that some of the Christian-on-Christian massacres France offers as comparisons reached the same level of intensity: Kedar, 'The Jerusalem massacre', 68. For further discussion on this theme see: Kedar, 'The Jerusalem massacre', 63–75; Housley, *Fighting for the cross*, pp. 213–21.

[329] For references see: (Ma'arra) Ibn al-Qalanisi, *The Damascus Chronicle*, p. 47; RA, pp. 94–102; Kamal al-Din, 'Extraits de la Chronique d'Alep', pp. 586–587; (Albara) RA, p. 91. Kamal al-Din gives a slightly different account of the taking of Albara: Kamal al-Din, 'Extraits de la Chronique d'Alep', p. 586. I am indebted to Ian Wilson for his advice on this subject.

the city's fall could be explained with this same martial logic, arguing that – as France suggests (following Albert of Aachen) – the crusaders had become aware that a Fatimid army would arrive imminently and they could not afford to leave the remnants of a hostile populace in Jerusalem in their rear.[330]

Nevertheless, the matter cannot be left here. As shown earlier, the crusaders regarded their massacre to be profoundly exceptional and unprecedented. Even if one rejects any claim that the apocalyptic-type imagery drawn upon by multiple authors has much of a basis in reality, the accounts of butchery and violence committed against non-combatants, both on the day of conquest itself and over the days that followed, are very unusual.[331]

Weighing up these various points, it seems likely that the crusaders' behaviour can be ascribed *in part* to long-standing military traditions. The crusaders' conviction that they had rights over conquered cities comes across clearly in the sources, not least when these rights were denied in the aftermath of the conquest of Nicaea.[332] Nevertheless, the crusaders' sense of martial entitlement was evidently dilated by additional factors that drove them to go far beyond the bounds of conventional behaviour. In part Flori is undoubtedly correct that the explanation for this outpouring of violence, at least during the initial massacre, must reflect the fact that the conquest of Jerusalem was the culmination of years or toil, suffering, fear, disease, and hardship. Releasing the floodgates of these pent-up longings and tensions may well have played its part in the massacre of Jerusalem.[333]

There must also be a religious dimension.[334] Both before and after the conquest, the crusaders performed symbolic processions; indeed, the Franks' conduct during the entire siege spliced professional soldiering with acts of spiritual devotion. In a similar vein, for several authors, the massacre of Jerusalem represented a spiritual 'cleansing'. The conviction that Jerusalem was contaminated by a non-Christian presence is referenced in sources produced before the crusade (the charters) and in its aftermath (the chronicles). It was not simply a later interpretation. Fulcher of Chartres, along with many writers, described the massacre of Jerusalem in this way.[335] One particularly noteworthy text, which

---

[330] France, *Victory in the east*, p. 356; AA, p. 440. See also Murray, 'The siege and capture of Jerusalem', p. 214.

[331] Kedar, 'The Jerusalem Massacre', 15–75. See also, Kangas, 'Deus Vult', p. 164; Flori, *Pierre l'Ermite*, p. 422.

[332] OV, vol. 5, p. 56.

[333] Flori, *Pierre l'Ermite*, pp. 419–421. See also, Mayer, *The Crusades*, p. 56.

[334] Asbridge, *The First Crusade*, pp. 318–319.

[335] FC, p. 306. See also RA, p. 145. For discussion see: Cole, 'O God, the Heathen have come into your inheritance', p. 89; Schein, *Gateway to the heavenly city*, p. 16;

references this theme is a charter written at the Aquitanian abbey of Charroux in 1100. The document itself is not directly concerned with crusading and was written up simply to record a donation to the abbey. Nevertheless, it was dated to:

> The second year after the most brave knights and footsoldiers of Christ under Duke Godfrey, later appointed king of Jerusalem, and with him the most steadfast Count Raymond and many others captured the aforesaid city with divine power and virtue having killed no small number of Turks and pagans and cleansed that most holy place of their filth.[336]

The use of such a passage, referencing the notion of spiritual pollution, in a document dealing with the local concerns of an abbey in Western Francia, suggests that both the conquest of Jerusalem and the conviction that the massacre of its inhabitants constituted a spiritual cleansing had become a standard reference point in that region at least. In general, the fact that this theme of spiritual cleansing was foregrounded by so many authors both at the outset of the campaign, in its immediate aftermath, and in its later representation, suggests that this conviction played a role in inspiring the massacre they committed in the city. Of course, the belief that cities under non-Christian rule were polluted by their unbelieving citizens was neither new nor exclusive to medieval Christianity; Emperor Louis the Pious was shown to have 'cleansed' Barcelona when he wrested it from Muslim control back in 801. At times Muslim sources described the conquest of Christian cities in a similar way.[337] Nevertheless, this was a theme that was self-consciously prioritised in accounts of the First Crusade.

Returning to the question of hatred, and reviewing the earlier discussion, the deeds of 15–18 July 1099 might well appear to be indisputable proof that the crusaders were driven more generally by a sense of anti–Muslim loathing. Even so, this may not have been the case. Jerusalem was and is a place of enormous spiritual potency for the members of many religions. It is not a place that can be judged by ordinary rules, nor can people's behaviour within its walls be taken as a guide for how they will behave elsewhere. This point is underlined by a basic acquaintance with Jerusalem's history in any period, but it is also confirmed by recent

---

Riley-Smith, 'The idea of Crusading', pp. 156–157; Kedar, 'The Jerusaelm massacre', 15–75; Akbari, *Idols in the east*, pp. 235–240.

[336] *Chartes et Documents pour servir a l'histoire de l'abbaye de Charroux*, no. 22.

[337] Ermoldus Nigellus, *Poème sur Louis*, pp. 34, 46. The theme of religious pollution is also present in Islamic accounts of Christian-ruled Jerusalem. Following the crusader conquest, Muslim authors described Jerusalem as being contaminated by the Christian presence, citing in particular the presence of pigs and alcohol. Latiff, 'Qur'anic Imagery', p. 145; Mallett, *Popular Muslim Reactions*, pp. 66–67.

studies on the enormous psychological/spiritual/delusion-inducing effect Jerusalem can have upon modern-day tourists; some of whom require hospitalisation as a consequence.[338] Returning to the medieval period, it might be noted that even after many decades of Frankish rule, at a time when strong diplomatic ties existed between the Latin East and its Muslim neighbours, when Muslim communities lived peacefully under Christian rule, Muslims were still barred from living in Jerusalem.[339] It is also striking that Albert of Aachen saw nothing strange in reporting that 'Saracens, Arabs, and Turks' were among the grief-stricken mourners who attended Godfrey of Bouillon's funeral in July 1100. Clearly, their grief was both observed and valued, and yet this was the man whose forces had cut a bloody path through the holy city only a year previously.[340] Consequently, his troops' behaviour in Jerusalem was exceptional and did not prevent him building relationships with Muslims at other times. It might be added that the pilgrims' deeds in Jerusalem in 1099 are not of-a-piece with their conduct in the earlier stages of the crusade, which are punctuated with alliances, treaties, and even statements of admiration. Thus, their behaviour in the holy city seems to have been governed by a different set of priorities.

The key to this distinction seems to be an intense sense of Jerusalem's overwhelming spiritual significance. This was a place of long-standing longing, not merely for the crusaders themselves, but for Christendom as a whole. Its importance in the Bible requires no rehearsal. Throughout the eleventh century, growing veneration for Jerusalem in western Christendom had drawn the holy city into the centre-ground of contemporary piety; a fact which rendered its continued occupation by non-Christians increasingly intolerable. Religious buildings across western Europe were dedicated to the Holy Sepulchre, while others seem to have aped the rotunda (*Anastasis*) of the Holy Sepulchre; relics were transported from the east in ever increasing numbers; and there was a rising traffic on the pilgrim roads to the east at the very time when these same routes were coming under greater threat.[341] By 1095 the presence of a non-Christian power was deemed – even at the outset of the campaign – to be an unacceptable pollutant. This conviction comes across clearly in the crusade charters, several of which describe the need to cast out pagans

[338] M. Kalian and E. Witztum, 'Facing a holy space: Psychiatric hospitalization of tourists in Jerusalem', *Sacred space: shrine, city, land*, ed. B. Kedar and R. Zwi Werblowsky (Basingstoke: Macmillan, 1998), pp. 316–330. I am indebted to Professor Kedar for drawing my attention to this article. See also Rubenstein, *Armies of Heaven*, p. 279.

[339] WT, vol. 1, 536.

[340] AA, p. 516. A similar situation is reported by Orderic Vitalis after the death of Robert II, count of Flanders. See: OV, vol. 6, p. 162.

[341] Morris, *The sepulchre of Christ*, pp. 134–179.

and liberate Jerusalem from its non-Christian masters.[342] By extension, the crusaders' belief that the successful conclusion of the crusade constituted an unambiguous disproof of paganism may imply that its former occupation by Islam was similarly perceived as a spiritual barrier blocking the sustained advance of Christianity.[343] Certainly the conquest itself was viewed as a liberation from tyranny.[344] Evidently it was deemed insufficient for Christians to simply have visiting rights to Jerusalem, particularly if these same rights were being threatened by Turkish attacks. All these factors seem to have played their part in the resulting sack of the city.

Viewed from this perspective, whatever the crusaders might have thought about the non-Christians they encountered, Jerusalem existed in a unique spiritual environment; one that was governed by different rules and – for specific reasons that actually had very little connection to the crusaders' attitudes towards Muslims – it was deemed essential to eradicate any non-Christian presence. When these spiritual convictions are spliced with the pent up emotions of three years of suffering and death and the martial conviction that a city which had refused to surrender could rightfully be taken by storm, the resulting mix goes some way to explaining what happened on those three days. Within this, it seems likely that the specific religious identity of Jerusalem's defenders was largely irrelevant beyond the fact that they were not Christian.

Jerusalem was and is *different*.

Conclusion

"God does not make miracles for believers, but for the unbelievers."
Caffaro of Genoa[345]

Shortly before the First Crusade, (1050–1070) William of Jumieges wrote a history of the dukes of Normandy. This work, the *Gesta Normannorum Ducum*, was dedicated to William I of England and covered the history and heroic deeds of his forebears. According to his narrative the duke's actions and those of his ancestors had earned them the right to be described as 'most steadfast knights of Christ'[346] Likewise, those who rebelled against them were portrayed as having been

---

[342] Examples: *Actes des comtes de Flandre, 1071–1128*, no. 20; *Cartulaire de l'abbaye de Saint-Victor de Marseille*, vol. 1, no. 143; 'Cartulaire du prieuré de Saint-Pierre de La Réole', *Archives historiques du départment de la Gironde*, ed. C. Grellet-Balguerie, vol. 5 (Paris and Bordeaux, 1863), p. 140.

[343] RA, p. 151.   [344] *Kb*, pp. 178–179, 180.   [345] Caffaro, *Annali Genovesi*, p. 8.

[346] *The Gesta Normannorum Ducum of William of Jumièges, Orderic Vitalis and Robert of Torigni*, ed. E. Van Houts, vol. 1 (Oxford: Clarendon Press, 1992–1995), p. 6.

incited by the Devil.[347] Their enemies – the counts of Flanders in particular – are described as evil, wicked, cunning, Judas-like, and at one point 'breathing out dreadful venom'.[348] The murderers of Duke William Longsword (d.'942) received especial scorn and were presented as 'sons of the Devil'.[349] Had these enemies been non-Christians, especially Muslims, there would be a *prima facie* case for claiming that the author had adopted a structure of binary opposition between Christians and Muslims; one which intentionally sought to demonise and dehumanise the non-Christian 'other'. Nevertheless, all these protagonists are Christian. True, the use of such terminology leaves the reader in no doubt about where their sympathies should lie, but it also demonstrates that this kind of language – used so frequently by First Crusade chroniclers – was in no way reserved for wars against non-Christians.[350]

There is a binary-opposition structure that runs through both William of Jumieges' chronicle and those of the First Crusade but the dividing line between good and evil is not simply Christians-versus-non-Christians. The difference instead is defined by adherence to the will and word of God.[351] Those who recognise and walk in conformity with God's will are deemed eligible for an artist's palate of eulogy and celebration. Those who are described either to have turned away from God's law or who live in isolation from it are judged to be leading a sinful life, vulnerable to demonic influence. Thus William of Jumieges, a determined advocate of his patron's family and forebears, goes to great pains to demonstrate the Normans' pious subordination to God's will, whilst stressing the demonic inspiration, and stubborn impiety of their foes. His general message is that: the dukes of Normandy conduct God's will; their enemies rebel against it. This is his definition of good and evil. The First Crusade narratives paint exactly the same picture. There are moments when individuals are celebrated for having followed God's will, thus their behaviour sits on the 'good' side of this binary structure. These naturally include many crusaders and the mere fact that Guibert of Nogent chose the title *Dei Gesta per Francos* for his chronicle makes this point exactly. Some Muslims also fall into this category. To some extent Karbugha's mother fulfils this role. She is described positively because she was deemed both to have successfully identified the spiritual significance of God's work through the crusade and to have attempted to prevent her son from

---

[347] *Gesta Normannorum Ducum*, vol. 1, p. 78.
[348] *Gesta Normannorum Ducum*, vol. 1, p. 90.
[349] *Gesta Normannorum Ducum*, vol. 1, p. 92.
[350] This approach is can be found in many chronicles see: Bachrach, *Religion and the conduct of war*, pp. 70–71.
[351] Kangas, 'Deus Vult', p. 169.

marching against the Franks.[352] Qilij Arslan and Ahmed ibn Marwan also fall comfortably into this category. On the other hand, chroniclers also dwelt upon those who had failed to respond to God's commands. These include some Turkish rulers who are shown to embody the vices of pride and arrogance; terms which denote the idea of rebellion against God. Karbugha especially is shown as prideful for failing to recognise that the crusaders' fought for the true God.[353] There were also many crusaders depicted in this way.

This fundamental structure, defined by an individual's responsiveness to God's will, is expressed through many linked metaphors: good against evil; cleanliness against pollution; health against sickness but – again – the dividing line is not synonymous with Christian/non-Christian. Certainly many Turkish leaders are shown to be evil, but some crusaders are too. As mentioned earlier, Raymond of Aguilers includes an account of a vision of Christ in which He divides the crusaders into five ranks. The first rank contains the most faithful of the crusaders whilst the later ranks are populated by those who are increasingly lukewarm or are even, by the time He reaches the fifth rank, traitors to the faith.[354] Likewise, as shown earlier, the Turks are frequently depicted as contaminated or polluted by their beliefs and their actions are shown to be depraved, but some crusaders are also presented in precisely these terms. Albert of Aachen described how the pilgrims' decision to tightly regulate their moral behaviour at Antioch was an attempt to rid themselves of 'filth and impurity'.[355] Raymond of Aguilers reported a speech made by some leading crusaders who complained that the crusaders had alienated themselves from God through their 'depraved' (*pravus*) actions.[356] He also recalled that the late Adhemar of Le Puy appeared to Peter Desiderius in a vision and incited the crusaders to worship God and cast off all their depravity.[357] Thus it was entirely possible for anyone of any religion to be described in this way; the dividing line between them was their acknowledgement of God's will, not solely the faith boundary.

The spiritual picture painted by the various chroniclers does show variations between authors, but there is much that they had in common. In general Christians, Turks, and Arabs alike are shown to be imperfect human beings standing before God. Their imperfections and their propensity for sinfulness have the potential to lead them any of them into

---

[352] *GF*, pp. 53–56.
[353] AA, pp. 254, 258, 330, 320; *GF*, p. 66. For wider discussion see: Völkl, *Muslime – Märtyrer – Militia Christi*, p. 187–188; Schwinges, *Kreuzzugsideologie*, p. 164.
[354] RA, pp. 68–69.   [355] Translation taken from AA, p. 228.
[356] RA, p. 144.   [357] RA, p. 144.

depravity and alienation from God.[358] Likewise, through their common sinfulness, the Devil can exert his influence upon all parties. Turks and Arabs – because they have not committed themselves to the Christian religion – are shown to be especially vulnerable to demonic suggestion because they are not under the same divine protection, but they too are shown as capable of grasping spiritual truths; most importantly the spiritual significance of the crusade. They are also capable of virtuous behaviour and redemption. The crusaders are far more likely to be shown as righteous and pious, but they are also capable of turning their back on God and aligning themselves with the Devil.

Consequently, a sense of binary opposition between good and evil is present but it is transcendental – God against the Devil – not simply crusader against Muslim. Nevertheless, whilst Turks and Arabs were deemed capable of responding positively to God's will, they were always shown to do so through actions that drew them closer to Christianity and away from their own beliefs. A case in point is Ahmed ibn Marwan, whose virtues and discernment are said to lead him eventually to convert. The Muslim religion itself, by contrast, was perceived as irredeemably evil and a direct manifestation of demonic influence. Thus, the crusaders maintained the believer/belief dichotomy described earlier. Viewed from this perspective, it was not especially important *what* the Turks and Arabs believed. Indeed, knowledge of the tenets of non-Christian religions were deemed by some contemporaries to be inherently dangerous; a form of dabbling with evil.[359] It was sufficient to know that they did not accept Christianity as the complete truth. Baldric of Bourgueil expressed this concern explicitly in the prologue to his chronicle, stating that he would not write anything down which might draw his fellow Christians into error.[360]

The bulk of the more hostile statements made against non-Christians are directed against Turks. They were the crusade's principal foe and whilst the Franks were fully persuaded of their prowess, they were also: horrified by their barbarity; terrified by their tactics; and appalled by their prior conduct in Asia Minor and Syria. The Arabs were viewed and treated very differently. The pilgrims went to great lengths to avoid conflict with the Arabs and they made strenuous attempts to form a détente with the Fatimids. Within these diplomatic dealings, the crusaders even

---

[358] See also S. Throop, *Crusading as an act of vengeance, 1095–1216* (Aldershot: Ashgate, 2011), pp. 55–56. See also Buc's comments: Buc, *Holy War*, p. 178.

[359] See: Liudprand of Cremona, 'Antapodosis', p. 5; Housley, 'The Crusades and Islam', 198.

[360] BB, p. 4.

floated the idea of permanent co-operation between Christian Europe and Fatimid Egypt. The fact that Jerusalem was ultimately besieged and taken by storm should not belie that fact that this was very much a last resort. The distinctions between the crusaders' attitudes and behaviour towards Turks and Arabs demonstrate that their perceived enemy was not Muslims or even non-Christians *en bloc*, but rather the partially Islamicised Turks. They knew that the Arabs, like the Armenians and Byzantines, had suffered considerably during the Saljuq invasions and they seem to have hoped to make common cause with them against this foe.

Drawing these factors together, Islam's role (or the 'laws of Mohammed' as Raymond of Aguilers describes the 'Saracen' faith) in the crusaders' thought world was tangential.[361] It was vaguely identified as the belief system of their main opponents and some elements of crusade propaganda spoke of the need to defeat 'Saracens' (which in this context was a religious rather than an ethnic descriptor). Nevertheless, the crusaders did not direct their energies to seeking out the centres of Muslim power.[362] The many battles they fought along the way were perceived as spiritual hurdles that had to be overcome in the achievement of their goal: Jerusalem.

* * *

Changing ground to the First Crusade's wider status, to date, several historians have positioned the First Crusade, in a *longue-durée* context, as part of a wider Christian retaliatory campaign against centuries of Islamic aggression. To this end, the crusade has been grouped with other eleventh-century ventures such as the reconquest of Sicily, the Christian advances into Northern Iberia, and the growing Italian dominance in the Mediterranean as part of a wider anti-Islamic offensive. This argument has been reinforced with the observation that the First Crusade, like these other campaigns, was wreathed by the language of liberation; a shared terminology common to these ventures.[363] Likewise, from a medieval

---

[361] RA, p. 149.   [362] See also Asbridge, 'Knowing the enemy', p. 17.

[363] For discussion on this theme see: Riley-Smith, *The First Crusade and the idea of crusading*, pp. 16–18; S. Kangas, 'Inimicus Dei et Sanctae Christianitatis? Saracens and their Prophet in twelfth-century crusade propaganda and western travesties of Muhammed's life', *The Crusades and the Near East: cultural histories*, ed. C. Kostick (London: Routledge, 2011), p. 132; Mastnak, *Crusading peace*, p. 120; Morris, *The sepulchre of Christ*, p. 173–174; Riley-Smith, 'The idea of Crusading', p. 156. For a particularly convincing study, which makes a similar point whilst discussing Urban's use of Daniel 2:21 see: M. Gabriele, 'The last Carolingian exegete: Pope Urban II, the weight of tradition, and Christian reconquest', *Church History*, 81.4 (2012), 796–814.

Islamic perspective, several authors including al-Sulami and later Ibn al-Athir also felt that the crusade was simply an extension of European expansionism in the Mediterranean.[364]

These ideas are all perfectly accurate – as far as they go – and they do play their part in describing the crusaders' thought-worlds; even so, there are objections to positioning the crusade too squarely within a vector of expanding European power. There are grounds for seeing the expedition as a discontinuation at least as much as it was a continuation of this trend. The crusade's fundamental objective was not wide-scale territorial conquest, but the recapture of a single city. The fact that the crusade succeeded in establishing four states in the Middle East does not imply that this was the expedition's basic purpose. Indeed, if regional takeover was their main object, then these highly-experienced commanders showed little strategic logic when they marched hundreds of miles into hostile territory – far from help – and only then began to pursue this objective. In all probability, the permanent conquest of any region, bar Jerusalem itself, seems to have been an opportunistic side-effect of the campaign, rather than its objective. Likewise, the plain fact that the vast majority of crusaders did not settle, but returned home, reinforces the idea that they were concerned primarily with their personal piety and Jerusalem itself.

Even so, it is not surprising that, to a contemporary Muslim eye, the crusaders were perceived to be intent on conquest. Whatever the crusaders' intentions may have been, ultimately they *did* seize thousands of square miles of territories at a time when their co-religionists were advancing on many fronts. Thus the decision to judge the crusade by its consequences was perfectly logical, even if it does not bring the crusaders' initial intentions into focus. Another important discontinuity is the nature of the crusaders' enemy. Both the papacy and the crusaders fully understood that the Turks were a fundamentally new force, whose origins lay in distant lands. Peter the Venerable explicitly labelled them 'new enemies of the Christian name' (*novi hostes Christiani nominis*).[365] Whilst they may have been at least partially Islamicised, the Franks did grasp the fact that the Turks were also a very different kind of foe; one which was not simply synonymous with their old Muslim sparring partners. Indeed, the crusaders recognised that the Arabs felt every bit as threatened by the Turks as they did themselves. For this reason also

---

[364] *The book of the Jihad of 'Ali ibn Tahir al-Sulami (d. 1106): text, translation and commentary*, ed. and trans. N. Christie (Aldershot: Ashgate, 2015), 206–207; IAA, vol. 1, p. 13. For discussion on this passage see: Micheau, 'Ibn al-Athir', pp. 60–62. See also WM, vol. 1, p. 134. See also Bar Hebraeus, *The chronography*, vol. 1, 234.

[365] *The letters of Peter the Venerable*, vol. 1, p. 208.

the crusade was discontinued. Drawing these factors together, there is something very enigmatic about the crusade. It *was* in many ways a manifestation of resurgent Christendom and it was certainly enabled by an expanding culture of territorial expansion. Any yet it was also very different; characterised by a highly distinctive goal and separated both geographically and in some respects ideologically from the wars of the western Mediterranean.

4   Aftermath

Introduction

In the months and years following the fall of Jerusalem, as the pall of smoke dissipated over its hallowed grounds and the carrion birds ceased to circle over the bodies of the fallen, the peoples of western Christendom, Byzantium, Armenia, Georgia, and the Islamic World were confronted by a single indisputable fact: Jerusalem was now in western Christian hands.

For many in western Christendom, this was a source of unparalleled rejoicing. Still, once the initial shock had worn off, churchmen seem to have realised that they were now confronted with a series of very important questions that it was specifically their responsibility to answer. Chief among these was the overriding need to determine what exactly God had just done through the crusaders? The conviction that the crusade was an outworking of divine will was so ubiquitous as to be almost banal. But the question of the crusade's significance as a milestone in world history, from creation to Apocalypse, was a much more complex issue that required inspection. There were also a host of linked issues for these theologians to ponder including: How would the 'pagans' react to their sustained defeats? Was the crusade a sign that the end of the world was near? Was the crusade a fulfilment of biblical prophecy? (And, if so, which prophesies did it fulfil?) Alongside these questions were the problems surrounding this newly-encountered people: the Turks. For these clerics the process of identifying the Turks was not simply a matter of learning the names of their leaders, customs, and warcraft; this problem had spiritual implications. The Turks were not mentioned in Genesis among the peoples descended from Noah and his sons, nor were they listed in subsequent authoritative works, such as Isidore's *Etymologiae*; so who were they? Such concerns seem to have become a source of intense debate, particularly in monastic circles, as intellectuals and thinkers pored over the Bible, patristic works, and classical histories in search of answers. For many it was evidently not deemed sufficient simply to accept the observations made in the participant narratives; these were far too vague on such crucial points of theology. Guibert of Nogent in particular was dismissive of the *Gesta Francorum*'s simplicity and offered a distinctly hostile critique of Fulcher of Chartres' chronicle.[1] For him, at least, a new more learned explanation had to be given. Many other writers similarly felt that these accounts were unsatisfactory and offered either new works of their own devising or redactions based on existing chronicles.

Consequently, many narratives were produced in the decades following the crusade. They were often the products of long reflection during which monastic authors had first consumed the tales supplied by returning pilgrims (whether orally or in their 'simple' textual accounts) and then rendered them into highly erudite treatises that would satisfy the pressing theological questions that had emerged in the wake of the campaign. The fruits of their labours were a series of artistic masterpieces, painstakingly created from the charcoal sketches provided by the participants.

This chapter will discuss these works focusing specifically upon the conclusions they reached about the non-Christian peoples encountered by the crusaders. In some cases their views were simply more explicit and expanded versions of what the participant authors had already concluded themselves (which actually could be fairly sophisticated). They too presented the crusade as a test ordained by God, one which had both elevated some to the status of Christian champions whilst finding others wanting. Robert the Monk, for example, depicted Bohemond haranguing those pilgrims who were contemplating desertion during the famines experienced outside Antioch saying plainly, 'He [God] often tempts those faithful to him, so that he might know whether they love him. Now he tempts you through the vexation of poverty and burdens you with the relentless attacks of enemies'.[2] Likewise, Robert had also clearly internalised the belief, seemingly common among participants, that the crusade's undeniable success would lead some 'Saracens' to embrace Christianity. On several occasions he depicts Turks and Arabs crying out to Mohammed for aid, but then coming to the realisation that no help would be forthcoming.[3] Ralph of Caen drew the same conclusions announcing that the campaign had destroyed 'idolatry' (*idolatria*).[4] As we have seen these themes are central to the participant narratives.

Nevertheless, a common feature of these later works, one which separates them from the participant narratives, is their lack of precision in descriptions of the Turks, Arabs, and other peoples encountered by the crusaders. On occasion these inconsistencies take the form of minor factual errors. Henry of Huntingdon, for example, speaks of the '*Agulani*'

---

[1] GN, pp. 79, 329–332.   [2] RM, p. 39.   [3] RM, pp. 46, 107.   [4] RC, p. 3.

(*Ghulam* – slave soldiers) being armed with spears, when the *Gesta Francorum* states plainly that whilst heavily-armoured they were armed only with swords.[5] Likewise William of Malmesbury, discussing the earlier journey of Bernard the Monk to the Holy Land in the ninth century, stated that the land was under Turkish rule.[6] Seemingly he was unaware that the Turkish conquest of the Near East was an eleventh-century phenomenon. In other cases, these authors did not draw distinctions between ethnic/religious/political groups with anything like the same confidence as the crusaders themselves. They lacked the crusaders' experience and, besides, their purpose was not to produce technically accurate accounts of the pilgrims' day-to-day progress, but to ponder the spiritual truths made manifest through their actions. Naturally, none of these mistakes would have been made by participants for whom such information was not merely interesting detail, but knowledge contingent to their survival. These later authors compensated for their lack of direct experience with a deep contextual knowledge of biblical, classical, and patristic sources. With a solid grounding in these works they were often better able to grasp the historical and religious significance of the various sites visited by the crusaders, than the pilgrims themselves. They were also more familiar with the earlier chronicle histories describing Christendom's prior relations with the 'Saracen' world; texts which enabled them to set their own works within the broader canvas of the events of earlier centuries.

The level of interest and hostility shown to the Turks and 'Saracens' in these narratives varies considerably between authors. Robert the Monk's chronicle, for example, dwells frequently upon the details of battle and individual combat. It is filled with accounts of mighty sword blows, spear thrusts, and heroic encounters. In this case, as Sweetenham has demonstrated, his chronicle owes much to the interests of the knightly classes and the influence of the *chansons de geste*.[7] A similar proclivity can be found in Orderic Vitalis' work where at one point he brings to life a martial encounter at the siege of Antioch by showing how Godfrey of Bouillon cut his Turkish opponent in half 'like a tender leek'.[8] Interestingly, their terminology – Robert's in particular – is often more jocularly aggressive towards the crusade's opponents than the participant narratives themselves. A further theme that begins to creep into some chronicles is that of physiological stereotyping. Derogatory descriptions of 'monstrous'

---

[5] Henry of Huntingdon, *Historia Anglorum (history of the English people)*, ed. and trans. D. Greenway, OMT (Oxford: Clarendon Press, 1996), p. 426; *GF*, p. 49.

[6] WM, vol. 1, p. 642.   [7] Sweetenham, 'Crusaders in a hall of mirrors', pp. 49–64.

[8] OV, vol. 5, p. 84.

enemies or hostile references to skin colour (of the kind found in *chansons*) are almost entirely absent from the participant narratives, but they are present – albeit very rarely – in the later chronicles.[9] Ralph of Caen, for example, in his description of a group of Franks ramming Turkish heads onto stakes, explains how one Turk's eyes were half-a-foot apart.[10] It is possible that in this passage he is simply offering an exaggerated report of an extraordinary individual, certainly he does not turn this statement into an ethnic generalisation. On balance, however, it seems likely that he was attributing 'monstrous' qualities to his foes, of the kind found commonly in *chansons*. Certainly in the *Chanson of Roland* one of the Saracen king Marsile's dukes is described as having precisely the same physical attribute.[11] This is unlikely to be a coincidence. Gilo of Paris also refers briefly to the Turks' skin as being *ferrugo tinctus*, although he makes no judgement – hostile or otherwise – on this point.[12] This, however, is the sum of the passages found in crusade histories (excluding *chansons*) to touch upon this issue and perhaps their most striking feature is their scarcity. Many studies, particularly those discussing *chansons*, have placed skin colour at the heart of Europe's representations of Muslims and yet, even though the First Crusade histories were shot-through with motifs drawn directly from such epic poems, these authors manifested little interest in their enemies' physical features.

Many authors predictably took a more theological approach to the crusade's enemies and these include Ekkehard of Aura in his *Hierosolimita*. This short work touches only briefly on the pilgrims' opponents, but it does so in a particularly striking way. He described how the crusade had cleared the road to Jerusalem, by removing the 'obstacles of pagan hearts, which are harder than stones'.[13] This reference to hearts that are 'harder than stones' (*duriora saxis*) draws upon an important biblical theme that was widely discussed in medieval exegesis. In both the Old and New Testaments the stone-hearted are given as those who have heard God's commands but have refused to listen. They have therefore separated themselves from God through their wilful independence. Such scriptural passages often express the hope or prophetically foretell that God will transform their stone hearts into 'hearts of flesh' which will be responsive to God's word. In Ezekiel 11 19–21, for example, it is written:

---

[9] It is interesting to note that the crusaders were not isolated in this approach and Epstein has demonstrated that some of the early emissaries/missionaries to the Mongols revealed little interest in skin colour. Epstein, *Purity lost*, pp. 31, 51. There is one reference to skin colour in Fulcher of Chartres' chronicle, but it concerns the inhabitants of a village near the Dead Sea and not the crusaders' enemies. See: FC, p. 379.

[10] RC, p. 56.   [11] *SR*, p. 72.   [12] GP, p. 80.

[13] Ekkehard of Aura, 'Hierosolimita', *FE*, p. 330.

I will give them one heart, and put a new spirit within them; I will remove the heart of stone from their flesh and give them a heart of flesh, so that they may follow my statutes and keep my ordinances and obey them. Then they shall be my people, and I will be their God. But as for those whose heart goes after their detestable things and their abominations, I will bring their deeds upon their own heads, says the Lord God.

This theme was referenced frequently by patristic writers and in a homily on Luke 3, Pope Gregory I explained how the teaching of Christ had enabled those Jews and gentiles who followed Him to leave behind their 'hearts of stone'.[14] In another homily on Matthew 2, Gregory focused on those Jews at the time of Christ, who had both heard the Old Testament prophecies and knew of Jesus' miracles, but who had *not* acknowledged him as God. He then described them as having hearts that are 'harder than stone' (*duriora saxis*).[15] This is exactly the same formulation of words as that found in Ekkehard's *Hierosolimita*; a point that suggests that Ekkehard was inspired by this homily.[16] Seemingly he transposed this idea onto the Crusades. Given that this term *duriora saxis* refers to those who have heard the truth but refused to listen, Ekkehard's message seems to be that the crusaders' opponents had failed to recognise the crusade's significance as a divinely-led pilgrimage and persisted in their unbelief. This denial then left the crusaders with no alternative but to drive them away like boulders from a path. Ekkehard's message is substantially more pessimistic than that contained in many of the earlier crusading narratives. In these works, as shown earlier, there was a widespread hope that the crusade's opponents would recognise the crusade's spiritual significance and convert. Still Ekkehard describes no such expectation. Writing decades after the crusade, he seems to have abandoned the dream that a widespread conversion would take place.[17]

Consequently, the texts under discussion in this chapter are an eclectic group. They are manifestations of an ongoing conversation between monastic writers concerning the significance and implications of the First Crusade. They describe a process of theological rationalisation and contextualisation by which these authors first sifted and filtered the returning crusaders' information (and often quite sophisticated theology) and then worked it into their existing framework of ecclesiastical and scientific

---

[14] Gregory I, *Homiliae in Evangelia*, ed. R. Étaix, CCSL CXLI (Turnhout: Brepols, 1999), p. 160.

[15] Gregory I, *Homiliae in Evangelia*, p. 67.

[16] Certainly McCarthy believes he is drawing upon this sermon see: T. McCarthy, *Chronicles of the Investiture Contest: Frutolf of Michelsberg and his continuators* (Manchester: Manchester University Press, 2014), p. 257 (footnote 307).

[17] Baldric of Bourgueil similarly observes that Turks are difficult to convert because their non-Christian faith has rendered them spiritual blind. BB, p. 8.

knowledge. The major authors to be discussed here will be Guibert of Nogent, Bartolf of Nangis, Henry of Huntingdon, Ekkehard of Aura, Ralph of Caen, Robert the Monk, Baldric of Bourgueil, Gilo of Paris (and the so-called Charleville poet), and William of Malmesbury. Representations of the crusade expressed through epic verse will be considered briefly in the next chapter.

Identifying the Turks

Even before the completion of the crusade, the pilgrims seem to have become curious about the Turks' racial origins and, as they returned home bearing both palm branches and news of strange lands, many thinkers in the monastic establishment interested themselves in this new people and their origins. Their response to this problem was to delve into their archives in the search of clues or references to a race that for many was evidently entirely unknown. One of the most learned of these writers was Guibert of Nogent. His account (written in 1107/8 at the monastery of Saint-Germer de Fly) drew heavily upon the *Gesta Francorum*, although he also consulted returning pilgrims and other written accounts. Like many others, he seems previously to have been unfamiliar with the 'Turks' and he too consulted the works of late antiquity that deal with the origins of different ethnic groups in search of answers. At the end of his history he named the main texts that he had examined as: Solinus' *De Mirabilibus mundi*, Trogus-Pompeius' *Historiae Philippicae* (which survives only in third-century abbreviation by Justin), and Jordanes' *Getica*.[18] Having conducted his background reading, Guibert delivered himself of the verdict that the Turks were originally Parthians. Admittedly, this may not have been a conclusion he reached independently, rather his work suggests that he had discussed their origins and nomenclature with his monastic peers; still his background reading seems to have informed his view.[19]

Judged by contemporary reasoning, this conclusion was well-founded. He learnt from Pompeius Trogus that the Parthians had been a tribal group of highly-skilled archers from the east, who had conquered all the neighbouring civilisations. Pompeius Trogus noted in particular their use of feigned-flight tactics, slave-soldiers and also their general barbaric way of life.[20] These qualities certainly matched the descriptions Guibert

---

[18] GN, p. 352.
[19] Apparently he was advised to use the name 'Parthians' as his preferred term for Turks, but he rejected this counsel, using the word sparing. GN, p. 83.
[20] *Justin: Epitome of the Philippic history of Pompeius Trogus*, trans. J. Yardley (Atlanta, GA: Scholars Press, 1994), pp. 254–255; Loutchitskaja, 'Barbarae Nationes', p. 102.

had received from the first crusaders and seem to have given him the confidence to draw connections between the two. He wrote for example: 'The kingdom of the Parthians, who we identify by the corrupt name 'Turks', excels in military matters and equestrian ability and also in the virtue of courage'.[21]

Pompeius Trogus also claimed that the Parthians were descended from the Scythians. Jordanes tells a similar tale describing how the Parthians were descended from the Goths, who had themselves lived for a long time in a Scythian territory. He described how this land lay near the Maeotic Lake, which was itself next to the territory of the Amazons. According to Jordanes' account, a long time ago, the Goths advanced into Asia following a victorious war fought against the Egyptians. The Goths then gave the rule of their newly conquered land to the king of the Medes. The name 'Parthians' was apparently given to those Goths who chose to remain in this conquered Asian territory with the Medes. In the Scythian tongue the name 'Parthians' was said to make reference to the fact that they had deserted the land of their birth.[22] Again Jordanes' account may have confirmed Guibert in his view that the Turks were Parthians because the *Gesta Francorum* identified Amazonian territory on the borders of Turkish land. More suggestively, in one of his lesser works on the reign of Baldwin I, Guibert described the Turks as 'Parthians and Medes'.[23] The fact that he grouped the two together in this way suggests an awareness of the tradition, alluded to earlier, which stressed the links between these peoples.

The notion that the Turks were latter-day Parthians is widely referenced in many later narratives including those by Robert the Monk[24] and Bartolf of Nangis.[25] Henry of Huntingdon, like Guibert, also made this connection explicitly speaking of 'Parthians, who now are called Turks'.[26] The so-called Charleville Poet even elaborated on this association naming the Turks as 'Arsacids' (descendants of Arsaces, the first ruler of Parthia).[27] In Robert the Monk's chronicle this association only appears once, in a description of the Karbugha's siege of crusade-held Antioch.[28] Here it is used to refer to the Turks without explanation

[21] GN, p. 100.

[22] Jordanes, 'Getica', *MGH: Auctorum Antiquissimorum*, ed. T. Mommsen, vol. 5.1 (Berlin, 1882), pp. 65–67.

[23] Guibert of Nogent, 'Petite Chronique du Règne de Baudouin Ier', *GN*, p. 363.

[24] For discussion see: D. Kempf and M. Bull, 'Introduction', *The Historia Iherosolimitana of Robert the Monk* (Woodbridge: Boydell, 2013), pp. xvii–xl.

[25] Bartolf of Nangis, 'Gesta Francorum Expugnantium Iherusalem', pp. 495, 504.

[26] Henry of Huntingdon, *Historia Anglorum*, p. 426 (see also, 428). For a similar statement see GP, p. 82.

[27] GP, p. 138.   [28] RM, p. 84.

or context. Seemingly Robert was sufficiently confident that his reader would follow the logic of his terminology without further explanation. More suggestive are his references to 'Medes' among the ranks of his Turkish enemies. Medes are said, both by him and others, to have been among the warriors who opposed the crusaders at Dorylaeum, during the so-called Foraging Battle, and finally in their struggle against Kar-bugha's army.[29] This identification of 'Medes' among his foes implies that he too was applying the same reasoning as Guibert (founded ulti-mately on Jordanes) which drew a link between the two. Gilo of Paris likewise described the Turks as 'Parthians', although unlike Robert he explained the relationship between these two groups writing: 'for those who are now called Turks are the Parthians of old, and trusting in their arrows while fleeing away is their custom'.[30] In this description he drew upon Virgil's *Georgics*, which describes Parthian tactics in this way.[31] He too includes the Medes among the enemy ranks.[32]

Unlike so many aspects of the crusaders' attitudes towards the Turks, the conviction that the Turks were latter-day Parthians seems to have been reached unilaterally by western Christian authors, without east-ern Christian assistance. This association does not appear in Byzantine sources where the general consensus seems to have been that the Turks were descended from the Huns. As shown earlier, at other times Greek authors described them as 'Persians'. Moreover, many of the later writ-ers to describe the Turks as 'Parthians', such as Robert the Monk, were associated with Guibert (a fellow Benedictine) in some way, suggesting that this identification was a product of conversations being held among senior circles of monastic intellectuals. The abbey of Nogent, for exam-ple, had close links with Robert's abbey of St-Remi.[33]

Consequently, Western authors were evidently attempting to make sense of the Turks, by fitting them into the established ethnographi-cal structures formed in late antiquity.[34] Their conclusions were clearly influential and many later writers followed their lead, including – remark-ably – writers in the crusader states. As we have seen, none of the crusade narratives, written by participants in the immediate aftermath of the cam-paign characterised the Turks as either Parthians or Medes, nor did the Byzantines or the other Christian peoples of the eastern Mediterranean.

---

[29] RM, pp. 27, 37, 58; Bartolf of Nangis, 'Gesta Francorum Expugnantium Iherusalem', p. 504.
[30] Translation from GP, p. 82.
[31] Virgil, *Georgics*, trans. P. Fallon (Oxford: Oxford University Press, 2006), p. 50.
[32] GP, p. 7. Orderic Vitalis also described the Medes among the crusaders' enemies' ranks. See: OV, vol. 6, pp. 120–122.
[33] Kempf and Bull, 'Introduction', p. xli.
[34] Loutchitskaja, 'Barbarae Nationes', pp. 102–103.

Nevertheless, the Antioch-based author Walter the Chancellor (writing about the Antiochene wars of the 1110s) used this terminology frequently and, more importantly, so too did Fulcher of Chartres in the later parts of his history.[35] Fulcher's account is of especial interest because his work was written in phases. The first books, written directly after the First Crusade, did not describe the Turks as Parthians, but his later books dealing with the history of the Latin East (written between 1110 and 1127) occasionally refer to them in this way and also include references to 'Medes' within the Turkish ranks.[36] This can be seen in his account of King Baldwin II's attempt to relieve the besieged fortress of Zardana in 1122. Describing the subsequent skirmish he provided an account of Turkish tactics, naming them as a 'Parthian race' (*gens Parthica*).[37] The sudden injection of this terminology suggests that he learnt to describe the Turks and their allies in this way in the years following the crusade, presumably from a western source.[38] Certainly the identification of the Turks as Parthians allied to Medes has strong resonances with the earlier-mentioned works produced by Guibert and Robert. The possibility has to be entertained therefore that both Fulcher and Walter were relying upon the findings of western European intellectuals to help them to identify their Turkish neighbours. This is not implausible and some lines of transmission can be suggested. To take one example, Ralph of Caen, author of the *Gesta Tancredi*, travelled to the Latin East with Bohemond on his Greek campaign in 1107 and he later took service with Tancred. It is quite possible that whilst at Antioch he reported the growing consensus that the Turks were derived from Parthian stock; certainly he references this connection in his own chronicle.[39] Presumably he would have known Walter the Chancellor in person; they were in the same place at the same time. Kempf and Bull have also raised the possibility that Robert the Monk might have made a pilgrimage to the east.[40] Thus it seems that some individuals, who were well versed in the debates circulating in western Europe concerning the Turks' origins, subsequently visited the Latin East, informing the local churchmen and writers of their research-based deductions. If this interpretation is correct then it reflects an astonishing willingness among those, who lived only miles from the Turkish frontier,

---

[35] Walter the Chancellor, *Bella Antiochena*, p. 62 and *passim*.

[36] For references to Parthians and/or Medes see: FC, pp. 468, 631, 649–650, 653.

[37] FC, pp. 649–650.

[38] Other historians have similarly noted that elements of Fulcher's terminology change in the second part of his chronicle, see: Kostick, *Social structure*, p. 218.

[39] RC, pp. 75, 79; B. Bachrach and D. Bachrach, 'Introduction', *The Gesta Tancredi of Ralph of Caen: A history of the Normans on the First Crusade*, Crusade texts in translation XII (Aldershot: Ashgate, 2010), pp. 2–3.

[40] Kempf and Bull, 'introduction', p. xviii.

to rely upon the authority of thinkers living thousands of miles away, who had never encountered the Turks personally.[41]

The belief that the Turks were descended from the Parthians is referenced in the majority of western Christian sources produced following the crusade, but there was a different, if less popular, explanation in circulation. As shown earlier, the Byzantines did not describe the Turks as 'Parthians'. They thought them to be descended from the Hephthalite Huns; a people who had ruled much of Central Asia and Northern India during the fifth–sixth centuries AD.[42] The Byzantines believed that the Huns themselves could be divided into two parts; a western group comprising peoples such as the Avars and Hungarians and an eastern group including the Khazars and eventually the Saljuq Turks. Many Byzantine chroniclers, both before and after the first millennium, pause in their narratives to explain that the Huns are more typically known as Turks.[43]

The Byzantines were quite correct in their identification of strong bonds, whether cultural and/or ethnic, between the Saljuqs and the nomadic groups pressing on their Danube border. They had, after all, long experience in their dealings with these peoples. Even so, the crusaders, for the most part, seem only vaguely aware of any link uniting the tribes of the western Black Sea region to the Saljuqs. No participant narrative identifies a common ancestry between the two and none of them describes the Turks as 'Huns'. The tribes they encountered on their journey to Constantinople are named as Pechenegs, Cumans, or Bulgars, with no reference made to any relationship with the Saljuqs.[44] Having said this, there are a few implicit clues that these authors did come to see some kind of affinity between these peoples. Albert of Aachen noted that both the Saljuqs Turks and the Pechenegs used bows of 'horn and bone', while Fulcher's description of the Saljuqs as 'Eastern Turks' may imply that he was taking the Byzantine approach of dividing the Turks/Huns into western and eastern halves.[45] A slightly more promising reference however occurs in Peter Tudebode's *Historia*. In his account of Raymond of Toulouse's difficult journey through Slavonia he shows how the count was persistently waylaid by the ambushes of 'Turks, Pechenegs, Cumans,

---

[41] For discussion on a similar theme see: Lapina, *Warfare and the miraculous*, p. 36.

[42] MA, p. 77. Certainly these two peoples did have some common history and consequently were frequently conflated in eastern Christian source. For example in 559–560 the Turks conquered the Hephthalite Huns. See: Dickens, 'Turkāyē: turkic Peoples', pp. 15, 63; Beihammer, 'Die Ethnogenese', 597.

[43] See for example, *The chronicle of Theophanes Confessor*, p. 362; *The history of Theophylact of Simocatta*, trans. M. and M. Whitby (Oxford: Clarendon Press, 1986), p. 30.

[44] See for example, *GF*, p. 6; AA, pp. 18–20;   [45] FC, p. 180; AA, p. 20.

Slavs, Uzes and Athenasi'.[46] In this reference to 'Turks' he clearly did not mean the imperial turcopoles, who are described separately and his placement of Turks in this list of peoples, who in all other cases lived in the Black Sea region, may indicate an awareness of a connection between the two. Still it is equally possible that he was simply listing groups of Byzantine auxiliaries. Consequently, there is little here to suggest that the participants saw any relationship between the Turks and the peoples they encountered in the Balkans.

Most of the later chroniclers of the crusade similarly draw no comparison between the Turks and Huns but there are a few exceptions. In its account of the First Crusade, the *Chronicle of Montecassino* described Qilij Arslan, sultan of Rum, as 'king of Huns, who now we call Turks'.[47] This work mirrors the Byzantine practice both of describing the Turks as Huns and also explaining that the name Turks is the more up-to-date term. In his case at least he seems to have been guided in his presentation of the Turks by long-standing Byzantine practices. To take another instance, Frutolf of Michelsberg does not link the Turks explicitly to the Huns, but he does seem to have believed that there was some association with the Turks and their kin living north of the Danube. In his entry for the year 766 he mentioned briefly a war fought between the Turks who emerged '*a Caspiis portis*' and the Avars.[48] This very brief reference suggests an awareness on his part that the Turks' operations were not confined to the Near East alone. Again, this reference reveals a dependency on Byzantine authorities. As Meserve has demonstrated, Frutolf was drawing upon the work of Landulphus Sagax, who was in turn drawing upon Anastasius' translation of Theophanes' *Chronographia*.[49]

Identifying the Turks' Allies

A distinctive feature of the later First Crusade accounts is their lengthy lists of Turkish allies. As shown earlier, the *Gesta Francorum* identified contingents of Azymites (Armenians), *Agulani* (*Ghulam* slave-soldiers), Publicans (Paulicians) in the Turkish armies encountered by the pilgrims along with the more recognisable Persians and Arabs. Nevertheless,

---

[46] PT, p. 44. For discussion on the term 'Athenasi' see: PT, p. 44 (footnote 32); Loutchitskaja, 'Barbarae Nationes', p. 104.

[47] 'Chronica Monasterii Casinensis', *MGHS*, ed. H. Hoffmann, vol. 34 (Hanover, 1980), p. 478.

[48] Frutolf of Michelsberg, 'Chronicon', p. 160.

[49] Although as Meserve points out that some elements of Theophanes' original text were blurred or altered in the retelling. Meserve, 'Medieval sources for Renaissance theories', pp. 430–431. See also Sigebert of Gembloux, 'Chronica', *MGHS*, ed. G. Pertz, vol. 6 (Hanover, 1844), p. 302; Meserve, *Empires of Islam*, p. 79.

later authors list many more peoples among their enemies' ranks. These include Medes and Parthians, but some writers also mention Elamites.[50]

The Elamites themselves were an ancient people who lived in the southwest of what would later be called Iran, with their main city at Fars. The origins of their civilisation lie in the fourth millennium BC. They were later displaced by the Assyrians, who waged a series of decisive campaigns against them in the seventh century BC.[51] Naturally little of this would have been known to the crusaders. Their main source of information would have been the Bible. In the Old Testament the Elamites appear occasionally, for example in Jeremiah 49:35: 'Thus says the Lord of hosts: I am going to break the bow of Elam, the mainstay of their might', and Isaiah 22: 6 'Elam bore the quiver with chariots and cavalry'. The Elamites' association with archery may have recommended them to the chroniclers as a people connected to the Turks, but a more convincing link can be found in the book of Genesis. This lists Elam among the sons of Shem (son of Noah).[52] According to Isidore of Seville, Elam's descendants were the Elamites, and he was known as the 'prince of the Persians'.[53] In this way he may have been deemed to have been an ancestor of the Turks, who as shown earlier were often described as 'Persians'. Another possible link can be found in Acts 2:9 in its description of the day of Pentecost. In this account the author expresses his wonderment at the ability of the many peoples there-present to understand one another's languages through the intervention of the Holy Spirit. Listing the peoples who were present he names side by side 'Parthians, Medes and Elamites' (Acts 2:9). Again this association may have reinforced the perceived links between these groups as 'eastern' peoples. Thus it could be concluded that, as with the association with the Parthians, these western European authors allied the Turks to the Elamites based on their scriptural knowledge.

There is another explanation. Turks and Muslims are occasionally described as Elamites in the Armenian tradition. Matthew of Edessa presented the Turks in this way and it is possible that the early twelfth-century *Sermo de Antichristo* made this same association.[54] We learn little

---

[50] GP, p. 6; RC, p. 107; Bartolf of Nangis, 'Gesta Francorum Expugnantium Iherusalem', pp. 495, 504.

[51] M. Waters, *Ancient Persia: a concise history of the Achaemenid empire, 550–330 BC* (Cambridge: Cambridge University Press, 2014), pp. 21–25.

[52] Genesis, 10:22.   [53] Translation from Isidore of Seville, *The etymologies*, p. 192.

[54] *Pseudo Epiphanii Sermo de Antichristo*, ed. G. Frasson, Bibliotheca Armenica: Textus et Studia II (Venice, 1976), p. 17; Z. Pogossian, 'The last emperor or the last Armenian king? Some considerations on Armenian apocalyptic literature from the Cilician period', *The Armenian apocalyptic tradition: a comparative perspective: essays presented in honor of Professor Robert W. Thomson on the occasion of his eightieth birthday*, ed. K. Bardakjian and S. La Porta (Leiden: Brill, 2014), p. 483.

from these references about their rationale for establishing such a connection but the notion must be entertained that, as with so many of their ideas concerning their Turkish enemies, these authors were guided, in these cases probably at second hand, by their contacts with eastern Christians.[55]

Other groups whose cohorts reportedly marched within the Turkish hordes against the first crusaders include: Indians,[56] Chaldeans,[57] Assyrians,[58] Philistines,[59] Libyans,[60] Phoenicians,[61] Cilicians,[62] and Caspiadeans.[63] Some of these names require only a brief explanation. The inclusion of Philistines surely references the crusaders' widely-held conviction that they were imitating or even recreating the Old Testament wars. Indians, Assyrians, Phoenicians, and Libyans are likely to have been included for no other reason than they were peoples who were thought to have originated in the Near East, East and/or North Africa. Indeed, it seems that in some cases the author's purpose in supplying such voluminous lists of enemy peoples was more to give the impression of a vast agglomeration of foes confronting the crusader host than to make a specific theological or ethnological point through each of their constituent names. The Charleville poet, for example, claims that the crusaders were opposed by a thousand different races of people, who dwelt in the Euphrates, Nile, and Tigris river basins.[64] Describing the battle of Antioch, Ralph of Caen gives the names of ten races arrayed against the pilgrims, but goes on to say that he has supplied a mere sample of the total.[65] Likewise in his version of the battle of Dorylaeum, Robert the Monk, drawing upon Psalm 105, presents the enemy host as locusts, who 'covered the surface of the land'.[66] By the time that the *Chanson d'Antioche* came to be written down, the Turks were said to have

---

[55] ME, p. 83.   [56] RC, pp. 75, 79.   [57] See discussion later in this chapter.

[58] RC, pp. 75, 124; GN, p. 300. Baldric later compared the Turks to the Jebusites. He presumably selected this particular Old Testament people because the Jebusites controlled Jerusalem at the time when the Israelites reached the Promised Land (BB, p. 9).

[59] GP, p. 6. Note also that Orderic Vitalis referred to the Turks/'Saracens' as *Allophilos* (see, for example: OV, vol. 4, p. 166). There has been some discussion on what precisely this word means. Throop is of the opinion that it can be translated as 'lovers of dirt' (Throop, *Crusading as an act of vengeance*, p. 50). Nevertheless, Forester who translated Orderic's work back in the mid-nineteenth century advanced the case that it is biblical in origin and intimates that a individual/group is 'of another race'. He also points out that Sulpitius Severus used the similar term 'Allophyli' to describe Philistines and Syrians: T. Forester, *The ecclesiastical history of England and Normandy by Ordericus Vitalis*, vol. 3 (London, 1854), p. 178.

[60] RC, p. 75.

[61] RC, p. 75. Note that Liudprand of Cremona refers to Muslims as 'Phoencians' in his chronicle: Liudprand of Cremona, 'Antapodosis', pp. 55, 98.

[62] Henry of Huntingdon, *Historia Anglorum*, p. 426.   [63] GP, p. 6.

[64] GP, p. 6.   [65] RC, pp. 75–76.   [66] RM, p. 27.

confronted the crusaders assisted by Slavic auxiliaries. This inclusion is probably sheer fantasy, although the possibility remains that it reflects the sustained employment of Slavic warriors by various Muslim rulers in the eastern Mediterranean.[67] In any event, these listed names have the effect of depicting an overwhelmingly powerful enemy, whose eventual defeat naturally makes the crusaders' own victory more spectacular.

Having said this, whilst some of the names seem to have been included primarily to 'bulk-out' the enemy host, a few of the peoples included in these lists warrant further attention, in particular the 'Caspiadeans' and 'Chaldeans'. The *Caspiadae* do not make a regular appearance in the sources for either the Middle Ages (i.e. a keyword search on the MGH database will return no references) or the Classical period and this alone makes them unusual. Only one crusading chronicler mentions them in his list of Turkish allies and this is the so-called Charleville poet.[68] His most obvious source was Valerius Flaccus' work *Argonautica*, which retells the story of Jason and the Argonauts. The *Caspiadae* appear in the ranks of Perses, usurper to the throne of Colchis (a kingdom situated on the east coast of the Black Sea).[69] Nothing more is said about them in this text, but they are surrounded by Scythian peoples which alone is significant. Seemingly the Charleville poet was stressing the Turks' supposed Scythian connections.

'Chaldeans' and Descriptions of the 'Saracen' Religion

Fulcher of Chartres and Robert the Monk also number Chaldeans within the ranks of their Turkish enemies and these references too deserve closer scrutiny.[70] The Chaldeans were an ancient Babylonian people, famed for their magical arts, who settled on the northern shores of the Persian Gulf at the beginning of the first millennium BC. Following the fall of the Assyrian Empire in the seventh century BC, the Chaldeans and Medes established the Neo-Babylonian Empire which reached the height of

---

[67] 'La Chanson d'Antioche', p. 65 and *passim*; J. Moran-Cruz, 'Popular attitudes towards Islam in medieval Europe', *Western views of Islam in medieval and early modern Europe*, ed. D. Blanks and M. Frassetto (Basingstoke: Macmillan, 1999), p. 57. See also D. Pipes, *Slave soldiers and Islam: the genesis of a military system* (New Haven, CT: Yale University Press, 1981), pp. 47, 183.

[68] GP, p. 6.

[69] Valerius Flaccus, *Argonautica*, ed. and trans. J. Mozley, Loeb classical library CCLXXXVI (Cambridge, MA: Harvard University Press, 1963), p. 308.

[70] Fulcher of Chartres identifies them in his account of the early history of the Latin East: FC, p. 468. Robert the Monk includes a group called the *Candei* in his list of enemies present at Dorylaeum. Sweetenham has noted that in some manuscripts this name is given as 'Chaldeans', see RM, p. 27; Sweetenham, *Robert the Monk's history of the First Crusade: Historia Iherosolimitana*, p. 111.

its power under the command of the famous Nebuchadnezzar (604–561BC).

The most likely explanation for references to this people among the Turkish armies in the crusade sources lies in their contemporary associations, both with the magical arts and with Islam.[71] Certainly the Chaldeans' knowledge of magic and astrology was widely acknowledged and Isidore of Seville observed that whilst the Egyptians were the first to learn astronomy, the Chaldeans had been the first to teach astrology.[72] This link also has a biblical basis. One particularly important reference can be found in the book of Daniel, where the young Jewish captive Daniel succeeded in interpreting King Nebuchadnezzar's prophetic dream following the failure of his magicians and 'Chaldeans' to render any satisfactory explanation (Daniel 2, 1–45). Again they appear here in the company of sorcerers.

The connection drawn between Chaldeans and Muslims similarly predates the crusade and has its roots in early-medieval Iberia. Many writers in the ninth century used Chaldean as a synonym for Muslim, including Eulogius of Cordoba and Paul Alvarus.[73] Tieszen's explains this link by suggesting that the Iberian Christians may have drawn parallels between their own plight under Islam and that of the Israelites and King Nebuchadnezzar.[74] The Chaldean association with magic may also have resonated with these authors who frequently linked the 'Saracens' with sorcery, divination, and the occult. As shown earlier, magic and the occult practices were widely attributed to the 'Saracens'. Karbugha's mother, for example, is ubiquitously represented as a practitioner of astrology, who consulted omens and the signs of the Zodiac.[75] Robert the Monk likewise depicted her immersed in ancient prophesies and all kinds of pagan superstitions.[76] Other allegations of occult practices are made by Raymond of Aguilers who described two women hurling down curses upon one of the crusaders' catapults during the siege of Jerusalem.[77] He later identified astrologers (*constellatores*) and soothsayers (*augures*) among Fatimid army.[78] Albert of Aachen notes the discovery of occult texts in Karbugha's camp following the crusaders' victory at Antioch.[79] Describing later events, Orderic Vitalis' chronicle included

---

[71] It is not impossible that these were references to Nestorian Christians (often described as 'Chaldeans') but this is not likely given that they do not seem to have been a major presence in the Levantine region and that they are not generally described as hostile by later authors.

[72] Isidore of Seville, *The etymologies*, p. 99.

[73] Tolan, *Saracens*, pp. 88, 94, 99–100; C. Tieszen, *Christian identity amid Islam in medieval Spain*, Studies on the Children of Abraham III (Leiden: Brill, 2013), pp. 81, 127.

[74] Tieszen, *Christian identity*, p. 127.   [75] *GF*, p. 55.   [76] RM, p. 63.

[77] RA, p. 149.   [78] RA, p. 158.   [79] AA, p. 336.

the tale of a Turkish sorceress using astrology to foretell the death of Geoffrey, lord of Marash, and her own brother Balak of Sororgia.[80] Reflecting upon these examples it is likely that the listing of Chaldeans within Turkish armies reflects a widely-held belief among western Christians that the 'Saracens' were latter-day Chaldeans with a penchant for magic.

They may also have been encouraged to associate Muslims with magic by the Byzantines. Greek authors frequently make observations of this kind. Leo the Deacon, for example, retelling the Byzantine siege of Candia (Crete) in 961, speaks of a prostitute among the Muslim defenders, behaving shamelessly, casting spells, and making incantations. He points out that the Cretens often practiced 'divination' and 'wrongful beliefs' which they learned from the 'Manicheans and from Muhammed'.[81] The Byzantines were not alone among the eastern Christians to hold such views. The Armenians also report such practices. Matthew of Edessa's chronicle includes an account of the transportation of Armenian captives to Persia following a Turkish attack in the 1060s. He explained that having arrived in Persia, the Muslim women of that land asked the Armenian captives why they had not responded to various signs foretelling their defeat and capture. They pointed out that during the previous evening a cock had crowed and sheep had 'squatted to defecate'; tell-tale signs apparently of impending assault.[82]

In a similar vein, the broad association of eastern religions with the astrology had a long pedigree in western Christendom. In both classical and patristic texts the *east* is often represented as a hotbed of astrology and sorcery and it maintained this reputation well into the medieval period.[83] The New Testament itself helped to embed this view with the gospel of Matthew's account of the Magi from the east, who followed the star to bring gifts to the baby Jesus. These Magi were long thought to have been astrologers who had used their arts to locate Christ; a point which provoked much debate among the patristic writers. The fact that these travellers had *successfully* followed a star to locate Christ drew a great deal of interest. Most intellectuals were generally at pains to emphasise

---

[80] OV, vol. 6, p. 124. See also Walter the Chancellor, *Bella Antiochena*, pp. 66–67.

[81] Translation from *The history of Leo the Deacon*, pp. 76–77. Ducellier, *Chretiens d'Orient*, p. 64. See also Brand, 'The Turkish element', 7.

[82] Translation from ME, p. 99. See also MS, vol. 3, p. 183. Several other Latin Eastern/crusading narratives describe female Islamic mystics, see: N. Hodgson, *Women, crusading and the Holy Land in historical narrative* (Woodbridge: Boydell, 2007), p. 193. It might be worth pointing out that the pre-Islamic Turks also studied astrology. See: Peacock, *Early Seljūq History*, p. 125.

[83] C. Saunders, *Magic and the supernatural in medieval English romance* (Cambridge: D.S. Brewer, 2010), pp. 14–50.

that the guidance provided by Magi's star did not constitute proof of the efficacy of astrology. St Peter Chrysologus (First metropolitan bishop of Ravenna, d. 454) tackled this topic in his sermons. He presented the Magi as spiritual travellers, passing from the darkness of their former astrological superstitions to the light of Christ. He wrote 'Christ transformed standard-bearers of the Devil, that is, the Magi, into his own most loyal generals'.[84] He showed how Herod (representing the Devil's will) attempted to manipulate them, but to no avail. He explains the star's role in guiding the Magi, with reference to God's omnipotent control over all creation (including the star). He reminds his audience that the stars do not establish a fatalistic structure for mens' lives (in the astrological sense); they are not co-equal with God in ruling mankind, but rather are instruments of God's will to be deployed according to His will.[85] Ignatius of Antioch similarly argued that the presence of the star did not serve to endorse astrology, but marked the end of this practice through the coming of Christ.[86] Pope Gregory I observed likewise that the star was God's chosen beacon to the gentiles revealing the coming of Christ.[87] Thus the thrust of patristic wisdom was to confirm that the east did dabble with astrology, but that these practices were evil and dangerous and had been conspicuously negated by the birth of Jesus.

Eastern astrology would continue to fascinate western Christendom's theologians and intellectuals for centuries and the Islamic world played a pivotal role in stoking this attraction. By the time of the crusade, astrology was viewed by most as a science – one of the liberal arts – rather than a magical practice, although its pursuit remained hedged in theological anxiety.[88] The Islamic world helped to stimulate this interest through the provision of its own astrological texts, which were themselves adaptations of earlier Persian, Indian, and Greek works.[89] The Islamic polities of Iberia seem to have been western Europe's main source of such manuscripts – a point which may help to explain why Iberian Christian intellectuals came to refer to their Muslim neighbours as Chaldeans. William of Malmesbury referenced this association of Iberian Islam with astrology when he told a scurrilous tale of a renegade monk (who would later rise to claim the papacy) sneaking away from his monastery to learn

---

[84] Translation from *St. Peter Chrysologus: selected sermons volume 3*, trans. W. Palardy (Washington, DC: Catholic University of America Press, 2005), p. 254.

[85] *St. Peter Chrysologus: selected sermons*, pp. 254, 275–276, 268–269.

[86] Saunders, *Magic and the supernatural*, p. 47.

[87] Gregory I, *Homiliae in Evangelia*, pp. 66–67.

[88] Gilbert, bishop of Lisieux, is said to have made astrological predictions about the future course of the First Crusade (see: OV, vol. 5, p. 8).

[89] R. Kieckhefer, *Magic in the Middle Ages* (Cambridge: Cambridge University Press, 1989), pp. 116–119.

astrology from the Muslims of Seville who – so he claims – customarily conduct such occult practices.[90] Many of the crusade authors themselves seem to have been thoroughly familiar with astrology and Fulcher of Chartres' chronicle frequently (and at times Ralph of Caen's *Gesta*) includes astrological terminology.[91] Thus is seems likely whilst Christendom's authors knew little enough about Islam or the lands of the east, they probably did approach these parts holding the conviction that its inhabitants conducted astrological practices.

One significant element in the crusaders' descriptions of Islamic astrology is that it is often depicted as accurate. Karbugha's mother is ubiquitously portrayed *correctly* predicting her son's downfall. Curiously, in some versions she is shown attempting to dissuade her son from marching on the crusaders, using arguments supported both by scripture and conclusions drawn from pagan auguries.[92] Guibert of Nogent took a particular interest in this subject. He discussed the episode with Karbugha's mother, but he also explained that before the crusade an old 'Saracen' man made the astrological prediction for Count Robert of Flanders (then on pilgrimage) that the Christians would shortly be victorious in that region. Guibert then offered a brief defence of such astrological practices. His argument was rooted in the earlier employment of such practices by famous figures in the Christian tradition, such as the Emperor Heraclius and the Three Magi. In this case he outlined a very different stance on this topic to the earlier-mentioned patristic sources, and he seems to have felt that such superstitions were compatible with the Christian faith.[93] His tone in this passage, however, is defensive (answering his critics); thus it seems that he knew he was not simply name-checking a normative truth, but championing views that would have furrowed the brows of his intended readership.[94]

From these points it seems that the inclusion of Chaldeans reflects a widely held conviction among these authors – both participants and later commentators – that the crusade had entered a very different spiritual topography when it crossed into 'Saracen' territory, in which it was believed that there was a widespread fascination with astrology and the occult.

[90] WM, vol. 1, p. 280.   [91] RC, pp. 54, 73.   [92] RM, p. 63.

[93] GN, pp. 319–321. Incidentally other Christian sources depict Muslims correctly foretelling future events. In the epic poem *Gormont and Isembart*, the renegade Christian knight Isembart whilst on the point of death explained how Moorish fortune-tellers had correctly foreseen his death. *Gormont et Isembart: Fragment de Chanson de Geste du XIIe Siècle*, ed. A. Bayot (Paris: Librairie Ancienne Honore Champion, 1914), p. 59.

[94] Another Magi-related story is told by Michael the Syrian in which a dog led the Turks during their incursions into the Near East. He later compared the dog to the star which guided the Magi. Dickens, 'The sons of Magog', 441–442; MS, vol. 3, pp. 153–155.

At this point it is necessary to offer one point of caution. This is that it should not be assumed from the foregoing that peoples such as Chaldeans and Medes were included in these lists of foes simply for narrative purposes or to make a theological point. It is quite possible that these authors sincerely believed that they were quite literarily describing 'living' peoples. Strikingly, well over a century later in 1260, in a decidedly no-nonsense letter, the Templar Master, Thomas Bérard (master, 1256–1273), wrote to the west underlining the threat posed by the Mongols. His correspondence had few literary pretentions; this was a military report dealing in tactical specifics and containing a dire warning. Even so, he still listed Persians, Medes, Assyrians, and Chaldeans among the peoples recently conquered by the Mongols.[95] Clearly, he at least thought that there were *really* peoples to the east who bore these names. Thus, if the head of an institution, which could draw upon well over a century of experience in dealing in eastern affairs, could seriously believe that there were such peoples *out there* then the possibility must be entertained that the First Crusade authors thought so too.

In addition to their presentation as practitioners of the occult, Muslims were also often depicted as adherents of the pantheistic religions of Ancient Greece and Rome. This trend surfaces occasionally in the participant narratives but also in the later texts.[96] The *Gesta Francorum*, for example, includes an accusation made by Karbugha to his mother that she has been influenced by the 'furies'.[97] Likewise, the *Gesta Tancredi* alluded to Pluto, Mars, and Apollo in its representations of the religious practices and afterlife of 'Saracens' and Turks.[98] In his description of the 'idol' of Mohammed in the *Templum Domini* Ralph of Caen also asked rhetorically whether it was a statue to Mars or Apollo before stating that it was a portrayal of Mohammed. Mohammed himself is described immediately afterwards as a 'slave of Pluto'.[99] The chroniclers are not uniform in their employment of such terminology and Ralph of Caen is exceptional in his enthusiasm for linking Islam with classical religions, still it is necessary to weigh the seriousness with which these authors advanced these ideas. On one hand it could be concluded that they are simply rhetorical flourishes intended to show off the authors' classically-educated credentials; on the other, these authors may actually have believed that the 'Saracen' religion was rooted in classical paganism.

[95] 'Annales Monasterii de Burton', *Annales Monastici*, ed. H. Luard, Rolls Series XXXVI, vol. 1 (London, 1864), p. 492.
[96] For further discussion on this theme see: Völkl, *Muslime – Märtyrer – Militia Christi*, pp. 189–214.
[97] *GF*, p. 53.   [98] RC, pp. 79, 107.   [99] RC, p. 107.

The answer seems to lie at an indeterminate point between these two poles. Certainly there is nothing too implausible about the idea that these medieval authors drew such connections whilst believing that they were stating an empirical fact. As we have seen there was a long-standing conviction among western European writers that Islam was a polytheistic religion and this belief may have led some conclude that it was an outgrowth of classical pantheistic faiths. Many earlier pre-crusade authors had also described Muslims and Turks as worshipping classical Gods. The pre-Islamic Turks, for example, were presented in the *cosmography of Aethicus Ister* as worshipping Saturn.[100] Even back in the fourth century, Jerome portrayed the pre-Islamic 'Saracens' as worshippers of Venus and Lucifer (referred to in the sense of Lucifer as the 'morning star', not the Devil).[101] Moreover, in the *chansons*, Muslims are frequently portrayed as worshipping a group of 'gods' including Mohammed, Apollo, and the mysterious Tervagant. The accounts of the First crusade were influenced by vernacular epic verse and the *Chanson d'Antioche* actually describes Muslims worshipping this same trio of 'deities'.[102] The crusaders themselves may also have been encouraged in forging such connections by the Byzantines. Certainly Greek authors frequently described Muslims both as idolaters and worshippers of classical Gods. Anna Comnena depicted the 'Ishmaelites' as slaves of Aphrodite and worshippers of Astarte and Ashtaroth (classical-era Middle Eastern goddesses).[103]

Nevertheless, other evidence serves as a caution against the idea that medieval authors were serious in making these connections. Ralph of Caen may have elaborated his account of Islam with references to classical deities, but significantly the author of the *Hystoria Antiochiae atque Ierusolymarum*, who drew at times upon his work, stripped out many of these allusions. In his reworking of Ralph's description of the 'statue' of Mohammed in Jerusalem, the author makes no reference to any of the earlier-mentioned classical gods contained in Ralph's account.[104] Seemingly he thought them to be either superfluous or misleading. In addition, references to classical gods in Ralph's original account and those of other

---

[100] *The cosmography of Aethicus Ister*, p. 32.

[101] Scarfe Beckett, *Anglo-Saxon perceptions*, p. 107. In the Eastern tradition it was also said that the pre-Islamic Arabs had worshipped the morning star and Aphrodite: John of Damascus, 'On heresy', p. 153.

[102] 'Chanson d'Antioche', p. 171.

[103] AC, p. 276. See also Tolan, *Saracens*, p. 118. The accusation that Muslims worshipped Aphrodite had been made before by John of Damascus and Nicetas of Byzantium: Ducellier, *Chrétiens d'Orient*, pp. 161–162; J. Meyendorff, 'Byzantine views of Islam', *Dumbarton Oaks papers* 18 (1964), 118–119; John of Damascus, 'On heresy', pp. 153, 157.

[104] *HAI*, pp. 123–124; RA, p. 85.

chroniclers were not confined to descriptions of Muslims, but could also be made in descriptions of crusaders. Ralph of Caen presented Eberhard of Le Puiset as a 'hero of Mars', while Raymond of Aguilers tells how, after his death, Adhemar of Le Puy was briefly assailed by the 'servants of Tartarus' (*ministri Tartharei*).[105] Obviously Ralph is not describing the Christian-crusader Eberhard to be literally a devotee of Mars, his meaning here is clearly rhetorical, emphasising his martial prowess. Likewise, Raymond's reference to Tartarus is simply a synonym for Hell.

Consequently, it is difficult gauge the spirit with which these authors linked Islam to classical religions: whether humorous, rhetorical or in earnest. The reality probably lies in some indeterminate point between these positions. Perhaps the most helpful explanation is that medieval contemporaries knew very little about Islam (and generally had very little interest in it); so there was both scope for the imagination to run wild and no pressure upon them to conform to a precise established framework. As shown earlier, there was also a widely held view that almost all non-Christian religions, through their common rejection of Christ, were united by their common exposure to demonic influence.[106] Viewed from this perspective, it may well have been believed that Islam and classical religions were united by this shared characteristic.

Overall, the portrayals offered by these later authors concerning the spiritual milieu of the Near East are multi-faceted. They constitute a merging of classical descriptions of cults from the ancient world with the more recent reports of pilgrims. This splicing of the classical with the contemporary was perhaps inevitable. The monastic authors of western Christendom had many sources at their disposal for the classical period and some reports from returning crusaders and pilgrims, but little information covering the intervening centuries. Thus it is not surprising that they concertinaed history to create accounts where the Parthians and Philistines of old could rub shoulders with the Saljuqs and Fatimids of the eleventh century. In a similar vein, Islam seems to have been recast in a classical and Old Testament mould as a continuation of the idolatrous faiths of the ancient world.[107] Ralph of Caen even compares it to the worship of Baal.[108]

Within this vivid scene, virtually none of these later authors reveal any actually factual information about Islam itself. Most follow the standard

---

[105] RC, p. 110; RA, p. 85.   [106] Köhler, *Alliances and treaties*, pp. 31–32.

[107] See also Tolan, *Saracens*, pp. 105–134.

[108] RC, p. 78. It might be pointed out however that clerical writers often depicted themselves protecting the Church against the 'worshippers of Baal' when describing their struggles with many enemies including western European Christians: See, for example: OV, vol. 5, p. 252.

line of presenting it as a polytheistic religion which worships Mohammed as one of its Gods.[109] There are however some exceptions to this pattern, most notably Guibert of Nogent. He is among the handful of writers to take an interest in Islam and its origins. His views are polemical in the extreme and he single-handedly dispels the popular modern notion that individuals tend to be more favourably disposed towards a different belief system once they have learnt more about it. The gist of his account of the rise of Islam is as follows: Guibert explains that following the death of a patriarch of Alexandria, at some point in the recent past, the various factions of the Church eventually decided that he would be succeeded by a hermit living nearby. Still, on closer inspection, it transpired that the hermit's theology was severely at variance with orthodox Catholicism and consequently his election was rejected. The hermit was distressed at these events and, like Arius, is said to have wanted revenge. This hermit is then depicted receiving a visitation from the Devil who promised him power and authority. The Devil told him to look for a certain young man who he should train and instruct. Guibert states that this youth was Mohammed (*Mathomus*). In time, so his story goes, under the hermit's guidance, Mohammed began to draw people away from Christianity by teaching them that God existed only in one person (effectively rejecting the Holy Trinity) and that Jesus was solely human and not divine. He is also said to have ordered his followers: to be circumcised, to fast and then he permitted them to carry out all kinds of immoral and lustful behaviour. The hermit is also reported to have sought wealth by marrying the young Mohammed to a rich widow. He goes on to discuss some of Mohammed's later alleged actions and deeds, arguing that he developed epilepsy which would often send him into fits. Mohammed is also shown supplying his people with a written law which he contrived to deliver to them in a manner that was intended to appear miraculous in their eyes. He is said to have trained a cow to respond to his voice and then to have tied this book of law between its horns. Subsequently, when surrounded by a crowd, the cow (hidden in a tent nearby) is shown to have heard Mohammed's voice and to have come into their midst; an act which convinced the crowd that a miraculous act had taken place. Guibert's story concludes with a lengthy and mocking reflection on Mohammed's death; he reports that Mohammed fell into an epileptic fit and was then eaten by pigs.[110]

Even from this brief outline, it is evident that Guibert sought to ridicule and deride the Islamic faith, but he also wanted to dispel the idea that Mohammed could genuinely have had any divine experiences. Describing

[109] RM, pp. 46, 51, 60, 73, 106, 107; RC, pp. 73, 107.   [110] GN, pp. 94–100.

Mohammed as a man suffering from epilepsy, who deceived his followers into thinking that he had been given the Koran by God, clearly marks his attempt to provide an alternative explanation for these claims. It is also noteable that deep beneath the layers of polemic and denunciation lies some genuine knowledge.[111] Unlike many of his contemporaries he was aware that Muslims believe Mohammed to be a prophet, not a God. Other practices and events such as circumcision and polygamy, and also Mohammed's marriage to a wealthy widow are referenced, albeit in highly hostile and distorted forms.

Exactly where Guibert acquired his material on Mohammed is unclear. He tells his readers that the written sources at his disposal were silent on this subject, compelling him to rely upon verbal reports.[112] This is not surprising; by the early twelfth century few authors in western Christendom had written much on the origins of Islam. Even so, it is not impossible to identify the ultimate source of at least some of Guibert's assertions. Many of his stories bear distinctive eastern Christian hallmarks raising the possibility that these tales had worked their way across the Mediterranean into Northern France.[113] For example, Guibert's report that Mohammed was instructed by a heretic hermit, who was following in the footsteps of the ancient heresiarch Arius (d.336), references several themes commonly found in eastern Christian texts. A particularly early example of this allegation can be found in the eighth-century work of John of Damascus. This eastern Christian author is the first to suggest that Mohammed conversed with an Arian monk. In making this claim he was presumably attempting to explain why Muslims, like Arians, reject the divinity of Christ.[114] The ultimate root of these legends about a monk encountering Mohammed is the Islamic tradition that a Christian monk named Bahira was the first to identify Mohammed as a prophet. Nevertheless, Muslim authors have strenuously denied that Bahira provided any kind of instruction to Mohammed because this would imply that Mohammed's message was not solely founded on the received word of God.[115] Thus, this theme of a monk-instructor emerged within the early Eastern-Christian tradition.[116]

---

[111]   Rubenstein, *Armies of Heaven*, pp. 123–125.   [112]   GN, p. 94.

[113]   Leclercq, *Portraits* croisés, p. 230.

[114]   John of Damascus, 'On heresy', p. 153. Interestingly Muslim authors were also aware of the connection between their own theology and Arianism and spoke approvingly of Arius' doctrines. B. Roggema, *The legend of Sergius Bahīrā: eastern Christian apologetics and apocalyptic in response to Islam*, History of Christian-Muslim Relations IX (Leiden: Brill, 2009), pp. 168–169, 172–173. Ademar of Chabannes also made this association, see: Frassetto, 'The image of the Saracen', p. 87.

[115]   Roggema, *The legend of Sergius Bahīrā*, pp. 151–154.

[116]   Although it should be pointed out that the idea of Islam as an Arian heresy was also present in Pisan circles. This conviction appears in the *Carmen in victoriam Pisanorum*

Other aspects of Guibert's work similarly find their echo in earlier Byzantine or Armenian writings.[117] His assertion that Mohammed suffered from epilepsy draws upon a tradition found in the *Chronographia* of Theophanes Confessor (d.818) – a work that was translated into Latin by Anastasius Bibliothecarius in the ninth century.[118] Moreover, Guibert's description of the reassurance offered to Mohammed's wife by the hermit after his alleged epileptic fits sounds very similar to the comfort offered to her by a 'false monk' in Theophanes' work.[119] Perhaps the most bizarre part of Guibert's account is his description of a trained cow delivering the Koran to Mohammed. Again, he was not the originator of this tale, indeed it seems to have been in wider circulation in western Europe at this time.[120] Its basic elements derive ultimately from the eastern Christian tradition, for example the Syriac *Legend of Sergius Baḥīrā*.[121] Assertions that the Islamic religion encourages carnality, feature in multiple traditions and seem to be a response to the Muslim practice of polygamy and the promises of the afterlife. Exactly where Guibert's story about Mohammed being eaten by pigs originated from is unclear, but again it appears in several other contemporary sources and it may have derived ultimately from the Iberian tradition where similar stories had been told in the past. It was certainly to have a long afterlife.[122]

---

commemorating the Pisan campaign against Mahdia (1087). See: Campopiano, 'La culture pisane', p. 84. For further discussion and the text see H. Cowdrey, 'The Mahdia campaign of 1087', *English Historical Review* 92 (1977), 1–29 (reference to Arius p. 27). For further discussion on Byzantine influences on Western attitudes towards the Islamic religion see: M. d'Alverny, 'La connaissance de l'Islam en Occident du IXe au milieu du XIIe siècle', *L'Occidente e l'Islam nell'alto medioevo*, vol. 2 (Spoleto, 1965), pp. 577–602; Loutchitskaja, 'L'image des musulmans', 722.

[117] For further discussion see: Loutchitskaja, 'L'image des musulmans', 724–727.

[118] *The chronicle of Theophanes Confessor*, p. 464. Several authors adopted this view including Guibert's contemporary Sigebert of Gembloux. See: Sigebert of Gembloux, 'Chronica', p. 323.

[119] Translation from *The chronicle of Theophanes Confessor*, pp. 464–465. Roggema has suggested that Theophanes' 'false monk' should not automatically be identified as Bahira. She also points out that in Anastasius' translation, this false monk is named as an adulterer, not a monk (Roggema, *The legend of Sergius Baḥīrā*, pp. 183, 185).

[120] Tolan, *Saracens*, p. 141.

[121] Roggema, *The legend of Sergius Baḥīrā*, pp. 194, 282–285. Strikingly several features of Guibert's account, including Mohammed's alleged epilepsy and the story about him being eaten by pigs also appear in the roughly contemporary work of Embrico of Mainz. A cow is central to his account as well although it plays a rather different role. See: J. Tolan, 'Embrico of Mainz', *Christian-Muslim relations: a bibliographical history, volume 3 (1050–1200)*, ed. D. Thomas and A. Mallett (Leiden: Brill, 2011), pp. 592–594; J. Tolan, 'Antihagiography: Embrico of Mainz's *Vita Mahumeti*', *Sons of Ishmael: Muslims through European eyes in the Middle Ages* (Gainesville, FL: University Press of Florida, FL: 2008), pp. 1–18. This story among others was dismissed by the contemporary author Petrus Alfonsi, see: Petrus Alfonsi, *Dialogue against the Jews*, pp. 153–154.

[122] Daniel, *Islam and the West*, pp. 18–19, 126–127; Tolan, *Saracens*, pp. 142–143; Roggema, *The legend of Sergius Baḥīrā*, p. 191; J. Tolan, 'Un cadavre mutilé: le déchirement

Overall, we should probably believe Guibert's claim to have gathered – orally – as many ideas and rumours as possible about Mohammed and then to have compiled them into a single account. His deeply antagonistic account contains a jigsaw puzzle of different influences and traditions, but many of these share the common trait of deriving either recently or historically from eastern Christian sources.

An important aspect of Guibert's account is that he does not present the rise of Islam as a unique event. Rather he depicts Mohammed as simply the last in a line of eastern heresiarchs and the Near East itself as a long-standing incubator of religious error. He observes that the faith of 'Orientals' (*orientales*) has always been inconstant and he builds upon this idea by painting a vivid picture of Eastern spirituality within which Mohammed and the 'Saracen' religion is surrounded by lacklustre and sinning Christian priests, heretics, and pagans. He shows how generation after generation of heresy has caused the faith of this region to fall further and further from the true faith until it reached its contemporary condition, exemplified by the religion propounded by Mohammed.[123] Within this portrayal he was clearly aware that some explanation was required to account for the formation of this remarkable religious environment. His view was that the air in the Near East is purer than in other climes and that this produces humans with lighter bodies and greater intelligence. He builds on this predicate by arguing that equipped with this enhanced intellect, the people of this region long ago became too theologically curious and began to dabble with unorthodox beliefs; a process culminating ultimately in the formation of dangerous heresies. In this way, Guibert's explanation for Islam and the religions of the east is founded in contemporary 'scientific' convictions – ultimately derived from the Hippocratic school of thought – concerning the effect of different climates/geographies upon physiology. This thinking was centred on the belief that the heat and humidity of different regions will affect a people's humoural balance (four humours: blood, phlegm, yellow bile, and black bile) which will in turn affect their behaviour and physical constitution.[124] A similar influence can be found in William of Malmesbury's *Gesta* where he speculated that the Turks' reliance on the bow was

polémique de Mahomet', *Le Moyen Âge: Revue d'Histoire et de Philologie* 104.1 (1998), 53–72. See also J. Tolan, 'European accounts of Muḥammad's life', *The Cambridge companion to Muhammed*, Cambridge Companions to Religion (Cambridge: Cambridge University Press, 2010), pp. 226–250. Notably in the *Chanson de Roland* a statue of Mohammed is said to have been thrown to the ground and then bitten and trampled by pigs and dogs: *SR*, p. 119.

[123] GN, pp. 89–92.

[124] For an introduction to this subject see: N. Arikha, *Passions and tempers: a history of the humours* (New York: Ecco, 2007). For further discussion, see also Akbari, *Idols in the east*, pp. 155–199.

linked to their physiology. He argued that because the Turks were raised in an eastern climate they were so dehydrated from the sun that there was very little blood in their veins and that consequently they could not risk the blood-loss involved in close-combat.[125]

New Information and Classical Influences

At many points in these narratives, the later chroniclers of the First Crusade supply 'new' information about the Turks which does not appear in the participant narratives. Ralph of Caen, for example, noted that the Turks used small crescent-shaped shields in battle – a statement that is probably accurate.[126] Orderic Vitalis described a number of Turks as drunks – statements that could either be casual defamation but are quite likely to be based on observed fact (many Muslim and eastern Christians allude to drunken Turks).[127] Gilo of Paris styled the Turks wearing purple -plumes on their heads – a statement straight out of the *Aeneid* which finds no echo in contemporary sources.[128] Robert the Monk and Gilo of Paris both speak of Jana ad-Daulah, ruler of Homs, sending the first crusaders a selection of gifts including a golden bow – a statement that is probably true given the centrality of the 'bow' in Turkish symbology.[129]

Regarding such material it is not often so easy to divide factual obser-vation (perhaps acquired from a conversation with a returning crusader) from imaginative embellishment. In some cases, as with the earlier cases, a reasonably confident identification can be made. To take another exam-ple, no source written by any participant in the First Crusade corrobo-rates the widely held belief among later writers that the Turks stocked their quivers with poisoned arrows; references of this kind only occur in the works of monastic chroniclers in western Christendom writing some time later.[130] It is hard to believe that had the Turks actually used poi-soned weapons this detail would have been overlooked when participants (and writers from other cultures across the Near East), who had seen

---

[125] WM, vol. 1, pp. 600–602.   [126] RC, p. 28.

[127] OV, vol. 5, pp. 92 (vol. 6), 112. See for example: *The history of the Seljuq Turks*, p. 32; Usama ibn Munqidh, *The book of contemplation*, p. 71; AC, 179. For discussion see: Peacock, *The great Seljuk empire*, p. 174.

[128] GP, p. 162; Virgil, *Aeneid*, trans. F. Ahl (Oxford: Oxford University Press, 2008), p. 213.

[129] RM, p. 91; GP, p. 220; Clauson, 'Turks and wolves', 18. There are similar stories about the Turks giving such gifts. Orderic Vitalis, for example, described the sultan of Baghdad giving a group of imprisoned Franks their freedom with the gift of a golden arrow: OV, vol. 6, p. 122. See also Rashid al-Din, 'The compendium of chronicles', *Classical writings of the medieval Islamic world: Persian histories of the Mongol dynasties, volume III*, trans. W. Thackston (London: I.B. Tauris, 2012), p. 23.

[130] RM, pp. 23, 25, 75; GP, p. 72; WM, vol. 1, p. 602.

them in battle, came to write their accounts. Still, it is difficult to be certain on this point. The tenth-century traveller Ibn Faqih al-Hamadhani, describing various Turkic communities in Central Asia, mentioned that one group of Turks employed poisoned arrows, although this seems to have been exceptional.[131] There is, however, another explanation. The Turks do not generally seem to have used poison but, according to the *Aeneid*, the Parthians did. Virgil speaks of Jupiter sending down one of his two evil handmaidens to visit death and destruction on mankind and describes them through the following simile:

> Much like an arrow, propelled through a cloud by the torque of a
>   bowstring,
> Armed with a savagely virulent poison and fired by a Parthian.[132]

Needless to say, many First Crusade authors were familiar with Virgil's work, citing him in many contexts, and, given that they deemed the Turks to be latter-day Parthians, the possibility has to be entertained that they simply assumed that the alleged practices of this ancient people would still have been implemented by their Turkish 'descendants'.[133]

The Turks and the Apocalypse

Shortly after the crusader conquest, a Russian abbot named Daniel made the arduous journey from his northern homeland to Jerusalem. His expedition took several years, seemingly between 1106 and 1108; during which time he travelled extensively in the Holy Land, winning favour with King Baldwin I. Among the many places he visited was the ancient town of Capernaum on the shores of the Sea of Galilee. Daniel could see from the ancient remains that it had once been a major settlement but now it was deserted.[134] The abandonment of so prominent a biblical site clearly sparked his curiosity and, upon enquiry, he learnt that the Franks did not wish to settle there for a specific reason: they believed that the future Antichrist would arise from Capernaum.[135] The scriptural basis

---

[131] Ibn Faqih al-Hamadhani, 'On the Turks and their lands', p. 51.

[132] Translation from Virgil, *Aeneid*, p. 324.

[133] Plutarch also mentions the Parthians use of poison. See: *Plutarch's Moralia*, trans. W. Helmbold, vol. 6 (Cambridge, MA: Harvard University Press, 1939), p. 373.

[134] Archaeological evidence has shown that there was a very small native village in Capernaum that was occupied 'more or less continuously' from the first century BC until the thirteenth. See: D. Pringle, *Secular buildings in the crusader kingdom of Jerusalem: an archaeological gazetteer* (Cambridge: Cambridge University Press, 1997), p. 46.

[135] Daniel the Abbot, 'The life and journey of Daniel, abbot of the Russian land', *Jerusalem pilgrimage, 1099–1185*, ed. and trans. J. Wilkinson, J. Hill and W. F. Ryan (London: Hakluyt Society, 1988), p. 152.

for this conviction can be found in the gospels of Matthew and Luke where Christ rebukes several towns, including Capernaum, whose populations had failed to repent upon hearing His message and seeing His works of power (Matthew, 11: 23; Luke, 10: 15). Nevertheless the gospel writers make no reference to the Antichrist in this context; this association was forged far later in the Syriac *Apocalypse* by Pseudo-Methodius which states that the Antichrist will rule over Capernaum.[136] This eschatological work was well known in both western Europe and the Levant and clearly it was taken so seriously that no one among the Franks wished to settle in Capernaum.

Abbot Daniel's tale is striking, but it is also rare; only a handful of authors suggest that the Franks were preoccupied with eschatological considerations. As the First Crusade progressed the pilgrims seem rapidly to have become aware that something truly momentous was happening. Their tales describe a world in which the tides of the heavenly and earthly realms were flowing swiftly together towards their culmination in Jerusalem. During their journey, the frontiers between earth and heaven are depicted being endlessly crossed and re-crossed by: warrior saints and martyrs descending to do battle; the souls of fallen pilgrims first ascending to heaven and then descending to give sage advice to their living comrades; and portents sent by God to lead the campaign to its culmination. At the crusade's conclusion the pilgrims could reflect upon the enormity of their achievement: Jerusalem was in Christian hands and, in their eyes, 'paganism' had been revealed to be utterly devoid of power. For these reasons they may well have felt that their deeds had heralded a new phase in mankind's history; some even saw it as a fulfilment of prophecy.[137] Even so, the question of whether they saw themselves as actors in an apocalyptic end-times narrative is more problematic.

The role of eschatological ideas in the first crusaders' thought world has long been a source of controversy and debate.[138] The crux of the problem is that on one hand there are only a few conspicuous allusions to eschatological themes in the main narratives, particularly those drawn up by the participants. On the other, there are rather more passages in these chronicles which could be interpreted as communicating apocalyptic overtones through their descriptions of events and uses of biblical

---

[136] Pseudo-Methodius, *Apocalypse*, pp. 63–65.   [137] *FE*, pp. 132, 140–142.

[138] For a sample of the key works to deal with this topic see: Rubenstein, *Armies of Heaven*, *passim*; Riley-Smith, *The First Crusade and the idea of Crusading*, p. 143 (see also p. 35); N. Cohn, *The pursuit of the Millennium: revolutionary millenarians and mystical anarchists of the Middle Ages* (London: Paladin, 1970); Housley, *Fighting for the cross*, p. 198; J. Flori, *L'Islam et la Fin des temps: L'interprétation prophétique des invasions musulmanes dans la chrétienté médiévale* (Paris: Seuil, 2007), pp. 250–265; Flori, *Pierre l'Ermite*, pp. 175–177.

citation and exegesis.[139] It is not the purpose of this section to fully explore the claims made by the protagonists in this particular debate, but rather to examine those passages which situate Turks or 'Saracens' within an end times narrative.

To begin, whatever the crusaders may themselves have felt about the end times, they were entering a region where many of the Christian and Muslim communities they encountered enroute were convinced that the rise of the Saljuqs and/or the advent of the crusaders represented formative stages in the coming apocalypse. One crucial element in contemporary eastern Christian and Muslim apocalyptic thought was that the Turks were the embodiment of the famous 'peoples of the North', Gog and Magog.

These races appear in several places in the Bible. Among the most important references are those found in the book of Ezekiel (chapters 38 and 39) which explains the prophecy that God will instigate an invasion by these northern peoples against the Israelites as a punishment for their sins. In Revelation 20 (verses 7–8), Gog and Magog appear again in this end-times narrative as the allies of Satan, released from his thousand-year imprisonment. Their depredations will finally be brought to an end when they are consumed by fire from heaven and when Satan is thrown into a lake of fire and sulphur.

In the centuries following the writing of these biblical books, many authors in the eastern Mediterranean attempted to identify the peoples of Gog and Magog, whilst speculating about the location of their northern

---

[139] For further discussion see: J. Rubenstein, 'Godfrey of Bouillon versus Raymond of Saint-Gilles: how Carolingian kingship trumped millenarianism at the end of the First Crusade', *The legend of Charlemagne in the Middle Ages: power, faith and crusade*, ed. M. Gabriele and J. Stuckey (New York: Palgrave Macmillan, 2008), pp. 59–75. J. and L. Hill have also pointed out that Raymond of Aguilers draw upon imagery from Revelation in his account of the conquest of Jerusalem, see RA, p. 150. There are also several further materials which relate to this debate. See for example discussion on the Jewish chronicle of Bar Simson and its report of Emich of Leningen's eschatological claims: Riley-Smith, 'The First Crusade and the persecution of the Jews', 59–60. Benzo of Alba also suggested that Henry IV should rule in Jerusalem, a claim which calls to mind notions of the 'Last Emperor'. For discussion on the theme of the 'Last Emperor' during the pre-crusade period see: Gabriele, *Empire of memory*, pp. 107–128 and *passim*. See also Tolan's discussion on Peter Tudebode (Tolan, *Saracens*, p. 111). For pre-crusading apocalyptic ideas concerning Jerusalem, see: D. Callahan, 'Al-Hākim, Charlemagne and the destruction of the church of the Holy Sepulcher in Jerusalem on the writings of Ademar of Chabannes', *The legend of Charlemagne in the Middle Ages: power, faith and crusade*, ed. M. Gabriele and J. Stuckey (New York: Palgrave Macmillan, 2008), pp. 41–57; M. Frassetto, 'The image of the Saracen as heretic in the sermons of Ademar of Chabannes', *Western views of Islam in medieval and early modern Europe*, ed. D. Blanks and M. Frassetto (Basingstoke: Macmillan, 1999), pp. 83–96. Buc similarly expresses rather neatly the problems engaged with studying this theme: Buc, *Holy War*, p. 9 (see also pp. 101–105).

homelands. The Jewish historian Josephus in his *Antiquities* made a particularly influential contribution to this debate, linking Gog and Magog to the Scythians living north of the Caucasus.[140] He also described in his *Jewish War* how Alexander the Great constructed his famous Iron Gates to prevent the incursions made by Scythian peoples.[141] These ideas soon appeared in the Christian tradition, being widely popularised in the seventh century by Pseudo-Methodius.[142] With this background, it is perhaps not surprising that many saw the inrush of the Saljuq Turk as the peoples of Gog and Magog, or even the harbingers of the coming apocalypse. In the Syriac tradition the Turks were identified specifically as the peoples of Magog by several authors, most strikingly by Michael the Syrian who argued that the Turks were – like the people of Magog – descendants of Noah's son Japheth (Genesis 10).[143] Michael the Syrian's work depicts the Turks as the embodiment of the prophecy of Ezekiel although he does not place their invasions in the apocalyptic context described in Revelation.[144] Exactly when Syriac authors first made this association between the Turks and Magog is unclear. Michael was the first author to unambiguously make this connection, although there seems to have been a growing identification between the two that might date back as far as the work of Jacob of Edessa (d.708).[145]

Several Georgian and Armenian writers drew similar conclusions, associating the Turks with the peoples of Gog and Magog including the author of the early-twelfth-century Armenian eschatological work, *Sermo de Antichristo*.[146] Matthew of Edessa did not draw this connection explicitly, but in a similar vein, he felt that the events unfolding across the region during his lifetime were proof that Satan had been released

---

[140] Many later authors associated the lands of Gog and Magog with Scythian territory. See, for example, Isidore of Seville, *The etymologies*, p. 288.

[141] Van Donzel and Schmidt, *Gog and Magog*, pp. 9–11; A. Anderson, *Alexander's gate, Gog and Magog, and the inclosed nations*, Monographs of the Medieval Academy of America V (Cambridge, MA: The Medieval Academy of America, 1932), pp. 15–19.

[142] Van Donzel and Schmidt, *Gog and Magog*, p. 32.

[143] Dickens, 'The Sons of Magog', 435. The Turks were widely considered to be the sons of Japhet in Islamic sources. See, for example: Rashid al-Din, 'The compendium of chronicles', p. 20.

[144] Dickens, 'The Sons of Magog', 436. Interestingly, as Dickens has shown, Michael's presentation of the Turks as the sons of Magog is not a solely hostile description and in some respects portrays the Turks in a 'positive' way. He acknowledges the brutality of their invasions but also shows how they conducted a God-led assault upon the Greek persecutors of the Syriac Church and even that they had a divine mandate to rule. Dickens, 'The Sons of Magog', *passim*.

[145] Dickens, 'Turkāyē: turkic Peoples', pp. 72–75; Dickens, 'The Sons of Magog', 436–438. Dickens points out that it is difficult to identify which parts of Jacob of Edessa's text are his own and which are the introductions of later redactors.

[146] Rapp, *Studies in medieval Georgian historiography*, p. 257; *Sermo de Antichristo*, pp. 19, 109; Pogossian, 'The last emperor', pp. 457–502.

from his thousand year confinement, bringing calamity and ultimately the end times.[147] In this he was following the prophecies made in 1030 and 1036/7 by Yovhannes Kozern.[148] Van Donzel and Schmidt have also shown how these ideas filtered into Islamic thought, eventually prompting the remarkable mission launched by Caliph al-Wathiq to discover the legendary wall created by Alexander the Great (842–845) to prevent the invasions of these northern peoples.[149] By the ninth century many Muslim authors saw the Turks as synonymous with Gog and Magog, although some argued more specifically that the Turks were the only one of the races of Gog and Magog who had not been successfully entrapped by Alexander's wall.[150] Reflecting upon these various traditions, it is striking that a significant proportion of the peoples encountered by the crusaders during their journey to Jerusalem believed that the advent of the Saljuqs was an event of eschatological significance.

Writers in western Christendom had similarly been interested in the identification of Gog and Magog and in earlier centuries, Huns, Goths, Alans, and Magyars had all been presented in this way at various points.[151] Shortly before the first millennium it seems that rumours were circulating that the Hungarians were the peoples of Gog and Magog.[152] Even the notion that the Turks were linked to Gog and Magog was present in the early-medieval western European tradition. The *cosmography of Aethicus Ister* (written in the early eighth century) described the Turks in this way, although this anonymous author was drawing heavily upon eastern Christian ideas rather than on an established western European tradition.[153]

Nevertheless, the crusading chronicles, at least those written by participants, do not make this connection. They mention the Caucasus, and the Turks are certainly portrayed as wild, mounted, numerous, and barbaric

---

147 MacEvitt, 'The chronicle of Matthew of Edessa', 175; La Porta, 'Conflicted coexistence', pp. 108–110. Although importantly Matthew of Edessa does not describe the Turks explicitly as the races of Gog and Magog. He identifies them rather as descended from Noah's son Ham (rather than the descendants of Noah's son Japheth who is said to be the forefather of the people of Magog). MacEvitt, 'The chronicle of Matthew of Edessa', p. 167; ME, p. 59. See also Van Donzel and Schmidt, *Gog and Magog*, pp. 38–45.

148 T. Andrews, 'The new age of prophecy: the chronicle of Matthew of Edessa and its place in Armenian historiography', *The medieval chronicle VI*, ed. E. Kooper (Amsterdam: Rodopi, 2009), pp. 110–111. See also Beihammer, 'Die Ethnogenese', 596–599; Pogossian, 'The last emperor', p. 461.

149 Van Donzel and Schmidt, *Gog and Magog, passim.*

150 Van Donzel and Schmidt, *Gog and Magog*, pp. 74–103.

151 Anderson, *Alexander's gate*, pp. 12–14.

152 R. Huygens, 'Un témoin de la crainte de l'an 1000: La lettre sur les Hongrois', *Latomus: revue d'études latines* 15 (1956), 225–239.

153 *The cosmography of Aethicus Ister*, pp. 28–32.

(all characteristics referenced in eastern Christian depictions of the 'peoples of the north'), but they are not explicitly linked to Gog and Magog. The only chronicler who might have attempted to make such allusions was the continuator of Frutolf of Michelsberg's chronicle. Describing the rise of the Saljuqs he explains that they suddenly appeared in huge numbers 'from the north' under the leadership of four sultans.[154] He makes no specific mention of Gog and Magog, but contextually the reference to the invasion of numerous northern peoples fits with this prophecy, whilst the reference to the Turks serving under four leaders may distantly call to mind the four horsemen of the book of Revelation. It might also be added that in Frutolf of Michelsberg's original chronicle (the work this author was extending) there is a reference to an ancient raid by the Turks launched in 766 emerging from the 'Caspian gates', which again calls to mind an eschatological theme.[155] Nevertheless, this evidence is thin ice; too vague and implicit to support any definite conclusion.

The other chronicles are silent on this matter. The seeming lack of interest among crusaders on so fundamental and topical a theme in contemporary eastern Christian thought is significant, particularly given their deep dependence on these same authorities elsewhere (and the fact that some of the eastern Christian apocalyptic narratives cast the crusaders as their saviours!)[156] This matter becomes even more striking given that Raymond of Aguilers' chronicle actually reports two instances when Syrian Christians (*Suriani*) communicated to the crusaders that they believed the crusade to be the fulfilment of biblical prophecy. One Syrian apparently even predicted the finding of the holy lance to the Frankish priest Eberhard while he was in Tripoli.[157] Evidently, the Franks had access to these eschatological beliefs so their unwillingness to draw heavily upon them is all the more conspicuous, particularly given their readiness to borrow elsewhere. In Raymond's case the explanation may lie in the evident contempt he held for the Christian Syrians (although this did not stop him from recording their views).

Perhaps the fact that the crusaders did not draw upon such themes demonstrates that whilst they relied heavily upon their Eastern co-religionists for information and guidance, they were not drawing wholesale upon their thought-worlds. There are several other major elements of Byzantine and other eastern Christian attitudes towards Islam that are conspicuous by their absence from crusading narratives (either those

---

[154] *FE*, p. 132.   [155] Frutolf of Michelsberg, 'Chronicon', p. 160.

[156] It is noteworthy that the presentation of the Turks as Scythians trapped by Alexander the Great behind the Iron Gates would gain currency in later centuries. Meserve, 'Medieval sources for Renaissance theories', pp. 414–415.

[157] RA, pp. 118, 129–130; Flori, *L'Islam et la Fin des temps*, pp. 268–269.

written by crusaders or by later authors). For example, the crusaders hardly ever described their foes as 'Hagarenes' or 'Ishmaelites' (despite the fact that they used many other names); yet as Hugh of Fleury observed, this was standard terminology in Byzantine sources.[158] They also did not accuse Muslims of being Manicheans – another typical Byzantine accusation.[159] Rather, their interests and borrowings are selective and suggest that it was they who were asking the questions; setting out an agenda of topics that they considered to be of interest, rather than passively receiving instruction on what their eastern teachers thought relevant.

The later authors of crusade narratives show fractionally more interest in apocalyptic material of this kind in their descriptions of the Turks, but even here this theme is generally marginal. This is certainly the case in Robert the Monk's chronicle. He too viewed the crusade as an immensely important event and said so in his prologue.[160] He retold the tale of the expedition complete with a heavenly trumpet, spiritual warriors in white, the appearances of saints, divine fire, and ultimately a serious defeat for the Devil.[161] Even so, specific references to a future apocalypse, implicit or explicit, are few. He certainly saw the campaign as the fulfilment of biblical prophecy (drawing upon Isaiah 60), but he did not explicitly fit it into a pre-existing eschatological schema.[162] There are, however, a couple of passages which require closer attention. One of these has been discussed earlier (his reference to *Chorozaim*). Another occurs in his description of Karbugha's famous meeting with his mother. In his account, Robert drew heavily upon the *Gesta Francorum*, but he included some new material in their alleged conversation including a biblical reference with strong apocalyptic overtones: Deuteronomy 32: 30.[163]

> How could one have routed a thousand, and two put a myriad to flight, unless their Rock had sold them, the Lord had given them up?

This verse was included as part of Karbugha's mother's attempt to convince her son that if he should march against the crusaders then his defeat will inevitably follow. Her fundamental argument, embroidered with this

---

[158] Hugh of Fleury, 'Historia regum Francorum', *MGHS*, vol. 9 (Hanover, 1851), p. 397. The exceptions to this pattern are all authors writing in western Christendom in later years, see: 'Gesta Adhemari', p. 354; WM, vol. 1, p. 412; OV, vol. 5, passim; BB, p. 41.

[159] Ducellier, *Chrétiens d'Orient*, pp. 165–166; Beihammer, 'Orthodoxy and religious antagonism', 23.

[160] RM, p. 4.   [161] RM, pp. 8, 51–55, 68, 69.   [162] RM, p. 110.   [163] RM, p. 62.

verse, was that the crusader army was supported by God and therefore could not be defeated even by vastly superior forces. This exchange occurs at a pivotal point in Robert's text. The crusaders' victories at Antioch are represented as the turning point for the entire campaign and Karbugha's defeat is the climax of these events. Thus this conversation discusses the tipping point when the fortunes of war swung decisively in favour of the Christians. Although this verse is not – in and of itself – explicitly eschatological, the possibility has to be entertained that it was included with this intent. Significantly, the famous *Apocalypse* of Pseudo-Methodius also includes this passage in a very similar context.[164] This seventh-century Syriac text, which purported to be the work of the fourth-century martyr Methodius, laid out a schema for history which focused on the rise of Islam, its supremacy over Christian lands, and finally its eventual collapse. The irrevocable defeat of the 'Ishmaelites' at the hands of a resurgent Christianity would then usher in the end times. Crucially, Deuteronomy 32:30 is introduced by Pseudo-Methodius at the very moment when the fortunes of war turn suddenly against the Muslims.[165] Thus, this verse underlines a vital juncture in his history. Placed side by side then it is striking that both Pseudo-Methodius and later Robert the Monk employ this verse to pinpoint and spiritually contextualise the specific moment when the Muslim armies will suddenly suffer a catastrophic defeat that will result in their expulsion from the Holy Land. Although Robert the Monk does not allude explicitly to Pseudo-Methodius, the parities between these texts are substantial.

On these grounds it seems likely that Robert was drawing in some way upon the Pseudo-Methodian tradition. Still, the line of transmission from the original text to Robert is unclear. Pseudo-Methodius' *Apocalypse* was widely known in western Europe both in Latin translations and later redactions.[166] Perhaps the most famous text (pre-crusade) influenced by his work was Adso of Montier-en-Der's *De Ortu et Tempore Antichristi*. Adso's work was written in *c.* 950 and was widely disseminated.[167]

---

[164] Flori has also noted similarities between the reports of Karbugha's conversation with his mother and the Pseudo-Methodian tradition although he does not focus on this biblical passage. Flori, *L'Islam et la Fin des temps*, p. 268.

[165] Pseudo-Methodius, *Apocalypse*, p. 57. This verse was clearly in circulation during the late seventh-century. It also appears in John bar Penkāyē's Rīš Mellē', although here is occurs in a rather different context, elaborating the rapid advance of the Arab Muslim forces, rather than foretelling their future defeat. S. Brock, 'North Mesopotamia in the late seventh century: book XV of John bar Penkāyē's Rīš Mellē', Jerusalem Studies in Arabic and Islam 9 (1987), 58.

[166] See for example: Peter the Monk's redaction: Pseudo-Methodius, *Apocalypse*, pp. 74–139.

[167] *Adso Dervensis de Ortu et Tempore Antichristi*, ed. D. Verhelst, CCCM XLV (Turnhout: Brepols, 1976).

Nevertheless, if Robert was following the Pseudo-Methodian tradition, it seems that he had not acquired his information through these western European redactions because both Adso's work and the earlier Latin translation edited out the reference to Deuteronomy 32:30. Another explanation is required. An alternative is that Robert – or perhaps the returning pilgrims he interviewed – had been influenced in some way by the eastern Christians they encountered. Certainly, this same verse was widely employed by Armenian and Georgian authors in similar contexts during this same period. The Armenian translation of the Georgian *History of David, King of Kings* paraphrased this verse in a description of King David II of Georgia's (d.1125) wars against the Turks fought shortly after the First Crusade.[168] Matthew of Edessa did not include this verse, but his work has strong apocalyptic themes which draw heavily upon the Pseudo-Methodian tradition; demonstrating that these ideas were still very much in circulation.[169]

The final alternative is that Robert was guided to use this verse by other western Christian chroniclers who were using it in a less complex fashion, simply to embroider accounts of heroic victories against insurmountable odds. It certainly occurs in several histories of the Normans in Italy and Sicily and, perhaps more importantly, Paschal II included it in his letter informing Christendom of the victories of the First Crusade.[170] Nevertheless these sources lack the prophetic context that is so striking in Robert's chronicle. On this point it is impossible to be certain, but it does seem that Robert was capturing – possibly unknowingly – a distant echo of this Syriac eschatological tradition.

Another apocalyptic association referenced in several further sources was the contemporary belief that Mohammed was the Antichrist. Robert himself names Muslims at one point as attendants (*satellites*) of the Antichrist, while Ralph of Caen describes Mohammed as the 'earliest Antichrist' (*pristinus Antichristus*).[171] Naturally, according to apocalyptic

---

[168] 'The history of David', p. 320. See also 'The history of King Vaxt'ang Gorgasali', *Rewriting Caucasian history: the medieval Armenian adaptation of the Georgian chronicles*, trans. R. Thomson (Oxford: Clarendon, 1996), p. 243.

[169] MacEvitt, 'The chronicle of Matthew of Edessa', 158.

[170] See: Amatus of Montecassino, *Storia de' Normanni*, pp. 44, 141; Geoffrey of Malaterra, *De Rebus Gestis Rogerii*, p. 43; *Kb*, p. 178 (Pope Paschal II's letter to the crusaders in Asia); GN, pp. 158, 258. Although it might be pointed out that these authors may themselves have been influenced by the Greek tradition given the strong bonds between the Byzantine Empire and Italy/Sicily and especially its long-standing relationship with the monastery of Montecassino. G. Loud, 'Anna Komnena and her sources for the Normans of southern Italy', *Church and chronicle in the Middle Ages: essay presented to John Taylor*, ed. I. Wood and G. Loud (London: Hambleton, 1991), p. 42. See also 'Gesta Adhemari', p. 355.

[171] RM, p. 72; RC, p. 107.

tradition, the rise of the Antichrist is one of the final phases of world history, nevertheless Ralph's comment that Mohammed was the 'earliest Antichrist' implies that he thought him to be one of many Antichrists who will appear throughout history.[172] He reinforces this idea immediately afterwards by saying that if Mohammed's 'companion' (*socius*) had been in the Temple that day – presumably the final Antichrist – then both Antichrists (*Antichristi*) would have been destroyed.

He is not alone in identifying multiple Antichrists; this idea is well evidenced in Christian theology dating back to the early patristic era. Tertullian, Lacatantius, Polycarp, and Irenaeus are among these who speak of multiple Antichrists.[173] Augustine and Pope Gregory I argued that anyone among the faithful could become an Antichrist by denying Christ; thus establishing a host of Antichrists. From this time, many heretics were described as 'Antichrists' for their opposition to Christianity. References of this kind can be found in Gregory VII's letters pertaining to those who had separated themselves from Christ.[174] Gregory also spoke of 'precursors of Antichrist', a theme found repeatedly in medieval eschatology.[175]

Among the earliest presentations of Mohammed in this way in the western Christian tradition can be found in ninth-century Iberia. Eulogius of Cordoba for example described Mohammed as a false Christ, of the kind forewarned by Jesus (Matthew 24: 11) when he told his disciples that many false prophets would arise and lead people astray.[176] His contemporary Paul Alvarus went one stage further to describe Mohammed as an Antichrist, noting that there were many.[177] In a similar vein, in the eleventh century, the Muslim ruler of Mahdia was compared to an Antichrist in the *Carmen in victoriam Pisanorum*.[178] Such ideas also had deep roots in the eastern Christian tradition and the notion of Islam as a precursor to the Antichrist developed soon after the rise of Islam and the Arab conquest of much of the Near East.[179] In this way, Ralph's identification of Mohammed as an Antichrist need not be interpreted as proof

---

[172] RC, p. 107
[173] This section has drawn extensively upon: B. McGinn, *Antichrist: two thousand years of the human fascination with evil* (New York: Columbia University Press, 2000), pp. 66–125; R. Emmerson, *Antichrist in the Middle Ages: a study of medieval apocalypticism, art and literature* (Seattle: University of Washington Press, 1984), pp. 62–73.
[174] *The Register of Gregory VII*, pp. 238, 370.   [175] *The Register of Gregory VII*, p. 12.
[176] Tolan, *Saracens*, p. 87; Emmerson, *Antichrist in the Middle Ages*, p. 67.
[177] Tolan, *Saracens*, pp. 87–93; Flori, *La Guerre Sainte*, pp. 242–243.
[178] Cowdrey, 'The Mahdia campaign of 1087', 27.
[179] John of Damascus, 'On heresy', p. 153. For discussion see: Tolan, *Saracens*, pp. 45–50, 51–52; Hoyland, *Seeing Islam*, pp. 57–58. Note also that Matthew of Edessa used the label 'precursor of the abominable Antichrist' in his description of the Armenian lord Philaretos Brachamios, who formed a small state in Northern Syria in the 1070s-1080s: ME, pp. 137–138.

that he believed the world was now nearing its end; he clearly believed that Mohammed was among a number of earlier manifestations of the ultimate Antichrist who would appear at some unidentified point in the future.

East and West

Both in public and academic histories, the Crusades have been interpreted as a vital stage in an alleged war that has taken place between 'east' and 'west' since time immemorial. The question of whether the twain are doomed never to meet has been batted around for decades, but the debate took on a fundamentally new character following the publication of Edward Said's *Orientalism* (1978). This work advanced the case that 'western' approaches towards the 'east' have been characterised by a perpetual (and perpetually self-reinforcing) discourse asserting cultural supremacy and imperialist dominance over the oriental 'other'.[180] His work is concerned predominantly with the modern era, but he offers this as a long-standing truth stretching back to the classical era. In recent years, Said's *Orientalism* has found both its advocates and opponents, but more than anything else it challenges historians to compare his arguments against the contemporary evidence. This section will explore how the crusaders and their later narrators perceived 'the east', examining the paradigms which shaped their attitudes towards its geography and theological significance.

To begin, the crusaders' concept of 'the east' was multi-faceted and in some cases contradictory. Medieval authors referred confidently to the 'east' and yet they rarely explained precisely where this 'east' lay, what it encompassed, or where it ended.[181] The reason for this must lie partly in the fact that the 'east' was in some respects synonymous with the 'unknown'. These were lands of legends about which much was speculated but little was known for certain. The Holy Land itself lay on western Christendom's knowledge horizon. Pilgrims offered some reports about its towns and shrines but these were mere glimpses largely confined to biblical sites. Beyond the river Jordan lay mysterious places dimly recalled only in classical or biblical memory. Constantinople represented one

---

[180] Said, *Orientalism*.

[181] For a stimulating discussion on the definition of the 'Orient' and its attendant historiography see: M. O'Doherty, *The Indies and the medieval west: thought, reform, imagination*, Medieval voyaging II (Turnhout: Brepols, 2013), pp. 3–5. Lapina has also performed an excellent analysis on the development of medieval representations of the four cardinal points and their manifestations in the First Crusade chronicles: Lapina, *Warfare and the miraculous*, pp. 122–142.

among a handful of further known fixed points in the eastern quadrant of this largely-blank world map, lying as it did at the crossroads between the known world of the west and the distant lands beyond. Robert the Monk described it both as the capital of the east and the refuge for its native Christians.[182] For Ralph of Caen and the Charleville poet it marked the frontier between Europe and Asia (reflecting the contemporary tripartite division of the world into Europe, Asia, and Africa).[183]

Jerusalem was another of these fixed points but its global location was more ambiguous. On one hand the crusaders had no doubt that it lay in the east. On this point they are unanimous. Both papal and crusading correspondence speaks of the crusaders' deeds *in Orientam*.[184] The very title of Caffaro's chronicle *De liberatione civitatum Orientis* captures this point.[185] Still, viewed from another perspective, Jerusalem was emphatically not in the east. Rather it was the world's centre; the crosshairs, both of the four cardinal points and of the world's history. As Guibert of Nogent observed, it was the fount and source of all Christian preaching; a statement which tallies well with the many world maps produced across the medieval period which situate Jerusalem at the world's heart, not in its eastern margins.[186]

The crusaders' approach to these lands then was multi-faceted. Spiritually, it was the beating heart of Christianity; the site of events from both Testaments and the principal theatre in which the biblical stages of mankind's relationship with God had unfolded. Sanctified by the blood of Christ, the land itself was and is the sacred epicentre of history and consequently a place of incredible spiritual potency. In this context, viewed from the Franks' perspective, the Holy Land was not foreign territory, rather it was the homeland to which they were returning. As William of Malmesbury observed:

There in earlier days the branches of our religion sprouted; there all the apostles, except two, sanctified this place with their deaths; there, today's Christians – those who are left-, surviving by impoverished farming, contemplate starvation through tribute to these heinous ones or yearn with silent sighs for experience of our liberty because they have lost their own.[187]

According to this view, the Holy Land was not simply the domain of the 'Oriental other'. In many ways it was more central and vital to the pilgrims' thought-worlds than their own native soil; a point evidenced

---

[182] RM, p. 21. See also WM, vol. 1, p. 624.   [183] GP, p. 30.

[184] *Kb, passim.* See also, BB, p. 3.   [185] Caffaro, *De Liberatione.*

[186] GN, p. 113. He is even more explicit in his *De Vita Sua* where he explicitly names Jerusalem as the world's centre. Guibert of Nogent, 'De Vita Sua', *PL*, vol. 156 (1853), col. 896.

[187] WM, vol. 1, p. 600. For similar sentiments see: OV, vol. 5, p. 156.

by the fact that many chose to abandon their old lives and settle in the newly-founded crusader states. Nevertheless, this sense of spiritual and biblical familiarity is immediately juxtaposed against the bald fact that the vast majority of pilgrims had never been there before.

During their journey the pilgrims encountered: strange beasts (like camels), rare fabrics (like silk and purple cloth), precious foods (like sugar-cane, pepper, and 'Turkish delicacies'), and strange places (like the Dead Sea).[188] Many pilgrims returned to their homes bearing curiosities and religious items, such as relics, and palm branches. In the year following his release from captivity in 1103 Bohemond I of Antioch journeyed back to western Europe where, according to Orderic Vitalis, he laid silks and relics from the Holy Land on many altars.[189] Turkish hats (*pilleum Turcorum*) became so popular among the Frankish nobility in the kingdom of France that attempts were made to ban them.[190] Gouffier of Lastours even tried to return home with a pet lion. According to this tale, while he was out raiding he happened to hear a lion roar and he went to investigate. He eventually found the beast at the mercy of a great snake which was tightly encircling its body. Gouffier then waded in and freed the lion, which then became quite tame, following him like a dog. As might be imagined, such a pet subsequently proved a formidable ally in battle, springing enthusiastically upon Gouffier's enemies. When Gouffier eventually embarked for his return voyage, the lion was unwilling to be parted from him and tried to board the ship. The sailors however were understandably concerned at the thought of having a lion for a shipmate. Consequently when Gouffier departed, it was without his new friend, who nonetheless swam out to sea in pursuit of his beloved master for some distance.[191]

Such sights would have been entirely new for the vast majority of pilgrims; certainly they were far removed from the familiar landscape of their former lives. The Franks were also aware that they were marching along the outer perimeter of the known world. Beyond Jerusalem, so

---

[188] Bartolf of Nangis, 'Gesta Francorum Expugnantium Iherusalem', p. 505; FC, pp. 329, 339; RC, pp. 79, 106; BB, p. 34; WM, vol. 1, p. 664.

[189] OV, vol. 6, p. 68.

[190] *Constitutiones canonicorum regularium ordinis Arroasiensis*, ed. L. Milis and J. Becquet, CCCM XX (Turnhout: Brepols, 1970), p. 213. See also Scarfe Beckett, *Anglo-Saxon perceptions*, pp. 191–192. Turkish hats seem to have had a broad fashion appeal. They had previously 'caught on' in China. See: Stepanov, *The Bulgars and the Steppe Empire*, pp. 54–55. By the thirteenth century, Simon of St Quentin reports that there was a brisk trade in Turkish hats between Anatolia and England and France. See: Simon of St Quentin, *Histoire des Tartares*, ed. J. Richard (Paris: Paul Geuthner, 1965), p. 69.

[191] 'Notitiae duae Lemovicenses de Praedicatione crucis in Aquitania', *RHC: Oc*, vol. 5 (Paris, 1895), p. 351. Apparently, he was not the only Frank to acquire a pet lion and in 1102 Baldwin I sent two to the Byzantine emperor as gifts, AA, p. 636.

it was believed, lay the unknown; lands inhabited by distant peoples as strange as Amazons, Indians, and Elamites. True, they were not entirely without assistance in interpreting their new surroundings. Some among their number had read classical works which could provide some illumination and, as we have seen, they received some guidance from eastern Christians. There is little doubt however that fundamentally they knew themselves to be pilgrims in a foreign land.

The product of these two conflicting influences – the juxtaposed familiarity and foreignness of the Levantine region – seems to have been an emerging sense of rediscovery and renewal as the crusaders identified, visited, commemorated, and – in time – built-upon the locations where key biblical and historical events had taken place. This sense of wide-eyed spiritual curiosity about these recently-discovered/long-known lands is well evidenced in the sources which devote considerable attention to the locations visited by the crusaders. Fulcher of Chartres for example explained how the city of Antioch had been founded by Seleucus, son of Antiochus, on the banks of the Orontes (other authors erroneously claimed that its founder was Antiochus himself). He went on to describe its buildings, including the famous church dedicated to St Peter. He also referenced the contemporary belief that Peter founded Antioch's episcopal seat having been given the keys to Heaven by Christ.[192] This passage is illuminating because Fulcher was not merely 'describing' Antioch and its history, rather he was forging connections between the scriptural and textual knowledge of his own education/childhood and his own recent experiences in contemporary Syria. To take another example the author of the *Gesta Francorum* turns away from his tale of the Frankish advance on Jerusalem to explain how there is a church near Ramla [in Lydda] where the body of St George is buried.[193] All the crusading narratives are studded with such descriptions and they reveal the crusaders' joy at their discovery of religious sites, which were so fundamental to their faith.

The posture assumed by these authors at such points is crudely analogous to that of modern-day travellers setting out to visit sites of intense family significance, perhaps a location where an ancestor served or died during a World War. They may have heard about this ancestor all their life, but the place itself where his/her deeds took place is entirely unfamiliar. Even so, however new that location may be, it is simultaneously important, extremely intimate, and from their perspective at least – indisputably *theirs*. The crusaders seem to have felt these same sensations acutely, but with one difference. They did not consider themselves solely

---

[192] FC, pp. 215–217.   [193] *GF*, p. 87.

to be visiting a mausoleum or a monument to the past, but rather a site throbbing with God's spiritual power that transcended past, present, and future.

Later authors of First Crusade histories embroidered on the existing descriptions of religious sites, reinforcing their significance. William of Tyre added the detail that the church in Lydda had been constructed by the emperor Justinian.[194] The importance of the city of Antioch was ubiquitously underlined; William again – who drew upon Fulcher's work – was able to make a far more detailed statement of its history and spiritual significance.[195] In doing so he implicitly emphasised the notion that these were not merely distant and strange places, worthy of curiosity but little more; rather these sites were foundational pillars to the very heart of Christendom.

In their dealings with the Christians of the east the crusaders seem to have encountered again a blend of both the strange and familiar. On one hand they were generally prepared to accept eastern Christians broadly as co-religionists, and yet many of their practices and customs were strange. As shown earlier, it was believed by some authors, especially Guibert of Nogent, that the 'east' existed in a very different spiritual climate; one which was especially prone to the development of heresies. Guibert is the main source of such ideas, although they are briefly referenced by Gilo; still clearly many authors felt that this was a region in the grip of heretical beliefs because they listed Paulicians or other heretics among the crusaders' foes.[196] The tendency of Easterners towards heresy was not considered to be simply an inexplicable phenomenon, but, as we have seen, a manifestation of the region's specific climate.

These factors contextualise the crusaders' attempts to situate the non-Christians they encountered within their concept of the 'east'. As far as they were concerned the east was not simply the 'Oriental' stronghold of the Muslim other. Unbelief of any form was deemed to be merely a transitory presence within its bounds. The crusaders were emphatic in their conviction that the east rightfully – and historically – belonged to Christianity.[197] In this way, Guibert of Nogent speaks of the crusaders

---

[194] WT, vol. 1, p. 373. Pringle has shown that it is not possible to verify whether or not this statement is true. Pringle, *Churches of the crusader kingdom: volume II*, p. 10.

[195] WT, vol. 1, pp. 244–245.

[196] Although as Biddlecombe points out Guibert took a far more negative view of eastern Christians than many other authors of crusade histories, particularly Baldric of Bourgueil, see: S. Biddlecombe, 'Baldric of Bourgueil and the familia Christi', Writing the early Crusades: Text, transmission and memory, ed. M. Bull and D. Kempf (Woodbridge: Boydell, 2014), pp. 9–23.

[197] Scarfe Beckett has shown that early-medieval authors viewed the area in much the same way. Scarfe Beckett, *Anglo-Saxon perceptions*, p. 68. See also Daniel, *The Arabs*

restoring (*restituere*) the east.[198] Robert the Monk describes the crusaders seeking to 'illuminate' (*illustrare*) the 'Orient' by 'dispelling' (*depellere*) its spiritual 'blindness'; he compared the campaign's conquest of the Holy Land to the restoration of a dismembered limb to a human body.[199] He later related a conversation between the Franks and Egyptian ambassadors in which the Christian princes are reported to have said: 'This land does not belong to your people. They may have possessed it for many years but it was ours in former times and your aggressive people, because of their malice, seized it from them. So it cannot be yours however long you have held it'.[200] Such claims were contextualised with stories told of Constantine, Heraclius, Jesus and the disciples and other Biblical and Christian leaders who had lived in the region before the advent of Islam. With the foundation of the kingdom of Jerusalem, newly established churchmen were cast as continuators of ancient lines of clerics. William of Malmesbury, for example, drew up a list of all the patriarchs of Jerusalem which stretched back to Jesus' brother James; making the point that this was an office with deep historical roots.[201] In these ways these authors presented the campaign as a liberation; one which would return the east to its former sanctified condition. As Prawer pointed out, to the crusaders' eye, the campaign 'was actually a movement of [Muslim] decolonization!'[202]

From this perspective, the 'Saracens' were not perceived as indigenous inhabitants, but as interlopers to be 'illuminated' or removed. This does not mean that the crusaders saw themselves as the instruments of divine vengeance against the descendants of those who had conquered the region many centuries before. As Throop has shown, the authors of the participant narratives did occasionally refer to the campaign as an instrument of vengeance, but this was rare.[203] Rather, the chroniclers described their actions instead in more evangelical terms. The continuator of Frutolf's chronicle explained the campaign's purpose with reference to the parable of the lost sheep (Luke 15.4). In this parable, Christ compared the shepherd's search for his one lost sheep to God's care and

and mediaeval Europe, pp. 116–118; Völkl, Muslime – Märtyrer – Militia Christi, pp. 172–173.

[198] GN, p. 235.   [199] RM, pp. 13, 24.

[200] RM, p. 48. See Lapina's thoughts on this theme: Lapina, Warfare and the miraculous, pp. 132–142.

[201] WM, vol. 1, pp. 642–644.

[202] J. Prawer, 'The roots of medieval colonialism', The meeting of two worlds: cultural exchange between east and west during the period of the Crusades, V. Goss and C. Bornstein, Studies in medieval culture XXI (Kalamazoo, MI: Medieval Institute Publications, 1986), p. 24.

[203] Although Throop points out that it occurs with greater frequency in the later narratives of the crusade. Throop, Crusading as an act of vengeance, pp. 47–70.

celebration over the salvation of a single sinner. In a similar vein, the continuator presented the crusaders as shepherds going out in search of the 'lost sheep' of the east. From this perspective the crusade was constructed as a missionary enterprise within which the supremacy of the Christian message was demonstrated through the deeds of the protagonists.[204] Guibert similarly stated the crusaders' purpose as that of rebuilding of the faith in Eastern Lands, while Robert the Monk showed how the conquest of Jerusalem caused the power of Christ's crucifixion to shine like a light in 'infidel minds' (*mentes infidelium*).[205] Thus, the 'liberation' of the east was presented not merely as an act of restoration for faithful in those regions, but also as a campaign of brutal spiritual enlightenment for non-Christians.

In sum, these chroniclers offer their readers an image of a Christian army from the west, travelling at God's request to liberate: the lost eastern heartlands of their own Christian faith, the Christian peoples of the east, and the heretic and pagan peoples in that area. They generally go on to show how these objectives were achieved largely through a series of battles in which the peoples of the east ('Saracens') suffered repeated reverses at the hands of the crusader host. These defeats are given as proof of the falsity of these peoples' faiths. Ralph of Caen, for example, presents the battle of Antioch as a struggle between the east and west winds (personified through the Greek Gods of the east and west winds) in which the east wind initially gains the upper hand, but is eventually overthrown by a gust from the north-west.[206] Fulcher of Chartres described how at Heraclea the crusaders saw a sign in the sky in the shape of a spear pointing towards the east.[207] Frutolf's continuator likewise speaks of blood-coloured clouds from east and west vying with one another for supremacy in the centre of the sky during the opening stages of the campaign.[208] All these images convey this idea of contestation between the peoples of east and west.

Drawing these points together, the crusade does not emerge from the pages of these chronicles as an imperialistic enterprise. The crusaders did not consider themselves to be simply invaders subjugating a foreign land, but rather warriors who were cutting a warlike path back to their spiritual homeland. The peoples and places they encountered were at once foreign and familiar. They contained many exotic sights and spectacles, but they were also the sites of biblical events with which these pilgrims were long familiar through scripture. Thus the east was not their 'other', they

---

[204] *FE*, p. 132.   [205] GN, p. 113; RM, p. 101.   [206] RC, pp. 77–78.

[207] FC, p. 205. See also Bartolf of Nangis, 'Gesta Francorum Expugnantium Iherusalem', p. 498.

[208] *FE*, p. 142.

believed it to be fundamentally their own. They knew that the Holy Land had long been ruled by Christian emperors before the advent of Islam and their campaign was intended to restore the region to its former state. This ambition is communicated both explicitly in these texts and also through metaphors that are widely referenced: the cleansing of pollution, light displacing darkness, freedom replacing slavery, health succeeding sickness.

5   The Impact of the Crusade

Introduction

The First Crusade's status as a major turning point in European/Islamic and Mediterranean history is beyond dispute. Its effects were far reaching and scores of historians have emphatically underlined this point, both historically and in recent years. The crusade also added a fundamentally new dimension to western Christendom's relationship with the Islamic world. The formation of the crusader states created its first border zone with Turkish territory; one which – over the next two centuries – would host a variety of interactions between these two civilisations. As these Frankish states grew in strength, conquering port after port along the Levantine littoral, Italian merchants swiftly achieved dominance across the eastern Mediterranean's sea lanes bringing ever-larger cargoes of goods to eager buyers in western Christendom. Growing trade, enhanced by periodic improvements in maritime architecture and technology, naturally strengthened the commercial networks between Christendom and its Islamic neighbours. There had of course been some European involvement in the eastern Mediterranean before the crusade and many pilgrims, traders and mercenaries had set sail for the Levant in earlier years, but hardly on a comparable scale. The establishment of the Latin East fundamentally redefined both the nature and scale of Christendom's involvement in the area.

Reflecting upon these points and contemplating the First Crusade's lasting impact, many historians have advanced the case that the crusade provoked a substantially more antagonistic engagement between Christendom and the Islamic world. The consensus among these historians seems to be that whilst the pre-crusade period was defined by friction between these two civilisational tectonic plates, as they chaffed uncomfortably against one another, the First Crusade drove them into greater opposition.[1] The purpose of this chapter is to discuss and in part to contest this characterisation of inter-civilisational relations.

---

[1] Mastnak, 'Europe and the Muslims', p. 206; Housley, 'The Crusades and Islam', 194; Asbridge, *The First Crusade*, p. 2. See also A. Maalouf, *The Crusades through Arab eyes*, trans. J. Rothschild (Saqi Books: London, 2012), p. 15.

When engaging with this issue, one question that immediately becomes apparent concerns the fundamental 'civilizational' terms of the debate. There are serious objections to the idea of grouping the partially-converted Turks, the Shia Fatimid caliphate, the North African emirates, and the fractured world of al-Andalus into a monolithic civilisational bloc entitled 'Islam'. In discussion on Huntington's thesis (which deals with current-day blocks of this kind) Edward Said offered serious and perfectly justifiable concerns about the collapsing of highly diverse groups of modern societies into civilisational units entitled the 'west' or 'Islam' and such concerns can be applied with equal force to the medieval period.[2] As we have seen already, the crusaders viewed the Turks and Arabs differently and, whilst they observed that they had some shared allegiance to the 'Saracen religion', they also seem to have understood that there were sectarian differences dividing them. It has also been shown that – to a contemporary Catholic eye – the line dividing the 'Saracen religion' from tribal paganism, such as that practiced in the eastern European or Baltic regions, was vague and contemporary awareness of the notion that Islam could be defined as a distinctive monotheistic religion was patchy at best and hedged with uninterest even among intellectuals. These problems are encapsulated by a passage in William of Malmesbury's *Gesta Regum Anglorum* where he explains to his readers that whilst the Egyptians had formerly, at the time of Jerome, worshipped idols in the same manner as the Wends and Letts of eastern Europe, the Turks and Saracens now believe in a single God and a prophet named Mohammed (*Mahumet*).[3] The fact that such an explanation was needed – demonstrating why Christendom's enemies in eastern Europe should be viewed as distinct from the Turks and 'Saracens' – shows how vaguely contemporaries differentiated between the religions of their non-Christian neighbours.

Nevertheless, there probably are *just* sufficient grounds, for discussing monolithic civilisational entities like the 'Islamic World' in a way that meaningfully brings us closer to contemporary thought-worlds, albeit with the earlier caveats. Pope Urban II seems to have viewed the 'Turks', 'Saracens' and 'Moors' as manifestations of the same threat and said as

---

[2] E. Said, 'The clash of ignorance', *The Nation*, 273.12 (2001), 11–14. Although Huntington does himself show an awareness of this problem: Huntington, *The clash of civilizations*, pp. 19–55. Grabar also discusses the problems involved in reducing diverse groupings of different ethnic groupings into monolithic civilisational blocks. See: O. Grabar, 'Patterns and ways of cultural exchange', *The meeting of two worlds: Cultural exchange between east and west during the period of the Crusades*, ed. V. Goss and C. Bornstein, Studies in medieval culture XXI (Kalamazoo, MI: Medieval Institute Publications, 1986), pp. 441–442.

[3] WM, vol. 1, pp. 338–340. For discussion see: Thomson, 'William of Malmesbury', 179–180. See also BB, p. 19.

much in a letter to the bishop of Huesca in 1098.[4] Muslim writers for their part, such as Ibn al-Athir, likewise viewed the wars of both Iberia and India to be matters of direct concern for the Muslim faithful despite the great distances and cultural differences involved. Thus there are grounds for dealing in civilisational blocs, albeit with caution. Moreover, if one is to engage directly with arguments that are specifically founded, in their basic premises, upon civilisational blocs then it is necessary to some extent to take these terms of reference at their own valuation.

This chapter will assess the way in which the First Crusade redefined Christendom's general stance towards the Islamic world. It will do so with broad brush strokes. The investigative methodologies employed here are intentionally sweeping, seeking to characterise Christendom's changing perspective as *en bloc*. More detailed regional studies would be desirable going forwards and doubtlessly will add a greater level of detail, but this present chapter seeks to assess the widely-referenced but rarely-explained notion that the crusade provoked or dilated within Christendom a sense of antagonism towards the Islamic world.[5]

It will begin by examining this relationship from a purely military perspective, enquiring whether the period from *c.* 1050 to 1150 saw an escalation in conflict between these two civilizations. It will then apply quantitative techniques to a range of sources to evaluate whether there is a discernible shift in Christendom's interest in the Islamic world in the wake of the First Crusade.

The Military Situation, 1050–1150

By the mid-eleventh century, Christendom had three major zones of military interaction with Islamic societies: western Mediterranean (Iberia and the western isles of the Mediterranean), the central Mediterranean (Italy, Southern France, Sicily, and North Africa), and the eastern Mediterranean (Anatolia, Egypt, and the Holy Land). The overall trajectory of Christian/Islamic military confrontations during the late eleventh and early twelfth centuries will now be assessed.

Western Mediterranean (sustained warfare): The first of these zones remained the scene of intense fighting as the Reconquista gathered pace during this period. The advent of the Almoravids and subsequently the Almohads likewise ensured that Iberia remained a major theatre of war throughout the twelfth century. Naturally there were times of treaty,

---

[4] Pope Urban II, 'Epistolae et Privilegia', col. 504.
[5] Crawford explains this notion and discusses some of its proponents. He too does not find this thesis convincing and in the article here-cited he also offers counter-arguments: Crawford, 'The First Crusade: unprovoked offense of overdue defense', pp. 1–4.

trade, and inter-civilisational alliance, but this should not obscure the underlying and protracted conflict that persisted before, during, and after the period of the First Crusade.

Central Mediterranean (declining conflict): By contrast, the 'central zone' saw a decline in inter-civilisational warfare beginning from the end of the eleventh century. Muslim naval attacks on Southern France declined as the Italian cities steadily achieved maritime supremacy (although occasional raids still took place into the late twelfth century). The remaining Muslim positions in the Alps by this stage had already been destroyed in 972. By 1100 Sicily and Italy were firmly in Norman hands and Christian control grew in later decades. There were some moments of unrest and short-lived Norman conquests in North Africa, but these were not comparable either to the previous periods of intense fighting which took place either on Sicily in the mid-eleventh century or on the Italian/French mainland in the ninth or tenth centuries.

Eastern Mediterranean (escalation): Placed within this wider context, the First Crusade took place at a time when some of Christendom's previously *hot* frontiers with Islam were just beginning to *cool*. Spain naturally remained an important theatre of war well into the thirteenth century, but the Islamic world's ability to conduct naval warfare was in steep decline. Thus the suggestion that the crusade suddenly drew Christendom and the Islamic world into an unprecedented and deeply-entrenched conflict is problematic. The crusade *did* open a new and often embattled frontier in the Levant, but while this was taking place in the first decades of the twelfth century, many other maritime border zones across the Mediterranean were slowly stabilising. Thus, from a purely military perspective, the overall intensity of the conflict between Christian and Islamic societies may have changed in geographical focus, but taken as a whole remained broadly stable when judged overall.

It might be added that in the Holy Land, as with elsewhere, the battle-lines were seldom as simple as Christian vs. Muslim. There was a deep-seated inter-religious conflict – this is undeniable – but as shown earlier, there were moments even during the First Crusade when the members of different faiths fought alongside one another and drew up treaties and alliances. Ibn al-Athir, admittedly writing long after the First Crusade, took seriously the notion that the campaign was a Fatimid/Frankish plot against the Saljuqs – an argument that sits uncomfortably with the view that the crusade represented some species of inter-faith 'Clash of Civilizations'.[6]

[6] IAA, vol. 1, p. 14.

Islam's Place on Christendom's Agenda, Before and After the First Crusade

This section will explore Christendom's evolving stance towards Islam predominantly in its 'core' regions (defined broadly as: Northern Italy, France, the German Empire, and England). It will examine in particular whether the First Crusade caused decision makers in western Christendom to turn their gaze more directly upon the Muslim world in the decades following the crusade. Should historians, for example, imagine a post-crusade scenario in which the corridors of ecclesiastical and secular power were suddenly humming with discussion about the wars with the 'Saracen' in a way in which they had not been previously? Were bishops and princes suddenly re-examining the priorities and radically revising their dealings with the Muslim world up their agenda papers? In short, was Christendom's engagement with its various Muslim neighbours a greater priority for magnates after the crusade, than before?

Answering this question in a meaningful way requires a judicious choice of methodologies. Previously when historians have commented on Islam's changing role within Christendom's world view they have focused their attention predominantly on intellectual life, discussing the growing scholarly interest shown in the 'Saracen religion', or at least classical texts housed in Muslim archives, during the course of the twelfth century. Nevertheless, this is a process that is only tangentially relevant to this present discussion. As several studies have shown, the overwhelming bulk of this scholarly exchange took place along Sicilian or Iberian vectors. Few scholars set out for the Holy Land, which in any case did not boast many centres of learning.[7] Thus this trend is liminal to our present discussion on the impact of the First Crusade.[8]

This work will take a new approach which essentially borrows from the practices of researchers studying modern-era history, who often judge an issue's importance by the number of column inches devoted to it in a specific newspaper or magazine. If, for example, one wished to learn how prominently *say* the Panama Canal figured in the British popular consciousness during the twentieth century, and how this changed over time, then one approach would be to gather a number of widely-disseminated British periodicals which span the period and then to see how many inches of text they devote to this subject in issues published over the century. By producing a chart showing the result it would be

---

[7] Irwin, *For the lust of knowing*, pp. 36–37.
[8] For an excellent analysis of the historiography on this process see: Frakes, *The Muslim other*, pp. 147–159. See also Prawer, 'the roots of medieval colonialism', p. 33.

possible to gain an insight into the evolution of the Panama Canal's perceived importance over time. The operative principle here is that authors tend to devote more ink to subjects that concern them acutely (or their readers) than those which do not.

This investigation into Islam's changing importance in pre/post-crusade Christendom will apply a broadly similar approach to the various surviving letter collections for leading – predominantly ecclesiastical – figures from the tenth and twelfth centuries. These letter collections are varied in composition and purpose, but even so they provide an invaluable insight into the issues that were consuming decision-makers of this age.[9] Written correspondence offered perhaps the primary channel by which leading abbots, archbishops, kings, counsellors, and other important figures: shared news, discussed polices and theologies, advanced their own causes, won supporters, appealed to allies, or chastised the disloyal. As Constable has observed, they were very rarely concerned with 'private affairs', being intended rather as quasi-public documents.[10] Thus, the content of these letter collections can help to characterise the heart-beat of international discourse for this era by identifying the issues that were troubling the councils of the mighty. As Rosenthal has observed: 'the collected letters of the great letter-writers are a window into their world view'.[11] Consequently, in any single letter collection it seems reasonable to suppose that the number of letters to namecheck a specific subject will be roughly proportionate to that subject's importance both to the author and – to some extent – his network of correspondents. This can certainly be seen in Pope Gregory VII's surviving correspondence. His sustained contest with the German emperor is reflected in the large number of letters which touch upon this subject (16% of all his known correspondence). By contrast only 0.9 per cent of his surviving letters mention Lanfranc, archbishop of Canterbury, who was naturally a lesser priority (and who seems to have stayed away from the papal curia anyway). Therefore it should be possible to gain an insight into the importance attached to a specific issue (in this case the Muslim world) by identifying the percentage of letters in any given collection to namecheck this specific theme.

To this end, in this present enquiry into the changing importance attached to Islam during the central medieval period, a large selection

---

[9] For discussion see: G. Constable, *Letters and letter-collections*, Typologie des Sources du Moyen Âge Occidental XVII (Turnhout: Brepols, 1976), pp. 57–62.

[10] Constable, *Letters and Letter-Collections*, p. 11.

[11] J. Rosenthal, 'Letters and letter collections', *Understanding medieval primary sources*, ed. J. Rosenthal (London: Routledge, 2012), p. 76.

of letter collections have been gathered, dating from the late-tenth to the twelfth century, and all the letters within these collections which reference Muslims ('Saracens', 'Pagans', 'Gentiles, 'Arabs', 'Ishmaelites', 'Hagarenes' etc.) have been identified and expressed as a percentage of the overall collection. The intention here being to create an indicator for the amount of interest and debate that circled around this specific issue. The results of this investigation are shown in Table 3.

Such an analysis is not without its limitations. The authors of these letter collections are not evenly spread across Christendom's heartlands; there are both clusters (particularly in Norman England) and wide vacant spaces. Moreover, there are very few collections for secular figures, the bulk of surviving material is located in ecclesiastical collections. Still it is necessary to work with the surviving material and, if enough of these letter collections for these centuries are gathered and compared, then it will be possible at least to create an indicator of the changing significance that elites – primarily clerical – attached to a specific issue.

It might be added that such collections do not merely give us an insight into these specific individuals' thought-worlds; rather each collection represents a nodal point in a pan-Christendom elite network of communications. They contain: replies to other peoples' enquiries, letters received from other correspondents, references to courtly gossip, or tidings passed on from friends and colleagues. They also capture the changing language, exegesis, and terminology of their day. Thus they offer snapshot into elite discourse. That is not to say that the pre-occupations of any single letter collection will perfectly reflect the concerns of 'Christendom' as a whole. This is too great a claim. Still, if enough collections are analysed simultaneously then it is possible to glean an impression of an issue's overall importance.

Table 3 shows the results of this investigation. It records the frequency with which references to Muslims or the Islamic world – however slight – occur in a variety of collections compiled during this period. The most important conclusion is immediately apparent: Muslims in any context are scarcely mentioned. References to dealings with Muslims (present or historic), or the use of Muslim-themed metaphor or simile, are very rare indeed. Many letter collections, which include hundreds of lengthy and detailed documents dealing with vital matters of Church and royal *realpolitik*, mention them scarcely, if at all. This is true of the majority of these sources including those of John of Salisbury, Fulbert of Chartres, Lanfranc of Canterbury, and Peter of Celle. Herbert of Losinga is a particularly striking case because, even though he lived through the First Crusade, he made no reference to the 'Saracen' world, despite showing a

Table 3. *References to Muslims in Western European letter collections from the late tenth to twelfth centuries*

Owner of letter collection	Percentage of documents to mention/ allude to Muslims in any context
Rather of Verona (d. 974)[12]	0% (0 documents in collection of 33)
Gerbert of Reims (letters pertain to the years before his accession to the papacy.)[13]	0.45% (1 document in a collection of 220)
Froumund of Tegernsee (d. 1012)[14]	0% (0 documents in a collection of 93)
Fulbert of Chartres (d.1028)[15]	0% (0 documents in a collection of 131)
Bern of Reichenau (d. 1048)[16]	0% (0 documents in a collection of 26)
Peter Damien (d. 1072)[17]	2% (4 documents in a collection of 180)
Pope Gregory VII (d. 1085)[18]	4% (19 documents in a collection of 466)
Lanfranc, archbishop of Canterbury (d. 1089)[19]	0% (0 documents in a collection of 61)
Emperor Henry IV[20] (d. 1106)	0% (0 documents in a collection of 42)
Anselm of Canterbury[21] (d. 1109)	0.4% (2 documents in a collection of 475)
Lambert, bishop of Arras[22] (d. 1115)	0.7% (1 document in a collection of 144)
Ivo of Chartres[23] (d.1115)	0.3% (1 document in a collection of 292)
Hildebert, bishop of Le Mans[24] (d.1133)	3% (1 document in a collection of 39)

(cont.)

[12] 'Die Briefe des Bischofs Rather von Verona', *MGH: Die Briefe der Deutschen Kaiserzeit*, band I (Weimar, 1949).

[13] Gerbert of Reims, 'Die Briefsammlung', *MGH: Die Briefe der Deutschen Kaiserzeit, band II*, ed. F. Weigle, vol. 2 (Weimar, 1966).

[14] Codex 1 only: 'Die Tegernseer Briefsammlung (Froumund)', *MGHES*, vol. 3 (Berlin, 1925).

[15] *The Letters and Poems of Fulbert of Chartres*, ed. F. Behrends, OMT (Oxford: Clarendon Press, 1976).

[16] *Die Briefe des Abtes Bern von Reichenau*, ed. F.-J. Schmale (Stuttgart, 1961).

[17] Peter Damian, 'Die Briefe des Petrus Damiani', *MGH: Die Briefe der Deutschen Kaiserzeit, band IV*, ed. K. Reindel, 4 vols (München, 1983–1993).

[18] Sources: *The Register of Pope Gregory VII* and *Epistolae Vagantes*.

[19] *The Letters of Lanfranc, archbishop of Canterbury*, ed. H. Clover and M. Gibson, OMT (Oxford: Clarendon Press, 1979).

[20] 'Die Briefe Heinrichs IV', *MGH: Deutsches Mittelalter*, ed. C. Erdmann (Leipzig, 1937).

[21] *S. Anselmi Cantuariensis Archiepiscopi Opera Omnia*, vols 3–5.

[22] Lambert of Arras, 'Epistolae', *PL*, vol. 162 (1889), cols. 647–700.

[23] Ivo of Chartres, 'Epistolae', *PL*, vol. 162 (1889), cols. 9–289.

[24] Hildebert of Le Mans, 'Epistolae', *PL*, vol. 171 (1893), cols. 135–310.

Table 3 (*cont.*)

Owner of letter collection	Percentage of documents to mention/ allude to Muslims in any context
Bernard of Clairvaux (d. 1153)[25]	0.6% (3 documents in a collection of 500)
Herbert of Losinga, bishop of Norwich[26](d. 1119)	0% (0 documents in a collection of 60)
Abbot Geoffrey of Vendôme[27] (d.1132)	0% (0 documents in a collection of 184)
Peter the Venerable, abbot of Cluny (d. 1156)[28]	4% (8 documents in a collection of 195)
Thomas Becket, archbishop of Canterbury[29] (d. 1170)	0.3% (1 document in a collection of 329)
John of Salisbury (d. 1180)[30]	0.3% (1 document in a collection of 325)
Peter of Celle (d. 1183)[31]	0% (0 documents in a collection of 183)
Arnulf of Lisieux[32] (d.1184)	0% (0 documents in a collection of 141)
Gilbert Foliot, bishop of London[33] (d. 1187)	0.7% (4 letters in a collection of 520)

marked interest in themes of spiritual warfare.[34] Ivo of Chartres (d. 1115) also lived through these tumultuous times but his letters contain only one reference in which he compares the behaviour of Adela, countess of Blois, towards the local canons of St Mary, to that of the Turks.[35] Clearly these authors spent very little time discussing the 'Saracen' threat. They were peripheral to their thought-worlds and in

[25] Bernard of Clairvaux, 'Epistolae', *Sancti Bernardi Opera*, ed. J. Leclercq and H. Rochais, vols 7–8 (Rome: Editiones Cistercienses, 1974–1977). For discussion on the number given for the total number of letters here see: B. Kienzle, 'Introduction', *The letters of St Bernard of Clairvaux* (Stroud: Sutton, 1998), p. xv.

[26] Hertbert of Losinga, *Epistolae Herberti de Losinga, Osberti de Clara et Elmeri*, ed. R. Anstruther (Brussels, 1846).

[27] Geoffrey of Vendôme, 'Epistolae', *PL*, vol. 157 (1899), cols. 33–211.

[28] *The letters of Peter the Venerable*

[29] *The correspondence of Thomas Becket, archbishop of Canterbury*, ed. A. Duggan, OMT, 2 vols (Oxford: Clarendon Press, 2000).

[30] *The letters of John of Salisbury*, ed. and trans. H. Butler, W. Millor, revised by C. Brooke, OMT, 2 vols (Oxford: Clarendon Press, 1979–1986).

[31] *The letters of Peter of Celle*, ed. J. Haseldine, OMT (Oxford: Clarendon Press, 2002).

[32] *The letters of Arnulf of Lisieux*, ed. F. Barlow (London, 1939).

[33] Gilbert Foliot, 'Epistolae', *PL*, vol. 190 (1803), cols. 745–1072.

[34] Hertbert of Losinga, *Epistolae Herberti de Losinga*, pp. 22–26; E. Goulburn and H. Symonds, *The life, letters and sermons of Henry of Losinga*, vol. 1 (London, 1878), pp. 98–99.

[35] Ivo of Chartres, 'Epistolae', col. 180.

this context the notion that they were somehow Christendom's primary 'other' looks decidedly out of place.

It might be objected at this point that people such as Thomas Becket or John of Salisbury are well known to have been preoccupied with other matters, such as the rivalry between secular and ecclesiastical authority, and were scarcely involved in inter-civilisational warfare. This is entirely true, for the most part they were not. But this serves only to underline the fact that Christendom's elites had other worries on their mind than the threat from the distant 'Saracens'. Moreover, for the reasons given earlier, these letter collections do not solely reflect their authors' ideas, but capture a wider pool of opinion.

Another conclusion that can be drawn from this analysis is that the post-crusade letter collections do not reveal any greater enthusiasm for discussing 'Saracen' affairs than their pre-crusade forebears. It seems then that neither the First Crusade nor the other events of this period drove 'Islam' any further up Christendom's agenda paper. There are exceptions. Peter the Venerable discussed Islam more than his contemporaries, as might be expected given his involvement in the first Latin translation of the Koran. Even here, however, only a small minority of his letters discuss this subject (8/195 letters), reflecting the fact that his interests embraced a far wider portfolio of issues. Moreover, he seems to have been a rather isolated figure and, as several historians have pointed out, his curiosity about Islam and, his translation of the Koran, does not seem to have sparked much interest among his peers, some of whom thought in any case that it was dangerous to show any interest in the 'Saracen' religion.[36]

Another dimension of this analysis is that whilst many of these authors revealed little interest in Islam, several demonstrate a greater interest in Jerusalem and the crusading movement. Anselm of Canterbury, for example, wrote ten letters, either to (or about) prospective crusaders or to leaders in the Latin East, but only one of these included a single brief allusion to 'infidels' (which in this context seems to refer to Turks).[37] Likewise, Bernard of Clairvaux, the great advocate of the Second Crusade, wrote huge numbers of letters to members of the military orders, dignitaries in the east, and crusading magnates, but scarcely ever mentions Muslims in his correspondence (3/500 letters). Even on the rare occasion when they do appear in Bernard's letters, the references are brief and vague, generally alluded to through euphemisms like 'the malignant'.[38]

[36] Irwin, *For the lust of knowing*, pp. 26–27.
[37] *S. Anselmi Cantuariensis Archiepiscopi Opera Omnia*, vol. 3, pp. 252–255; (vol. 4) 85–86, 142–143, 174, 175, 179, 183 (vol. 5) 255, 355, 423.
[38] Bernard of Clairvaux, 'Epistolae', vol. 8, p. 435.

The letters of Arnulf of Lisieux fall into a similar category, in that he participated in the Second Crusade (and he mentioned the campaign in his letters) but he does not make any reference to Islam. This striking pattern calls to mind a comment R.H.C. Davis once made when discussing why William of Tyre's *Gesta orientalium principum* aroused so little attention in the west: 'Crusades were interesting, but Muslims were not'.[39]

Speaking for the letter collections as a whole, their primary concerns are largely local (issues of church discipline, news, or appointments). There is often a lively correspondence between the main author and his secular ruler and sometimes with his ecclesiastical superiors. Technical discussions – often heated – on the separation of secular and ecclesiastical power feature prominently as do debates of a theological nature. Nevertheless, the one subject that appears more than any other is also the most obvious: God. References to God appear in multitudinous forms with almost uniform regularity across all collections and this provides a useful point of reference for this discussion on Islam. Contemporaries in Christendom, whether they were intellectuals gazing wonderingly into the Cosmos, or serfs praying for rain, seem to have spent a great deal more time contemplating God's will than they did on any other subject. The next most pressing set of affairs were predominantly local, or at least confined to their specific kingdom or county. This was not, after all, an age where long distance communications were well developed so, even for elites, detailed information on the world beyond their borders would have been scarce or at times even inaccessible (particularly in the late-autumn/winter). The papacy, at the helm of Christendom's wider policy, naturally had to look further afield but even in Gregory VII's case, there are four times more letters dealing with Henry IV than there are even mentioning Islam. Moreover, a large proportion of Gregory's letters discussing the emperor, focus upon him alone, while the majority of letters to mention Muslims do so only in passing; often a single fleeting reference. Indeed, taken as a whole, the number of letters across all these collections which are actually *about* 'Saracens' – rather than briefly referring to them whilst talking about something else – could comfortably be counted on the fingers of two hands. To take an example, the only reference to Muslims found in Thomas Becket's collection is a letter written by Cardinal Otto of Brescia to Thomas in May 1165 which is primarily intended to relay the affairs of Genoa and Northern Italy. The single reference to 'Saracens' occurs in a brief aside where he mentions that the archbishop of Magdeburg was captured during his return journey from

---

[39] R.H.C. Davis, 'William of Tyre', *Relations between east and west in the Middle Ages*, ed. D. Baker (Edinburgh: Edinburgh University Press, 1973), p. 71.

Jerusalem.[40] Reflecting on these conclusions it seems that Christendom's clerical elites spent a lot more time staring upwards at God than they did looking sideways at their Muslim neighbours. It is likely that if a parallel analysis was carried out for the Muslim world then it would report much the same pattern. Overall, the 'Saracen' world was not particularly important to western European ecclesiastical elites before the crusade and it was not particularly important afterwards.

'Saracens' in Medieval Narratives Written Away from the Frontier

If 'Saracen affairs' only rarely consumed the deliberations of princes of the Church, either before or after the First Crusade, then it is necessary to discuss those contexts in which contemporaries *did* take an interest in their Islamic neighbours. There are a number of types of source which can serve as indicators on this point, with perhaps the most useful being the narrative histories and chronicles written between the ninth and twelfth centuries. These works, generally written by monastic or clerical authors, are not unambiguous measures of the kinds of information that were circulating about the Muslim world in western European communities. Their authors' religious profession and perspective naturally guided both their selection of material and the subjects in which they took an interest. These chronicles also range in scope and coverage from narratives preoccupied largely with local affairs, to chronicles written by authors situated at the heart of royal government. Thus they are a diverse, rather than a homogenous, source group. Nevertheless, taken as a whole, they do demonstrate some interesting patterns of knowledge. They give some indication as to the kinds of news concerning the 'Saracens' that had filtered through either to their monastic cloisters or to royal/ecclesiastical courts. There are also some consistent trends that are communicated clearly when chronicles from different centuries are read side by side.

Table 4 provides a general overview of the contexts in which medieval chroniclers wrote about Islam between *c.* 900 and 1187 CE. Whilst it is not possible to describe in detail every reference to the Muslim world contained in these sources, the broad focus of every episode discussing 'Saracen' affairs has been grouped under a series of headings. In all cases, chronicles and narratives have been selected that were written by authors living away from the border. As explained earlier, the purpose of this section is not to examine the ongoing conflicts and perceptions of frontier societies but rather to analyse the interest shown in 'Saracens'

---

[40] *The correspondence of Thomas Becket*, vol. 1, p. 206.

Table 4. *References to the Muslim world in Western European chronicles between c. 900 and 1187*

Details of work	Passages/sections discussing Muslims / Muslim world in narrative sources							Among these, sections of over 100 words in length discussing topics directly connected to Muslims or the Islamic world.	Reference
	War and diplomacy in west Med. (Spain, Balearics)	War and diplomacy in Central Med. (France/Italy/Sicily)	War and diplomacy in eastern Med. (Crusades/Byzantium)	Historic (over 100 yrs before chronicle's completion).	Muslims mentioned in the context of pilgrimage to Jerusalem (pre–First Crusade)	Trade and trade goods	Curiosities / Culture / Rhetoric		
Annales of Saint Bertin (multiple authors including Prudentius and Hincmar of Reims; covers the period up to 882)	17% (5)	70% (21)	3% (1)			3% (1)	7% (2)	1. An account of Louis II's campaign against the Saracens of Bari. 2. An account of the capture of Roland, archbishop of Arles.	*Annales de Saint-Bertin*, pp. 4, 24, 43, 46, 49–68, 73, 104, 114, 124, 126, 153, 164–165.

Annales of Fulda (uncertain authorship – covers events up to the early tenth century)	4% (1)	17% (4)	17% (4)	62% (15)		'Annales Fuldenses', *MGHS*, ed. G. Pertz, vol. 1 (Hanover, 1826), pp. 337–415.
Flodoard of Reims (*Annales*) d. 966		100% (10)				*Les Annales de Flodoard*, ed. P. Lauer (Paris, 1905), pp. 5, 19, 44–45, 47, 57, 74, 65, 79.
The chronicle of Regino of Prüm (d. 915) (chronicle completed in c. 908)	5.5% (1)	11% (2)	5.5% (1)	78% (14)	1. An account of Louis II's campaign against Muslim forces in Italy.	Regino of Prum, 'Chronicon', pp. 30, 31, 32, 36, 52, 60, 61, 63, 66, 70, 93.
Richer of St Rémi (writing 991–998)	100% (1)					Richer of Saint-Rémi, *Histories*, vol. 2, p. 224.

(*cont.*)

Table 4 (*cont.*)

Details of work	Passages/sections discussing Muslims / Muslim world in narrative sources							Among these, sections of over 100 words in length discussing topics directly connected to Muslims or the Islamic world.	Reference
	War and diplomacy in west Med. (Spain, Balearics).	War and diplomacy in Central Med. (France/Italy/Sicily)	War and diplomacy in eastern Med. (Crusades/Byzantium)	Historic (over 100 yrs before chronicle's completion).	Muslims mentioned in the context of pilgrimage to Jerusalem (pre–First Crusade).	Trade and trade goods	Curiosities / Culture / Rhetoric		
Liudprand of Cremona		70% (7)	30% (3)					1. Account of the construction of La Garde Freinet in Provence. 2. Account of ongoing raids against Italy and Provence 3. Several further accounts of ongoing attacks by/against the garrison of La Garde Freinet	Liudprand of Cremona, 'Antapodosis', pp. 6–7, 53–57, 77–78, 80, 97–98, 128, 129, 131, 132.
Thietmar of Merseburg (*Historia*) written c. 1012–1018		50% (2)	25% (1)		25% (1)			1. Account of Otto II's defeat by the Fatimids in 982. 2. Account of a Muslim attack on Luni in 1016.	Thietmar of Merseburg, 'Chronicon', pp. 70, 96, 122, 126

					Content	Reference
Ralph Glaber (d. c. 1046)	50% (4)	25% (2)	25% (2)		1. An account of the captivity and ransom of Mayol, abbot of Cluny. 2. A description of a raid from al-Andalus to Italy in c. 900. 3. There are two lengthy accounts of the ongoing wars in Iberia in the early eleventh century 4. A story describing how the souls of Christian warriors fallen in battle in Iberia celebrated mass in the church of St Maurice. 5. A report of the destruction of the Holy Sepulchre 6. An account of the pilgrimage of Ulric, bishop of Orleans to Jerusalem and an incident that occurred during the Holy Fire ceremony.	RG, pp. 18–22, 32, 80–85, 132–136, 206–208.
Ademar of Chabannes (d. 1034)	11% (3)	4% (1)	4% (1)	81% (21)	1. Several reasonably lengthy accounts of wars between the Franks and Iberian Muslim polities during the eighth–ninth centuries. 2. Account of Charlemagne's reception of the envoys of Harun al-Rashid. 3. The depredations of the Caliph al-Hakim against Christians of the Near East and the destruction of the Holy Sepulchre.	Ademar of Chabannes, 'Chronicon', pp. 63, 65–66, 84, 95, 96, 97, 99, 103, 105, 107, 108, 109, 114, 116, 120, 127–130, 144, 159, 166–168, 174, 189.

(cont.)

Table 4 *(cont.)*

Details of work	War and diplomacy in west Med. (Spain, Balearics)	War and diplomacy in Central Med. (France/Italy/Sicily)	War and diplomacy in eastern Med. (Crusades/Byzantium)	Historic (over 100 yrs before chronicle's completion).	Muslims mentioned in the context of pilgrimage to Jerusalem (pre–First Crusade)	Trade and trade goods	Curiosities / Culture / Rhetoric	Among these, sections of over 100 words in length discussing topics directly connected to Muslims or the Islamic world.	Reference
	Passages/sections discussing Muslims / Muslim world in narrative sources								
Hugh of Flavigny (writing at the start of the twelfth century)			8.3% (1)	75% (9)	8.3% (1)		8.3% (1)	4. Attack on the town of Narbonne in c. 1018. 5. Account of the deeds of Roger of Tosny in warfare against Iberian Muslims. 1. An account of the early life of Mohammed and the rise of Islam. 2. A report of the pilgrimage made by Abbot Richard of St Vanne to the Holy Land in 1026–1027.	'Chronicon Hugonis monachi Virdunensis et Divionensis', pp. 323–325, 339, 342, 351, 359, 394–395, 464, 481.

Source						Content	Reference
William of Poitiers (late eleventh century)		50% (2)			25% (1)	25% (1)		William of Poitiers, *Gesta Guillelmi*, ed. R.H.C. Davis and M. Chibnall, OMT (Oxford: Clarendon Press, 1998), pp. 96, 156, 174, 176, 452–453
Adam of Bremen (late eleventh century)		50% (1)	50% (1)	50% (1)				Adam of Bremen, 'Gesta Hammaburgensis Ecclesiae Pontificum', pp. 82, 225.
Sigebert of Gembloux (d. c. 1112)		12% (7)	88% (50)				1. An account of Mohammed's life 2. An account of the First Crusade	Sigebert of Gembloux, 'Chronica', pp. 311–367
William of Malmesbury *Gesta regum Anglorum* (completed c.1135)	11% (2)	44% (8)	39% (7)			6% (1)	1. A legendary account of the life of one Gerbert of Aurillac (later Pope Sylvester II), describing his education in Islamic Iberia. 2. An explanation of the difference between paganism and the 'Saracen' religion	WM, vol. 1, pp. 100, 114, 134, 218, 280–282, 308, 338–340, 365, 380, 410–412, 438, 466, 476, 480, 484, 592–704.

(*cont.*)

Table 4 (*cont.*)

Details of work	Passages/sections discussing Muslims / Muslim world in narrative sources							Among these, sections of over 100 words in length discussing topics directly connected to Muslims or the Islamic world.	Reference
	War and diplomacy in west Med. (Spain, Balearics)	War and diplomacy in Central Med. (France/Italy/Sicily)	War and diplomacy in eastern Med. (Crusades/Byzantium)	Historic (over 100 yrs before chronicle's completion).	Muslims mentioned in the context of pilgrimage to Jerusalem (pre-First Crusade)	Trade and trade goods	Curiosities / Culture / Rhetoric		
								3. A description of King Edward IV's prophecies including future wars between Christians and 'pagans'. This is followed by a brief account of the Turkish attacks on Byzantium. 4. Fulk of Anjou's pilgrimage to Jerusalem. 5. Edgar the Atheling's activities in the Holy Land 6. A lengthy account of the First Crusade and the foundation of the Latin East	

Source						Notes	References
Abbot Suger of St Denis	20% (1)		60% (3)		20% (1)		Suger, *Vie de Louis VI*, pp. 44, 48, 142, 202, 222.
Gesta Stephani (mid twelfth century)			100% (2)			1. This work provides a brief account of the Second Crusade.	*Gesta Stephani*, ed. K. Potter, intro. R. H. C. Davis, OMT Texts (Oxford: Clarendon Press, 1976), pp. 178, 192.
Otto of Freising	13% (1)		62% (5)		38% (3)	1. Otto includes a copy of *Quantum Praedecessores*. 2. Otto includes a copy of a letter sent by Bernard of Clairvaux concerning the Second Crusade 3. There is a rather mysterious account of a Saracen poisoner seeking to murder Emperor Frederick I	Otto of Freising, 'Gesta Friderici I. Imperatoris', pp. 9, 55–57, 61, 81,119, 141, 229, 285

in Christendom's heartlands (north of the Pyrenees and away from the embattled western Mediterranean coastline and Levant). It should be stated from the outset however that there are many works which do not mention them at all in any context, but they are too numerous to list here. Table 4 captures instances where writers discussed contemporary relations with Muslims as well as historic references and also moments where Muslims were alluded to rhetorically for some purpose or other.

Drawing conclusions from this motley collection of sources is not an exact science. They certainly do not resemble anything near a complete data set. Still, some patterns begin to emerge. One important conclusion is that 'Saracens' were only of marginal interest in almost every chronicle. Hardly any author devoted a substantial proportion of their time to the peoples or cultures of the Muslim world while in many cases the vast majority of references are historic (typically dealing with the affairs of the Carolingian era). If these historic references were removed, then the list of references would be thin indeed. Naturally those chronicles which include lengthy First Crusade narratives reference Turks and Arabs frequently within their accounts of the campaign, but they too show little more than a passing interest in their identity or culture and rarely reference them in other contexts. Typically, contemporary Muslims are mentioned perhaps half a dozen times and then only briefly as 'walk-on' roles in tales devoted to other subjects (i.e. 'while the knight was away fighting the 'Saracens', all these other things happened that I will now tell you about . . . '). Thus the evidence supplied by the chronicles reinforces the conclusions already drawn from the letters: the Muslim world did not attract a great deal of attention.

Even so whilst Muslims may only occasionally have caused ripples across Christendom's heartlands at any point during this period, attitudes towards them did not remain unchanged. There is a clear perceptional shift that took place during this period. In the earliest chronicles, the overwhelming message communicated by authors about the 'Saracens' is one of continual – if distant – attack and danger. Works such as the *Annals of St Bertin*, *Annals of Fulda* or Flodoard of Reim's *Annals* provide their readers essentially with a register of burning ports, raids, and forays against pilgrims crossing the Alps. There is little sense that these assaults posed an existential challenge to Christendom's survival, and their tone is bland and matter-of-fact, nonetheless their cumulative effect is to portray Muslims as an ongoing threat to mainland Christendom's frontiers. Muslims are referenced only rarely in any other context (aside from a few references to inter-civilisational diplomacy under the declining Carolingian Empire). Taken as a group, the cumulative impression given by these authors is one of Christendom on the defensive. To describe

Christendom as being under siege during the tenth century is to go too far; nonetheless it was under attack on almost every quarter and many societies may well have felt themselves to be living under permanent threat of attack.

The early-eleventh-century chronicles propitiate many of these themes. Certainly, there are references to Muslim raids and attacks. Thietmar of Merseburg described Otto II's failed attempt to block Fatimid incursions on the Italian peninsula in 982 and he also discussed the later sack of Luna in 1016. Ralph Glaber likewise drew attention to multiple raids and attacks along the Mediterranean coastline. One rather striking character-istic, both of these chronicles and their tenth-century predecessors, is that they spend a great deal more time discussing Muslim attacks on Southern France and Italy than they do on Iberia. The wars of the Spanish marches are rarely mentioned; seemingly these were deemed to be a lesser con-cern, or more likely the Spanish kingdoms were not as integrated into western Christendom's networks of communication (thus information was harder to acquire) as its core countries.

There is, however, a new theme that begins to appear with greater regularity during the eleventh century, which is pilgrimage to Jerusalem. Allusions to pilgrim parties travelling to the Holy Land and their experi-ences with the local Muslim authorities appear with far greater frequency and Ralph Glaber famously offered an account of al-Hakim's destruction of the Holy Sepulchre in 1009. Thietmar likewise reports the departure of pilgrim parties for the east. By the late eleventh century the general tone of the chronicles has changed still further. There are far fewer references to any kind of Islamic threat on any frontier, with only a few chronicles (often Norman), such as William of Apulia's *Gesta Guillelmi* mentioning mercenaries fighting in defence Byzantium. Allusions to Muslim raids or invasions in Iberia, France, or Italy tend to be solely historic, often referencing the wars of Charlemagne. Moreover, these writers began to include tales of Christendom taking the offensive against the Muslim world. Herman of Reichenau, for example, mentions the Norman inva-sions into southern Italy and Sicily.[41] Another theme, which had always been present, but which grows in volume at this time, is a sense of curios-ity about – and at times admiration for – the peoples and topography of the east. Returning to William of Poitiers, in a section of his work where he praised the virtues of the Normans' newly-conquered kingdom of England, he compared its wealth to that of Arabia. Clearly Arabia pro-vided him with a benchmark for wealthiness that he felt his readers would

---

[41] Herman of Reichenau, 'Chronicon', *MGHS*, ed. G. Pertz, vol. 5 (Hanover, 1844), p. 132.

understand. Shortly afterwards, when praising William the Conqueror's liberality and his patronage of churches, he claimed that the buildings constructed at this time would have impressed even the 'Greeks or Arabs'; evidently Greek and Arab workmanship set a recognisable standard for William and his immediate circle.[42] These brief references are important because they underline a series of judgements concerning the Muslim world. In this case he used the Arabs as an exemplar for wealth and high-quality workmanship. References of this kind are not absent in earlier works and the presentation of the 'east' as exceptionally wealthy had a long pedigree; still their proliferation, particularly in highly contemporaneous contexts (such as the earlier cases) are suggestive.

Moving into the twelfth century, these kinds of statements become even more common. Otto of Freising expended little ink describing the Genoese ventures against Muslim ports in al-Andalus, but on the one occasion when he did so, his main interest seems to have been in their exotic plunder which included many strange beasts such as: lions, ostriches, and parrots.[43] William of Malmesbury offers many 'curiosity' tales about 'Saracen' territory including stories of Islamic astrology, Turkish physiology, and the topography of the east alongside his descriptions of more military encounters. He also included a series of reports about 'strange' animals and places. He described for example the effects of a leopard bite, warning his readers that anyone so misfortunate as to suffer such a misadventure would need to be on their guard against the swarms of mice, who always attempt to urinate on people bitten by leopards. His source for this story apparently claimed that one man – who had suffered just such a leopard bite – had been forced to take to sea to avoid these mice, but even there he had not been safe because the mice had followed him out onto the water by sailing on hollowed-out pomegranate rinds.[44] Incidentally, medieval authors clearly found such tales to be of interest, but they should not necessarily be ascribed to the authors' over-active imagination, or even to the garbled repetition of 'strange news from far away'. In the case of the earlier tale, William of Malmesbury was absolutely correct that it was received wisdom in the Near East that mice seek to urinate in wounds caused by leopard bites; Usama ibn Munqidh reported the same phenomenon. Thus, this tale at least was anchored ultimately upon eastern sources.[45]

Cumulatively, these references depict a civilisation whose relations with its Muslim neighbours were no longer characterised solely by fear

[42] William of Poitiers, *Gesta Guillelmi*, pp. 174, 176.
[43] Otto of Freising, 'Gesta Friderici I. Imperatoris', p. 119.
[44] WM, vol. 1, p. 524.
[45] Usama Ibn Munqidh, *The book of contemplation*, p. 124.

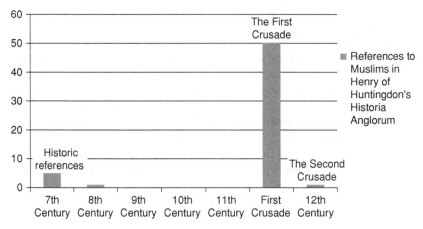

Figure 1. References to Muslims in Henry of Huntingdon's *Historia Anglorum*

(whether proximate for frontier societies or distant for communities in Christendom's heartlands). This was, after all, the crucial century where the tides of war began to run against a deeply divided Muslim world and in favour of an increasingly powerful Christendom. In this new environment, the chronicles reflect a wider range of cross-cultural experiences. They still convey a sense of danger and peril but these are mixed with interactions that speak of new prospects, admiration, and emulation. Almost all border regions by this stage were militarily contestable by Christian frontier societies and, for the adventurous, they represented a zone of considerable opportunity. Seemingly the defensiveness of the earlier period was allowed to slowly ebb away to be replaced with a more open-eyed opportunistic approach (even if the memory of former suffering was retained).[46] Again, this position seems to have filtered back into Christendom's heartlands to be included in the works written by authors far from the frontier.

The First Crusade was both a product of these great political and sociological forces, and also a vital driver in their future trajectory. For some writers it is almost the only event in their entire chronicle which discusses the Muslim world in any context. Henry of Huntingdon, for example, offers a lengthy description of the crusade. He shows some interest in 'Saracens' within this crusade narrative, but his interest is not maintained. Describing events, both before and after the crusade, Muslims are hardly referenced (see Figure 1 above). They appear briefly

[46] Daniel, *The Arabs and mediaeval Europe*, p. 55.

in a short account of the Second Crusade and there are few historic references, but that is all.

It is almost as though the crusade and its battles against the Turks seem for a brief instant to have caused Henry to put down his tools, look up from his private concerns, and stare wonderingly towards the east. Yet, his contemplation of the great events that were shaping his world was not sustained and the nagging demands of local concerns and responsibilities swiftly reasserted themselves. This pattern can be found in many chronicles where the crusade appears as a magnificent anomaly; suddenly and briefly intruding the distant wars of the east into an account that is otherwise concerned with neighbouring elite networks dominated by fractious noble families and ecclesiastical squabbles. It is quite possible that the way in which the crusade was reported (along with its stories about the Muslim world) reflects the lived experience of many contemporaries across Christendom's core territories. For many, this event may have been the only occasion in their entire life when the affairs of the Muslim world impinged meaningfully into their daily existence.

A similar pattern can be found in many chronicles, even those written by authors at the summit of the social pyramid. In his own way, Abbot Suger's (d. 1151) *Vie de Louis VI le Gros* mirrors this trend. He wrote his history of Louis VI's reign (1108–1137) at a time when many Frankish nobles were setting out on the road to Jerusalem, while the Latins of the east were engaged in the process of building and defending viable states amidst the chaos of the post-crusade Levant. Nevertheless, despite Suger's considerable eminence, his chronicle reflects little interest in any of these distant affairs. He mentions Muslims briefly at only five points in his work. The first is rhetorical and has been discussed earlier. The second simply describes why the coastal settlement of Maguelonne (near Montpellier) had originally been fortified to ward off 'Saracen' raiders. The remaining three – all brief – concern the First Crusade and its immediate aftermath. Near the beginning of his chronicle Suger shows how Bohemond had won glory for himself in the east and was renowned among the 'Saracens', who praised his deeds. Immediately afterwards he shows how Bohemond's union with Constance, sister of Louis VI, caused fear among the Saracens because of the great valour of the Frankish people. Finally he mentions briefly how Robert II of Flanders had become famous among the 'Saracens' during the First Crusade.[47] If the way in which he writes about Muslims in any way reflects his own attitudes then it seems that they primarily impinged upon Suger's thought world in the

[47] Suger, *Vie de Louis VI*, pp. 44, 48, 142, 202, 222.

context of the First Crusade and its immediate aftermath and, even then, only in-so-far as they provided opportunities for Western nobles to win renown.

Admittedly, this approach is not universal. For some chroniclers, the First Crusade (and consequently its interactions with the Muslim world) is not simply treated as an extraordinary one-off event. A handful of chroniclers show some interest in the establishment of the Latin East and its wars. The most outspoken example here is Orderic Vitalis, who was writing in Normandy in the first half of the twelfth century. He seems to have been fascinated by the First Crusade and to have gathered as much information as possible about the subsequent affairs of the Levantine region. He dwells at length on the campaign and includes a large number of colourful tales about the political world of the Near East (so many that he has not been included in Table 4). His work however reflects the enormous gap of time, space, topography and experience between Normandy and the eastern Mediterranean. Despite a few moments of rather remarkable accuracy, his stories about the principality of Antioch and Northern Syria at times bear a closer resemblance to the *chansons de geste* than to the work of a monastic historiography. They are populated with beautiful Saracen maidens, tyrannous Turkish rulers, and noble Christian warriors. There are imprisonments, battles, plucky escapes, romances, fabulous wealth, and all manner of knightly escapades. In short, his chronicle, which in most other areas represents the serious work of a dedicated monastic historian, depicts a Latin East of knightly dreams; a place of adventure, far removed from everyday life.[48]

Orderic's chronicle captures an important transition that is communicated clearly through many chronicles written at this time. In the decades before the crusade, the Muslim world impinged upon western Christendom's core countries as a proximate – if declining – military threat to its shores (Iberia does not seem to have caused nearly the same level of concern). During and after the crusade however, Christendom's gaze was drawn dramatically eastwards (this pattern is confirmed by Table 4). It was widely understood that there was conflict with the 'Saracens' in the Latin East, but these wars were now far removed indeed, taking place in lands that lay on the frontiers of knowledge. As Chibnall observed in her work on Orderic Vitalis, 'the Saracens in the Holy Land were distant peoples, who to most men and women in western Europe inhabited a world of fantasy'.[49] In this way, the crusade seems to have had

---

[48] For discussion see: F. Warren, 'The enamoured Moslem princess in Orderic Vital and the French epic', *Publications of the Modern Language Association of America* (1914), pp. 341–358.
[49] Chibnall, *The world of Orderic Vitalis*, p. 151.

the effect of bringing about a dramatic geo-perceptional shift in Christendom's attitudes towards Islam; where previously 'Saracens' had been generally described as neighbouring maritime marauders, now the inter-civilisational relationship was typified by the distant – but vital – struggle for Jerusalem.

The Holy Land under Christian Control

For the most part then, the chroniclers depict western European societies that, even after the crusade, could still pass from one year to the next with scarcely a thought about contemporary dealings with the 'Saracens'. Even so, the passing of the First Crusade played a greater role in shaping Europe's relationship with Islam than merely creating a new, but distant, frontier zone. After all, Jerusalem lay within these newly conquered lands and the holy city was a matter of acute concern. This section will consider how possession of Jerusalem recast Christendom's wider relationship with the Muslim world.

Reviewing the general history of the world's civilisations, there is a discernable tendency for societies to locate their most precious shrines at the very heart of their territory; in the safest possible location. The central position of such sacred spaces is often a natural consequence of the fact that they mark the point of origin for the subsequent expansion or flourishing of a people-group. Consequently it is only natural that this sacred space will swiftly find itself becoming incubated from hostile neighbours by hundreds of miles of friendly territory. Mecca and Medina, for example, lie so deep within Muslim territory that no non-Muslim army has ever come even close to threatening them. The centre of the Avar civilisation – its famous 'ring' – likewise lay at the heart of its territory and it took a series of hard-won campaigns for Charlemagne to threaten this vital site. Typically any invader even contemplating a strike at such a location would have to fight their way through line after line of fortification and/or pass through whole landscapes of hostile territory even to get close. The reason for the elaborate care taken to safeguard such places lies in the fact that they are so incalculably precious and any threat to their survival will inevitably provoke an immediate and overwhelming hostile reaction.

Jerusalem was and is such a sacred site but, from a western Christian perspective, unlike the sacred sites of many other faiths and societies, Christendom's hold over the city after 1099 was precarious and so far from being sheltered by whole landscapes of friendly territory, it lay directly on the frontier. Thus, it may have been Christendom's beating heart, but it lacked the protective rib-cage that guarded the sacred sites of other faiths. The kings of Jerusalem endeavoured almost immediately to construct such a ribcage through the geographical expansion of the kingdom, the construction of strongholds, and the repeated attempts to seize any major invasion points, particularly Ascalon and Damascus. Nevertheless, this should not obscure the fact that Christendom's greatest point of sensitivity – its soft spot – now lay within a few days march of Turkish and Egyptian forces. In this way, the First Crusade created a dangerous 'pressure point' lying on a contested frontier. As we have seen the first crusaders do not seem to have been especially interested in Islam and, concerning the Muslim inhabitants in the newly-formed Latin East, Prawer's statement probably still holds true that they 'knew little and wanted to know even less about the population they ruled'.[50] Even so, should the Muslims of the Near East come to pose a genuine threat to Jerusalem itself then they could suddenly become very interesting indeed.

Certainly this pattern is borne out by many groups of sources. Shortly after the capture of Jerusalem, the returning pilgrims and their fellows in western Europe seem to have been content to resume their business and, as the earlier analyses have demonstrated, there is little to suggest that the affairs of the Muslim world were of any greater consequence to them than before. Admittedly many more Christians may have set out for Jerusalem now that the route was in Christian hands, but these pious travellers appear to have been remarkably uninterested in the Muslim inhabitants of the lands they were visiting. They scarcely mentioned them in their accounts and on the rare occasion that they do appear it is normally only because of they had previously caused damage to a holy site.[51]

Jerusalem remained, however a subject of sensitivity and when it was seriously threatened, it had an immediately galvanising effect, causing warriors who may never have had any dealings previously with the Muslim world to shake themselves free from their daily affairs and risk their lives and fortunes buttressing Jerusalem's defences. Preachers wishing to raise warriors for the east, clearly knew that *this* was an issue that would provoke a significant reaction and when Bernard of Clairvaux attempted to rally forces for the Second Crusade, following the fall of Edessa (1144), in his *Sermo mihi ad vos* he did not mention Edessa but focused his audience's attention specifically on the impending threat now posed to Jerusalem itself (even though, as Phillips points out, Jerusalem

---

[50] Prawer, 'The roots of medieval colonialism', p. 33.

[51] Scarfe Beckett has observed a similar trend in earlier accounts of Anglo-Saxon pilgrimages to the east. She writes that such accounts 'ignore the Saracens or present them as irrelevant except where their actions impinge upon Christians'. (Scarfe Beckett, *Anglo-Saxon perceptions*, p. 71).

was c.450 miles south of Edessa).[52] Strikingly the author of the *Gesta Stephani*, in a brief account of the Second Crusade written shortly after the event, also presented the perceived threat to Jerusalem as the main stimulus for the campaign.[53] The rulers of the Latin East were also aware of the reaction that could be provoked by any threat to Jerusalem and, when seeking aid from western Europe after a battlefield defeat, they were generally careful to show in their letters how such a reverse imperilled Christendom's continued control of the city and the surrounding pilgrim sites.[54]

A linked consideration which compounded Jerusalem's spiritual significance was the intense admiration felt across Christendom for the first crusaders. They were presented as idealised exemplars of Christian knighthood and their legend persisted for centuries. The reverence felt for warriors such as Godfrey or Bouillon, Bohemond of Taranto, and Raymond of Toulouse did not serve merely to provide Christendom with crusading role models, it also placed a permanent obligation upon later generations to defend and extend the achievements of their forefathers (i.e. Jerusalem). Thus any attack upon the holy city was not merely a threat to Christendom's sacred heartlands, it also challenged Christendom's elites to ask themselves whether they were prepared to allow the city which their fathers had secured at such cost, to be conquered through their own indolence. Again this theme was repeatedly drawn upon in papal propaganda and it formed a central component of Eugenius III's crusading bull *Quantum Praedecessores* (December 1145) where he observed:

It will be seen as a great token of nobility and uprightness if those things acquired by the efforts of your fathers are vigorously defended by you, their good sons. But if, God forbid, it comes to pass differently, then the bravery of the fathers will have proved diminished in the sons.[55]

In a sense the many noble-led expeditions to the east, along with the big crusading campaigns, were not really concerned with the Turks or Fatimids. Their objective was the security and retention of Jerusalem. 'Saracens' were only relevant to this objective in so far as they posed a threat to these sites. Even so, the consistent threat posed by the Zangids and Ayyubids to pilgrim sites under Frankish protection may well have

---

[52] J. Phillips, *The Second Crusade: Extending the frontiers of Christendom* (New Haven, CT: Yale University Press, 2007), p. 72.
[53] *Gesta Stephani*, p. 192.
[54] For a good sample of these letters see: *Letters from the East: Crusaders, passim.*
[55] Translation from Phillips, *The Second Crusade*, p. 54 (see also pp. 53–54).

had the effect of drawing greater attention to Islam along the vector of concern for the security of the Holy Land.

The military orders encapsulate this approach clearly. They were prepared to: conduct diplomacy with Muslims, fight alongside Muslims, employ Muslims in a variety of capacities including as warriors and doctors. Muslims also worked their estates, received medical care in the Hospital in Jerusalem, and were permitted to visit Muslim religious sites which were under their control. A particularly striking piece of evidence is the Hospitallers' readiness seemingly to accommodate Muslim dietary requirements in their hospital. Patients who were unwilling to eat pork would be served with chicken, a clause which may indicate a sensitivity to those who were prohibited from eating such meat.[56] Moreover, as Riley-Smith has shown, the military orders did not seek to demonise Turks or Saracens in their letters of appeal. He has pointed out rather that these letters were pragmatic in tone and rarely resorted to polemics.[57] Still, there is no doubt whatsoever that they were prepared to fight (often to the last man) to protect Jerusalem and the Christian frontier. Again, it seems that it was Jerusalem itself that defined their approach to neighbouring Muslim rulers.[58]

A crude, if slightly bizarre, analogy that perhaps captures the crux of western Christendom's approach towards the Muslim polities threatening Jerusalem during the twelfth century can perhaps be seen in modern-day attitudes towards African elephant hunters. On the whole, contemporary western Europeans scarcely think about elephant hunters and they generally show little interest in them. Yet they care passionately about the elephants they endanger. Elephants appear in children's books, films, the education system, and artwork, not to mention zoos which can be found across Europe and which permanently remind visitors of the precarious position of the species. Thus Europeans are born and raised to care passionately about elephants. We are aware that they are hunted, but the hunters are liminal to our world view. Some among us might travel to visit the elephants and, when we hear about the dangers of hunting, we will shake our heads in disapproval, but generally take no further action. A handful of Europeans will take matters into their own hands, either through raising awareness in Europe, or by travelling to Africa in person,

---

[56] S. Edgington, 'Administrative regulations for the Hospital of St John in Jerusalem dating from the 1180s', *Crusades* 4 (2005), 29.

[57] J. Riley-Smith, 'The military orders and the east, 1149–1291', *Knighthoods of Christ: essays on the history of the Crusades and the Knights Templar, presented to Malcolm Barber* (Aldershot: Ashgate, 2007), pp. 143, 147.

[58] For more detailed discussion see: N. Morton, 'Templar and Hospitaller attitudes towards Islam in the Holy Land during the Twelfth and Thirteenth centuries: Some historiographical reflections', *Levant* 47:3 (2015), 316–327.

and many more will make donations. But that will be all. Responsibility for guarding the elephants will be left primarily with the local authorities. Even so, if Europeans were to become sufficiently convinced that the *permanent* extinction of all African elephants was imminent then it seems likely that swift and decisive action would take place at governmental and popular levels against the most proximate threat – the elephant hunters.

Muslims in the Holy Land in 1187 seem to have occupied a broadly similar position. They were not deemed to be particularly important in themselves; their significance lay in the threat they posed to Jerusalem. Jerusalem itself was absolutely vital and a wide selection of ecclesiastical and monastic orders stood as permanent reminders of its significance; the military orders even built some of their chapels in a form that would call to mind the architecture of the Holy Sepulchre. Nevertheless, aside from the dedicated few who were prepared to set out for the east, the defence of the holy sites was primarily left to local forces and western Christendom's magnates generally remained preoccupied with their own affairs. They might send a few contingents of troops and almost certainly donate financial aid (either to rulers of Jerusalem or to the military orders) but that is all. Still, as the Second and Third Crusades demonstrate, if they felt that the Holy Land was truly threatened, or worse still, if a crusader state or major site (i.e. the holy city itself) had actually been lost, then this neglected priority would suddenly jump to the top of their agenda paper.

It might be added that if at some future point, European governments should intervene decisively to save the elephants and then find themselves bogged down in a long-term guerrilla war against the elephant hunters, then the European public might end up hearing – and therefore thinking – a great deal more about these hunters.

Consequently, the First Crusade (and the establishment of the Latin East) does not seem to have provoked a greater interest or engagement with Muslims, certainly no more than any other Christian/Islamic frontier. During the bulk of the period under discussion here, the Muslim world rarely posed an existential threat to the crusader states. Life and diplomacy in the Latin East went on and western European rulers rarely paused their own squabbles long enough to take a measured look at their eastern cousins, who for the most part proved more-or-less capable of defending themselves. Still, the latent potential for substantial western intervention was always there. To a European eye, the retention of Jerusalem was an existential absolute. While the city and its protective kingdom prospered (or at least limped along) then the defensive passion that any serious challenge to Jerusalem could provoke remained dormant, but the events of 1144–1149 – and still more the actual loss of the holy city in 1187 – revealed the blast furnace of fury that could erupt very suddenly if Christendom's elites grasped hold of the notion that a genuine threat existed. In this way, the attitudes and level of interest shown in the 'Saracens' in the Near East seem to have been broadly proportionate to the level of threat they posed to the holy city. Should the threat level become critical then the cobwebs surrounding this 'red button' in the European mentality would be swept away and a deeply hostile reaction provoked against the aggressor, whoever it may be.

Crusading Fantasy

The evidence thus far has tended towards the view that while Christendom's general stance towards the Muslim world was slowly opening and evolving, the First Crusade did not play much of a role in stimulating interest in 'Saracens', at least among elites in Christendom's core countries. There is one other group of sources, however, which requires closer scrutiny.

Through its conquest of much of the Levantine region, the First Crusade established a new and incredibly exciting topography in the minds of European Christians. This was a land populated by strange beasts, miraculous birds, fabulous wealth, and the luxuries of the spice trade. As Ansell, cantor of the Holy Sepulchre, pointed out in his letter to the bishop and archdeacon of Paris in 1120: to the north of Jerusalem lay the Iron Gates of the Caucuses, built by Alexander the Great to prevent the invasions of Gog and Magog.[59] Nearby flowed the rivers of Paradise, whilst out to the east lay the lands of the Amazons. Moreover, this was also the land of Christ, sanctified by the blood of His passion. Within this spiritually-charged arena was an ongoing conflict between the defenders of Jerusalem and the Turks, an enemy that was perceived to be both noble and cruel. In short, this was a land of knightly dreams, a gift to the writers of epic verse and knightly poetry. It may well be imagined how the *chansons* and chronicles, which reported the adventures of crusaders or pseudo-crusaders, would have electrified the imaginations of men-at-arms living out the drudgery of garrison duty in damp Normandy or pious footsoldiers confronting the moral tensions posed by their lord's depredations against a local monastery. This section will turn away from the role of 'Saracens' in Christendom's *realpolitik*, diplomacy and day-to-day concerns and look instead at how the campaign repositioned them in its fantasy worlds.

---

[59] 'Epistola Anselli Cantoris S. Sepulcri', *PL*, vol. 162 (1899), cols. 729–732. For discussion see: G. Bautier, 'L'envoi de la relique de la Vraie Croix à Notre-Dame de Paris en 1120', *Bibliothèque de l'écoledes chartres* 129 (1971), 387–397.

The immense popularity and proliferation of the crusading chronicles demonstrates the receptiveness of western Christians to epic tales of war against Saracens and it seems likely that, for many, the recitation of works such as Robert the Monk's *Historia Hierosolimitana* would have been their main source of news about the distant Turks. Of course the crusading chronicles themselves, as we have seen, drew heavily upon themes commonly found in *chansons* and epic verse, which offered adventurous tales of warfare waged against Islam, generally during the Carolingian period. In later years specifically crusading-themed *chansons* such as the *Les Chetifs*, *La Chanson d'Antioche*, and *La Chanson de Jerusalem* emerged to slake the contemporary thirst for crusading epics while even *chansons* which were not concerned specifically with crusading show the imprint of knowledge brought home by returning crusaders. To take one example, the *Chanson de Roland*, which is concerned with Charlemagne's wars in Iberia, includes 'Turks' among the ranks of Christendom's enemies.[60] As shown earlier, the Turks were almost wholly unknown pre-crusade, but very quickly came to Christendom's attention in later years; a point which suggests that the *chanson* was informed, at least in its post 1100 manifestations, by news brought home by crusaders. Other allusions to: eastern trade goods, pepper, the Bedouin, silks, and gold similarly speak of the burgeoning communications spreading in the wake of the crusade across the Mediterranean.

Clearly the First Crusade reshaped the topography of Christendom's fantasy worlds and naturally the Turks or, more generally, 'Saracens' provided the requisite opponents against whom the epic heroes would prove their valour. For these reasons therefore it is necessary to consider whether the First Crusade and its legacy inspired greater interest in epic tales of warfare fought against Muslims. Or, to restate the question: did the First Crusade cause 'Saracens' to become the quintessential *enemy* in the fantasy worlds created for the amusement of Christendom's elites?

Caution is needed on this point. Clearly the campaign added new foes (the Turks) to the existing armies of 'pagandom' deployed in such epics and new Levantine battlefields were devised to backlight their clashes with fictional Christian heroes. Still, popular interest in hearing stories about Christian knights defeating Muslim armies far predates the Council of Clermont. Admittedly we know very little about pre-crusade *chansons*; this genre only really began to take a written form during the twelfth century, still we know enough to be sure that such songs were sung long before the crusade and that they too focused their attention on combat with Islam. To take one example, the famous

---

[60] *SR*, pp. 289, 308, 318, 326, 328, 330, 339, 343, 352, 363, 365, 375.

Chanson de Roland in its earliest written form may post-date the crusade, but a succinct narration of the story still exists in the *Nota Emilianense* (1065–1075) suggesting that it had long been in circulation. Moreover, there is a report that this same song was recited in the preparations for the Battle of Hastings in 1066.[61] Thus whilst later manifestations of the *chanson* may have been influenced by crusading, its core ideas and the centrality it accorded to the struggle with Islam were already firmly established in Christendom's cultural repertoire.

Without more evidence on the pre-1095 *chansons* it is impossible to know exactly how much the crusade remoulded depictions of Muslims in epic verse but, based on the available information, care is needed before concluding that the crusaders dramatically introduced a new genre of anti-Islamic epic verse. The song of Roland especially is often presented as the embodiment of crusading ideology and yet with only brief glimpses of its pre-1095 form it is very unclear how much it was influenced by 'new' crusading ideas. Moreover, the labelling of specific terminology found in this and other *chansons* as 'crusader-inspired' raises many concerns. The crusade did not generate a new pallet of polemical anti-Muslim language and this present study has demonstrated that phrases such as 'enemies of Christ' or the notion that the conquest of a Muslim city constituted a spiritual cleansing can be found as far back as the Carolingian sources. Thus the inclusion of such terms in the *chansons* is not admissible as proof of a 'crusader' influence. Therefore it is necessary to be careful before concluding that *chansons* were the product of a newly-created crusading lexicon. Indeed it is possible that the reverse is true: that the mentality manifested by the crusade chroniclers (both participants and later authors) drew heavily upon existing norms found in orally-transmitted epic verse (thus: the *chansons* shaped the crusade, rather than the crusade shaping the *chansons*). After all, as we have seen, many of the structures employed by crusaders – including participants – reflect patterns manifested in *chansons*.

Another component in this equation is the fact that whilst there were some *chansons* which were concerned with crusading (along with crusading chronicles which exhibited some *chanson*-like qualities) the vast majority of *chansons* written during the twelfth century continued to centre their attention upon Carolingian-era events set in Iberia, France, or Italy. They deal with the sack of Rome or Charlemagne's exploits south of the Pyrenees, or the burning of Christian coastal cities. They look to

---

[61] C. Jones, *An introduction to the chansons de geste*, New perspectives on medieval literature: authors and traditions (Gainesville: University Press of Florida, 2014), pp. 5, 63, 143. For the text of *Nota Emilianense* see: *La Chanson de Roland: Texte original et traduction*, ed. G. Moignet (Paris: Bordas, 1969), pp. 293–294.

the early-medieval period and the invasions of Islam along the southern European coastland rather than the later events of the crusade and twelfth-century Syria. Thus, the epicentre of the imagined historic confrontation between Christendom and Islam as manifested in the *chansons* was Roncevalles, not Antioch or Jerusalem.

In this way, the crusade may have created a new and exciting arena in which imagined Christian heroes could swing their imagined swords against the shields of imagined 'Saracen' foes, but it is far from clear that the crusade popularised the fictional depiction of Christian/Islamic warfare. We are hamstrung in this analysis by a lack of pre-crusade written sources but those indictors which can be identified suggest that these kinds of stories had been around for a long time and far pre-dated the crusade. The mere fact that the First Crusade authors drew so heavily upon paradigms reminiscent of the *chansons* implies that they – along with their notions of warfare against the 'Saracens' – were already circulating widely. The most likely scenario is that the crusade merely added a few extra dimensions and some exciting stage-sets to an existing fictional paradigm in which tales of Christian/Islamic warfare were already foregrounded.

Perhaps the strongest conclusion here is also the most obvious: that Muslims were *important* to the *chanson* genre – whether this *importance* was a product of the crusade or not – and this alone is significant. As shown earlier, in other sources, including pilgrim narratives, ecclesiastical letter collections, and chronicles, Muslims were referenced either scarcely or never. The *chansons* by contrast provide a staple diet of Muslim enemies. Some – it must be said – discuss unruly barons or Christian traitors, but Muslims (and to a lesser extent Slavs – who are always shown to be allied to Muslims) appear with routine consistency. This point tends towards the conclusion that the popular idea of the 'Saracen' – insofar as one existed at all in medieval Europe – was kept alive predominantly in the realms of fantasy.

Conclusion

Overall, the First Crusade does not seem to have had the effect of convulsing western Christendom into a more hostile stance towards Islam. In most cases, Turks and Arabs remained as marginal to the chronicles written by monastic authors in the decades following the crusade as they had been in former years. Likewise, the letter collections written by contemporaries demonstrate that the elites of this period were far more concerned with spiritual matters and their dealings with neighbouring Christian magnates than with the distant 'Saracens'. A new frontier with

Islam may have been created, but these wars lay in the distant east. Meanwhile, the long-standing threat posed by Muslims in the Central Mediterranean was in decline and only rarely did elites in Christendom's core countries have to confront raids against the Italian or French coastline; military confrontations were now remote: either far beyond the Pyrenees or in distant Jerusalem.[62] Thus there was no dramatic escalation in overall inter-civilisational conflict.

By extension, this pattern to some extent seems to be broadly mirrored on the Muslim side of the border. As we have seen already, some Saljuq histories did not trouble even to mention the First Crusade or the foundation of the Frankish states and even those which did often thought that the First Crusade was simply a larger-than-usual Byzantine raid.[63] The Byzantines had successfully taken the offensive previously, particularly under Basil II, so a successful invasion from the north was hardly unprecedented. These points should not obscure however the ongoing and renewed tension surrounding possession of Jerusalem, brought about in large part by the crusade, which always had the latent potential to break into major inter-civilisational conflict.

[62] B. Lewis, *The Muslim discovery of Europe* (London: W.W. Norton, 1982), p. 300.

[63] Mecit, *The Rum Seljuqs*, p. 32; Hirschler, 'The Jerusalem conquest', 49–51. Although when Alexius I wrote to the Egyptians in 1098 he would have disabused them at least of this fact. Köhler, *Alliances and treaties*, p. 53. See also Christie, 'Motivating listeners in the *Kitab al*-Jihad', 10.

Concluding Remarks

It has been insightfully observed that medieval thinkers were incessant model-builders, permanently preoccupied with understanding, defining, and labelling the structures – whether spiritual, administrative, or hierarchical – that moulded both this life and the beyond.[1] St Anselm (d. 1109), like so many others, fits this definition exactly and in his *De Humanis Moribus* he offered his readers a general model for western Christendom as a whole. With broad brush strokes he represented it as a beleaguered city, ruled by a great king, but beset upon all sides by enemies. These foes lurked just outside the walls awaiting the foolhardy whilst even within the ramparts there was always the danger that a sudden attack would break through the defences. At such times of crisis, a few virtuous citizens would flee their homes and take refuge in the city's citadel, whilst the many sinful inhabitants would fall prey to the invaders. In the citadel the survivors were entirely protected, although should they leave its sanctuary then they would again be vulnerable.

Through this metaphor, Anselm offers a world view in which the city of Christendom, ruled by God, is constantly beset by the Devil who seeks every opportunity to attack the faithful. His evil machinations take many forms. He corrupts the hearts of the faithful, whose only hope is to seek the protection of the city's spiritual defenders: the monks. He also corrupts and perverts the minds of non-Christians (who are defenceless against his demonic will), driving them before him in a cruel assault on the city.[2] Thus, Christendom is an existential battlefield in which the contest between God and the Devil is played out with mankind's only hope being to cling to both God's teaching and protection.

Anselm's model was neither innovative nor original. He simply provided a workmanlike metaphor for a widely held view. The people of

---

[1] Lewis, *The discarded image*, p. 11.

[2] St Anselm, 'De Humanis Moribus per Similitudines', Memorials of St. Anselm, ed. R. Southern and F. Schmitt, *Auctores Britannici Medii Aevi* I (London, 1969), pp. 66–67. Interestingly Baldric of Bourgueil used a similar analogy, albeit briefly in his account of the crusade, see: BB, p. 42.

270

Christendom had long known that they were in a permanent state of war and, to this end, by the time of the First Crusade, they were midway through one of the most ambitious armament campaigns in history. Across the land, monasteries and churches sprang up like fortresses populated by spiritual warriors ready to throw down the strongholds of the Devil. A sustained industrial revolution in prayer spread across Europe, stimulated and encouraged by contemporaries at every level of society, eager to erect a spiritual shield against the darkness that assailed them. Priests and churchmen worked to shepherd the faithful from the wolves of sin, whilst reforming their own practices and purging themselves of – among other things – the sins of clerical marriage, lay investiture, and simony. The people themselves helped drive this effort, demanding that their ecclesiastical shepherds live out the moral code which they preached. This was medieval Christendom's war and it took place almost entirely on a spiritual plain. Outlining this wider battle is important because it places contemporary attitudes towards non-Christians (including 'Saracens') in a meaningful context.[3] This was not a world in which Christendom and Islam were locked in an existential conflict; the main battle was fought primarily between God and the Devil. To a contemporary Christian eye, Turks and Arabs were only ever marginal to this struggle. They were distant peoples, simultaneously to be feared and pitied; feared because they had limited means to resist the urgings of demonic will that hurled them against Christendom's ramparts; pitied because their God-given humanity was deemed so deeply subverted that they had only a slight chance of escaping the clutches of evil.

This model lies at the core of many crusading histories, both participant narratives and later redactions. It draws together much of the earlier discussion and establishes an additional layer of meaning to many of the conclusions reached by modern historians. As has been shown, it was fully understood that both Christians and Muslims shared a common humanity and as such they were both open to divine inspiration and vulnerable to demonic activity. Contemporaries may have considered Muslims to be particularly susceptible to evil influence because they lay outside the Christian fold, but the faithful themselves were hardly immune and almost every hostile epithet flung against the Turks and Arabs was also applied to fellow Christians. They knew their own weakness and fallibility. In the chroniclers' eyes, the Muslims may have been hostile to the Church, but Guibert of Nogent was equally content to level

---

[3] For interesting remarks on the crossover between reform and crusade see: Buc, *Holy war*, pp. 98–105.

this same accusation against King William Rufus of England.[4] Muslims may have been compared to aggressive or unclean beasts, but so too were the crusaders.[5] Turks were described gnashing their teeth like barbarians, but so too were some crusaders (and also some heroes in *chansons*).[6] The Turks were often depicted as vulnerable to demonic suggestion, so were some crusaders.[7] In addition, sinfulness, theological error, cruelty, consignment to Hell, and straightforward bad behaviour are all amongst the qualities applied by the chroniclers both to their co-religionists and their Turkish and Arab enemies. Thus, the First Crusade was not simply a contest between pure crusaders and the impure Turks. It was instead a struggle in which fallen and sinful Christians sought to attain redemption and avert their own damnation through the quest for Jerusalem. In pursuit of this goal they were required to fight against peoples who were alienated from God in the hope that these foes might see the Christian Truth manifested through in their actions. In short, the battlelines were not painted as white vs. black, rather they were dark grey versus darker grey. To a contemporary eye, at the outset of the campaign, both the Christian knights fighting vendettas in the kingdom of France and the Turks laying waste to Anatolia were headed for a common fate: perdition. Through the crusade both parties, whether by manifesting the Christian truth or observing it, had a chance to mend their ways and redeem themselves.[8]

In this model, the crusaders' 'other' was aspirational: God. Their primary war was against error, sin, and the Devil, not their worldly enemies. The crusaders firmly believed that their campaign was a self-conscious, self-sacrificing imitation of Christ (*imitatio Christi*).[9] They knew that they would suffer (like Him); serve their fellows (like Him); carry their cross (like Him); and show their faith in God the Father (like Him). Jesus was the fundamental point of reference against which they measured their own actions and they often found themselves wanting. Within this paradigm, the behaviour of their enemies – good or bad – was not especially important. Believing the Muslims to be bad did not mean that

---

[4] Guibert of Nogent, 'De Vita Sua', col. 887.

[5] BB, pp. 9, 50. Leclercq discusses at length the depiction of Muslims in an animalistic way, both in the crusade chronicles and *chansons*: Leclercq, *Portraits croisés*, pp. 289–297. Sweetenham notes this parallel: 'Crusaders in a hall of mirrors', p. 55.

[6] BB, p. 50; RM, p. 42; RC, p. 110.   [7] See for example: GN, pp. 323–327.

[8] For recent discussion on the theme of redemption in the Old French Crusade Cycle see: C. Sweetenham, 'Count and the cannibals', pp. 307–328.

[9] Purkis, *Crusading spirituality, passim*. In a similar way Housley has described the First crusade as a 'Euro-centric' venture in which the participants were far more preoccupied with their own spirituality than their Muslim opponents. Housley, 'The Crusades and Islam', 195–196; Bysted, *Crusade indulgence*, pp. 215–235.

their own actions compared any more favourably with Christ's example. Underlining the 'perfidy' of their enemies might indicate the scale of the obstacles that the pilgrims were compelled to surmount during the expedition, just as it might show the depths of sin from which their foes would have to be drawn if they were to be saved; still such considerations brought their own souls no closer to salvation. Ultimately, their enemy was of only tangential importance to their assessment of their own character and their own salvation. Spiritually, they were hurdles to be crossed on the road to Jerusalem. Militarily they were the enemy against whom Christian knights would prove their valour. Still, such roles were liminal when set against their primary objective: the imitation of Christ. The paradigm of 'othering', at least in an earthly sense, does not work. Christ was the only reference point that mattered.

When the crusaders' chroniclers bothered to think about Turks or Arabs at all, they interpreted them according to their intellectual apparatus. Their frames of reference were not purpose-built for the crusade or even for warfare with Islam but can be traced back to the Church fathers, particularly Jerome, Orosius, and St Augustine, or even to the pagan writers of the Classical period. These intellectual giants cast a long shadow and their centuries-old approaches to topics such as non-Christian peoples, non-Christian religions, the identity of the 'Saracens', the geography of the east, define in part the crusaders' own approaches. After all, medieval writers *en bloc* were – to quote Lewis – 'overwhelmingly bookish' and it was to these ancient tomes that medieval theologians returned when seeking inspiration or answers.[10] Even when these works did not supply the chroniclers with explicit answers to their questions, they still had unswerving faith that the resolution lay somewhere within their pages; a conviction that led them to splice the Turks with latter-day Parthians.

Nevertheless, the crusaders' dependence on long-standing discourses, inherited from antiquity, should not be construed as evidence for a Saidian-type 'Orientalist' approach stretching from Troy to the twentieth century in which the 'east' was approached with arrogant superiority. Medieval European contemporaries, both crusaders and later commentators, may have reverenced their classical forebears, but they did not consider themselves to be their worthy successors. This self-effacing view was all but universal and produced the trope by which medieval chroniclers customarily opened their works by proclaiming their inferiority to the writers of old. They knew themselves to be living in a fallen society situated on the margins of the world of antiquity that was

---

[10] Lewis, *The discarded image*, p. 5.

merely a shadow of Ancient Greece and Rome.[11] Their cumulative effort through the phenomena now described as the 'Carolingian Renaissance', 'Ottonian Renaissance', and 'Twelfth Century Renaissance' (perhaps we should speak of a generic 'medieval Renaissance?) was to restore some glimmer of the imagined greatness of these former empires. Indeed, a renewed flourishing of interest in the Church Fathers and ancient Rome seems to have occurred whenever a princely court acquired sufficient social and financial capital to patronise a band of writers, grammarians, and theologians.

Consequently, neither they nor the crusaders viewed Islam with cultural superciliousness.[12] Chronicles and *chansons* are littered with references to Cordoban leather, Valencian lances, eastern pepper, Arab architecture, and Muslim gold: all spoken of with considerable reverence.[13] Assertions of European cultural/technological supremacy are conspicuous by their absence. Consequently it might be appropriate to pose the question that Tolan asked when reflecting on western Europeans' awareness that their lands lay on the outer margins of the known world: 'should we attribute their [medieval Christians'] worldview to a subaltern consciousness rather than to a colonialist one?'[14] Thus when the crusaders crossed Christendom's frontier into the lands which lay beyond they knew themselves to be entering the realms which produced these much-coveted luxuries. The contemporary admiration for the *cultural* achievements of Islamic society, however, was spliced with an equally strong conviction of their own *spiritual* superiority. In their eyes, Islam was at best an *error*. The outworking of these twin divergent trajectories has been the work of this study and explains in part how the crusaders could simultaneously admire and deprecate the 'Saracens'.

Drawing these points together, the model proposed in this work – the basic frame of reference by which the first crusaders approached their Turkish and Arab foes – is a composite structure. There are certain features and moral/theological judgements that are common to all (or almost all) the authors:

- The convertibility of the Turks and all non-Christians;
- The decidedly evil nature of the Turkish/Arab/'Saracen' religion;
- The Turks' ethnic distinctiveness in comparison with the Arabs;

[11] D. Tinsley, D., 'Mapping the Muslims: images of Islam in middle high German literature of the thirteenth century', *Contextualizing the Muslim other in medieval Christian discourse*, ed. J. Frakes (New York: Palgrave Macmillan, 2011), pp. 65–101.

[12] For discussion see: Scarfe Beckett, *Anglo-Saxon perceptions*, p. 199.

[13] Montgomery Watt, *The influence of Islam*, pp. 23–26.

[14] Tolan, 'Afterword', p. 175. Said does himself briefly shows an awareness that medieval Europeans may have been aware of the Islamic world's cultural ascendency: Said, *Orientalism*, p. 74.

- The non-Christian potentiality for virtue through natural law (but equally their tendency towards vice);
- A pronounced lack of interest in the specific theology of the 'Saracen' religion;
- A deference towards the authority of the Church Fathers, the Bible, and classical writers for guidance on approaches to non-Christians.

These features are constants in the sources produced by participants. Nevertheless, whilst these conceptual landmarks are omnipresent, each text displays variations in texture and emphasis. Some authors accept the Turks' potential for conversion full-heartedly; for others it is begrudged. Some stress ethnic divisions among the 'Saracens'; for others they are less important. Some struggle with the concept of non-Christian virtue and dwell on Saracen atrocities; others are more comfortable with such ideas. Some are interested in the Turks' history and background; most are not. Some clearly spent a lot of time seeking guidance from eastern Christians about the Turks; some did not. In the final analysis these textual variations represent the merging of mainstream discourses with the perceptions, interests, and lived experiences of individual writers drawn from very different – if always Catholic Christian – backgrounds. The works they produced reflect their authors' character whilst simultaneously bearing the unmistakable stamp of basic Catholic Christian theology.

The interpretive lenses described in these chronicles are not exclusive to the First Crusade. As has been shown the crusaders' ideas and beliefs cast deep roots into long-standing Latin traditions. Many of the terms and expressions they employed to describe the various non-Christian people they encountered were long-standing tropes, identifiable in works dating back to the Carolingian era (if not before). Likewise, these same tropes continued to characterise works produced long after the crusade's conclusion. The crusaders' proclivity for recognising ethnic differences between their Islamic neighbours, for example, was sustained in many later works concerning the crusader states.[15] The distinctions drawn between Muslim believers and their Islamic faith (believer/belief) also manifest themselves in subsequent histories including William of Tyre's famous *Historia*; a work incidentally which testifies to its author's readiness to appreciate virtues among non-Christians.[16]

These later authors – like their forebears on the First Crusade – also drew heavily upon eastern Christian authorities. Byzantine and Armenian

---

[15] See, for example: A. Murray, 'Franks and indigenous communities in Palestine and Syria (1099–1187): A hierarchical model of social interaction in the principalities of Outremer', *East meets west in the Middle Ages and early modern times: Transcultural experiences in the premodern world*, ed. A. Classen (Berlin: De Gruyter, 2013), p. 298.

[16] Morton, 'William of Tyre's attitude towards Islam', pp. 13–24.

influences especially would continue to shape the ideas, culture, and policies of Franks living in the east throughout this period and multitudinous studies have drawn attention to this trend in the subsequent formation of the kingdom of Jerusalem. They have underlined the guiding presence of such influences in matters as diverse as: law-making, diplomatic culture, architecture, art, coinage, church ornamentation, and the prestige items and clothing worn by Frankish elites.[17] Placed within this framework, the First Crusade emerges – viewed in the *longue-durée* – simultaneously as a continuator, compiler, and mediator of cultural traits; handing on western Christendom's received wisdom, but not without leaving its mark; agglomerating and passing on the wisdom of many other cultures, but doing so according to its own interests and concerns (neither slavishly, nor at random).

The mentalities manifested by the crusaders in their writings are complex; every bit as sophisticated as modern thought-worlds and certainly they cannot be reduced *en bloc* to any kind of simplistic notion of Manichean binary opposition (us and them / good and evil). This work proposes instead a model whereby – conceptually borrowing from Foucault/Scott – the crusader approached his Turkish foe through a dispersed constellation of conflicted priorities.[18] Crusade texts, in so far as they relate to non-Christians, are a bundle of competing imperatives: I must convert my foe; I must defend my family/home/religion/co-religionists; I must love my enemies; I must reach Jerusalem; I must accept that my enemy is a human being; I want to kill my enemy for the atrocities he has inflicted; I am a holy warrior and have a right to take the life of non-Christians. The ultimate origin of these thoughts lies ultimately in the disputed territory of the Christian soul. On one hand there is the instinctive human desire to protect one's own, to beat down interlopers, even to kill and hate; on the other the injunction to follow Jesus by loving strangers and enemies, teaching them the Christian message and recognising that they are loved manifestations of God's creation. The hybrids

---

[17] B. Kedar, 'On the origins of the earliest laws of Frankish Jerusalem: The canons of the council of Nablus, 1120', *Speculum* 74.2 (1999), 310–335; S. Salvadó, 'Icons, crosses and liturgical objects of Templar chapels in the crown of Aragon', *The debate on the trial of the Templars (1307–1314)*, ed. J. Burgtorf, P. Crawford and H. Nicholson (Aldershot: Ashgate, 2010), pp. 183–198; J. Folda, 'Mounted warrior saints in crusader icons: images of the knighthoods of Christ', *Knighthoods of Christ: Essays on the history of the Crusades and the Knights Templar, presented to Malcolm Barber*, ed. N. Housley (Aldershot: Ashgate, 2007), pp. 87–107; K. Weitzmann, 'Icon painting in the crusader kingdom', *Dumbarton Oaks papers* 20 (1966), 49–83; Folda, *The art of the Crusaders, passim.*

[18] See: M. Foucault, *The history of sexuality: Volume 1, an introduction*, trans. R. Hurley (London: Penguin, 1990); Joan W. Scott, 'Gender: A useful category of historical analysis', *The American historical review*, 91.5 (1986), 1067.

formed by these two groups of influences, which are the classic features of crusader spirituality (or indeed the spirituality of so many perpetrators of Christian violence), are also perhaps what have made these wars so fascinating for so many people across so many generations.

Changing ground slightly, the crusaders' approach to their foes may have been multi-faceted, but Turks and Arabs were also marginal to their thought-worlds. The crusade's target was Jerusalem. This is the overwhelming conviction of all the sources: papal letters, crusade charters, and the crusade chronicles. The crusaders arrived in the east knowing that they would have to fight to reach the Holy Land and were prepared to lend their assistance to the Byzantines in the opening phases of their campaign in Asia Minor. Nevertheless, their loyalty to Alexius proved disposable, whilst their commitment to Jerusalem was not. Battles with Turks, like bad weather or illness, were considered to be the tests by which the crusaders' proved their faith. Thus this was hardly a Christian/Islamic 'Clash of Civilizations'; this kind of association can be rejected on the following grounds.[19]

From the crusaders' perspective . . .

- The crusaders were not particularly interested in Islam and did not know much about it;
- they tended to avoid their enemies in the latter stages of the campaign and worked with local Muslim potentates when possible, even writing to the rulers of Damascus and Aleppo stressing that they had no desire to threaten their lands;
- their primary objective was Jerusalem, a target that the crusaders only associated with Islam (the 'Saracens') in so far as the Fatimids possessed it at the time of their advance (and they tried hard to take control by treaty – slaughter was never inevitable);
- their Turkish enemy was only partially Islamified, thus the commonly-voiced Christian vs. Islamic binary is problematic;
- the crusaders drew clear lines between the various ethnic groups they encountered (they did not treat 'Muslims'/'Saracens' as an undifferentiated group);
- the crusaders' identity did not require the Turks/Muslims to serve as its polar opposite, their eyes were focused on Christ;

---

[19] For some thought-provoking reflections on the applicability of the term 'Clash of Civilizations' to the crusades see: K. Jensen, 'Cultural encounters and clash of civilizations: Huntington and modern crusading histories', *Cultural encounters during the Crusades*, ed. K. Jensen, K. Salonen and H. Vogt (Odense: University Press of Southern Denmark, 2013), pp. 15–26. See also Asbridge 'Knowing the enemy', p. 17.

From the Turkish/Arab/Muslim perspective ...
- many Muslim commentators simply saw the crusade as yet another Byzantine campaign from the north, of a kind that had been conducted for centuries – hardly a new form of conflict;
- The conquest of Jerusalem was not initially perceived as a landmark event in the relationship between Christianity and Islam, at least by commentators writing in Arabic in the decades directly after 1099.[20]
- Ibn al-Athir thought the crusade might have been a Fatimid/Frankish project (in which case the dividing lines were not Christian/Muslim).
- Many Islamic commentators were simply not interested in the crusaders and did not mention them in their histories.

In addition, there are many contextualising details which support this interpretation; for example, the fact that Bohemond recruited his crusading forces from within an army that contained a large Muslim contingent chaffs rawly against the notion that he was setting out on some kind of anti-Islamic war.

If anything, the crusade was an odyssey: a campaign launched hundreds of miles inside enemy territory, often avoiding confrontation where possible, and seeking to take and hold a single city. It conformed neither to military, economic, or political logic. The fact that its leaders bent military, economic, and political logic sufficiently to achieve this goal is perhaps their greatest achievement.

Even if the First Crusade did not constitute a 'Clash of Civilizations' between Christianity and Islam, there are grounds for claiming that a rather different 'Clash' was taking place across the Near Eastern region at this time. During the eleventh century the greater part of Southern Eurasia was in turmoil through the invasion of multiple Turkic peoples. India, Persia, Iraq, Syria, the Jazira, Asia-Minor, Egypt, the Caucuses: all were affected. The crusade in many ways was simply a collateral consequence of this colossal Clash of Civilisations between the steppe peoples of Central Asia and the settled peoples along their margins. The confrontation of the 'pastoral' and the 'agricultural' – the pre-modern world's great faultline – was the 'Clash' of this era and it redefined the future trajectory of many cultures. Of course in this historic struggle against nomadic incursion, the Abbasid Caliphate and western Europe were emphatically on the same side. The tendency among historians of the Crusades to discuss the titanic events which were reshaping the Eurasian world as simply background information to the First Crusade vastly overestimates the crusade's importance in a global context, reflecting a tendency to view world history through a European lens. It would be fairer to say that

---

[20] Hirschler, 'The Jerusalem conquest', 38.

the crusade was a contextual detail of the Saljuq invasions, rather than
vice versa.

As we have seen, the First Crusade in-and-of-itself cannot be described
as a Christian versus Muslim 'Clash of Civilizations', but there is the
wider question of whether it caused one to come about in the longer term.
Certainly the crusade had lasting consequences for Christian/Islamic
relations and perhaps the most important of these lies in the domain of
memory. The First Crusade's conquest of Jerusalem swiftly became an
iconic moment in the popular history of the relationship between both
civilisations. It was not the first 'iconic moment' of this kind. In the European tradition at least, the battle of Poitiers 732/3 qualifies for inclusion
in this category, as does the famous diplomatic exchange between Charlemagne and Harun al-Rashid (although this event barely registered on the
Muslim side of the border).[21] A case could also be made for the sacking
of St Peters in Rome by a Muslim fleet in 846, although the memory of
this event seems to have had less of an impact.

Even so, as an iconic moment within Christian/Islamic relations, the
First Crusade casts all these earlier events into the shade. It has had a profound impact upon all parties that far exceeds issues like 'what actually
happened?' or 'what were the crusaders/Turks trying to achieve?' This
debate is closely meshed with a fundamental question underpinning this
work: Does the First Crusade represent a 'Clash of Civilizations' between
Christianity and Islam? Much of the contemporary evidence considered
earlier tends against such a characterisation and by now should require
little rehearsal. Nevertheless, in a narrow and anachronistic sense perhaps the First Crusade *can* be described as such as 'Clash'. This is not
to say that any of the major protagonists in the events that took place
between 1095 and 1099 felt that they were participating in anything
that we would recognise today as a 'Clash of Civilizations'. Still, the
belief that the First Crusade was an event that instigated a prolonged,
hate-filled conflict between the leading proponents of two diametrically
opposed religions, both bent on the other's degradation or destruction,
(i.e. a 'Clash of Civilizations') has been common currency in multiple
civilisations throughout the modern era (if not before). It has pervaded
these societies, affecting whole zones of lived existence and memory. It
has acquired a toxic life of its own, acting as a stimulus for action in
its own right. The serious historiographical and evidential objections to
such a characterisation based on the actual eleventh-century events are
irrelevant; the myth has overtaken the event and become a fact in its
own right. On these grounds, the First Crusade did instigate a 'Clash of

---

[21] Lewis, *The Muslim discovery of Europe*, p. 92.

Civilizations'; not because such an event actually occurred at the time, but because – centuries later – multiple societies have assumed that it had – and then built their history and identities around that 'fact'.[22]

---

[22] For further discussion on this theme see: M. Hammad and E. Peters, 'Islam and the Crusades: A nine hundred-year-long grievance', *Seven myths of the Crusades*, ed. A. J. Andrea and A. Holt (Indianapolis, IN: Hackett Publishing Company), pp. 127–149.

Bibliography

ABBREVIATIONS

AA Albert of Aachen, *Historia Ierosolimitana: History of the journey to Jerusalem*, ed. S. Edgington, OMT (Oxford: Clarendon Press, 2007).

AC Anna Comnena, *The Alexiad*, trans. E. Sewter, revised by P. Frankopan (London: Penguin, 2009).

AST Ibn al-Athir, *The annals of the Saljuq Turks*, trans. D. S. Richards, RSIT (Abingdon: Routledge, 2002).

BB *The* Historia Ierosolimitana *of Baldric of Bourgueil*, ed. S. Biddlecombe (Woodbridge: Boydell, 2014).

CC Corpus Christianorum.

CCCM Corpus Christianorum: Continatio Mediaeualis.

CCSL Corpus Christianorum: Series Latina.

FC Fulcher of Chartres, *Historia Hierosolymitana (1095–1127)*, ed. H. Hagenmeyer (Heidelberg, 1913).

FE *Frutolfi et Ekkehardi chronica necnon anonymi chronica Imperatorum*, ed. F.-J. Schmale and I. Schmale-Ott (Darmstadt: Wissenschaftliche Buchgesellschaft, 1972).

GF *Gesta Francorum: The deeds of the Franks and the other pilgrims to Jerusalem*, ed. R. Hill, OMT (Oxford: Clarendon Press, 1962).

GP *The Historia vie Hierosolimitane of Gilo of Paris and a second author*, ed. C. Grocock and J. Siberry, OMT (Oxford: Clarendon Press, 1997).

GN Guibert of Nogent, *Dei Gesta per Francos et cinq autres textes*, ed. R. Huygens, CCCM CXXVIIA (Turnhout: Brepols, 1996).

HAI *Hystoria de via et Recuperatione Antiochiae atque Ierusolymarum (olim Tudebodus Imitatus et Continuatu): I Normanni d'Italia alla prima Crociata in una cronaca cassinese*, ed. E. D'Angelo, preface by J. Flori (Florence: SISMEL, 2009).

IAA *The chronicle of Ibn al-Athir for the Crusading period from al-Kamil fi'l-Ta'rikh*, ed. and trans. D. S. Richards, 3 vols, Crusade texts in translation XIII, XV, XVII (Aldershot: Ashgate, 2006–2010).

JS John Skylitzes, *A synopsis of Byzantine history, 811–1057*, ed. and trans. J. Wortley (Cambridge: Cambridge University Press, 2010).

Kb   *Die Kreuzzugsbriefe aus den Jahren, 1088–1100: Eine*
        Quellensammlung zur Geschichte des ersten Kreuzzuges ed. H.
        Hagenmeyer (Innsbruck, 1901).
MA   Michael Attaleiates, *The history*, trans. A. Kaldellis and D. Krallis,
        Dumbarton Oaks Medieval Library (Cambridge, MA: Harvard
        University Press, 2012).
ME   Matthew of Edessa, *Armenia and the Crusades: Tenth to twelfth*
        centuries: The chronicle of Matthew of Edessa, trans. A. Dostourian
        (Lanham, MD: University Press of America, 1993).
MGH   *Monumenta Germaniae Historica*
MGHES   *Monumenta Germnaiae Historica: Epistolae Selectae*, 5 vols
        (1916–1952).
MGHS   *Monumenta Germaniae Historica: Scriptores*, 39 vols (1826–2009).
MGH   *SRG: Monumenta Germaniae Historica: Scriptores Rerum*
        Germanicarum, 78 vols (1871–2007).
MGH   *SRGNS: Monumenta Germaniae Historica Scriptores Rerum*
        Germanicarum Nova Series, 24 vols (1927–2009).
MS   Michel Le Syrien, *Chronique de Michel Le Syrien, Patriarche*
        Jacobite d'Antioche (1166–1199), ed. J.-B. Chabot, 4 vols (Paris,
        1899–1910; rpr. Culture and Civilisation, 1963).
OMT   Oxford Medieval Texts
OV   Orderic Vitalis, *The ecclesiastical history of Orderic Vitalis*, trans. M.
        Chibnall, 6 vols, OMT (Oxford: Clarendon Press, 1969–1990).
PL   *Patrologia Latina*, 221 vols (1844–1865).
PT   Peter Tudebode, *Historia de Hierosolymitano Itinere*, ed. J. Hill
        and L. Hill (Paris: Librairie Orientaliste Paul Geuthner,
        1977).
RA   *Le <<Liber>> de Raymond D'Aguilers*, ed. J. Hill and L. Hill
        (Paris: Librairie Orientaliste Paul Geuthner, 1969).
RC   Ralph of Caen, *Tancredus*, ed. E. D'Angelo, CCCM CCXXXI
        (Turnhout: Brepols, 2011).
RG   *Rodulfi Glabri Historiarum Libri Quinque (Rodulfus Glaber: The five*
        books of histories), ed. J. France, OMT (Oxford: Clarendon Press,
        1989).
RHC   *Recueil des Historiens des Croisades*
RHC   *Oc: Recueil des Historiens des Croisades: Historiens Occidentaux*
RM   *The Historia Iherosolimitana of Robert the Monk*, ed. D. Kempf and
        M. Bull (Woodbridge: Boydell, 2013).
RSIT   Routledge studies in the history of Iran and Turkey
SR   *The song of Roland*, trans. J. Duggan and A. Rejhon (Turnhout:
        Brepols, 2012).
WM   William of Malmesbury, *Gesta Regum Anglorum: the history of the*
        English kings, ed. R. Mynors, 2 vols (Oxford: Clarendon Press,
        1998).
WT   William of Tyre, *Chronicon*, ed. R. Huygens, 2 vols, CCCM
        LXlll(A) (Turnhout: Brepols, 1986).

PRIMARY

Abbo of Saint-Germain-des-Prés, *Viking attacks on Paris: The bella parisiacae urbis*, ed. and trans. N. Dass (Paris: Peeters, 2007).

Abu Dulaf, 'Pseudo-travel', *The turkic peoples in medieval Arabic writings*, trans. Y. Frenkel, RSIT (Abingdon: Routledge, 2015), pp. 54–60.

Actes des comtes de Flandre, 1071–1128, ed. F. Vercauteren (Brussels, 1938).

Adam of Bremen, 'Gesta Hammaburgensis Ecclesiae Pontificum', *MGH: SRG*, ed. B. Schmeidler, vol. 2 (Hanover, 1917).

Adam of Bremen, *History of the archbishops of Hamburg-Bremen*, trans. F. Tschan (New York: Columbia University Press, 2002).

Ademar Dupuis, 'Le siège du Rhodes', *Hospitaller piety and crusader propaganda: Guillaume Caoursin's description of the Ottoman siege of Rhodes, 1480*, ed. T. Vann and D. Kagay (Aldershot: Ashgate, 2015), pp. 216–283.

Ademar of Chabannes, *Chronicon: Ademari Cabannensis Opera Omnia Pars I*, ed. P. Bourgain and R. Landes, G. Pon, CCCM CXXIX (Turnhout: Brepols, 1999).

Adso Dervensis de Ortu et Tempore Antichristi, ed. D. Verhelst, CCCM XLV (Turnhout, 1976).

Aethicus Ister, *The cosmography of Aethicus Ister*, ed. and trans. by M. Herren, Publication of the journal of medieval Latin VIII (Turnhout: Brepols, 2011).

al-Muqaddasi, *The best divisions for knowledge of the regions*, trans. B. Collins (Reading: Garnet, 1994).

al-Sulami, *The book of the Jihad of 'Ali ibn Tahir al-Sulami (d. 1106): Text, translation and commentary*, ed. and trans. N. Christie (Aldershot: Ashgate, 2015).

Albert of Aachen, *Historia Ierosolimitana: history of the journey to Jerusalem*, ed. S. Edgington, OMT (Oxford: Clarendon Press, 2007).

Alcuin of York, 'Epistolae', *MGH: Epistolae Karolini Aevi*, ed. E. Duemmler, vol. 2 (Berlin, 1895).

Alcuin of York, 'Carmina', *MGH: Poetae Latini, Aevi Carolini*, ed. E. Duemmler, vol. 1 (Berlin, 1881), pp. 160–351.

Pope Alexander II, 'Epistolae et Diplomata', *PL*, vol. 146 (1884), cols. 1279–1470.

Pope Alexander III, 'Instructio fidei Catholicae ad soldanum Iconii missa', *PL*, vol. 207 (1904), cols. 1069–1078.

Aliscans, ed. C. Régnier, vol. 1 (Paris, 1990).

Amatus of Montecassino, *Storia de' Normanni*, ed. V. de Bartholomaeis, Fonti per la Storia d'Italia LXXVI (Rome, 1935).

Ammianus Marcellinus, ed. and trans. J. C. Rolfe, 3 vols, Loeb Classical Library CCC, CCCXV, CCCXXXI (Cambridge, MA: Harvard University Press, 1935–1940).

Anna Comnena, *The Alexiad*, trans. E. Sewter, revised by P. Frankopan (London: Penguin, 2009).

Annales de Saint-Bertin, ed. F. Grat, J. Vielliard, S. Clémencet (Paris, 1964).

'Annales Fuldenses', *MGHS*, ed. G. Pertz, vol. 1 (Hanover, 1826).

'Annales Monasterii de Burton, 1004–1263', *Annales Monastici*, ed. H. Luard, vol. 1, Rolls Series XXXVI (London, 1864), pp. 183–500.

'Annales Sancti Rudberti Salisburgenses', *MGHS*, ed. G. Pertz, vol. 9 (Hanover, 1851), pp. 758–810.

Anonymi auctoris chronicon ad A.C.1234 pertinens II, trans. A. Abouna, Corpus Scriptorum Christianorum Orientalium: Scriptores Syri CLIV (Leuven: Secretariat du CorpusSCO, 1974).

'Anonymous Syriac chronicle', trans. A. Tritton, *Journal of the Royal Asiatic Society* 65 (1933), 69–101.

St Anselm, *S. Anselmi Cantuariensis Archiepiscopi Opera Omnia*, ed. F. Schmitt, 6 vols (Edinburgh, 1946–1961).

St Anselm, 'De Humanis Moribus per Similitudines', *Memorials of St. Anselm*, ed. R. Southern and F. Schmitt, Auctores Britannici Medii Aevi I (London, 1969).

Anselm, cantor of the Holy Sepulchre, 'Epistola Anselli Cantoris S. Sepulcri', *PL*, vol. 162 (1889) cols. 729–732.

Aristakēs Lastivertc 'I's history, trans. R. Bedrosian (New York: Sources of the Armenian Tradition, 1985).

Arnulf of Lisieux, *The letters of Arnulf of Lisieux*, ed. F. Barlow (London, 1939).

St Augustine, *Confessionum: Libri XIII*, ed. L. Verheijen, CCSL XXVII (Turnhout: Brepols, 1981).

St Augustine, *De civitate Dei*, ed. B. Domart and A. Kalb, CCSL XLVIII, vol. 2 (Turnhout: Brepols, 1955).

St Augustine, *City of God*, trans. H. Bettenson (London: Penguin, 2003).

St Augustine, 'De Praedestinatione Sanctorum', *PL*, vol. 44 (1865), cols. 959–992.

Badr al-Din Mahmud (al-Ayni), 'Genealogy and tribal division', *The Turkic peoples in medieval Arabic writings*, trans. Y. Frenkel, RSIT (Abingdon: Routledge, 2015), pp. 66–68.

Baldric of Bourgueil, *The Historia Ierosolimitana of Baldric of Bourgueil*, ed. S. Biddlecombe (Woodbridge: Boydell, 2014).

Bar Hebraeus, *The chronography of Gregory Abû'l Faraj: the son of Aaron, the Hebrew physician commonly known as Bar Hebraeus*, trans. E. Wallis Budge, 2 vols (Oxford: Oxford University Press, 1932).

Bartolf of Nangis, 'Gesta Francorum Expugnantium Iherusalem', *RHC: Oc*, vol. 3 (Paris, 1866), pp. 487–543.

Bede's ecclesiastical history of the English people, ed. B. Colgrave and R. Mynors, OMT (Oxford: Clarendon Press, 1998).

Bede, *Opera pars II: opera exegetica 1: libri quatuor in principium Genesis*, CCSL CXVIIIa (Turnhout: Brepols, 1967).

Benjamin of Tudela, 'The travels of Rabbi Benjamin of Tudela', *Early travels in Palestine*, ed. T. Wright (London, 1848), pp. 63–126.

Benzo of Alba, 'Ad Heinricum IV. Imperatorem libri VII', *MGH: SRG*, ed. H. Seyffert, vol. 65 (Hanover, 1996).

Bernard of Clairvaux, 'Epistolae', *Sancti Bernardi Opera*, ed. J. Leclercq and H. Rochais, vols 7–8 (Rome: Editiones Cistercienses, 1974–1977).

Bernard of Clairvaux, 'De Gradibus Humilitatis et Superbiae', *Sancti Bernardi Opera*, ed. J. Leclercq and H. Rochais, vol. 3 (Rome, 1963), pp. 13–59.

Bernard the Frank, 'Itinerarium', *Itinera Hierosolymitana et descriptiones Terrae Sanctae*, ed. T. Tobler and A. Molinier (Geneva, 1879), pp. 309–320.

'Bernoldi chronicon', *MGHS*, ed. G. Pertz, vol. 5 (Hanover, 1844), pp. 385–467.

Boniface of Mainz, 'S. Bonifatii et Lulli epistolae', *MGHES*, vol. 1 (Berlin, 1916).

Die Briefe des Abtes Bern von Reichenau, ed. F.-J. Schmale (Stuttgart, 1961).

Three Byzantine military treatises, trans. G. Dennis (Washington D.C.: Dumbarton Oaks, 1985).

Caffaro, *Annali Genovesi di Caffaro e de' suoi continuatori*, ed. L. Belgrano, Fonti per Storia D'Italia XI (Rome, 1890).

Caffaro, *De Liberatione Civitatum Orientis*, ed. L. Belgrano, Fonti per Storia D'Italia XI (Rome, 1890).

Cartulaire de l'abbaye de Saint-Victor de Marseille, ed. M. Guérard, 2 vols (Paris, 1857).

Cartulaire de Marmoutier pour le Dunois, ed. E. Mabille (Ch â teaudun, 1874).

'Cartulaire du prieuré de Saint-Pierre de La Réole', *Archives historiques du départment de la Gironde*, ed. C. Grellet-Balguerie, vol. 5 (Paris and Bordeaux, 1863), pp. 99–186.

Cartulaire de Sauxillanges, ed. M. Doniol (Clermont, 1864).

'La Chanson d'Antioche', *The old french crusade cycle: volume IV*, ed. J. Nelson (Tuscaloosa, AL: University of Alabama Press, 2003).

Chanson de Guillaume, ed. P. Bennett, vol. 2 (London: Grant and Cutler, 2000).

La Chanson de Roland: Texte original et traduction, ed. G. Moignet (Paris: Bordas, 1969).

Chartes et Documents pour servir a l'histoire de l'abbaye de Charroux, ed. P. de Monsabert, Archives Historiques du Poitou XXXIX (Poitiers, 1910).

'Christodoulos: rule, testament and codicil of Christodoulos for the monastery of St. John the Theologian on Patmos', *Byzantine monastic foundation documents*, ed. J. Thomas and A. Hero, trans. P. Karlin-Hayter, vol. 2 (Washington D.C.: Dumbarton Oaks Research Library, 2000).

'Chronica Monasterii Casinensis', *MGHS*, ed. H. Hoffmann, vol. 34 (Hanover, 1980).

'Chronicon Hugonis monachi Virdunensis et Divionensis', *MGHS*, ed. G. Pertz, vol. 8 (Hanover, 1848), pp. 288–502.

'Chronicon monasterii Sancti Petri Aniciensis', *Cartulaire de L'abbaye de St Chaffre du Monastier*, ed. U. Chevalier (Paris, 1891), pp. 151–166.

'The conquest of Orange', *Guillaume d'Orange: four twelfth century epics*, trans. J. Ferrante (New York: Columbia University Press, 2001).

Constantine Porphyrogenitus, *De Administrando Imperio*, ed. G. Moravcsik, trans. R. Jenkins (Washington: Dumbarton Oaks Center for Byzantine Studies, 1967).

Constantine Porphyrogenitus, *The book of ceremonies*, trans. by A. Moffatt and M. Tall, vol. 2 (Canberra: Australian Association for Byzantine Studies, 2012).

Constitutiones canonicorum regularium ordinis Arroasiensis, ed. L. Milis and J. Becquet, CCCM XX (Turnhout: Brepols, 1970).

'The coronation of Louis', *Guillaume d'Orange: four twelfth century epics*, trans. J. Ferrante (New York: Columbia University Press, 2001).

Cosmas of Prague, 'Die Chronik der Böhmen des Cosmas von Prag', *MGH: SRGNS*, ed. B. Bretholz, vol. 2 (Berlin, 1923).

Le Couronnement de Louis: Chanson de Geste du XIIe Siècle, ed. E. Langlois, 2nd ed. (Paris: Honoré Champion, 1984).

Daniel the Abbot, 'The life and Journey of Daniel, abbot of the Russian land', *Jerusalem pilgrimage, 1099–1185*, ed. and trans. J. Wilkinson, J. Hill and W. F. Ryan (London: Hakluyt Society, 1988), pp. 120–171.

'La Destruction de Rome: Première Branche de La Chanson de Geste de Fierabras', ed. G. Goeber, *Romania* 2 (1873), 1–48.

Digenis Akritis: the Grottaferrata and Escorial versions, ed. E. Jeffreys, Cambridge medieval classics VII (Cambridge: Cambridge University Press, 1998).

Ekkehard of Aura, 'Hierosolimita', *Frutolfi et Ekkehardi Chronica necnon Anonymi Chronica Imperatorum*, ed. F.-J. Schmale and I. Schmale-Ott (Darmstadt: Wissenschaftliche Buchgesellschaft, 1972), pp. 268–333.

Ermoldus Nigellus, *Poème sur Louis le Pieux*, ed. E. Faral (Paris, 1932).

Eugenius III, 'Epistolae et privilegia', *PL*, vol. 180 (1855), cols. 1013–1648.

Eusebius, *The ecclesiastical history, books I-V*, ed. and trans. by K. Lake, Loeb classical library CLIII (Cambridge, MA: Harvard University Press, 2001).

De expugnatione Lyxbonensi: The conquest of Lisbon, ed. C. Wendell David (New York: Columbia University Press, 2001).

Fierabras: chanson de geste, ed. A. Kroeber and G. Servois, Les Anciens Poetes de la France (Paris, 1860).

Fierabras and Floripas: a French epic allegory, ed. and trans. M. Newth (New York: Italica Press, 2010).

Flodoard of Reims, *Les Annales de Flodoard*, ed. P. Lauer (Paris, 1905).

Count Fulk Le Réchin of Anjou, 'Fragmentum historiae Andegavensis', *Chroniques des comtes d'Anjou et des seigneurs d'Amboise*, ed. L. Halphen and R. Poupardin (Paris, 1913).

'Fredegarii et aliorum chronica', *MGH: Scriptores rerum Merovingicarum*, ed. B. Krusch, vol. 2 (Hanover, 1888).

Froumund of Tegernsee, 'Die Tegernseer Briefsammlung (Froumund)', *MGHES*, vol. 3 (Berlin, 1925).

Frutolf of Michelsberg, 'Chronicon', *MGHS*, ed. G. Waitz, vol. 6 (Hanover, 1844), pp. 33–231.

Frutolf of Michelsberg, *Chronicles of the investiture contest: Frutolf of Michelsberg and his continutors*, trans. T. McCarthy (Manchester: Manchester University Press, 2014).

Frutolfi et Ekkehardi chronica necnon anonymi chronica Imperatorum, ed. F.-J. Schmale and I. Schmale-Ott (Darmstadt: Wissenschaftliche Buchgesellschaft, 1972).

The Letters and Poems of Fulbert of Chartres, ed. F. Behrends, OMT (Oxford: Clarendon Press, 1976).

Fulcher of Chartres, *Historia Hierosolymitana (1095–1127)*, ed. H. Hagenmeyer (Heidelberg, 1913).

Fulcher of Chartres: a history of the expedition to Jerusalem, 1095–1127 (New York: W.W. Norton, 1973).

Fulk Le Réchin of Anjou, 'Fragmentum historiae Andegavensis', *Chroniques des comtes d'Anjou et des seigneurs d'Amboise*, ed. L. Halphen and R. Poupardin (Paris, 1913).

'Gesta Adhemari, Episcopi Podiensis', *RHC: Historiens Occidentaux*, vol. 5 (Paris, 1895), pp. 354–355.

Gesta Francorum: The deeds of the Franks and the other pilgrims to Jerusalem, ed. R. Hill, OMT (Oxford: Clarendon Press, 1962).

Gesta Stephani, ed. K. Potter, intro. R. H. C. Davis, OMT (Oxford: Clarendon Press, 1976).

Geoffrey of Malaterra, De Rebus Gestis Rogerii Calabriae et Siciliae Comitis et Roberti Guiscardi Ducis fratris *eius*, ed. E. Pontieri, Rerum Italicarum Scriptores V part1 (Bologna, 1927).

Geoffrey of Malaterra, *The deeds of Count Roger of Calabria and Sicily and of his brother Duke Robert Guiscard by Geoffrey Malaterra*, trans. K. Baxter Wolf (Ann Arbor: University of Michigan Press, 2005).

Geoffrey of Vendôme, 'Epistolae', *PL*, vol. 157 (1899), cols. 33–211.

George Akropolites, *The history: introduction, translation and commentary*, ed. R. Macrides, Oxford studies in Byzantium (Oxford: Oxford University Press, 2007).

Gerbert of Reims, 'Die Briefsammlung', *MGH: Die Deutschen Geschichtsquellen des Mittelalters, 500–1500, Die Briefe der Deutschen Kaiserzeit*, ed. F. Weigle, vol. 2 (Weimar, 1966).

Gilbert Foliot, 'Epistolae', *PL*, vol. 190 (1803), cols. 745–1072.

The Historia vie Hierosolimitane of Gilo of Paris and a second author, ed. C. Grocock and J. Siberry, OMT (Oxford: Clarendon Press, 1997).

Gormont et Isembart: Fragment de Chanson de Geste du XIIe Siècle, ed. A. Bayot (Paris: Librairie Ancienne Honore Champion, 1914).

Gratian 'Decretum', *Corpus Iuris Canonici*, ed. A. Friedberg, vol. 1 (Graz, 1959: reprint of 1879–1881 edition).

Gregory I, 'Epistolarum libri quatuordecim', *PL*, vol. 77 (1862), cols. 431–1326.

Gregory I, *Homiliae in Evangelia*, ed. R. Étaix, CCSL CXLI (Turnhout: Brepols, 1999).

Gregory VII, *The Epistolae Vagantes of Pope Gregory VII*, ed. and trans. by H. Cowdrey, OMT (Oxford: Clarendon Press, 1972).

Gregory VII, *The register of Pope Gregory VII, 1073–1085*, ed. and trans. H. Cowdrey (Oxford: Oxford University Press, 2002).

Gregory VIII, 'Epistolae et privilegia', *PL*, vol. 202 (1855) cols. 1537–1564.

Gregory of Tours, 'Decem Libri Historiarum', *MGH: Scriptores Rerum Merovingicarum*, ed. B. Krusch (Hanover, 1951).

Guibert de Nogent, *Dei Gesta per Francos*, ed. R. Huygens, CCCM CXXVII (Turnhout: Brepols, 1996).

Guibert of Nogent, 'De Vita Sua', *PL*, vol. 156 (1853), cols. 837–1016.

Henry IV, emperor of Germany, 'Die Briefe Heinrichs IV', *MGH: Deutsches Mittelalter*, ed. C. Erdmann (Leipzig, 1937).

Henry of Huntingdon, *Historia Anglorum (history of the English people)*, ed. and trans. D. Greenway, OMT (Oxford: Clarendon Press, 1996).

Hertbert of Losinga, *Epistolae Herberti de Losinga, Osberti de Clara et Elmeri*, ed. R. Anstruther (Brussels, 1846).

Herman of Reichenau, 'Chronicon', *MGHS*, ed. G. Pertz, vol. 5 (Hanover, 1844), pp. 67–133.

Hildebert of Le Mans, 'Epistolae', *PL*, vol. 171 (1893), cols. 135–310.

'The history of David, king of kings', *Rewriting Caucasian history: the medieval Armenian adaptation of the Georgian chronicles*, trans. R. Thomson (Oxford: Oxford University Press, 1996).

'The history of King Vaxt'ang Gorgasali', *Rewriting Caucasian history: the medieval Armenian adaptation of the Georgian chronicles*, trans. R. Thomson (Oxford: Clarendon, 1996).

History of the patriarchs of the Egyptian Church, ed. and trans. A. Atiya et al., vol. 2, part 3 (Cairo, 1959).

The history of the Seljuq state: a translation with commentary of the Akhbār Al-dawla Al-saljūqiyya, ed. and trans. by C. Bosworth, RSIT (Abingdon: Routledge, 2011).

The history of the Seljuq Turks, ed. C. Bosworth, trans. K. Luther (Richmond: Curzon, 2001).

'Historia peregrinorum euntium Jerusolymam', *RHC: Oc*, vol. 3 (Paris, 1866), pp. 165–229.

'Hrotsvithae Opera', *MGH: SRG*, ed. P. de Winterfeld, vol. 34 (Berlin, 1902).

Hugeburc of Heidenheim, 'Vita Willibaldi', *MGHS*, ed. O. Holder-Egger, vol. 15,1 (Hanover, 1887), pp. 80–117.

Hugh of Fleury, 'Historia regum Francorum', *MGHS*, vol. 9 (Hanover, 1851), pp. 395–406.

Hugh of Fleury, 'Liber qui modernorum regum Francorum continet actus', *MGHS*, vol. 9 (Hanover, 1851), pp. 376–395.

Hugh of St Victor, 'Priorum Excerptionum libri decem', *PL*, vol. 177 (1854) cols. 191–284.

Hystoria de via et Recuperatione Antiochiae atque Ierusolymarum (olim Tudebodus Imitatus et Continuatu): I Normanni d'Italia alla prima Crociata in una cronaca cassinese, ed. E. D'Angelo, preface by J. Flori (Florence: SISMEL, 2009).

Ibn al-Athir, *The annals of the Saljuq Turks*, trans. D.S. Richards, RSIT (Abingdon: Routledge, 2002).

The chronicle of Ibn al-Athir for the Crusading period from al-Kamil fi'l-Ta'rikh., ed. and trans. D.S. Richards, Crusade texts in translation XIII, XV, XVII, 3 vols (Aldershot, 2006–2010).

Ibn Fadlān and the land of darkness: Arab travellers in the far north, trans. and intro. by P. Linde and C. Stone (London: Penguin, 2012).

Ibn Faqih al-Hamadhani, 'On the Turks and their lands', *The turkic peoples in medieval Arabic writings*, trans. Y. Frenkel, RSIT (Abingdon: Routledge, 2015), pp. 41–53.

Ibn Khaldun, *The Muqaddimah: an introduction to history*, trans. F. Rosenthal (Princeton, NJ: Princeton University Press, 2005).

Ibn al-Qalanisi, *The Damascus chronicle of the Crusades*, ed. and trans. H. Gibb (Mineola, NY: Dover, 2002).

Isidore of Seville, *The etymologies*, trans. S. Barney et al. (Cambridge: Cambridge University Press, 2010).

Ivo of Chartres, 'Epistolae', *PL*, vol. 162 (1889) cols. 9–289.

Pope John VIII, 'Iohannis VIII. Papae Epistolae', *MGH: Epistolae*, vol. 7 (Berlin, 1928), pp. 1–333.

St John of Damascus, 'On heresy', *St John of Damascus: writings*, trans. F. Chase jr, The fathers of the Church XXXVII (Washington: The Catholic University of America Press, 1958).

John Kinnamos, *Deeds of John and Manuel Comnenus by John Kinnamos*, trans. C. Brand (New York: Columbia University Press, 1976).

John of Salisbury, *The letters of John of Salisbury*, ed. and trans. H. Butler, W. Millor, revised by C. Brooke, OMT, 2 vols (Oxford: Clarendon Press, 1979–1986).

John Skylitzes, *A synopsis of Byzantine history, 811–1057*, ed. and trans. J. Wortley (Cambridge: Cambridge University Press, 2010).

'John of Würzburg', *Peregrinationes Tres*, ed. R. Huygens, CCCM CXXXIX (Turnhout: Brepols, 1994), pp. 78–141.

Jordanes, 'Getica', *MGH: Auctorum Antiquissimorum*, ed. T. Mommsen, vol. 5.1 (Berlin, 1882).

Justin: Epitome of the Philippic history of Pompeius Trogus, trans. J. Yardley (Atlanta, GA: Scholars Press, 1994).

Kamal al-Din, 'Extraits de la Chronique d'Alep', *RHC: Historiens Orientaux*, vol. 3 (Paris, 1884), pp. 577–690.

Die Kreuzzugsbriefe aus den Jahren, 1088–1100: Eine Quellensammlung zur Geschichte des ersten Kreuzzuges ed. H. Hagenmeyer (Innsbruck, 1901).

Lambert of Arras, 'Epistolae', *PL*, vol. 162 (1889), cols. 647–700.

Lanfranc of Canterbury, *The Letters of Lanfranc, archbishop of Canterbury*, ed. H. Clover and M. Gibson, OMT (Oxford: Clarendon Press, 1979).

Leo the Deacon, *The history of Leo the Deacon: Byzantine military expansion in the tenth century*, trans. A.-M. Talbot and D. Sullivan (Washington D. C.: Dumbarton Oaks, 2005).

Letters from the east: crusaders, pilgrims, and settlers in the 12th-13th centuries, ed. and trans. M. Barber and K. Bate, Crusade texts in translation XVIII (Aldershot: Ashgate, 2010).

The life of King Edward who rests at Westminster, ed. F. Barker, OMT, 2nd ed. (Oxford: Clarendon Press, 1992).

Liudprand of Cremona, 'Antapodosis', *Liudprandi Cremonensis Opera Omnia*, ed. P. Chiesa, CCCM CLVI (Turnhout: Brepols, 1998).

Livy, *History of Rome*, trans. E. T. Sage, Loeb classical library CCCXIII, 14 vols (Cambridge, MA: Harvard University Press, 1919–1959).

Lupus Protospatarius, 'Annales', *MGHS*, ed. G. Pertz, vol. 5 (Hanover, 1844), pp. 52–63.

Matthew of Edessa, *Armenia and the Crusades: tenth to twelfth centuries: the chronicle of Matthew of Edessa*, trans. A. Dostourian (Lanham, MD: University Press of America, 1993).

Matthew Paris, *Chronica Majora*, ed. H. R. Luard, Rolls Series LVII, 7 vols (London, 1872–1883).

Maurice's Strategikon: handbook of Byzantine military strategy, trans. G. Dennis (Philadelphia, PA: University of Pennsylvania Press, 1984).

Michael Attaleiates, *The history*, trans. A. Kaldellis and D. Krallis, Dumbarton Oaks Medieval Library (Cambridge, MA: Harvard University Press, 2012).

Michael Psellus, *Fourteen Byzantine rulers*, trans. E. Sewter (London: Penguin, 1966).

Michel Le Syrien, *Chronique de Michel Le Syrien, Patriarche Jacobite d'Antioche (1166–1199)*, ed. J.-B. Chabot, 4 vols (Paris, 1899–1910; rpr. Culture and Civilisation, 1963).

Nicéphore Bryennios, *Historiarum Libri Quattuor*, ed. P. Gautier, Corpus Fontium Historiae Byzantinae IX (Brussels, 1975).

Nicholas I, patriarch of Constantinople, *Letters*, trans. R. Jenkins and L. Westerink (Washington: Dumbarton Oaks Center for Byzantine Studies, 1973).

Nikephoros, patriarch of Constantinople, *Short history*, trans. C. Mango, Corpus Fontium Historiae Byzantinae XIII (Washington: Dumbarton Oaks, 1990).

'Notitiae duae Lemovicenses de Praedicatione crucis in Aquitania', *RHC: Oc*, vol. 5 (Paris, 1895), pp. 350–351.

Oliver of Paderborn, 'Historia Damiatina', *Die Schriften des Kölner Domscholasters, Späteren Bishofs von Paderborn und Kardinal-Bischofs von S. Sabina*, Bibliothek des Litterarischen Vereins in Stuttgart, CCII (Tübingen, 1894).

Orderic Vitalis, *The ecclesiastical history of Orderic Vitalis*, trans. M. Chibnall, OMT, 6 vols (Oxford: Clarendon Press, 1969–1990).

'Ottonis de Sancto Blasio Chronica', *MGH: Scriptores rerum Germanicarum in usum scholarum*, ed. A. Hofmeister, vol. 47 (Hanover, 1912).

Otto of Freising, 'Chronica sive Historia de Duabus Civitatibus', *Monumenta Germaniae Historica: SRG*, ed. A. Hofmeister, vol. 45 (Hanover, 1912).

Otto of Freising, 'Gesta Friderici I. Imperatoris', *MGH: SRG*, ed. G. Waitz, vol. 46 (Hanover and Leipzig, 1912).

'Papsturkunden in Florenz', *Nachrichten von der Gesellschaft der Wissenschaften zu Göttingen philologisch-historische klasse*, ed. Wiederhold (G ö ttingen, 1901), pp. 306–325.

Papsturkunden in Spanien: Vorarbeiten zur Hispania Pontificia: I Katalanien, ed. P. Kehr (Berlin, 1926).

'Passio Thiemonis Archiepiscopi', *MGHS*, vol. 11 (Hanover, 1854), pp. 51–62.

Paulus Orosius, 'Historiarum Libri Septem', *PL*, vol. 31 (1846), cols. 664–1174.

Peter Abelard, *Collationes*, ed. and trans. J. Marenbon and G. Orlandi, OMT (Oxford: Clarendon Press, 2001).

Peter of Celle, *The letters of Peter of Celle*, ed. J. Haseldine, OMT (Oxford: Clarendon Press, 2002).

Peter Damian, 'Die Briefe des Petrus Damiani', *MGH: Die Briefe der Deutschen Kaiserzeit, band IV*, ed. K. Reindel, 4 vols (München, 1983–1993).

St. Peter Chrysologus: selected sermons volume 3, trans. W. Palardy (Washington: Catholic University of America Press, 2005).

Peter Tudebode, *Historia de Hierosolymitano Itinere*, ed. J. Hill and L. Hill (Paris: Librairie Orientaliste Paul Geuthner, 1977).

Peter the Venerable, *The letters of Peter the Venerable*, ed. G. Constable, 2 vols (Cambridge, MA: Harvard University Press, 1967).

Petrus Alfonsi, *Dialogue against the Jews*, trans. I. Resnick (Washington D.C.: Catholic University of America Press, 2006).

Pliny (the Elder), *Natural history II, Libri III-VII*, ed. H. Rackham, vol. 2 (London: Heinemann, 1942).

Plutarch's Moralia, trans. W. Helmbold, 15 vols (Cambridge, MA: Harvard University Press, 1986–2004).

Poetry of the Carolingian renaissance, ed. and trans. P. Goodman (London: Duckworth, 1985).

Pomponius Mela's description of the world, ed. and trans. F. Romer (Ann Arbor: University of Michigan Press, 2001).

Pseudo Epiphanii Sermo de Antichristo, ed. G. Frasson, Bibliotheca Armenica: Textus et Studia II (Venice, 1976).

Pseudo-Methodius, *Apocalypse*, ed. and trans. B. Garstad, Dumbarton Oaks Medieval Library (Cambridge, MA: Harvard University Press, 2012).

Ralph of Caen, *Tancredus*, ed. E. D'Angelo, CCCM CCXXXI (Turnhout: Brepols, 2011).

Ralph Glaber, *Rodulfi Glabri Historiarum Libri Quinque (Rodulfus Glaber: The five books of histories)*, ed. J. France, OMT (Oxford: Clarendon Press, 1989).

Ramon Muntaner, *The Catalan expedition to the east: from the chronicle of Ramon Muntaner*, trans. R. Hughes and J. Hillgarth (Woodbridge: Boydell, 2006).

Rashid al-Din, 'The compendium of chronicles', *Classical writings of the medieval Islamic world: Persian histories of the Mongol dynasties, volume III*, trans. W. Thackston (London: I.B. Tauris, 2012).

Rather of Verona, 'Die Briefe des Bischofs Rather von Verona', *MGH: Die Briefe der Deutschen Kaiserzeit, band I* (Weimar, 1949).

Les Rédactions en vers de La Prise d'Orange, ed. C. Régnier (Paris: Klincksieck, 1966).

Raymond of Aguilers, *Le <<Liber>>de Raymond D'Aguilers*, ed. J. Hill and L. Hill (Paris: Librairie Orientaliste Paul Geuthner, 1969).

Regino of Prüm, 'Chronicon', *MGH: SRG*, ed. F. Kurze, vol. 50 (Hanover, 1890).

Regino of Prüm, *History and politics in late Carolingian and Ottonian Europe: the chronicle of Regino of Prüm and Adalbert of Magdeburg*, trans. S. Maclean (Manchester: Manchester University Press, 2009).

Richer of Saint-Rémi, *Histories*, ed. J. Lake, Dumbarton Oaks Medieval Library, 2 vols (Cambridge, MA: Harvard University Press, 2011).

Robert the Monk, *The Historia Iherosolimitana of Robert the Monk*, ed. D. Kempf and M. Bull (Woodbridge: Boydell, 2013).

Robert the Monk's history of the First Crusade: Historia Iherosolimitana, Crusade texts in translation XI (Aldershot: Asgate, 2005).

Robert of Clari, *La Conquête de Constantinople*, ed. P. Noble, British Rencesvals Publications III (Edinburgh: British Rencesvals Publications, 2005).

Rudulf of Fulda, 'Translatio S. Alexandri', *MGHS*, ed. G. Pertz, vol. 2 (Hanover, 1829), pp. 673–681.

The sea of precious virtues (Baḥr al-Favā'id): a medieval mirror for princes, trans. J. S. Meisami (Salt Lake City, UT: University of Utah Press, 1991).

Sigebert of Gembloux, 'Chronica', *MGHS*, ed. G. Pertz, vol. 6 (Hanover, 1844), pp. 300–374.

Simon of St Quentin, *Histoire des Tartares*, ed. J. Richard (Paris: Paul Geuthner, 1965).

Snorri Sturluson, *Edda*, trans. A. Faulkes (London: J.M. Dent, 2004).

The song of Roland, trans. J. Duggan and A. Rejhon (Turnhout: Brepols, 2012).

'The song of William', *Heroes of the french epic*, ed. and trans. M. Newth (Woodbridge: Boydell, 2005).

Suger, *Vie de Louis VI le Gros*, ed. H. Waquet, Le Classiques de l'histoire de France au Moyen Age XI (Paris: Les Belles-Lettres, 1964).

Theophanes Confessor, *The chronicle of Theophanes Confessor: Byzantine and near eastern history, AD284–813*, trans. C. Mango and R. Scott (Oxford: Clarendon Press, 1997).

Theophylact of Simocatta, *The history of Theophylact of Simocatta*, trans. M. and M. Whitby (Oxford: Oxford University Press, 1986).

Thietmar of Merseburg, 'Chronicon', *MGH: SRGNS*, ed. R. Holtzmann, vol. 9 (Berlin, 1935).

St Thomas Becket, *The correspondence of Thomas Becket, archbishop of Canterbury*, ed. A. Duggan, OMT, 2 vols (Oxford: Clarendon Press, 2000).

Pope Urban II, 'Epistolae et Privilegia', *PL*, vol. 151 (1853), cols. 283–561.

Usama Ibn Munqidh, *The book of contemplation: Islam and the Crusades*, trans. P. Cobb (London: Penguin, 2008).

Valerius Flaccus, *Argonautica*, ed. and trans. J. Mozley, Loeb classical library CCLXXXVI (Cambridge, MA: Harvard University Press, 1963).

Virgil, *Aeneid*, trans. F. Ahl (Oxford: Oxford University Press, 2008).

Virgil, *Georgics*, trans. P. Fallon (Oxford: Oxford University Press, 2006).

Walter the Chancellor, *Bella Antiochena*, ed. H. Hagenmeyer (Innsbruck, 1896).

William of Apulia, 'Gesta Roberti Wiscardi', *MGHS*, ed. R. Wilmans, vol. 9 (Hanover, 1851), pp. 239–298.

William of Jumièges, *The Gesta Normannorum Ducum of William of Jumièges, Orderic Vitalis and Robert of Torigni*, ed. E. Van Houts, 2 vols (Oxford: Clarendon Press, 1992–1995).

William of Malmesbury, *Gesta Regum Anglorum: the history of the English kings*, ed. R. Mynors, 2 vols (Oxford: Clarendon Press, 1998).

William of Poitiers, *Gesta Guillelmi*, ed. R.H.C. Davis and M. Chibnall, OMT (Oxford: Clarendon Press, 1998).

William of Rubruck, *The mission of Friar William of Rubruck*, trans. P. Jackson, Hakluyt Society: Second Series CLXXIII (London: Hakluyt Society, 1990).

William of Tyre, *Chronicon*, ed. R. Huygens, CCCM LXlll(A), 2 vols (Turnhout: Brepols, 1986).

SECONDARY

Adair, P., 'Flemish comital family and the Crusades', *The Crusades: other experiences, alternative perspectives*, ed. K. Semaan (Binghampton: Global Academic Publishing, 2003), pp. 101–112.

Akbari, S., *Idols in the east: European representations of Islam and the orient, 1100–1450* (Ithaca: Cornell University Press, 2009).

d'Alverny, M., 'La connaissance de l'Islam en Occident du IXe au milieu du XIIe siècle', *L'Occidente e l'Islam nell'alto medieoevo*, vol. 2 (Spoleto, 1965), pp. 577–602.

al-Azmeh, A., 'Barbarians in Arab eyes', *Past and present* 134 (1992), 3–18.

al-Imad, L., *The Fatimid vizierate*, Islamkundliche Untersuchungen CXXXIII (Berlin: Schwarz, 1990).

Anderson, A., *Alexander's gate, Gog and Magog, and the inclosed nations*, Monographs of the Medieval Academy of America V (Cambridge, MA: The Medieval Academy of America, 1932).

Andrews, T., 'The new age of prophecy: the chronicle of Matthew of Edessa and its place in Armenian historiography', *The medieval chronicle VI*, ed. E. Kooper (Amsterdam: Rodopi, 2009), pp. 105–123.

Arikha, N., *Passions and tempers: A history of the humours* (New York: Ecco, 2007).

Asbridge, T., *The Crusades: the authoritative history of the war for the Holy Land* (New York: Ecco, 2010).

Asbridge, T., *The First Crusade: a new history* (Oxford: Oxford University Press, 2004).

Asbridge, T., 'Knowing the enemy: Latin relations with Islam at the time of the First Crusade', *Knighthoods of Christ: essays on the History of the Crusades and the Knights Templar, presented to Malcolm Barber* (Aldershot: Ashgate, 2007), pp. 17–26.

Bachrach, B., 'On the origins of William the Conqueror's horse transports', *Transport and culture* 26.3 (1985), 505–531.

Bachrach, B., and Bachrach, D., 'Introduction', *The Gesta Tancredi of Ralph of Caen: A history of the Normans on the First Crusade*, Crusade texts in translation XII (Aldershot: Ashgate, 2010), pp. 1–17.

Bachrach B. and Bachrach, D., Ralph of Caen as a military historian', *Crusading and warfare in the Middle Ages*, ed. S. John and N. Morton, Crusades subsidia VII (Aldershot: Ashgate, 2014), pp. 87–99.

Bachrach, D., *Religion and the conduct of war, c.300-c.1215* (Woodbridge: Boydell, 2003).

Barber, M., *The Crusader states* (New Haven, CT: Yale University Press, 2012).

Başan, A., *The great Seljuqs: a history*, RSIT (Abingdon: Routledge, 2010).

Bautier, G., 'L'envoi de la relique de la Vraie Croix à Notre-Dame de Paris en 1120', *Bibliothèque de l'écoledes chartres* 129 (1971), 387–397.

Scarfe Beckett, K., *Anglo-Saxon perceptions of the Islamic world*, Cambridge studies in Anglo-Saxon England XXXIII (Cambridge: Cambridge University Press, 2003).

Beech, G., The abbey of Saint-Florent of Saumur, and the First Crusade', *Autour de la Première Croisade: Actes du Colloque de la Society for the Study of the Crusades and the Latin East*, ed. M. Balard (Paris: Publications de la Sorbonne, 1996), pp. 57–70.

Beihammer, A. 'Christian views of Islam in early Seljuq Anatolia: perceptions and reactions', *Islam and Christianity in medieval Anatolia*, ed. A. Peacock, B. de Nicola and S. Nur Yildiz (Aldershot: Ashgate, 2015), pp. 51–76.

Beihammer, A., 'Defection across the border of Islam and Christianity: apostasy and cross-cultural interaction in Byzantine-Seljuk relations', *Speculum* 86 (2011), 597–651.

Beihammer, A., 'Die Ethnogenese der Seldschukischen Türken im Urteil Christlicher Geschichtsschreiber des 11. und 12. Jahrhunderts', *Byzantinische Zeitschrift* 102.2 (2009), 589–614.

Beihammer, A., 'Orthodoxy and religious antagonism in Byzantine perceptions of the Seljuk Turks (eleventh and twelfth Centuries)', *Al-Masōq* 23.1 (2011), 15–36.

Bennett, M., 'First crusaders' images of Muslims: the influence of vernacular poetry', *Forum for Modern Language Studies* 22 (1986), 101–122.

Berend, N., *At the gate of Christendom: Jews, Muslims and 'pagans' in medieval Hungary, c.1000–c.1300* (Cambridge: Cambridge University Press, 2001).

Berend, N., 'The concept of Christendom: A rhetoric of integration or disintegration?', *Hybride Kulturen im mittelalterlichen Europa: Vorträge und Workshops einer internationalen Frühlingsschule*, ed. M. Borgolte and B. Schneidmüller, Europa im Mittelalter XVI (Berlin: Akademie Verlag, 2010), pp. 51–61.

Biddlecombe, S., 'Baldric of Bourgueil and the familia Christi', *Writing the early Crusades: text, transmission and memory*, ed. M. Bull and D. Kempf (Woodbridge: Boydell, 2014), pp. 9–23.

Blanks, D., and Frassetto, M., 'Introduction', *Western views of Islam in medieval and Early Modern Europe: perception of other* (Basingstoke: Macmillan, 1999), pp. 1–9.

Blanks, D., 'Western views of Islam in the premodern period: a brief history of past approaches', *Western views of Islam in medieval and early modern Europe*, ed. D. Blanks and M. Frassetto (Basingstoke: Macmillan, 1999), pp. 11–53.

Bosworth, C., 'Introduction', *The Turks in the early Islamic world*, ed. C. Bosworth, The formation of the classical Islamic world IX (Aldershot: Ashgate, 2007), pp. xiii–xlv.

Bosworth, C., 'The origins of the Seljuqs', *The Seljuqs: politics, society and culture*, ed. C. Lange and S. Mecit (Edinburgh: Edinburgh University Press, 2011), pp. 13–21.

Bosworth, C., 'The Turks in the Islamic lands up to the mid-11 century', *The Turks in the early Islamic world*, ed. C. Bosworth, The formation of the classical Islamic world IX (Aldershot: Ashgate, 2007), pp. 193–212.

Bosworth, E., 'The steppe peoples in the Islamic World', *The new Cambridge history of Islam: volume 3 The eastern Islamic world, eleventh to eighteenth centuries*, ed. D. O. Morgan and A. Reid (Cambridge: Cambridge University Press, 2010), pp. 21–77.

Bouchard, C., *"Every valley shall be exalted" The discourse of opposites in twelfth-century thought* (Ithaca: Cornell University Press, 2003).

Bowlus, C. R., *The battle of Lechfeld and its aftermath: the end of the age of migrations in the Latin West* (Aldershot: Ashgate, 2006).

Brand, C., 'The Turkish element in Byzantium, eleventh-twelfth centuries', *Dumbarton Oaks papers* 43 (1989), 1–25.

Brock, S. P., 'North Mesopotamia in the late seventh century: book XV of John bar Penkāyē's Rīš Mellē', *Jerusalem Studies in Arabic and Islam* 9 (1987), 51–74.

Bronstein, J., '1096 and the Jews: A historiographic approach', *Jerusalem the golden: The origins and impact of the First Crusade*, ed. S. Edgington and L. García-Guijarro, Outremer: studies in the Crusades and the Latin East III (Turnhout: Brepols, 2014), pp. 117–131.

Brundage, J., 'The hierarchy of violence in twelfth – and thirteenth-century canonists', *International history review* 17 (1995), 670–692.

Buc, P. *Holy war, martyrdom, and terror: Christianity, violence, and the West, ca. 70 c.e. to the Iraq war* (Philadelphia, PA: University of Pennsylvania Press, 2015).

Bull, M., 'The relationship between the *Gesta Francorum* and Peter Tudebode's *Historia de Hierosolymitana*: the evidence of a hitherto unexamined manuscript', *Crusades* 11 (2012), 1–18.

Bull, M., 'Views of Muslims and of Jerusalem in miracle stories, c.1000–c.1200: reflections on the study of the first crusaders' motivations', *The experience of crusading: volume one western approaches*, ed. M. Bull and N. Housley (Cambridge: Cambridge University Press, 2003), pp. 13–38.

Bysted, A. L., *The Crusade indulgence: spiritual rewards and the theology of the Crusades, c. 1095–1216*, History of warfare CIII (Leiden: Brill, 2014).

Cahen, C., 'An introduction to the First Crusade', *Past and present* 6 (1954), 6–30.

Cahen, C., *Orient et Occident au temps des Croisades* (Paris: Aubier Montaigne, 1983).

Cahen, C., *Pre-Ottoman Turkey: a general survey of the material and spiritual culture and history c.1071–1330*, trans. J. Jones-Williams (London: Sidgwick & Jackson, 1968).

Callahan, D., 'Al-Hākim, Charlemagne and the destruction of the church of the Holy Sepulcher in Jerusalem on the writings of Ademar of Chabannes', *The legend of Charlemagne in the Middle Ages: power, faith and crusade*, ed. M. Gabriele and J. Stuckey (New York: Palgrave Macmillan, 2008), pp. 41–57.

Campopiano, M., 'La culture pisane et le monde arabo-musulman: entre connaissance réelle et héritage livresque', *Bien Dire et Bien Aprandre: Revue de Médiévistique, Un exotisme littéraire médiéval?*, ed. C. Gaullier-Bougassas, Actes du colloque du Centre d'Études Médiévales et Dialectales de Lille III (Lille: Université Lille, 2008), pp. 81–95.

Carr, M., 'Between Byzantium, Egypt and the Holy Land: the Italian maritime republics and the First Crusade', *Jerusalem the golden: The origins and impact of the First Crusade*, ed. S. Edgington and L. García-Guijarro, Outremer: studies in the Crusades and the Latin East III (Turnhout: Brepols, 2014), pp. 75–88.

Catlos, B., *Infidel kings and unholy warriors: faith, power and violence in the age of Crusade and Jihad* (New York: Farrar, Straus and Giroux, 2014).

Chibnall, M., *The world of Orderic Vitalis: Norman monks and Norman knights* (Woodbridge: Boydell, 1984).

Christie, N., 'Ibn al-Qalānisī', *Medieval Muslim historians and the Franks in the Levant*, ed. A. Mallett (Leiden: Brill, 2014), pp. 7–28.

Christie, N., 'The origins of suffixed invocations of God's curse on the Franks in Muslim sources for the Crusades', *Arabica* 48 (2001), 254–266.

Ciggaar, K., 'Byzantine marginalia to the Norman Conquest', *Anglo-Norman Studies IX*, ed. R. Allen Brown (Woodbridge: Boydell, 1986), pp. 43–63.

Citarella, A., 'The relations of Amalfi with the Arab world before the Crusades', *Speculum* 42 (1967), 299–312.

Classen, A., 'The self, the other, and everything in between: xenological phenomenology of the Middle Ages', *Meeting the foreign in the Middle Ages*, ed. A. Classen (New York: Routledge, 2002), pp. xi–lxxiii.

Clauson, G., 'Turks and wolves', *Studia Orientalia*, 28.2 (1964), 1–22.

Cohn, N., *The pursuit of the Millennium: revolutionary millenarians and mystical anarchists of the Middle Ages* (London: Paladin, 1970).

Cole, P., '"O God, the heathen have come into your inheritance" (Ps. 78.1) The theme of religious pollution in crusade documents, 1095–1188', *Crusaders and Muslims in twelfth century Syria*, ed. M. Shazmiller, The medieval Mediterranean I (Leiden: Brill, 1993), pp. 84–111.

Cole, P., *The preaching of the Crusades to the Holy Land, 1095–1270* (Cambridge, MA: Medieval Academy of America, 1991).

Constable, G., 'Medieval charters as a source for the history of the Crusades', *Crusaders and crusading in the twelfth century* (Aldershot: Ashgate, 2008), pp. 93–116.

Constable, G., *Letters and letter-collections*, Typologie des Sources du Moyen Âge Occidental XVII (Turnhout: Brepols, 1976).

Cowdrey, H., 'The Mahdia campaign of 1087', *English Historical Review* 92 (1977), 1–29.

Cowdrey, H., 'New dimensions of reform: war as a path to salvation', *Jerusalem the golden: the origins and impact of the First Crusade*, ed. S. Edgington and L. García-Guijarro, Outremer: studies in the Crusades and the Latin East III (Turnhout: Brepols, 2014), pp. 11–24.

Crawford, P. F., 'The First Crusade: unprovoked offense or overdue defense', *Seven myths of the Crusades*, ed. A. J. Andrea and A. Holt (Indianapolis, IN: Hackett Publishing Company, 2015), pp. 1–28.

Cutler, A., 'The First Crusade and the idea of "conversion"', *The Muslim World* 58 (1968), 57–71.

Cyrino, M. S., *Aphrodite*, Gods and heroes of the ancient world (Abingdon: Routledge, 2010).

Dadoyan, S., *The Armenians in the medieval Islamic world, paradigms of interaction, seventh to fourteenth centuries, volume 1: the Arab period in Armīnyah, seventh to eleventh century* (New Brunswick, NJ: Transaction Publishers, 2011).

Daniel, N., *The Arabs and mediaeval Europe* (London: Longman, 1975).

Daniel, N., 'The Church and Islam II: The development of the Christian attitude to Islam', *The Dublin review* 231 (1957), 289–312.

Daniel, N., *Heroes and Saracens: an interpretation of the chansons de geste* (Edinburgh: Edinburgh University Press, 1984).

Daniel, N., *Islam and the West: the making of an image* (Edinburgh: Edinburgh University Press, 2009).

Davis, R. H. C., 'William of Tyre', *Relations between east and west in the Middle Ages*, ed. D. Baker (Edinburgh: Edinburgh University Press, 1973), pp. 64–76.

Dickens, M., 'The sons of Magog: the Turks in Michael's *chronicle*', *Parole de l'Orient* 30 (2005), 433–450.

Dickens, M., 'Turkāyē: turkic peoples in Syriac literature prior to the Seljuks', unpublished PhD thesis, University of Cambridge (2008).

Ducellier, A., *Chrétiens d'Orient et Islam au Moyen Age, VIIe-XVe siècle* (Paris: Armand Colin, 1996).

Duggan, L. G., '"For force is not of God"? compulsion and conversion from Yahweh to Charlemagne', *Varieties of religious conversion in the Middle Ages*, ed. J. Muldoon (Gainesville, FL: University Press of Florida, 1997), pp. 49–62.

Durak, K., 'Defining the 'Turk': mechanisms of establishing contemporary meaning in the archaizing language of the Byzantines', *Jahrbuch der österreichischen Byzantinistik* 59 (2009), 65–78.

Eastwood, W., et al., 'Integrating palaeoecological and archaeo-historical records: land use and landscape change in Cappadocia (central Turkey) since late Antiquity', *Archaeology of the countryside in medieval Anatolia*, ed. T. Vorderstrasse and J. Roodenberg (Leiden: Nederlands Instituut voor het Nabije Oosten, 2009), pp. 45–69.

Edgington, S., 'Administrative regulations for the Hospital of St John in Jerusalem dating from the 1180s', *Crusades* 4 (2005), 21–37.

Edgington, S., 'Albert of Aachen reappraised', *From Clermont to Jerusalem: The Crusades and crusader societies, 1095–1500*, ed. A. Murray (Turnhout: Brepols, 1998), pp. 55–67.

Edgington, S. 'Albert of Aachen and the chansons de geste', in *The Crusades and their sources: essays presented to Bernard Hamilton*, ed. J. France and W. Zajac (Aldershot: Ashgate, 1998), pp. 23–37.

Edgington, S., 'The doves of war: the part played by carrier pigeons in the Crusades', *Autour de la Première Croisade: Actes du Colloque de la Society for the Study of the Crusades and the Latin East*, ed. M. Balard (Paris: Publications de la Sorbonne, 1996), pp. 167–175.

Edgington, S., 'Espionage and military intelligence during the First Crusade, 1095–99', *Crusading and warfare in the Middle Ages: realities and representations. Essays in honour of John France*, ed. S. John and N. Morton, Crusades subsidia VII (Aldershot: Ashgate, 2014), pp. 75–86.

Ellenblum, R., *The collapse of the eastern Mediterranean: climate change and the decline of the East, 950–1072* (Cambridge: Cambridge University Press, 2012).

Emmerson, R., *Antichrist in the Middle Ages: a study of medieval apocalypticism, art and literature* (Seattle, WA: University of Washington Press, 1984).

Emilie Haspels, C., *The highlands of Phrygia: sites and monuments*, 2 vols (Princeton, NJ: Princeton University Press, 1971).

Engel, P., *The realm of St. Stephen: a history of medieval Hungary: 895–1526* (London: I.B. Tauris, 2005).

Epstein, A., 'The date and significance of the cathedral of Canosa in Apulia, South Italy', *Dumbarton Oaks papers* 37 (1983), 79–90.

S. Epstein, *Purity lost: transgressing boundaries in the eastern Mediterranean, 1000–1400* (Baltimore: The Johns Hopkins University Press, 2006).

Findley, C., *The Turks in world history* (Oxford: Oxford University Press, 2005).

Fletcher, R., *The barbarian conversion: From Paganism to Christianity* (Berkeley, CA: University of California Press, 1999).

Flori, J., *La Guerre Sainte: La formation de l'idee de croisade dans l'Occident chrétien* (Paris: Aubier, 2001).

Flori, J., *L'Islam et la Fin des temps: L'interprétation prophétique des invasions musulmanes dans la chrétienté médiévale* (Paris: Seuil, 2007).

Flori, J., 'Jérusalem terrestre, celeste et spirituelle: Trois facteurs de sacralisation de la première croisade', *Jerusalem the golden: The origins and impact of the First Crusade*, ed. S. Edgington and L. García-Guijarro, Outremer: studies in the Crusades and the Latin East III (Turnhout: Brepols, 2014), pp. 25–50.

Flori, J., *Pierre l'Ermite et la première croisade* (Paris: Fayard, 1999).

Flori, J., 'Première croisades et conversion des <<païens>>', *Migrations et Diasporas Méditerranéennes (Xe-XVIe siècles)*, ed. M. Balard and A. Ducellier (Paris: Publications de la Sorbonne, 2002), pp. 449–457.

Flori, J., 'Tares et défauts de L'Orient dans les sources relatives a la première croisade', *Monde Oriental et Monte Occidental dans la culture médiévale* (Greifwald, 1997), pp. 45–56.

Folda, J. *The art of the Crusaders in the Holy Land, 1098–1187* (Cambridge: Cambridge University Press, 1995).

Folda, J., 'Mounted warrior saints in crusader icons: images of the knighthoods of Christ', *Knighthoods of Christ: essays on the history of the Crusades and the Knights Templar, presented to Malcolm Barber*, ed. N. Housley (Aldershot: Ashgate, 2007), pp. 87–107.

Forester, T., *The ecclesiastical history of England and Normandy by Orderic Vitalis*, 4 vols (London, 1853–1856).

Foss, C., 'Strobilos and related sites', *Anatolian studies* 38 (1998), 147–174.

Foucault, M., *The history of sexuality: volume 1, an introduction*, trans. R. Hurley (London: Penguin, 1990).

Foucault, M., *The use of pleasure: The history of sexuality, volume 2*, trans. R. Hurley (London: Penguin, 1985).

Frakes, J., *Vernacular and Latin discourses of the Muslim other in medieval Germany*, The new Middle Ages (New York: Palgrave Macmillan, 2011).

France, J., 'Byzantium in western chronicles before the First Crusade', *Knighthoods of Christ: essays on the history of the Crusades and the Knights Templar presented to Malcolm Barber* (Aldershot: Ashgate, 2007), pp. 3–16.

France, J., *The Crusades and the expansion of Catholic Christendom, 1000–1714* (Abingdon: Routledge, 2005).

France, J., 'The destruction of Jerusalem and the First Crusade', *Journal of ecclesiastical history* 47 (1996), 1–17.

France, J., 'The First Crusade and Islam', *The Muslim world* 67 (1977), 147–157.

France, J., 'Moving to the goal, June 1098-July 1099', *Jerusalem the golden: the origins and impact of the First Crusade*, ed. S. Edgington and L. García-Guijarro, Outremer: studies in the Crusades and the Latin East III (Turnhout: Brepols, 2014), pp. 133–150.

France, J., 'The Normans and crusading', *The Normans and their adversaries at war: essays in memory of C. Warren Hollister*, ed. R. Abels and B. Bachrach (Woodbridge: Boydell, 2001), pp. 87–101.

France, J., 'The use of the Anonymous Gesta Francorum in the early twelfth-century sources for the First Crusade', *From Clermont to Jerusalem: the Crusades and crusader societies, 1095–1500*, ed. A. Murray (Turnhout: Brepols, 1998), pp. 29–39.

France, J., *Victory in the east: a military history of the First Crusade* (Cambridge: Cambridge University Press, 1994).

France, J., 'Warfare in the Mediterranean region in the age of the Crusades, 1095–1291: A clash of contrasts', *The Crusades and the Near East: cultural histories*, ed. C. Kostick (Abingdon: Routledge, 2011), pp. 27–54.

France, J., *Western warfare in the age of the Crusades: 1000–1300* (Ithaca, NY: Cornell University Press, 1999).

Frankopan, P., *The First Crusade: The call from the East* (London: Bodley Head, 2012).

Frassetto, M., 'The image of the Saracen as heretic in the sermons of Ademar of Chabannes', *Western views of Islam in medieval and early modern Europe*, ed. D. Blanks and M. Frassetto (Basingstoke: Macmillan, 1999), pp. 83–96.

Freely, J., *Storm on horseback: the Seljuk warriors of Turkey* (London: I.B. Tauris, 2008).

Frembgen, J., 'Honour, shame, and bodily mutilation: cutting off the nose among tribal societies in Pakistan', *Journal of the Royal Asiatic society* 16 (2006), 243–260.

Frye, R., and Sayili, A., 'Turks in the Middle East before the Saljuqs', *The Turks in the early Islamic world*, ed. C. Bosworth, The formation of the classical Islamic world IX (Aldershot: *The Cambridge history of early inner Asia*, 2007), pp. 179–212.

Gabriele, M., *An empire of memory: the legend of Charlemagne, the Franks, and Jerusalem before the First Crusade* (Oxford: Oxford University Press, 2011).

Gabriele, M., 'The last Carolingian exegete: Pope Urban II, the weight of tradition, and Christian reconquest', *Church History*, 81.4 (2012), 796–814.

Gat, S., 'The Seljuks in Jerusalem', *Towns and material culture in the medieval Middle East*, ed. Y. Lev (Leiden: Brill, 2002), pp. 1–39.

Gibbon, Edward, *The history of the decline and fall of the Roman Empire* (Ware, 1998).

Gil, M., *A history of Palestine, 634–1099*, trans. by E. Broido (Cambridge: Cambridge University Press, 1992).

Goitein, S., 'Geniza sources for the crusader period', *Outremer: studies in the history of the crusading kingdom of Jerusalem*, ed. B. Kedar, H. Mayer and R. Smail (Jerusalem: Yad Izhak Ben-Zvi Institute, 1982), pp. 306–322.

Goitein, S., *A Mediterranean society: the Jewish communities of the Arab world as portrayed in the documents of the Cairo Geniza, volume V the individual* (Berkeley, CA: University of California Press, 1988).

Goldberg, E., *Struggle for empire: kingship and conflict under Louis the German, 817–876* (Ithaca, NY: Cornell University Press, 2006).

Golden, P., 'The peoples of the Russian forest belt', *The Cambridge history of early inner Asia*, ed. D. Sinor (Cambridge: Cambridge University Press, 1990), pp. 229–255.

Golden, P., 'The peoples of the south Russian Steppes', *The Cambridge history of early inner Asia*, ed. D. Sinor (Cambridge: Cambridge University Press, 1990), pp. 256–284.

Golden, P., 'Religion among the Qıpčaqs of Medieval Eurasia', *Central Asiatic Journal*, 42.2 (1998), 180–237.

Goulburn, E., and Symonds, H., *The life, letters and sermons of Henry of Losinga*, vol. 1 (London, 1878).

Grabar, O., 'Patterns and ways of cultural exchange', *The meeting of two worlds: cultural exchange between east and west during the period of the Crusades*, ed. V. Goss and C. Bornstein, Studies in medieval culture XXI (Kalamazoo, MI: Medieval Institute Publications, 1986), pp. 441–445.

Green, D., *The Millstätter Exodus: a crusading epic* (Cambridge: Cambridge University Press, 1966).

Greenstone, J. H., 'The Turkoman defeat at Cairo by Solomon ben Joseph Ha-Kohen', *The American journal of Semitic languages and literatures* 22:2 (1906), 144–175.

Haldon, J., 'Humour and the everyday in Byzantium', *Humour, history and politics in late antiquity and the early Middle Ages*, ed. G. Halsall (Cambridge: Cambridge University Press, 2004), pp. 48–71.

Hamdani, A., 'Byzantine-Fātimid relations before the battle of Manzikert', *Byzantine Studies* 1–2 (1974), 69–79.

Hamilton, B., 'Knowing the enemy: western understanding of Islam at the time of the Crusades', *Journal of the Royal Asiatic Society* 7.3 (1997), 373–387.

Hamilton, B., 'Prester John and the three kings of Cologne', *Studies in medieval history presented to R.H.C. Davis*, ed. H. Mayr-Harting and R.I. Moore (London: Hambledon, 1985), pp. 177–192.

Hamilton, J., and Hamilton, B., *Christian dualist heresies in the Byzantine world, c.650-c.1450* (Manchester: Manchester University Press, 1998).

Hammad, M. and Peters, E., 'Islam and the Crusades: A nine hundred-year-long grievance', *Seven myths of the Crusades*, ed. A. J. Andrea and A. Holt (Indianapolis, IN: Hackett Publishing Company, 2015), pp. 127–149.

Haydock, N., and Risden, E., (eds), *Hollywood in the Holy Land: essays on film depictions of the Crusades and Christian-Muslim clashes* (Jefferson: McFarland & Company, 2009).

Herde, P., 'Christians and Saracens at the time of the Crusades: some comments of contemporary medieval canonists', *Studia Gratiana*, 12 (1969), 359–376.

Hill, R., 'The Christian view of Muslims at the time of the First Crusade', *The eastern Mediterranean lands in the period of the Crusades*, ed. P. Holt (Warminster: Aris and Phillips, 1977), pp. 1–8.

Hillenbrand, C., *The Crusades: Islamic perspectives* (Edinburgh: University Press, 2006).

Hillenbrand, C., 'Ibn al-Adīm's biography of the Seljuq sultan, Alp Arslan', *Actas XVI Congreso Union Européene des Arabisants et Islamisants* (Salamanca, 1995), pp. 237–242.

Hillenbrand, C., *Turkish myth and Muslim symbol: the battle of Manzikert* (Edinburgh: Edinburgh University Press, 2007).

Hillenbrand, C., 'What's in a name? Tughtegin – the 'minister of the Antichrist'?', *Fortresses of the intellect. Ismaili and other Islamic studies in honour of Farhad Daftary*, ed. Omar Ali-de-Onzaga (London: I.B. Tauris, 2011), pp. 463–475.

Hirschler, K., 'The Jerusalem conquest of 492/1099 in the medieval Arabic historiography of the Crusades: from regional plurality to Islamic narrative', *Crusades* 13 (2014), 37–76.

Hodgson, N., 'The role of Kerbogha's mother in the Gesta Francorum and selected chronicles of the First Crusade', *Gendering the Crusades*, ed. S. Edgington and S. Lambert (New York: Columbia University Press, 2002), pp. 163–176.

Hodgson, N., *Women, crusading and the Holy Land in historical narrative* (Woodbridge: Boydell, 2007).

Holt, A., 'Crusading against barbarians: Muslims as barbarians in Crusades era sources', *East meets west in the Middle Ages and early modern times: transcultural experiences in the pre-modern world*, ed. A. Classen, Fundamentals of medieval and early modern culture XIV (Berlin: De Gruyter, 2013), pp. 443–456.

Housley, N., 'The Crusades and Islam', *Medieval encounters* 13 (2007), 189–208.

Housley, N., *Fighting for the cross: crusading to the Holy Land* (Yale: Yale University Press, 2008).

Hoyland, R. G., *Seeing Islam as others saw it: a survey and evaluation of Christian, Jewish and Zoroastrian writings on early Islam* (Princeton, NJ: Darwin Press, 1997).

Huntington, S., *The clash of civilizations and the remaking of world order* (London: Simon & Schuster, 1996).

Huntington, S., 'The clash of civilizations', *Foreign affairs* 72.3 (1993), 22–49.

Huygens, R., 'Un témoin de la crainte de l'an 1000: la lettre sur les Hongrois', *Latomus: revue d'études latines* 15 (1956), 225–239.

Iogna-Prat, D., *Order & exclusion: Cluny and Christendom face heresy, Judaism, and Islam (1000–1150)* (Ithaca: Cornell University Press, 1998).

Irwin, R., *For the lust of knowing: the orientalists and their enemies* (London: Penguin, 2006).

Izdebski, A., 'The changing landscapes of Byzantine Anatolia', *Archaeologia Bulgarica* 16.1 (2012), 47–66.

Jacoby, D., 'Bishop Gunther of Bamberg: Byzantine and Christian pilgrimage to the Holy Land in the eleventh century', *Zwischen Polis, Provinz und Peripherie: Beiträge zur byzantinischen Geschichte und Kultur*, ed. L. Hoffmann (Wiesbaden: Harrassowitz, 2005), pp. 267–285.

Jacoby, D., 'Venetian commercial expansion in the eastern Mediterranean, 8–11 centuries', *Byzantine trade, 4ᵗʰ–12ᵗʰ centuries: the archaeology of local, regional and international exchange*, ed. M. M. Mango, Studies for the promotion of byzantine studies XIV (Aldershot: Ashgate, 2009), pp. 371–391.

Jensen, K., 'Cultural encounters and clash of civilizations: Huntington and modern crusading histories', *Cultural encounters during the Crusades*, ed. K. Jensen, K. Salonen and H. Vogt (Odense: University Press of Southern Denmark, 2013), pp. 15–26.

Jones, C., *An introduction to the chansons de geste*, New perspectives on medieval literature: authors and traditions (Gainesville, FL: University Press of Florida, 2014).

Joranson, E., 'The problem of the spurious letter of Emperor Alexius to the court of Flanders', *The American historical review* 55.4 (1950), 811–832.

Jotischky, A., 'The Christians of Jerusalem, the Holy Sepulchre and the origins of the First Crusade', *Crusades* 7 (2008), 35–58.

Jotischky, A., 'Pilgrimage, procession and ritual encounters between Christians and Muslims in the Crusader States', *Cultural encounters during the Crusades*, ed. K. Jensen, K. Salonen and H. Vogt (Odense: University Press of Southern Denmark, 2013), pp. 245–262.

Jubb, M., 'The Crusaders' perceptions of their opponents', *Palgrave advances in the Crusades*, ed. H. Nicholson (Basingstoke: Palgrave Macmillan, 2005), pp. 225–244.

Jubb, M., 'Enemies in the holy war, but brothers in chivalry: the Crusaders' view of their Saracen opponents', *Aspects de l'épopee romane: mentalités, idéologies, intertextualités*, ed. H. van Dijk and W. Noomen (Groningen: E. Forsten, 1995), pp. 251–259.

Kaeuper, R., *Holy warriors: the religious ideology of chivalry* (Philadelphia, PA: University of Pennsylvania Press, 2009).

Kalian M., and Witztum, E., 'Facing a holy space: psychiatric hospitalization of tourists in Jerusalem', *Sacred space: shrine, city, land*, ed. B. Kedar and R. Zwi Werblowsky (Basingstoke: Macmillan, 1998), pp. 316–330.

Kangas, S., 'First in prowess and faith. The great encounter in twelfth century crusader narratives', *Cultural encounters during the Crusades*, ed. K. Jensen, K. Salonen and H. Vogt (Odense: University Press of Southern Denmark, 2013), pp. 119–134.

Kangas, S., 'Inimicus Dei et Sanctae Christianitatis? Saracens and their Prophet in twelfth-century crusade propaganda and western travesties of Muhammed's life', *The Crusades and the Near East: cultural histories*, ed. C. Kostick (London: Routledge, 2011), pp. 131–160.

Kangas, S., 'Deus vult: violence and suffering as a means of salvation during the First Crusade', *Medieval history writing and crusading ideology*, ed. T. Lehtonen, K. Jensen, et al. (Helsinki: Finnish Literature Society, 2005), pp. 163–174.

Kedar, B., *Crusade and mission: European approaches toward the Muslims* (Princeton, NJ: Princeton University Press, 1988).

Kedar, B., 'De Iudeis et Sarracenis: on the categorization of Muslims in medieval canon law', *The franks in the Levant* (Aldershot: Ashgate, 1993), pp. 207–213.

Kedar B., 'The Jerusalem massacre of July 1099 in the western historiography of the Crusades', *Crusades* 3 (2004), 15–75.

Kedar, B., 'Multidirectional conversion in the Frankish Levant', *Varieties of religious conversion in the Middle Ages*, ed. J. Muldoon (Gainesville, FL.: University of Florida Press, 1997), pp. 190–199.

Kedar, B., 'On the origins of the earliest laws of Frankish Jerusalem: The canons of the council of Nablus, 1120', *Speculum*, 74.2 (1999), 310–335.

Kedar, B., and Aslanov, C., 'Problems in the study of trans-cultural borrowing in the Frankish Levant', *Hybride Kulturen im mittelalterlichen Europa: Vorträge und Workshops einer internationalen Frühlingsschule*, ed. M. Borgolte and B. Schneidmüller, Europa im Mittelalter XVI (Berlin: Akademie Verlag, 2010), pp. 277–285.

Kempf, D., and Bull, M., 'Introduction', *The Historia Iherosolimitana of Robert the Monk* (Woodbridge: Boydell, 2013), pp. ix–lxxiv.

Kendall, C., 'Bede and Islam', *Bede and the future*, ed. P. Darby and F. Wallis (Aldershot: Ashgate, 2014), pp. 93–114.

Kennedy, H., *The great Arab conquests: how the spread of Islam changed the world we live in* (London: Phoenix, 2008).

Kennedy, H., 'Medieval Antioch', *The city in late antiquity*, ed. J. Rich (London: Routledge, 1992), pp. 181–198.

Kennedy, H., *Muslim Spain and Portugal: a political history of al-Andalus* (London: Longman, 1996).

Kieckhefer, R., *Magic in the Middle Ages* (Cambridge: Cambridge University Press, 1989).

Kienzle, B., 'Introduction', *The letters of St Bernard of Clairvaux* (Stroud: Sutton, 1998), pp. vii–xxx.

Kim, H. *The Huns, Rome and the birth of Europe* (Cambridge: Cambridge University Press, 2013).

Köhler, M., *Alliances and treaties between Frankish and Muslim rulers in the Middle East: cross-cultural diplomacy in the period of the Crusades*, trans. P.M. Holt, revised by K. Hirschler (Leiden: Brill, 2013).

Kolbaba, T., 'Byzantine perceptions of Latin religious "errors": themes and changes from 850 to 1350', *The Crusades from the perspective of Byzantium and the Muslim world*, ed. A. Laiou and R. Mottahedeh (Washington D. C.: Dumbarton Oaks, 2001), pp. 117–144.

Korobeinikov, D., *Byzantium and the Turks in the thirteenth century*, Oxford studies in Byzantium (Oxford: Oxford University Press, 2014).

Kostick, C., 'Courage and cowardice on the First Crusade, 1096–1099', *War in History*, 20.1 (2013), 32–49.

Kostick, C., *The siege of Jerusalem: crusade and conquest in 1099* (London: Continuum, 2009).

Kostick, C., *The social structure of the First Crusade*, The medieval Mediterranen LXXVI (Leiden: Brill, 2008).

Kreutz, B., *Before the Normans: southern Italy in the ninth and tenth centuries* (Philadelphia, PA: University of Pennsylvania Press, 1991).

Laiou, Angeliki E., 'Economic and noneconomic exchange', *The economic history of Byzantium*, ed. A. Laiou, vol. 2, Dumbarton Oaks studies XXXIX (Washington D.C.: Dumbarton Oaks Research Library, 2002), pp. 697–770.

La Porta, S., 'Conflicted coexistence: Christian-Muslim interaction and its representation in medieval Armenia', *Contextualizing the Muslim other in medieval Christian discourse*, ed. J. Frakes (New York: Palgrave Macmillan, 2011), pp. 103–123.

Lapina, E., *Warfare and the miraculous in the chronicles of the First Crusade* (University Park, PN: University of Pennsylvania Press, 2015).

Latiff, O., 'Qur'anic imagery, Jesus and the creation of a pious-warrior ethos in the Muslim poetry of the anti-Frankish Jihad', *Cultural encounters during the Crusades*, ed. K. Jensen, K. Salonen and H. Vogt (Odense: University Press of Southern Denmark, 2013), pp. 135–151.

Lauranson-Rosaz, C., 'Le Velay et la Croisade', *Le Concile de Clermont de 1095 et l'Appel à la Croisade* (Rome: Ecole française de Rome, Palais Farnèse, 1997), pp. 33–64.

Leclercq, A., *Portraits croisés: L'image des Francs et des Musulmans dans les textes sur la Première Croisade*, Nouvelle Bibliothèque du Moyen Âge XCVI (Paris: HonoréChampion, 2014).

Leiser, G., 'The Turks in Anatolia before the Ottomans', *The new Cambridge history of Islam: volume 2 the western Islamic World, eleventh to eighteenth centuries*, ed. M. Fierro (Cambridge: Cambridge University Press, 2010), pp. 301–312.

Lightfoot, C., and Ivison, E., 'The Amorium project: the 1995 excavation season', *Dumbarton Oaks papers* 51 (1997), 291–300.

Lewis, B., *The Muslim discovery of Europe* (London: W.W. Norton, 1982).

Lewis, B., 'The roots of Muslim rage', *The Atlantic Monthly* 266.3 (1990), 47–60.

Lewis, C. S., *The discarded image: an introduction to medieval and Renaissance literature* (Cambridge: Cambridge University Press, 1964).

Lev, Y., 'A Mediterranean encounter: the Fatimids and Europe, tenth to twelfth centuries', *Shipping, trade and crusade in the medieval Mediterranean, studies in honour of John Pryor*, ed. R. Gertwagen and E. Jeffreys (Aldershot: Ashgate, 2012), pp. 131–156.

Loud, G., 'Anna Komnena and her sources for the Normans of southern Italy', *Church and chronicle in the Middle Ages: essay presented to John Taylor*, ed. I. Wood and G. Loud (London: Hambleton, 1991), pp. 41–57.

Loutchitskaja, S., 'Barbarae Nationes: Les peuples musulmans dans les chroniques de la Première Croisade', *Autour de la Première Croisade: Actes du Colloque de la Society for the Study of the Crusades and the Latin East*, ed. M Balard (Paris: Publications de la Sorbonne, 1996), pp. 99–107.

Loutchitskaja, S., 'L'idée de conversion dans les chroniques de la première croisade', *Cahiers de civilisation médiévale* 45 (2001), 39–53.

Loutchitskaja, S., 'L'image des musulmans dans les chroniques des croisades', *Le Moyen Âge* 105 (1999), 717–735.

Maalouf, A., *The Crusades through Arab eyes*, trans. J. Rothschild (Saqi Books: London, 2012).

MacEvitt, C., 'The chronicle of Matthew of Edessa: apocalypse, the First Crusade, and the Armenian diaspora', *Dumbarton Oaks papers* 61 (2007), 157–181.

MacEvitt, C., *The Crusades and the Christian world of the East: rough tolerance* (Philadelphia, PA: University of Pennsylvania Press, 2008).

Madden, T., 'Rivers of blood: an analysis of one aspect of the crusader conquest of Jerusalem in 1099', *Revista Chilena de Estudios Medievales* 1 (2012), 25–37.

Mallett, A., *Popular Muslim reactions to the Franks in the Levant, 1097–1291* (Aldershot: Ashgate, 2014).

Mastnak, T., *Crusading peace: Christendom, the Muslim world and western political order* (Berkeley, CA: University of California Press, 2002).

Mastnak, T., 'Europe and the Muslims: the permanent Crusade?', *The new Crusades: constructing the Muslim enemy*, ed. E. Qureshi and M. Sells (New York: Columbia University Press, 2003), pp. 205–248.

Mayer, H. E., *The Crusades*, trans. J. Gillingham, 2nd ed. (Oxford: Oxford University Press, 1990).

Mayr-Harting, H., *The coming of Christianity to Anglo-Saxon England*, 3rd ed. (London: Batsford, 1991).

McCarthy, T., 'Introduction', *Chronicles of the Investiture Contest: Frutolf of Michelsberg and his continuators* (Manchester: Manchester University Press, 2014), pp. 1–84.

McGinn, B., *Antichrist: two thousand years of the human fascination with evil* (New York: Columbia University Press, 2000).

McGinn, B., 'Iter Sancti Sepulchri: the piety of the first crusaders', *The Walter Prescott Webb lectures: essays in medieval civilization*, ed. R. Sullivan (Austin, TX: University of Texas Press, 1978), pp. 33–71.

McKitterick, R., *Charlemagne: the formation of a European identity* (Cambridge: Cambridge University Press, 2008).

Mecit, S., *The Rum Seljuqs: evolution of a dynasty*, RSIT (Abingdon: Routledge, 2014).

Menache, S., 'Emotions in the service of politics: another crusading perspective on the experience of crusading (1095–1187)', *Jerusalem the golden: the origins and impact of the First Crusade*, ed. S. Edgington and L. García-Guijarro, Outremer: studies in the Crusades and the Latin East III (Turnhout: Brepols, 2014), pp. 235–254.

C. Meredith Jones, 'The conventional Saracen of the songs of geste', *Speculum* 17.2 (1942), 201–225.

Meserve, M., *Empires of Islam in Renaissance historical thought* (Cambridge, MA: Harvard University Press, 2008).

Meserve, M., 'Medieval sources for Renaissance theories on the origins of the Ottoman Turks', *Europa und die Türken in der Renaissance*, ed. B. Guthmüller and W. Kühlmann (Tübingen: Niemeyer, 2000), pp. 409–436.

Metcalfe, A., *The Muslims of medieval Italy*, The new Edinburgh Islamic surveys (Edinburgh: Edinburgh University Press, 2009).

Meyendorff, J., 'Byzantine views of Islam', *Dumbarton Oaks papers* 18 (1964), 113–132.

Micheau, F., 'Ibn al-Athīr', 'Ibn al-Athīr', *Medieval Muslim historians and the Franks in the Levant*, ed. A. Mallett (Leiden: Brill, 2014), pp. 52–83.

Montgomery Watt, W., *The influence of Islam on medieval Europe* (Edinburgh: Edinburgh University Press, 1972).

Moore, R. I., *The formation of a persecuting society: authority and deviance in Western Europe, 950–1250*, 2nd ed. (Oxford: Blackwell, 2006).

Moran-Cruz, J., 'Popular attitudes towards Islam in medieval Europe', *Western views of Islam in medieval and early modern Europe*, ed. D. Blanks and M. Frassetto (Basingstoke: Macmillan, 1999), pp. 55–81.

Morris, C., *The sepulchre of Christ and the medieval West, from the beginning to 1600* (Oxford: Oxford University Press, 2005).

Morton, N., and France, J., 'Arab Muslim reactions to Turkish authority in northern Syria, 1085–1128', *Warfare, crusade and conquest in the Middle Ages*, Variorum collected studies series (Farnham: Ashgate, 2014), XV (pp. 1–38).

Morton, N., 'Encountering the Turks: The first crusaders' foreknowledge of their enemy: some preliminary findings', *Crusading and warfare in the Middle Ages: realities and representations. Essays in honour of John France*, ed. S. John and N. Morton, Crusades subsidia VII (Aldershot: Ashgate, 2014), pp. 47–68.

Morton, N., 'Templar and Hospitaller attitudes towards Islam in the Holy Land during the twelfth and thirteenth centuries: some historiographical reflections', *Levant*, 47:3 (2015), 316–327.

Morton, N., 'William of Tyre's attitude towards Islam: some historiographical reflections', *Deeds done beyond the Sea: essays on William of Tyre, Cyprus and the military orders presented to Peter Edbury*, ed. S. Edgington and H. Nicholson, Crusades subsidia VI (Farnham: Ashgate, 2014), pp. 13–24.

Mourad S.A., and Lindsay, J.E., *The intensification and reorientation of Sunni Jihad ideology in the crusader period* (Leiden: Brill, 2013).

Munro, D., 'The speech of Pope Urban II. at Clermont, 1095', *The American historical review*, 11.2 (1906), 231–242.

Muratova, X., 'Western chronicles of the First Crusade as sources for the history of art in the Holy Land', *Crusader art in the twelfth century*, ed. J. Folda (Oxford: British School of Archaeology in Jerusalem, 1982), pp. 47–69.

Murray, A., 'Coroscane: homeland of the Saracens in the chansons de geste and the historiography of the Crusades', *Aspects de l'épopée romane: mentalités, idéologies, intertextualités* (Groningen: E. Forsten, 1995), pp. 177–184.

Murray, A., 'Franks and indigenous communities in Palestine and Syria (1099–1187): a hierarchical model of social interaction in the principalities of Outremer', *East meets west in the Middle Ages and early modern times: transcultural experiences in the premodern world*, ed. A. Classen (Berlin: De Gruyter, 2013), pp. 291–309.

Murray, A., 'The siege and capture of Jerusalem in western narrative sources of the First Crusade', *Jerusalem the golden: The origins and impact of the First Crusade*, ed. S. Edgington and L. García-Guijarro, Outremer: studies in the Crusades and the Latin East III (Turnhout: Brepols, 2014), pp. 191–215.

Murray, A., 'William of Tyre and the origin of the Turks: observations on possible sources of the Gesta orientalium principum', *Dei Gesta per Francos: Etudes sur les croisades dédiés à Jean Richard: Crusade studies in honour of Jean Richard*, ed. M. Balard, B. Kedar and J. Riley-Smith (Aldershot: Ashgate, 2001), pp. 217–229.

Ní Chléirigh, L., 'Nova Peregrinatio: the First Crusade as a pilgrimage in contemporary Latin narratives', *Writing the early Crusades: text, transmission and memory*, ed. M. Bull and D. Kempf (Woodbridge, 2014), pp. 63–74.

Nilsson, B., 'Gratian on pagans and infidels: a short outline', *Cultural encounters during the Crusades*, ed. K. Jensen, K. Salonen and H. Vogt (Odense: University Press of Southern Denmark, 2013), pp. 153–163.

Nirenberg, D., *Communities of violence: persecution of minorities in the Middle Ages* (Princeton, NJ: Princeton University Press, 1996).

O'Doherty, M., *The Indies and the medieval west: thought, reform, imagination,* Medieval voyaging II (Turnhout: Brepols, 2013).

Papageorgiou, A., 'οἱ δέ λύκοι ὡς Πέρσάι: the image of the "Turks" in the reign of John II Comnenus (1118–1143)', *Byzantinoslavica* (2011), 149–161.

Peacock, A., *Early Seljūq history: a new interpretation,* RSIT (Abingdon: Routledge, 2010).

Peacock, A., *The great Seljuk Empire,* Edinburgh history of the Islamic empires (Edinburgh: Edinburgh University Press, 2015).

Petkov, K., 'The cultural career of a 'minor' vice: arrogance in the medieval treatise on sin', *Sin in medieval and early modern culture: the tradition of the seven deadly sins,* ed. R. Newhauser and S. Ridyard (Woodbridge: Boydell, 2012), pp. 43–64.

Phillips, J., *Holy warriors: a modern history of the Crusades* (London: Vintage Books, 2009).

Phillips, J., *The Second Crusade: extending the frontiers of Christendom* (New Haven, CT: Yale University Press, 2007).

Pipes, D., *Slave soldiers and Islam: the genesis of a military system* (New Haven, CT: Yale University Press, 1981).

Pogossian, Z., 'The frontier existence of the Paulician heretics', *Annual of medieval studies at CEU, vol. 6,* ed. K. Szende and M. Sebők (Budapest: Central European University, 2000), pp. 203–206.

Pogossian, Z., 'The last emperor or the last Armenian king? Some considerations on Armenian apocalyptic literature from the Cilician period', *The Armenian apocalyptic tradition: a comparative perspective: essays presented in honor of Professor Robert W. Thomson on the occasion of his eightieth birthday,* ed. K. Bardakjian and S. La Porta (Leiden: Brill, 2014), pp. 457–502.

Prawer, J., 'The roots of medieval colonialism', *The meeting of two worlds: cultural exchange between east and west during the period of the Crusades,* V. Goss and C. Bornstein, Studies in medieval culture XXI (Kalamazoo, MI: Medieval Institute Publications, 1986), pp. 23–38.

Preiser-Kapeller, J., 'A collapse of the eastern Mediterranean? new results and theories on the interplay between climate and societies in Byzantium and the Near East, ca. 1000–1200 AD' (unpublished).

Pringle, D., *The churches of the crusader kingdom of Jerusalem, a corpus,* 4 vols (Cambridge: Cambridge University Press, 1993–2009).

Pringle, D., *Secular buildings in the crusader kingdom of Jerusalem: an archaeological gazetteer* (Cambridge: Cambridge University Press, 1997).

Purkis, W., *Crusading spirituality in the Holy Land and Iberia, c.1095–c.1187* (Woodbridge: Boydell, 2008).

Purkis, W., 'Rewriting the history books: the First Crusade and the past', *Writing the early Crusades: text, transmission and memory,* ed. M. Bull and D. Kempf (Woodbridge: Boydell, 2014), pp. 140–154.

Ramey, L., 'Medieval miscegenation: hybridity and the anxiety of inheritance', *Contextualizing the Muslim other in medieval Christian discourse,* ed. J. Frakes (New York: Palgrave Macmillan, 2011), pp. 1–19.

Rapp, S., *Studies in medieval Georgian historiography: early texts and Eurasian contexts*, Corpus Scriptorum Christianorum Orientalium: Subsidia CXIII (Louvain: Peeters, 2003).

Riley-Smith, L. and J. (ed. and trans.), *The Crusades: idea and reality, 1095–1274* (London: Edward Arnold, 1981).

Riley-Smith, J., *The First Crusade and the idea of crusading* (London: Continuum, 2003).

Riley-Smith, J., 'The First Crusade and the persecution of the Jews', *Studies in Church history*, ed. W. Sheils, 21 (1984), 51–72.

Riley-Smith, J., *The first crusaders, 1095–1131* (Cambridge: Cambridge University Press, 1997).

Riley-Smith, J., 'The idea of crusading in the charters of the early Crusaders, 1095–1102', *Le Concile de Clermont de 1095 et l'Appel à la Croisade* (Rome: Ecole française de Rome, Palais Farnèse, 1997), pp. 155–166.

Riley-Smith, J., 'The military orders and the east, 1149–1291', *Knighthoods of Christ: essays on the history of the Crusades and the Knights Templar, presented to Malcolm Barber* (Aldershot: Ashgate, 2007), pp. 137–149.

Róna-Tas, A., *Hungarians and Europe in the early Middle Ages* (Budapest: Central European University Press, 1999).

Roggema, B., *The legend of Sergius Baḥīrā: eastern Christian apologetics and apocalyptic in response to Islam*, History of Christian-Muslim Relations IX (Leiden: Brill, 2009).

Lauranson-Rosaz, C., 'Le Velay et la Croisade', *Le Concile de Clermont de 1095 et l'Appel à la Croisade* (Rome, 1997), pp. 33–64.

Rosenthal, J., 'Letters and letter collections', *Understanding medieval primary sources*, ed. J. Rosenthal (London: Routledge, 2012), pp. 72–85.

Rubenstein, J., *Armies of Heaven: the First Crusade and the quest for the Apocalypse* (New York: Basic Books, 2011).

Rubenstein, J., 'Godfrey of Bouillon versus Raymond of Saint-Gilles: how Carolingian kingship trumped millenarianism at the end of the First Crusade', *The legend of Charlemagne in the Middle Ages: power, faith and crusade*, ed. M. Gabriele and J. Stuckey (New York: Palgrave Macmillan, 2008), pp. 59–75.

Rubenstein, J., 'Guibert of Nogent, Albert of Aachen and Fulcher of Chartres: three crusade chronicles intersect', *Writing the early crusades: text transmission and memory*, ed. M. Bull and D. Kempf (Woodbridge: Boydell, 2014), pp. 24–37.

Runciman, S., *A history of the Crusades*, 3 vols (Cambridge: Cambridge University Press, 1951–1954).

Runciman, S., 'Teucri and Turci', *Medieval and Middle Eastern studies: in honor of Aziz Suryal Atiya*, ed. S. Hanna (Leiden: Brill, 1972), pp. 344–348.

Russo, L., 'The Monte Cassino tradition of the First Crusade: from the Chronica Monasterii Casinensis to the Hystoria de Via et Recuperatione Antiochiae atque Ierusolymarum', *Writing the early Crusades: text, transmission and memory*, ed. M. Bull and D. Kempf (Woodbridge: Boydell, 2014), pp. 53–62.

Ryan, M., *A kingdom of stargazers: astrology and authority in the late medieval crown of Aragon* (Ithaca, NY: Cornell University Press, 2011).

Safi, O., *The politics of knowledge in premodern Islam: negotiating ideology and religious inquiry* (Chapel Hill, NC: University of North Carolina Press, 2006).

Sager, S., 'Hungarians as vremde in medieval Germany', *Meeting the foreign in the Middle Ages*, ed. A. Classen (New York: Routledge, 2002), pp. 27–44.

Said, E., 'The clash of ignorance', *The Nation*, 273.12 (2001), 11–14.

Said, E., *Orientalism* (London: Routledge and Kegan Paul, 1978).

Said, E., *Orientalism*, reprinted with new afterword (London: Penguin, 1995).

Salvadó, S., 'Icons, crosses and liturgical objects of Templar chapels in the crown of Aragon', *The debate on the trial of the Templars (1307–1314)*, ed. J. Burgtorf, P. Crawford and H. Nicholson (Aldershot: Ashgate, 2010), pp. 183–198.

Saunders, C., *Magic and the supernatural in medieval English romance* (Cambridge: D.S. Brewer, 2010).

Savvides A. G., 'Byzantines and the Oghuz (Ghuzz): some observations on nomenclature', *Byzantinoslavica* 54 (1993), 147–155.

Schaller, H. 'Zur Kreuzzugsenzyklika Papst Sergius' IV', *Papsttum, Kirche und Recht im Mittelalter: Festschrift für Horst Fuhrmann zum 65. Geburtstag*, ed. H. Mordek (Tübingen: Niemeyer, 1991), pp. 135–153.

Schein, S., *Gateway to the heavenly city: crusader Jerusalem and the Catholic west (1099–1187)*, Church, Faith and Culture in the Medieval west (Aldershot: Ashgate, 2005).

Schwinges, R.C., 'William of Tyre, the Muslim enemy and the problem of tolerance', *Tolerance and intolerance: social conflict in the age of the Crusades*, ed. M. Gervers and J. Powell (Syracuse, NY: Syracuse University Press, 2001), pp. 124–134.

Schwinges, R. C., *Kreuzzugsideologie und Toleranz: Studien zu Wilhelm von Tyrus* (Stuttgart: Hiersemann, 1977).

Scott, Joan W., 'Gender: a useful category of historical analysis', *The American historical review*, 91.5 (1986), 1053–1075.

Shepard, J., '>>How St James the Persian's head was brought to Cormery<<. A relic collector around the time of the First Crusade', *Zwischen Polis, Provinz und Peripherie: Beiträge zur byzantinischen Geschichte und Kultur*, ed. L. Hoffmann (Wiesbaden: Harrassowitz, 2005), pp. 287–335.

Shukurov, R., 'Harem Christianity: The Byzantine identity of Seljuk princes', *The Seljuks of Anatolia: court and society in the medieval Middle East*, ed. A. Peacock, and Sara Nur Yıldız (London: I.B. Tauris, 2013), pp. 115–150.

Sinor, D., 'The establishment and dissolution of the Türk empire', *The Cambridge history of early inner Asia*, ed. D. Sinor (Cambridge: Cambridge University Press, 1990), pp. 285–316.

Skottki, K., 'Medieval western perceptions of Islam and the scholars: what went wrong?', *Cultural transfers in dispute. Representations in Asia, Europe and the Arab world since the Middle Ages*, ed. J. Feuchter (Frankfurt: Campus Verlag, 2011), pp. 107–134.

Skottki, K., 'Of 'pious traitors', and dangerous encounters: historiographical notions of inter-culturality in the principality of Antioch', *Journal of transcultural medieval studies* 1 (2014), 75–116.

Somerville, R., *The councils of Urban II: Volume 1, Decreta Claromontensia* (Amsterdam: Adolf M. Hakkert, 1972).

Southern, R., *Western views of Islam in the Middle Ages* (Cambridge, MA: Harvard University Press, 1962).

Stepanov, T., *The Bulgars and the steppe empire in the early Middle Ages: the problem of the others*, trans. T. Stefanova and T. Stepanov (Leiden: Brill, 2010).

Stroll, S., *Symbols as power: the papacy following the Investiture Contest*, Brill's Studies in Intellectual History XXIV (Leiden: Brill, 1991).

Summerell, O. (ed.), *The otherness of God* (Charlottesville: University Press of Virginia, 1998).

Sweetenham, C., 'The count and the cannibals: the old French crusade cycle as a drama of salvation', *Jerusalem the golden: the origins and impact of the First Crusade*, ed. S. Edgington and L. García-Guijarro, Outremer: studies in the Crusades and the Latin East III (Turnhout: Brepols, 2014), pp. 307–328.

Sweetenham, C., 'Crusaders in a hall of mirrors: the portrayal of Saracens in Robert the Monks' *Historia Iherosolimitana*', *Languages of love and hate: conflict, communication, and identity in the medieval Mediterranean*, ed. S. Lambert and H. Nicholson, International Medieval Research XV (Turnhout: Brepols, 2012), pp. 49–63.

Sweetenham, C., '"Hoc enim non fuit humanum opus, sed Divinum": Robert the Monk's use of the Bible in the *Historia Iherosolimitana*', *The uses of the Bible in crusading sources*, ed. E. Lapina and N. Morton (forthcoming).

Sweetenham, C., 'What really happened to Eurvin de Créel's donkey? Anecdotes in sources for the First Crusade', *Writing the early Crusades: text, transmission and memory*, ed. M. Bull and D. Kempf (Woodbridge: Boydell, 2014), pp. 75–88.

Szádeczky-Kardoss, S., 'The Avars', *The Cambridge history of early Inner Asia* (Cambridge: Cambridge University Press, 1990), pp. 206–228.

Tetley, G., *The Ghaznavid and Seljuk Turks: poetry as a source for Iranian history*, RSIT (Abingdon: Routledge, 2009).

Throop, S., 'Combat and conversion: inter-faith dialogue in twelfth-century crusading narratives', *Medieval encounters* 13 (2007), 310–325.

Throop, S., *Crusading as an act of vengeance, 1095–1216* (Aldershot: Ashgate, 2011).

Tieszen, C., *Christian identity amid Islam in medieval Spain*, Studies on the Children of Abraham III (Leiden: Brill, 2013).

Tinsley, D., 'Mapping the Muslims: images of Islam in middle high German literature of the thirteenth century', *Contextualizing the Muslim other in medieval Christian discourse*, ed. J. Frakes (New York: Palgrave Macmillan, 2011), pp. 65–101.

Tolan, J., 'Afterword', *Contextualizing the Muslim other in medieval Christian discourse*, ed. J. Frakes (New York: Palgrave Macmillan, 2011), pp. 171–177.

Tolan, J., 'Antihagiography: Embrico of Mainz's Vita Mahumeti', *Sons of Ishmael: Muslims through European eyes in the Middle Ages* (Gainesville, FL: University Press of Florida, 2008), pp. 1–18.

Tolan, J., 'Un cadavre mutilé: le déchirement polémique de Mahomet', *Le Moyen Âge: Revue d'Histoire et de Philologie* 104.1 (1998), 53–72.

Tolan, J., 'The dream of conversion: baptizing pagan kings in the crusade epics', *Sons of Ishmael: Muslims through European eyes in the Middle Ages* (Gainesville, FL: University Press of Florida, 2008), pp. 66–74.

Tolan, J., 'Embrico of Mainz', *Christian-Muslim relations: a bibliographical history, volume 3 (1050–1200)*, ed. D. Thomas and A. Mallett (Leiden: Brill, 2011), pp. 592–595.

Tolan, J., 'European accounts of Muḥammad's life', *The Cambridge companion to Muhammed*, Cambridge Companions to Religion (Cambridge: Cambridge University Press, 2010), pp. 226–250.

Tolan, J., 'Introduction', *Sons of Ishmael: Muslims through European eyes in the Middle Ages* (Gainesville, FL: University Press of Florida, 2008), pp. ix–xvii.

Tolan, J. *Saracens: Islam in the medieval European imagination* (New York: Columbia University Press, 2002).

Tolan, J., 'Veneratio Sarracenorum: shared devotion among Muslims and Christians, according to Burchard of Strasburg, envoy from Frederic Barbarossa to Saladin (c.1175)', *Sons of Ishmael: Muslims through European eyes in the Middle Ages* (Gainesville, FL: University Press of Florida, 2008), pp. 101–112.

Tolan, J., Veinstein, G., and Laurens, H., *Europe and the Islamic world: A history* (Princeton, NJ: Princeton University Press, 2013).

Tor, D., '"Sovereign and pious": The religious life of the great Seljuq sultans', *The Seljuqs: politics, society and culture*, ed. C. Lange and S. Mecit (Edinburgh: Edinburgh University Press, 2011), pp. 39–62.

Tourneur, V., 'Un Denier de Godefroid de Bouillon Frappé en 1096', *Revue Belge de Numismatique* 83 (1931), 27–30.

Treadgold, W., *Byzantium and its army: 284–1081* (Stanford: Stanford University Press, 1995).

Tuley, K., 'A century of communication and acclimatization: interpreters and intermediaries in the kingdom of Jerusalem', *East meets west in the Middle Ages and early modern times: transcultural experiences in the pre-modern world*, ed. A. Classen, Fundamentals of medieval and early modern Culture XIV (Berlin: De Gruyter, 2013), pp. 311–339.

Turan, O., 'The ideal of world domination among the medieval Turks', *Studia Islamica* 4 (1955), 77–90.

Tyerman, C. (ed. and trans.), *Chronicles of the First Crusade: 1096–1099* (London: Penguin, 2012).

Tyerman, C., *God's war: a new history of the Crusades* (London: Allen Lane, 2006).

Tyerman, C., 'Paid crusaders: "pro honoris vel pecunie"; "stipendiarii contra paganos"; money and incentives on crusade', *The practices of crusading: image and action from the eleventh to the sixteenth centuries*, Variorum collected studies series (Aldershot: Ashgate, 2013), pp. 1–40 (article XIV).

van Donzel, E., and Schmidt, A., *Gog and Magog in early Christian and Islamic sources: Sallam's quest for Alexander's wall*, Brill's Inner Asian Library XXII (Leiden: Brill, 2010).

Völkl, M., *Muslime – Märtyrer – Militia Christi: Identität, Feindbild und Fremderfahrung während der ersten Kreuzzüge* (Stuttgart: Kohlhammer, 2011).

Vryonis, S., *The decline of medieval hellenism in Asia Minor and the process of Islamization from the eleventh through the fifteenth century* (Berkeley, CA: University of California Press, 1971).

Vryonis, S., 'Evidence on human sacrifice among the early Ottoman Turks', *Journal of Asian history* 5 (1971), 140–146.

Vryonis, S., 'Nomadization and Islamization in Asia Minor', *Dumbarton Oaks papers* 29 (1975), 41–71.

Walter, C., *The warrior saints in Byzantine art and tradition* (Aldershot: Ashgate, 2003).

Warren, F. 'The enamoured Moslem princess in Orderic Vital and the French epic', *Publications of the Modern Language Association of America* (1914), 341–358.

Waters, M., *Ancient Persia: a concise history of the Achaemenid empire, 550–330 BCE* (Cambridge: Cambridge University Press, 2014).

Weitzmann, K., 'Icon painting in the crusader kingdom', *Dumbarton Oaks papers* 20 (1966), 49–83.

Wink, A., 'The early expansion of Islam in India', *The new Cambridge history of Islam: volume 3 the eastern Islamic world, eleventh to eighteenth centuries*, ed. D. O. Morgan and A. Reid (Cambridge: Cambridge University Press, 2010), pp. 78–99.

Winroth, A., *The conversion of Scandinavia: Vikings, merchants, and missionaries in the remaking of Northern Europe* (New Haven, CT: Yale University Press, 2012).

Wright, D. C., 'The northern frontier', *A military history of China* (Lexington: University Press of Kentucky, 2012), pp. 57–80.

Zakkar, S., *The emirate of Aleppo, 1004–1094* (Beirut: Dar Al-Amanah & El-Risalah Publishing House, 1971).

Index